Sustainable Architectural Design

This book is a guide to a sustainable design process that moves from theory, to site and energy use, to building systems, and finally to evaluation and case studies, so you can integrate design and technology for effective sustainable building. Kuppaswamy Iyengar shows you how to get it right the first time, use free energy systems, and utilize technologies that minimize fossil fuel use. Each chapter has a sustainable design overview, technical details and strategies marked by clear sections, a summary, and further resources. Heavily illustrated with charts, tables, drawings, photographs, and case studies, the book shows technologies and concepts integrated into cohesive project types, from small and large office spaces to single and multi-use residences, hospitals, schools, restaurants, and warehouses to demonstrate implementing your designs to meet clients' needs now and for the future.

This book includes an overview of alternative assessment and evaluation systems such as BREEAM, CASBEE, GBTool, and Green Globes, alongside LEED®, ECOTECT™, energy 10, HEED, and eQuest simulation programs. The guide reveals the importance of the building envelope – walls, superstructure, insulation, windows, floors, roofs, and building materials – for the environmental impact of a building, and has a section on site systems examining site selection, landscape design, thermal impact, and building placement.

Kuppaswamy Iyengar is an Associate Professor, Associate Director, and Regents Lecturer in the architecture program at the University of New Mexico. Professor Iyengar is a highly skilled teacher and technical consultant, combining his degrees in civil and structural engineering and architecture with over fifty years' practical experience. In addition to developing academic courses of study, he has designed and presented over 50 seminars in professional settings, bringing his expertise to students in academic, governmental, and commercial locations in India, Barbados, the USA, England, Canada, Australia, the Philippines, and Thailand.

Sustainable Architectural Design

An Overview

Kuppaswamy Iyengar

Routledge
Taylor & Francis Group

NEW YORK AND LONDON

First published 2015
by Routledge
711 Third Avenue, New York, NY 10017

and by Routledge
2 Park Square, Milton Park, Abingdon, Oxon OX14 4RN

Routledge is an imprint of the Taylor & Francis Group, an informa business

© 2015 Taylor & Francis

The right of Kuppaswamy Iyengar to be identified as author of this work has been asserted by him in accordance with sections 77 and 78 of the Copyright, Designs and Patents Act 1988.

Every effort has been made to contact and acknowledge copyright owners, but the author and publisher would be pleased to have any errors or omissions brought to their attention so that corrections may be published at a later printing. Readers should be aware that local building codes and standards vary widely by region and may require verification and research.

Library of Congress Cataloguing in Publication Data
Iyengar, Kuppaswamy.
Sustainable architectural design : an overview / Kuppaswamy Iyengar.
pages cm
Includes bibliographical references and index.
1. Sustainable architecture. 2. Architectural design. I. Title.
NA2542.36.I94 2015
720'.47--dc23
2014031955

ISBN: 978-0-415-70234-8 (hbk)
ISBN: 978-0-415-70235-5 (pbk)
ISBN: 978-1-315-75847-3 (ebk)

Acquisition Editor: Wendy Fuller
Editorial Assistant: Grace Harrison
Production Editor: Jennifer Birtill

Typeset in 10.5/13.5 pt Adobe Caslon
by Fakenham Prepress Solutions, Fakenham, Norfolk NR21 8NN

This book is dedicated to my beloved wife, Lalitha.

Contents

Figures

Acknowledgments

I thank many authors for their dedication to educating future designers in sustainable architecture and many others all over the world for creating awareness about global warming and its consequences. I owe them my profound gratitude.

Katherine Enggass, my editor, while never wavering in her support of this project, relentlessly verified my writing and made sure that I mostly got it right.

I owe my gratitude to Professor Stephen Dent at the University of New Mexico for thoroughly reviewing an earlier draft for technical content, and Professor Andrew Pressman at the University of Maryland for guiding in framing the book and generally supporting my effort. I thank UNM Adjunct Professor Lawrence Schuster for detailed review and advice on the HVAC section. I am responsible for any errors of omission and/or commission.

I am grateful to my students Norian Ubechel, UNM Architecture (2007), for helping me in researching the book material; Mathew Frantz, UNM Architecture (2009), and Christopher Murphy, UNM Architecture (2014), for drawing all the figures and tables in the book; and Sarah Sheesley, UNM Language Studies (2014), for her patient efforts in obtaining permissions.

I thank Routledge/Taylor Francis: to my commissioning editor, Wendy Fuller, for her vision and her support for this book, and to Laura Williamson, Emma Gadsden, and Grace Harrison for their tireless encouragement and editorial support.

If I missed anyone to thank here, I apologize – it is not intentional.

Introduction

Current Approaches to Sustainable Design and Resource Efficiency

Sustainable Architectural Design: An Overview aims to assist teachers and designers to plan and create buildings that meet the needs of the present without compromising the ability of future generations to meet their own needs [1]. This notion of preserving the planet for present and future generations poses several fundamental issues. Of primary concern is the interaction between natural systems (the regenerative capacity of the Earth's biosphere) and human demands for natural resources. We humans are acting as though fresh resources will be discovered to satisfy our inexhaustible need, as if there is a second Earth waiting to provide for us when we run out of supplies. History reveals multiple examples alerting us that civilizations vanish when they out-strip their resources. Now we may be approaching just such a moment on a planetary level.

What is the response of the building and construction industry to these issues? Will the industry continue to contribute approximately 50 percent of greenhouse gas (GHG) emissions through its buildings as architect Edward Mazria contends [2]? Or will educators help designers learn how to make key sustainable decisions in the early stages of their projects, resolving to use passive and active green technologies to produce the least amount of carbon dioxide and other gases?

Specifically, as a teacher, I am writing this book as a tool to meet challenges of my students to relate technical information to the studio design process, all within the context of sustainability. For designing sustainable (Net Zero or Net Plus) architectural buildings I recommend a three-step approach: (1) *do it right first time* through awareness of cultural and formal aesthetics, environmentally sound practices

Figure I.1   Jean Marie Tjibaou Cultural Center for Kanak Population, New Caledonia.
(Source: © ADCK – Centre Culturel Tjibaou/RPBW/Architects.)

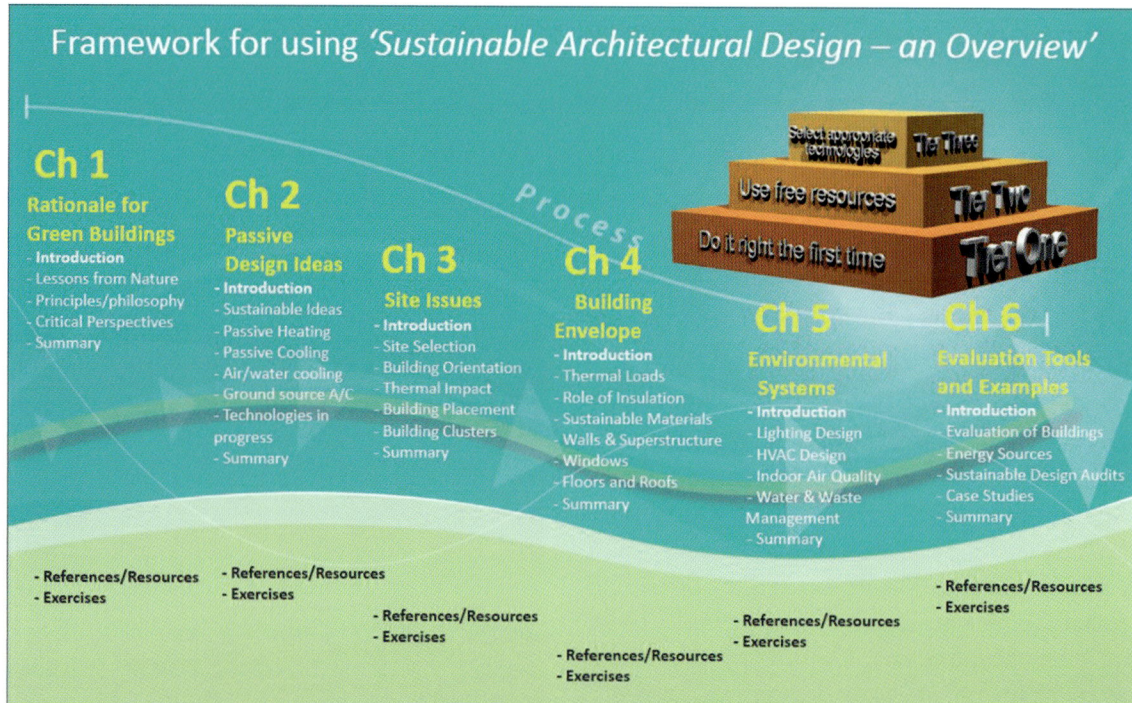

Figure I.2 A framework for using *Sustainable Architectural Design: An Overview.*
(Source: Kuppaswamy Iyengar.)

that take advantage of orientation, capturing the natural assets of the land, wind, and sun; (2) *use free energy* by understanding issues involved in sustainable design – the site, building envelope, materials used, indoor air quality, water management, and minimizing waste following some of the LEED® guidelines; and (3) *minimize fossil fuel energy* by using the most efficient technical systems possible.

The book's organization reflects this overall whole-system thinking design approach and gives students a simple framework for moving through a series of choices while learning to apply their design ideas. The intention of this book is to go beyond merely building sustainable buildings, but also to contribute to an attitude or habit of thought that is responsive to global environmental issues. Educators can use the material in this book to cover one semester as a seminar course in 16 weeks. The content is especially effective when accompanied by a studio design project as part of the learning process. The book's chapters correspond to the three-step approach outlined above.

At the forefront of change is the merging of two trends in sustainable design: *technological innovation* and a *cultural/formal aesthetic.* The resolution of these movements can be examined in the work of Renzo Piano, who used high-tech innovations while reflecting the Kanak spirit of place in the design of the Jean-Marie Tjibaou Cultural Center, New Caledonia (see Figure I.1). He used high-tech environmental principles to create a center that is a combination of spirit and culture of place, appropriate sustainable passive and active technologies, and suitable use of materials, similar to the three-step approach shown in Figure I.2.

It is hoped that through the above example and many others provided in the text, this book will inspire students to use the tools needed to integrate sustainable technology as an indistinguishable part of *the aesthetic harmony of the built environment.*

References

[1] UN Brundtland Report: http://conspect.nl/pdf/ Our_Common_Future-Brundtland_Report_1987. pdf

[2] Christopher Hawthorne, Turning down the global thermostat, *Metropolis Magazine*, 2003.

CHAPTER ONE

Rationale for Green Buildings

1.1 Rationale for Sustainable Architecture

Sustainable architectural design is part of an increasing awareness that we must use our ingenuity as creative humans to face the ecological and environmental concerns of our planet. An understanding of the global context informs "green" or ecologically responsive design. This section examines environmental and ecological issues that pertain to architecture and calls for a new social and global sense of responsibility.

Background

Architectural sustainability borrows from the widely accepted global definition, which aims to meet the needs of the present generation without compromising the ability of future generations to meet their own needs [5]. Understanding this broad definition provides a context that can then be narrowed to address architectural issues. Primarily it is important to understand the interaction between natural regenerative systems and the human need for resources. The question that arises here is the magnitude of resources we require to sustain ourselves in this world.

The aim of sustainability is to maintain ecological balance, allowing all life forms the opportunity to survive and flourish. A sustainable society can meet its needs by using the natural resources and ecological services of the planet without degrading the environment that supplies these services. Human demand placed on the environment has the potential to cause imbalance in ecological cycles and impede the production of renewable natural resources for future generations.

Biodiversity becomes crippled when the biosphere cannot keep up its productivity to support human and other life needs and to offset waste. The term *"ecological footprint"* was conceived at the University of British Columbia by Mathis Wackernagel and William Rees in 1990 to describe our impact on the planet. It is a measurement of how much land, water, and natural resources a person, city, country, or humanity as a whole requires to produce the resources it consumes. To leave no footprint would mean that a person replaces into the environment exactly what he or she takes out of it. Since the mid 1980s, humankind has been in ecological overshoot, meaning we are taking more than we are giving back. For example, according to the *Living Planet Report 2006*, the ecological footprint of the USA is 9.6 gha (global hectares) per capita × 300 million people = 2,880 gha, while the ecological footprint of India is 0.8 gha per capita × 1,200 million people = 960 gha. Even though the population of the USA is a quarter that of India, its demand for world resources is about three times greater. Other countries fall between these extremes [6]. In other words, we in the USA require far more resources than people in India to sustain our lifestyle, thus leaving a larger impact on the environment. What kind of equity should there be between developed, developing, and underdeveloped countries?

Some might wonder why we should care about sustainability. Prerequisites to healthy and stable societies depend on meeting basic human needs such as controlling unprecedented growth of human numbers and sensible management of vital natural resources (fresh water, forests). Living systems create essential materials such as wood and food. They also provide the services derived from these products (trees can provide building materials, for example). These renewable resources are more critical to human prosperity than nonrenewable resources [1]. Our well-being and our survival depend on our treatment of the planet.

Climatic changes occur as a net result of both internal and external forces. Carbon dioxide is known to absorb long-wave infrared radiation as it rebounds from the Earth's surface. This CO_2 absorption traps the heat in the Earth's atmosphere, causing a greenhouse effect, without which life on the planet cannot exist. Concentrations of atmospheric GHGs and their associated radiation forces on the Earth's climatic system have substantially increased as a result of human activities in the last few decades. Atmospheric concentrations of CO_2 have climbed from nearly 280 parts per million (ppm) in 1760, when the Industrial Revolution began, to 387 ppm in 2009. In 2008, some 7.9 billion tons of carbon were emitted from the burning of fossil fuels and 1.5 billion tons were emitted from deforestation, for a total of 9.4 billion tons. But since nature absorbs only about five billion tons per year in oceans, soils, and vegetation, nearly half of the remaining emissions stay in the atmosphere, pushing up CO_2 levels [2].

Unfortunately, several environmental concerns, including CO_2 emissions, water scarcity, population growth, pollution, and more, remain a threat to our planet. Scientists have conclusively declared that uncontrolled CO_2 emissions by human activities are the cause of many ecological problems facing the world now and will continue to be a major problem. *Climate Change 2007: Synthesis Report*, by the Intergovernmental Panel on Climate Change (IPCC), declared that warming of the climate system is unequivocal. As is now evident from observations

of increases in global average air and ocean temperatures, most of the global warming in the past 50 years is attributable to human activities. US emissions rose 18 percent in the last decade, while India and China are adding to this global pollution due to their recent tremendous growth. In addition, the updated synthesis document by the Copenhagen Climate Congress [7] concluded that IPCC projections of 2007 are underestimated by 50 percent for mean sea-level rise. A business-as-usual approach to emissions results in global warming that is likely to raise sea levels by several meters in coming centuries, leading to the loss of many major coastal cities and entire island nations, causing severe disruption and consequent damage that can also be expensive.

The latest report, AR4, from the IPCC declares that

> unmitigated climate change would, in the long term, be *likely* to exceed the capacity of natural, managed and human systems to adapt. Many impacts can be reduced, delayed or avoided by mitigation. Mitigation efforts and investments over the next two to three decades will have a large impact on opportunities to achieve lower stabilization levels. Delayed emission reductions significantly constrain the opportunities to achieve lower stabilization levels and increase the risk of more severe climate change impacts.

If the world continues business-as-usual, emissions will double by 2055. To prevent the worst consequences of global warming, scientists recommend freezing and reducing net global emissions at 2010 levels [3].

The difference between the business-as-usual scenario and the flat path of CO_2 emissions for the next 50 years can be shown as a triangle (Figure 1.1.1). Pacala and Socolow of Princeton University divided this hypothetical triangle into seven stabilization wedges, which represent different measures that must be taken to reduce emissions. By reducing the stabilization wedge of 14 gigatons of CO_2 into seven smaller wedges, the task is much easier to conceptualize. When speaking of different strategies to reduce emissions, the phrase "to reduce one wedge's worth" is often employed. Essentially, these wedges, each valued at 25 billion tons of carbon, fit broadly into the following four major categories [3]:

1 efficiency (four strategies)
2 decarbonization of power (five strategies)
3 decarbonization of fuel (four strategies)
4 forest and agricultural soils (two strategies).

Figure 1.1.1 also shows how important it is to begin managing the climate problem as soon as possible. Of particular interest here is that efficiency is one of the major contributors to reducing GHG emissions. Scientists and designers strongly recommend that actions be taken to reduce emissions of carbon dioxide and other GHGs. Adding scrubbers to power plants and catalytic converters to cars does not significantly limit the carbon dioxide we emit into the atmosphere. Using energy efficiently, however, is a far-reaching strategy that can make an important contribution to the reduction of greenhouse gases.

In addition to the problem of emissions, water scarcity affects one-third of the world at present, and this could dramatically change to two-thirds by 2025. Ten percent of the grain harvest is from pumped water in India, China, and the Great Plains in the USA. Without significant change in water-use practices, this harvest will be unavailable one day.

Current estimates indicate that the world population grew beyond seven billion in 2012. This causes enormous demands on global resources, and meeting those demands causes greater pollution to be emitted to the environment (see Figure 1.1.2).

The *Living Planet Report 2006* by WWF International confirms that we are using the planet's resources faster than they can be renewed. Our ecological footprint has tripled since 1961. Since we have already exceeded our limits to manage our resources, we must act now to bring some balance into our activities on this planet. It is time to make some critical choices to make the impact on the natural world manageable.

Human Perspectives and Social Responsibility

J. R. McNeill, in *Something New Under the Sun* [4] points to the unusual adaptability and cleverness of the human species in the twentieth century, but also reminds us that we have missed the evolutionary focus of interconnectedness and a mutually dependent world. In his opinion, our short-term focus on exploitation will eventually cause injury to the whole race.

Sustainable issues deserve long-term focus and should span several generations. As Figure 1.1.3 reveals, it is rare that human interest reaches the global level that is needed for the sustainable worldview.

Humankind has inherited 3.8 billion years of natural capital, vital and rich resources that also

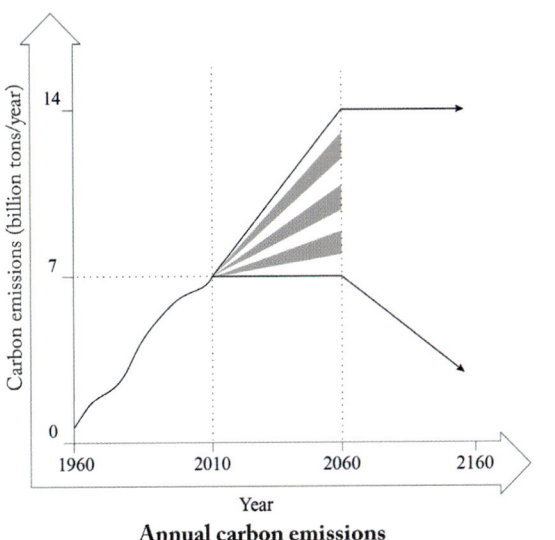

Annual carbon emissions

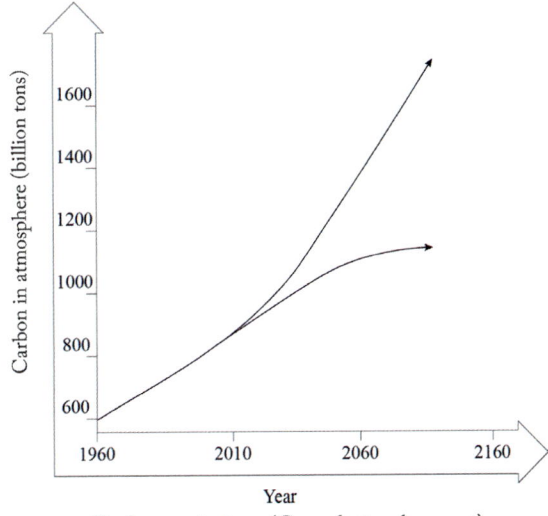

Carbon emissions (Cumulative Amount)

Figure 1.1.1 Managing climate change.
(Source: Energy Future Beyond Carbon, *Scientific American*, New York: 9/2006.)

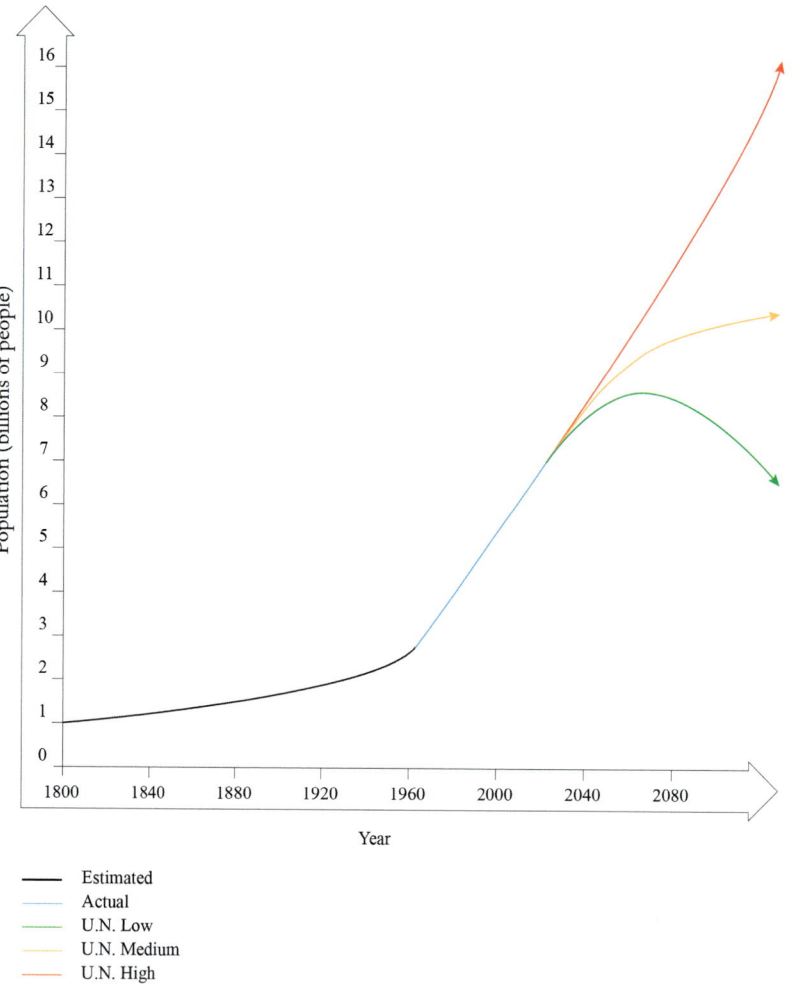

Figure 1.1.2 Exponential population growth.
(Source: this file is licensed under the Creative Commons Attribution Share Alike 3.0 Unported license. Data sourced from the United Nations, Department of Economic and Social Affairs, Population Division, Population Estimates and Projections Section, "World Population Prospects: The 2012 Revision," and the United States Census Bureau.)

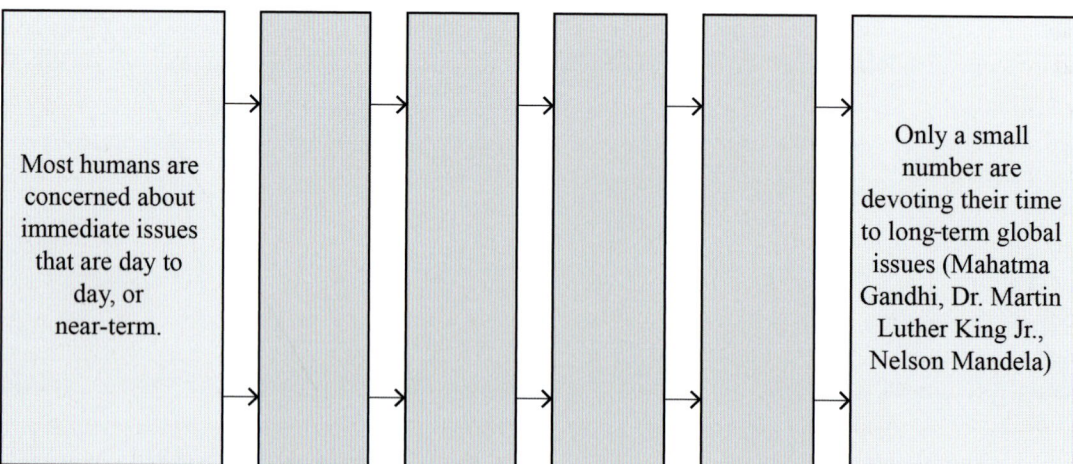

Figure 1.1.3 Human interest for the long haul: *What is closest is most important to us.*
(Source: Kuppaswamy Iyengar.)

present an opportunity for environmental responsibility [1]. The waste, reckless use of resources, and disproportionate distribution of vital natural capital based on the wealth of some nations continues to cause social unrest and injury to many people. This cannot go on for long without severe consequences. Elie Wiesel, a winner of the Nobel Peace Prize in 1986, tells a Midrashic story reflective of our situation. We now need to think of the larger picture:

> A man is on a boat. He is not alone, but acts as if he were. One night, he begins to cut a hole under his seat. His neighbors shriek: "Have you gone mad? Do you want to sink us all?" Calmly, he answers them, "What I am doing is none of your business. I paid my way. I'm only cutting a hole under my own seat." What the man will not accept, what you and I cannot forget is that all of us are in the same boat [8].

Nations cannot do whatever they please, even if they appear to have the means and resources to indulge at the present time. The actions of a nation affect the rest of the world and every nation must act responsibly.

Rationale for Sustainable Development

What does all this mean specifically in terms of architecture and all of us concerned with design and development of buildings? What can be done? Architecture and the building industry in North America alone contribute approximately 48 percent of GHG emissions [9] and consume nearly 50 percent of available resources over the life of a building. This kind of resource depletion is unsustainable. A building typically uses resources during its life to maintain comfort for its occupants through heat and cool energies, lighting, electricity, natural gas, and other energy sources. Sustainable and green building design employs strategies to reduce the collective negative environmental impact during the entire life of the building, from the mining of raw materials, to production of building components, construction, maintenance, and disposal phases.

Practitioners of sustainable building often seek to achieve ecological but also aesthetic harmony between a structure and its surrounding natural and built environment. Aesthetics need not suffer through

sustainable design. The appearance and style of sustainable design can bring forward a new aesthetic and a new idea of what is beautiful. Sustainable design and green buildings emphasize taking advantage of renewable resources, e.g., using sunlight through passive and active solar techniques, using plants and trees through green roofs, or adding rain gardens to minimize run-off. There are many other proven techniques available for the designer, which will be discussed later in this book. The point is, sometimes less is more and less is elegant!

As part of a new attitude toward the planet, it is encouraging that in the USA a certification process called LEED® (Leadership in Energy and Environmental Design) prompts designers to consider all available options to make new and existing buildings as sustainable as possible. Worldwide there are several assessment and rating systems such as Green Building Councils (GBCs) and Building Research Establishment Environmental Assessment Method (BREEAM), and several others to assist a designer (see more on these systems in Chapter 6). Designers can use their knowledge to illustrate to society that there are many possibilities for reducing the use of valuable fossil fuels and increasing the use of renewable resources.

To conclude, why is sustainability an imperative for architectural design? It:

1 is comfortable for the user;
2 uses fewer non-renewable resources;
3 can be less expensive, especially in the long term;
4 is responsible to the community as a whole;
5 reduces CO_2 emissions and global warming.

Summary

Many environmental concerns such as CO_2 emissions, water scarcity, population growth, waste, and pollution are straining our planet's ability to keep pace with our demand for resources. For our own well-being as well as that of other living things, we must work to bring balance to our activities on the planet. Since architecture is a big part of this drain on resources and also contributes nearly half of GHG emissions in North America, designers have an imperative to right some of the wrongs through sustainable building designs.

References

[1] Paul Hawken, Amory Lovins, and Hunter Lovins, *Natural Capitalism* (Boston, MA: Little, Brown and Company, 1999).

[2] Lester Brown, *Future at Risk on a Hotter Planet* (New York: W.W. Norton & Company, 2009).

[3] Energy Future Beyond Carbon, *Scientific American* (9/2006)

[4] J.R. McNeill, *Something New Under the Sun* (New York: W.W. Norton & Company, 2001).

[5] UN Brundtland Report: http://conspect.nl/pdf/Our_Common_Future-Brundtland_Report_1987.pdf.

[6] WWF, *Living Planet Report* (2006): assets.panda.org/downloads/living_planet_report.pdf.

[7] K. Richardson, Will Steffen, Hans Joachim Schellnhuber, Joseph Alcamo, Terry Barker, Daniel M. Kammen, Rik Leemans, Diana Liverman, Mohan Munasinghe, Balgis Osman-Elasha, Nicholas Stern, Ole Waever, *Climate Change: Synthesis Report: Global Risks, Challenges and Decisions, Copenhagen 2009* (Copenhagen: University of Copenhagen, 2009)

[8] Earth Journal, *Environmental Almanac and Resource Directory* (Boulder, CO: Buzzworm Books, 1993).

[9] Christopher Hawthorne, Turning down the global thermostat, *Metropolis Magazine*, 2003.

Further Reading

Donella Meadows and Dennis Meadows, *The Limits to Growth* (New York: Universe Books, 1972).

Rocky Mountain Institute, *Green Developments* (Westminster, CO: Rocky Mountain Institute, 2001).

Web Support

www.wri.org/chart/wedges-concept

Exercises

1 Describe how CO_2 and greenhouse gas (GHG) emissions affect global climate and the consequences for our human population.

2 Compare per capita ecological footprints between Canada and China.

3 How would you explain why your client should care about sustainable architectural design?

4 Search the Sustainable Building Alliance website to find six core indicators of sustainability. List them.

1.2   Lessons from Nature

Change begins with new thinking. How do aspiring designers synthesize sustainable elements of environmental responsiveness, resource efficiency, community and social sensitivity, and aesthetic quality? Sustainable designers must learn to allocate design priorities of architectural systems differently. This means understanding whole-system design thinking and developing a vision of what sustainability should look like in the future. Whole-system thinking involves recognition of the interconnectedness of several systems. Many solutions are sought and the final solution addresses many questions.

Systems are Interconnected

The concept of sustainable design recognizes that human civilization is an integral part of the natural world. Nature must be preserved, respected, and perpetuated if the human community itself is to survive. When we look at certain churches, cathedrals, temples, bridges, pyramids, and other man-made structures built a few centuries ago, our minds are filled with admiration and awe. And yet, nature has been building remarkable structures in a sustainable way for millions of years. Nature teaches us in countless examples about whole-system thinking. In his book *Animal Architecture*, Karl von Frisch [1] describes how different termite species build and air-condition their dwellings, requiring quite sophisticated building configurations. In the Ivory Coast, the species *Macrotermes bellicosus* builds mounds about 3–4 m high. These mounds withstand the effects of nature – sun, wind, rain, and other forces – and also control indoor climate very effectively using an ingenious ventilation system. What can we learn from these amazing structures? (See Figure 1.2.1.)

The conical shape of a termite mound resists wind forces, typical of a vertical cantilever, while

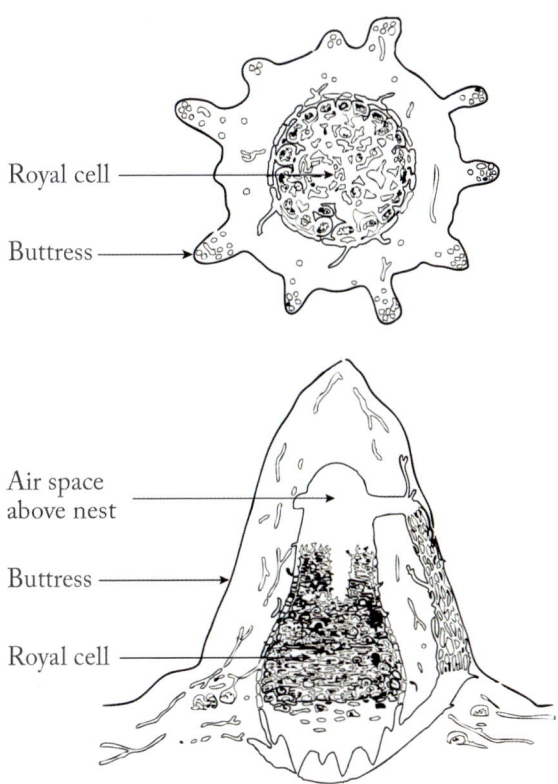

Royal cell

Buttress

Air space
above nest

Buttress

Royal cell

Figure 1.2.1   Animal architecture: air-conditioning in termite mounds. Termite mounds withstand the effects of sun, wind, rain, and other forces while controlling the indoor climate very effectively using an ingenious ventilation system. (Source: Karl von Frisch, *Animal Architecture* (New York and London: Harcourt Brace Jovanovich, Inc; 1974).)

also serving additional functions. Due to its radial porous ventilation ducts, the structure must extend outward to increase the moment of inertia (increase the geometrical shape), which, in turn, compensates for the loss of area of the cross-section due to porosity. This termite community of over two million consumes abundant oxygen. The exterior and interior walls are so porous that the exchange of carbon dioxide to oxygen is very efficient. This natural ventilation system is an engineering marvel that shows the interdependency of multiple parts, thus illustrating the concept of whole-system thinking.

Nature as a model, which studies natural systems and processes and then imitates them to solve human problems, can help us improve the efficiency of industrial processes. We need to question the value of manufacture when compared with natural processes. Natural processes are nearly 100 percent efficient and there is minimal waste. Waste of one species becomes a resource for another. Some scientists and researchers believe that our overall manufacture has a 1:100 ratio

of durable:waste products, while only 6 percent of materials actually end up in products. That is not a great story to tell our future generations.

In contrast, the next story *is* a great one. What if, for example, we decided to learn from and imitate nature rather than waste it? Take, for instance, the truly efficient construction technique used by the spider seen in the sketches in Figure 1.2.2, taken from Frisch's *Animal Architecture*. The spider first constructs a beam across two branches and bisects it to drop a vertical column to the ground. Then all the other members of the web are triangulated in the same fashion. The true marvel is that this construction material, silk produced by the spider, is supposed to be stronger than Kevlar and carbon steel, according to science writer Janine Benyus [2]! This realization has prompted scientists to investigate how we can duplicate the technique for human use in manufacturing and construction.

Consider, also, the example of a tree. It gives shade and fruit when it is alive; after that it can be

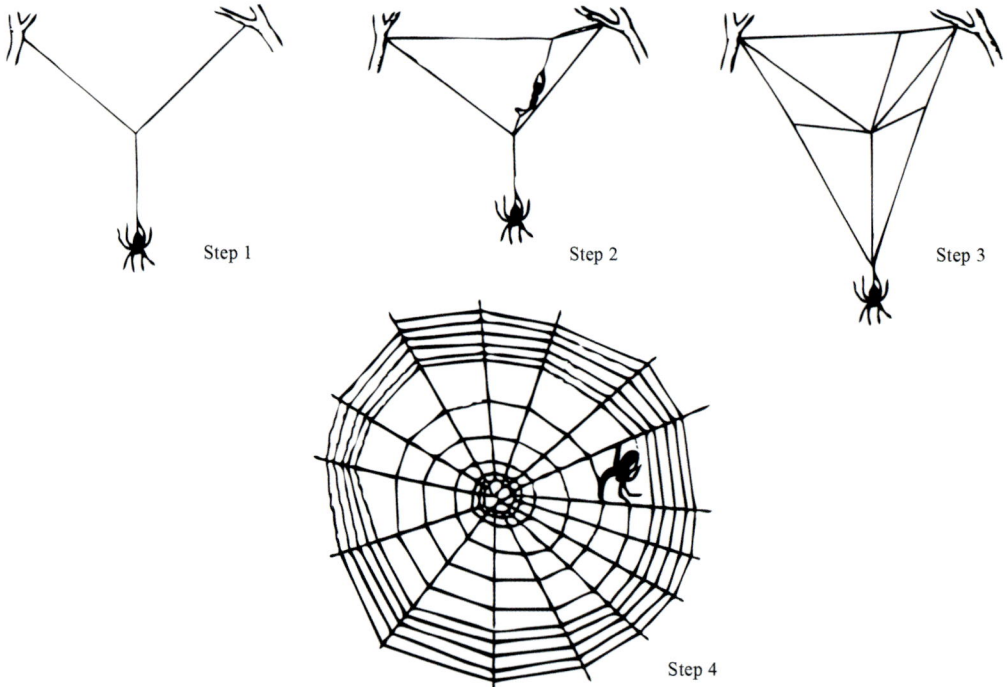

Figure 1.2.2   Animal architecture: the spider's web. *The truly efficient construction technique used by the spider.* (Source: Karl von Frisch, *Animal Architecture* (New York and London: Harcourt Brace Jovanovich, Inc; 1974).)

Figure 1.2.3   Thimmakka nurtured this avenue of massive trees (image courtesy of Professor Sreedhara Murthy, NMKRV Institute Bangalore).

a doorframe, furniture, or many other products. In the end, when it is done serving that purpose, it can become firewood or food for insects. We should learn from nature how to construct, deconstruct, and reconstruct again.

Even one individual can make a difference. Below is an inspiring story of a nurturing spirit that in the end has been rewarded many times over for her long efforts to help the planet.

Saalumarada Thimmakka, a native of Hulikal Village near Bangalore, India, received no formal education and worked as a casual laborer in a nearby quarry. She was married to a cattle herder but they unfortunately could not have children. It is said that Thimmakka started to plant *Ficus* (banyan) trees (Figure 1.2.3) in lieu of having children. She is referred to as Saalumarada ("of the row of trees" in the local language) because of her work in planting and tending to the 284 *Ficus* trees along a 4 km stretch of highway. For decades she walked many miles carrying pitchers of water to nurture the plants. Her work has been honored by the National Citizen's Award of India, and a US environmental organization based in California, Thimmakka's Resources for Environmental Education, is named after her.

A Vision of Environmental Sustainability

Building a more environmentally stable future clearly requires a holistic vision of that future. If fossil fuels are not to be used for power, then what? If forests are no longer to be cleared to grow food, then how is a larger population to be fed? If a throwaway culture leads inevitably to pollution and resource depletion, how will material needs be satisfied? In other words, as the authors of *Saving the Planet* ask, if the present path is obviously unsound, what picture of the future can be substituted to move toward a global community that can endure [3]? As highlighted in *Saving the Planet*, we need to address all the above questions through:

- prudent design of efficient buildings and infrastructures;
- city planning with care and concern for future generations;
- careful and appropriate management of resources;

- global equity and balance in use of resources;
- minimal waste at all levels;
- reuse, recycle, retrofit, and regeneration as a part of our daily existence; and
- production processes in our industries that rely on renewable energy.

To do this, we must emphasize in all of our educational institutions that it is crucial that we care for this planet.

The vision for ecologically and environmentally sensitive buildings is that they are by definition better buildings, offering comfort to occupants and profit to builders. They are healthier buildings, resulting in diminished risk to the user as well as to developers from reduced liability. In the long run they can be cheaper and more efficient than traditional architecture. These buildings use natural energy flows – e.g., sun, wind – to augment performance, and use non-renewable resources efficiently.

Our vision also must include the need for reaching carbon neutrality in buildings. Most buildings use energy in the form of electricity, natural gas, and other fossil fuels to operate, or in the case of industries, to manufacture. All of these fuels generate carbon dioxide (CO_2), producing greenhouse gases in the atmosphere. Buildings that plan to offset these CO_2 emissions can approach carbon neutrality by proper building design, use of trees and other vegetation, minimal use of fossil fuels, and other best practices such as use of non-toxic products in construction and maintenance.

Some Suggestions to Achieve Ecological Balance

Natural Capitalism, by Paul Hawken *et al.*, contains suggestions for dealing with complex concerns of global warming. Instead of viewing issues in isolation, this book is about the common link between nature, economics, environment, and society. It reveals how tomorrow a business will derive profits from its own realization and practice of environmental responsibility. Hawken's suggestions fall into four major categories: learning from nature (introduced briefly at the beginning of this chapter); resource management; appreciating value of service; and investing in natural capital.

Resource management concentrates on managing our existing resources more effectively to improve the quality of life for everyone across the globe – prudent agricultural practices, efficient lighting, comfortable travel by fuel-efficient vehicles, energy-efficient buildings (e.g. air-conditioning). If all of these are done well, they should cost less.

Resources do not exist for all the world population to attain Western standards of living, but radical improvements in resource productivity can support the efforts of sustainability in these countries.

Appreciation for value of service, rather than concentrating on selling commodities can improve the manufacturing process and minimize waste. This involves a shift in thinking. As we all know, keeping our offices environmentally comfortable requires chillers and heaters using, in most cases, electricity. We pay the utility company for the kilowatts and kilowatt-hours on a schedule. A different way of looking at this service is to say we are paying someone to guarantee a temperature of 70°F in all our rooms whenever we are in them. Such a concept eliminates the payment for a commodity (kwH) and replaces it with paying for results (comfortable temperature). This, in turn, opens up the door to alternative energy-management techniques for heating, cooling, and more. There are companies such as Interface, for example, who will lease carpeting to a customer for a period of time, say for 20 years. The company will maintain the carpet, repair it whenever necessary, and recycle the waste carpet. The idea here is that nothing in nature is exhausted in its first use and it can be reused and recycled. This model of a *service economy* was proposed in the mid 1980s by German scientist Michael Braungart, based on the nature of material cycles.

Hawken's fourth value of community and social sensitivity requires that we *invest in natural capital*. Stories of natural disasters and their human costs abound in this world. Hurricane Katrina, for example, caused over $200 billion in damages and untold amounts of grief to thousands of people. Years of neglect, mismanagement, and an uncaring attitude toward scientific advice contributed to this disaster. Ideally, all societies should support and maintain the vital flow of life-supporting services to all people in the world. Societies must adopt shared goals and enhance social values. When these values are not appreciated and acted upon, conflicts and resentments can result. Perhaps if the rest of the country had the foresight to adopt shared values by insisting on appropriate funding to strengthen the levees, then the effects of the Katrina disaster could have been minimized.

Avoid Waste: Recycle, Retrofit, Reuse, and Regenerate

In the USA, 50 trillion tons of solid waste is created each year [2]. If liquid waste is included, this number becomes a mind-boggling 250 trillion tons. Imagine the amount of waste produced by human beings as a whole in the entire world!

In *Lean Thinking*, James Womack illustrates the life of an aluminum soda can. A ton of bauxite ore is mined in Australia or elsewhere and goes through a smelting process, resulting in ingots of half tons. These are sent to another country for conversion to thick sheets and then to yet another country in Europe to reheat and create very thin rolled sheets. The thin sheets are shipped to factories in the USA, where they are made into 8- or 12-ounce cans, labeled, filled with the desired liquids, and fitted with pop-up lids. Typically, these drinks are consumed in less than 6–8 minutes and the cans are thrown away. Nearly 88 percent of these cans are discarded in the USA and 85 percent in the UK. According to the authors of *Natural Capitalism* these discarded aluminum cans in the USA, each one weighing 17 grams, could replace the entire fleet of commercial aircraft every three months, which comes to nearly 2.998 billion pounds or 1.5 million tons of aluminum that could be recycled.

The lesson is that designers should consider, at all levels, ways to recycle, retrofit, reuse, and regenerate just as nature does. For example, we can recycle scrap materials such as steel, brick, stone, and others for new buildings; retrofit a warehouse to become an elegant electronic industry; and reuse an abandoned jail by converting it into a delightful hotel. Once we start realizing that pure water, clean air, and healthy forests are not endless commodities and also have significant monetary and social merit, perhaps we will pay more attention and use our resources more appropriately.

Summary

Biomimicry is a thought process that examines nature and its incredibly efficient systems and then imitates them to solve human problems. Whole-systems thinking, or seeing the interrelatedness of many systems working together, is another tool that can help designers plan sustainable projects. Sustainable design requires a new way of thinking about productivity, waste, performance, and the impact of buildings on environmental conditions and human quality of life.

References

[1] Karl von Frisch, *Animal Architecture* (New York and London: Harcourt Brace Jovanovich, Inc; 1974).

[2] Paul Hawken, Amory Lovins, and Hunter Lovins, *Natural Capitalism* (Boston, MA: Little, Brown and Company, 1999).

[3] Lester R. Brown, Christopher Flavin, and Sandra Postel, *Saving the Planet* (New York: W.W. Norton & Company, 1991).

Further Reading

Donella Meadows and Dennis Meadows, *The Limits to Growth* (New York: Universe Books, 1972).

Energy Future Beyond Carbon, *Scientific American* (9/2006).

J.R. McNeill, *Something New Under the Sun* (New York: Norton, 2000).

Rocky Mountain Institute, *Green developments* (Westminster, CO: Rocky Mountain Institute, 2001).

James Womack and Daniel Jones, *Lean Thinking* (New York: Simon & Schuster, Inc, 1996).

US Department of Energy, *Energy Information Administration (EIA)* (May–July 2008).

Web Support

www.carbonfootprint.com/calculator
www.epa.gov/climatechange/ghgemissions/ind-calculator.html
www.redefiningprogress.org
www.deccanherald.com
www.topics.nytimes.com/timestopics/kyoto_protocol

Exercises

1 Find articles for and against global warming. Which arguments do you believe and why?
2 Search and sketch two examples of *animal architecture* and explain how these examples from nature might be used in building design.
3 Take a building system such as fenestration and use "whole-system thinking" to examine how it might contribute to the larger system of the building.

1.3 Principles and Philosophy

The theoretical underpinnings that inform green design decisions link environmental, social, and economic goals. The section contains a series of statements about designing with forethought and consideration of the environmental impact of our designs. It concludes with the importance of education and sharing knowledge as part of this quest.

A Unified Approach to Sustainable Decision-Making

Many environmental thinkers are convinced that the extent of climate change, species extinction, and other environmental degradation is due for the most part to the built environment and demands resulting from suddenly increasing populations in certain regions of the world. Political leaders have joined together to try to address this problem. The Kyoto Protocol, which the USA has not signed, entered into force in 2005 after intense negotiations between nations and final ratification by Russia. Among other issues, the Protocol required developed countries to reduce their GHG emissions by 5 percent against the baseline of 1990 by 2012. This Protocol introduced innovative market-based mechanisms in order to be flexible. They are (1) emissions trading, (2) joint implementation, and (3) the Clean Development Mechanism (CDM), which demands non-polluting growth. The intent is that these concepts will create opportunities to identify and act upon lowest-cost ways to reduce emissions by developed nations.

After the Kyoto Protocol, several international summits were held and promises were made. Years later, the world is still grappling with how to proceed with the problems and concerns of environment, energy, and global warming.

Designers are now asking what roles planning and design can have in improving the situation. A multi-faceted approach to sustainability in architecture is advisable.

Facets of Sustainability

Basic facets of sustainable design include:

- Solving for the problem – ideas of holistic design *(no particular style, different for different locations).*
- Seeing the trees *and* the forest – environmental responsiveness and respect for land *(respecting what is already there – landforms, sun, vegetation, etc.).*
- Resource efficiency *(land, fossil fuels, minerals, materials – doing more with less).*
- Cultural sensitivity *(avoiding long commutes, auto dependency, monotonous development, and compromised quality of life issues).*
- Avoiding redundancy – doing it right first time *(avoid waste – reuse, recycle, retrofit, and regenerate).*

Sustainable Building Design Principles

The basic facets of sustainable design can be incorporated as principles of sustainable buildings and objects with forethought about their environmental impact, their effects on sustainable growth, and their overall impact on society. Sustainable building design principles can be separated into six key areas:

1 *Site issues including site selection*: Minimize urban sprawl; be responsive and respectful to the land, the environment, habitat, and green space; and encourage high-density urban development over low-density development to preserve valuable green space and preserve key environmental assets. Designers can minimize site disturbance and regenerate and preserve valuable habitat, green space, and ecosystems.
2 *Building envelope responding to climate, architectural form, and material*: Select safe building materials suitable for the climate and for long-term value with maximum recycled and renewable content, and manage other resources such as energy and water through efficient aesthetic and engineering design, and thoughtful planning for construction by minimizing waste.
3 *Energy use and dealing with passive and active systems*: Recognize the interdependence of natural systems and maximize the use of renewable energy and other low-impact energy sources. Follow natural energy flows to minimize adverse impacts on the environment (air, water, land, natural resources) through climate-responsive building siting, optimized building design and envelope selection, material selection, and use of energy-efficient mechanical and electrical systems. Resultant building performance should approach Net Zero energy performance.
4 *Indoor environment*: Sustainable building design should incorporate the best possible healthy conditions in terms of indoor air quality, ventilation, and thermal comfort, access to natural ventilation and daylighting, and effective control of the acoustical environment without VOCs and other harmful agents.
5 *Water and waste management*: Minimize the unnecessary and inefficient use of potable water on the site and the building while maximizing the recycling and reuse of water, including harvested rainwater, storm water, and gray water.
6 *Overall evaluation including Net Zero aspects*: Formal rating systems used for evaluating design and energy performance of the buildings, include using Energy Target Finder to establish minimum technical performance and then exceeding it by cross-checking simple hand calculations and using computer simulations such as ECOTECT™, Energy 10, HEED, eQuest, and Energy Plus.

These six principles contribute to an attitude that respects nature as a teacher and views design decisions within a larger environmental, technical, economic, and social context. Newer sustainable designs pay attention to climatic conditions (bioclimatic design) through sophisticated technical simulation programs and the study of natural processes (biomimicry). The idea is to work with natural forces, rather than against them, when designing buildings.

Figure 1.3.1 Eastgate Office building, Harare, Zimbabwe, by architect Mick Pearce, in conjunction with Arup Associates. An example of a sustainable building reflecting biomimicry design concept from a termite hill (*Animal Architecture*, p. 140) by Karl Von Frisch.
(Source: photo by Mandy Patterson; this file is licensed under the Creative Commons Attribution Share Alike 3.0 Unported license.)

Need for Sustainable Architectural Designs

Well-known and contemporary architects such as Mick Pearce (see Figure 1.3.1), Sir Norman Foster, Thomas Herzog, Glen Mercutt, and Sir Richard Rogers have embraced sustainable architecture as part of their architectural practice. Their buildings are aesthetically stimulating, sustainable, and often employ biomimicry. Others in the profession could learn from their example. In essence, architectural offices must insist that architecture schools engage in sustainable design teaching.

Writing in *Harvard Design Magazine* in 2003 [1], Susannah Hagan points out that there are *intellectual*, *practical*, *technical*, *economic*, and *pedagogical* reasons for schools and architectural practices to adopt sustainable design principles. The following paragraphs have incorporated some of her thoughts.

Architects are beginning to *intellectually* appreciate nature and to apply its processes. For example, a tree's blooms appear to be alike, yet every flower is different. We can learn from nature's capacity to repeat itself without appearing identical. Imagine how this concept could be applied to our row houses and

the many repeated elements of a building, challenging the conventional boundaries of architecture. Nature, to whatever extent we understand it, is complex and non-linear. Designers can represent the dynamic nature of architecture, instead of the static aspect of representation of form.

At the present time sustainable design issues in architecture have taken two paths. One route follows with impressive success sustainable technologies, and the other track emphasizes abstract architectural aesthetics, the art and culture of architecture. Often these two approaches develop as parallel tracks without merging in any meaningful way.

However, there are exceptions. The new headquarters of Dutch courier TNT Express, designed by architect Paul de Ruiter, is truly a sustainable Dutch corporate building (Figure 1.3.2). The building's sustainability was recognized by LEED® Platinum and the Dutch GreenCalc system with a score of 1,005 points. The center is transparent, with appropriate orientation responding to site and urban conditions, social sense, logistics, and connectivity to sustainability in all dimensions of choice of materials, CO_2 emissions, healthy indoor air quality, and flexibility for the future tenants. An imposing atrium, terraced staircases, formal and informal coffee corners, and elegant meeting rooms make this building an interesting and effective design solution. The resultant architecture is a combination of spirit of place, appropriate use of materials and spaces, and sustainable design technology.

Figure 1.3.2 TNT Express Headquarters (TNT Center) Hoofddrop, Netherlands. Architect Paul de Ruiter acknowledges the spirit of this energy-positive building is "connectivity, comfort and health".
(Source: photo by Burg + Schuh, www.palladium.de.)

Sustainable design requires *technical* competence. Modern buildings are complex and must deal with demands of internal requirements while responding to ever-changing natural forces. The development of several new building materials having different and complex conductivities and other structural properties requires sophisticated software for modeling environmental performance. Architects must be competent in using these and other three-dimensional modeling techniques for integrating thermal behavior, acoustic performance, lighting qualities, impact of solar load, and final cost. The interactions between systems can result in delightful and architecturally complex buildings. Dr. Ken Yeang, a Malaysian architect, has incorporated all the above principles in many of his high-rise buildings. Yeang's Singapore Central Library (Figure 1.3.3) combines the dynamic aspects

Figure 1.3.3   Singapore Central Library, bioclimatic design by Dr. Ken Yeang. Yeang's design works with natural forces, resulting in a combination of dynamic aspects of architecture and bioclimatic techniques responding and adapting to the environment, much in the same way the human body does. (Source: photo by Nlannuzel; this file is licensed under the Creative Commons Attribution Share Alike 3.0 Unported license.)

of architecture and bioclimatic techniques, responding and adapting to the environment much in the same way the human body does, and working with natural forces rather than against them.

This ethic of being sustainable has added *economic* benefits. Many economists predict that thinking in terms of sustainability creates opportunities for jobs in new fields, transforming construction and industrial settings. A large cadre of new jobs all over the world will arise from development of new design software, new window designs, clean air technologies, and adaptive reuse of abandoned buildings. Technicians will be needed to operate new building and control systems and other sustainable technologies. In addition, if industry were to think of itself in biological terms, more attention could be paid to reducing waste and recycling, thus saving money.

Again, according to Hagan, a final reason for sustainable design is *pedagogical*. Architectural schools are just beginning to incorporate environmental design into the core curricula. New programs will require a combination of traditional design and sustainable practice, bringing together the ability to integrate aesthetics with proficiency in computer analysis and simulations. This also requires that faculty be better trained in sustainable design principles to meet the needs of today's environmentally aware architecture students. Several schools have already incorporated sustainable design education into their core curriculum, including Net Zero buildings.

Summary

Part of sustainable design is forethought and care for our future generations. If we approach projects with certain sustainable principles in mind (using natural energy flows, reducing waste, recycling, looking at the full cycle of use, and appreciation of technical innovations), we have a better chance of incorporating those principles into our designs. Theoretical discourse, modeled on some provisions of the Kyoto Protocol and other documents, brings together environmental, social, and economic concerns to create a multifaceted view of world problems and their possible solutions. Reasons for sustainable practice range from intellectual to practical, technical, economic, and pedagogical. The ultimate aim is for humanity and nature to coexist in harmony, and designers can contribute to that goal through sustainable design practices and sharing knowledge.

Reference

[1] Susannah Hagan, *Harvard Design Magazine* (Boston: Spring 2003).

Further Reading

Klaus Daniels and Ralph E. Hammann, *Energy Design for Tomorrow* (Germany: Edition Axel Menges, 2008).

Sustainable Development, Agenda 21, Kyoto Protocol (2001).

Jerry Yudelson and Ulf Meyer, *The World's Greenest Buildings* (Abingdon: Routledge, 2013).

Web Support

www.earthsummit2012.org

Exercises

1 Find a building example for each of the six sustainable principles listed in this section. Make a simple diagram of each and provide a caption that explains the principle shown.
2 Research and develop a chart showing principles used at Jean Marie Tjibaou Cultural Center for Kanak Population, New Caledonia, by Renzo Piano, and how these also reflect Kanak values.
3 Explain how two contemporary architects are using the principles of sustainable architecture in their practices.

1.4   Critical Perspectives

Current Global Efforts in Sustainable Designs

Several academic institutions and research organizations are putting forth their ideas and solutions to address the important issues involved in sustainable design. Already new constructions in the last two to three decades have made significant efforts to reduce CO_2 and GHG emissions.

To help accomplish this goal, *Architecture 2030*, a US organization, issued the challenge in 2005 for the global design community to meet fossil fuel, GHG-emitting, energy-consumption performance standards that would be 60 percent below the regional standard by 2010. Furthermore, for all new buildings, developments, and major renovations, the fossil fuel reduction standard shall increase to:

- 70 percent in 2015
- 80 percent in 2020
- 90 percent in 2025
- 100 percent carbon neutral in 2030.

In the spirit of Architecture 2030, the following institutions are also making remarkable efforts and offering hope to address the impact of global warming. Collectively, these examples illustrate that efficiency, cultural sensitivity, user behavior, cost-effectiveness, and integrated design methods support sustainable designs.

An independent nonprofit organization, *Rocky Mountain Institute* (RMI), a think-and-do-tank in Colorado, has been helping businesses to transition from a fossil fuel economy to efficiency and renewables. Their ambitious goal is to assist businesses in the USA to run on no oil, no coal, and no nuclear energy and to use one-third less natural gas by 2050. They are suggesting to US businesses three tools to become sustainable: (1) slash their own energy use and sell energy-saving products; (2) teach building users to be more sustainable in their behavior; and (3) urge designers to adopt integrative design methods.

RMI has consulted for the Byron Rogers Federal Building in Denver (Figure 1.4.1), an outstanding building for energy efficiency, with 27 kBtu/sq.ft/year energy use as compared to 166 kBtu/sq.ft/year.

As a member of a team of five key players (Clinton Climate Initiative, Empire State Building, Jones Lange LaSalle, Johnson Controls, and RMI), RMI developed an *integrated sustainability program* for the Empire State Building in New York, focused on energy efficiency and sustainability. In 2011 this building beat its year-one energy-efficiency guarantee by 5 percent, saving $2.4 million. In year two, the property surpassed its energy-efficiency guarantee by an additional 4 percent.

Figure 1.4.1 Byron Rogers Federal Building, Denver, Colorado. An outstanding energy-efficient building. (Source: photo by Hellmuth, Obata & Kassabaum, Inc.)

Solar Decathlon, started in 2002, is an award-winning US Department of Energy competitive program that challenges, on a national scale, college teams to design, build, and demonstrate solar-powered residences that are architecturally pleasing, appropriate, cost-effective, and energy efficient (Figure 1.4.2). This program has involved over 120 schools with over 18,000 students and has worldwide recognition for successful education in workforce development opportunities. It has educated the public on benefits, affordability,

and clean energy solutions. The program expanded to Europe and China in 2011.

Nationally recognized for its innovations in planning and sustainable design, *Prairie Crossing Conservation Community*, developed since 1987, is governed by essential guiding principles that include responsible development, preservation of open land and easy commuting, environmental protection, energy conservation, lifelong education, community diversity, and economic viability. Its developers believe that having a working organic farm on site is consistent with – even essential to – all of those principles. Accomplished architects developed single-family homes following Midwestern architectural tradition as well as being 50 percent more energy efficient than homes in the Chicago area. A "sense of place" is reinforced by preservation of historic buildings, open space trails, sustainable organic farms, and commuter trains (Figure 1.4.3).

Suzlon One Earth, Pune, India [1], home of the world's fifth largest wind energy company, is a three-story, 816,000 square foot commercial building that received a LEED® Platinum award and also the highest rating of five stars from India's GRIHA (Green Rating for Integrated Habitat Assessment). Suzlan serves as corporate headquarters for learning centers, with a wind energy museum, multimedia

Figure 1.4.2 2009 Solar Decathlon competition on the Washington Mall. (Source: US Department of Energy.)

Figure 1.4.3 Single-family homes at Prairie Crossing
(Source: Jeff Kingsbury, Greenstreet Ltd.)

rooms, theater, library, classrooms, and business halls. The design takes its inspiration from the traditional Indian town square, and includes a central water body and building-integrated PV panels. Owners of this facility take pride in conceptualizing and creating a self-sustaining ecosystem for managing its water, energy, and waste.

Other Global Efforts Through Certification Programs

Many green building certificate programs offer meaningful standards for sustainable design and development: Green Mark in Singapore; BREEAM in the UK and Europe; Green Star in Australia, New Zealand, and South Africa; and LEED®, developed by the US Green Building Council and used in over 130 countries. However, the elements used to measure building performance are not consistent across all continents and only focus on environmental factors. It would be useful in the future to integrate social and communal values and economic aspects into the standards.

Understanding the Present Energy Situation of the World

The exponential demand for energy worldwide requires a new emphasis on energy efficiency *and* rapid development of renewable energy resources. Active building technologies use both nonrenewable (coal, fuel oil, etc.) and renewable (solar, biomass, wind, etc.) technologies to create electricity for building operations. Optimum sustainable practices are required for both forms of energy.

Awareness of the energy situation for the planet must inform designers' future decisions. The most rapid growth in energy demand from 2007 to 2035 will occur in nations outside the Organization for Economic Cooperation and Development (in non-OECD nations). According to the *International Energy Outlook (EIA) 2010*, world marketed energy consumption will increase by 49 percent from 2007 to

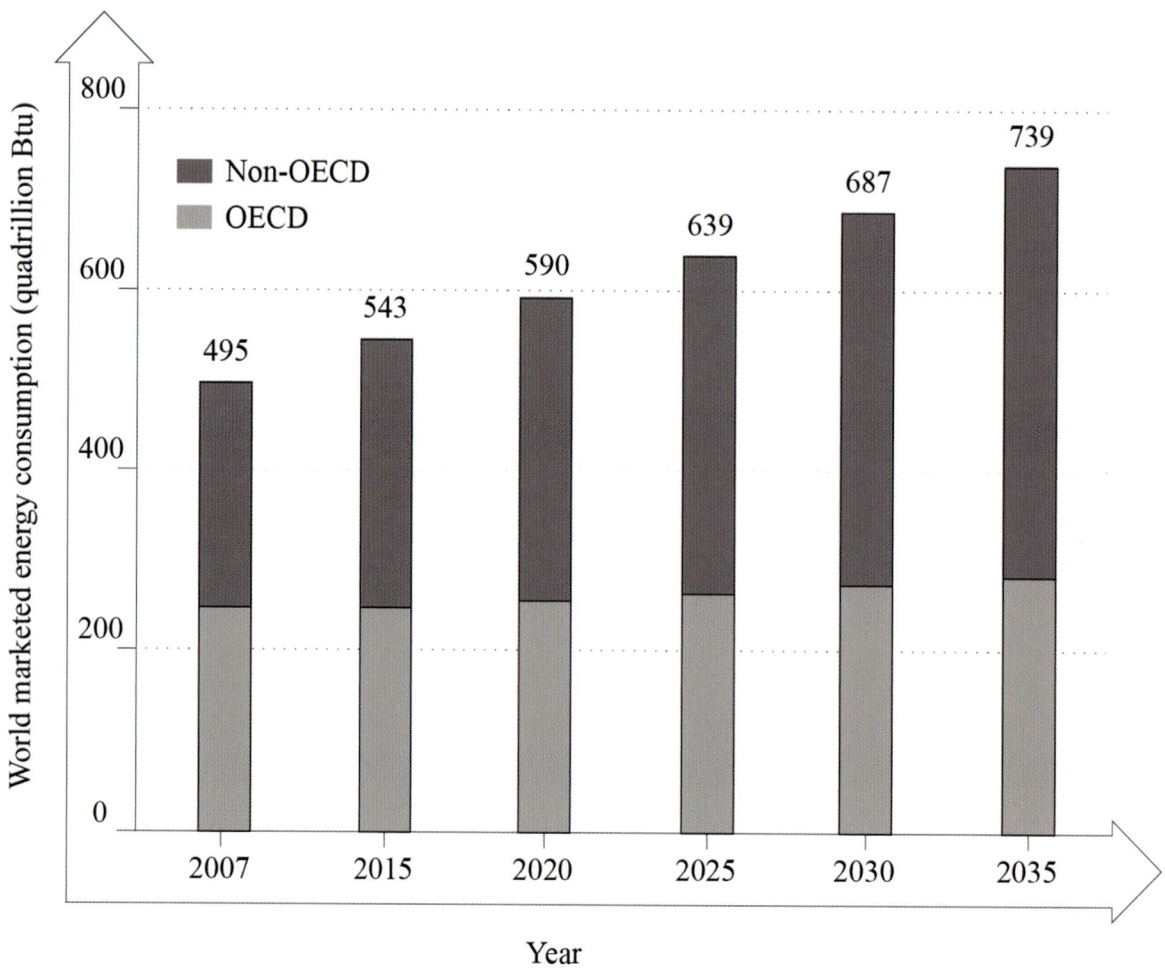

Figure 1.4.4 World marketed energy consumption 2007–2035, in quadrillion BTU. (Source: US Energy Information Administration, *International Energy Outlook 2010*.)

2035. Total energy demand in non-OECD countries will increase by 84 percent, compared with an increase of 14 percent in OECD countries (see Figure 1.4.4).

The Role of Increased Electricity Consumption

It would be unrealistic to expect that GHG emissions can be successfully reduced by energy-efficiency measures alone. The implication is that an increasing reliance on electricity will also increase demands for energy, which in turn contributes to increasing carbon emissions and their attendant impact on the planet.

World net electricity consumption will more than double from 14,781 billion kilowatt hours in 2003

to 21,699 billion kilowatt hours in 2015 and 30,116 billion kilowatt hours in 2030.

Consumption of electricity generated from nuclear power worldwide will increase from 2,523 billion kilowatt hours in 2003 to 3,299 billion kilowatt hours in 2030.

Increased electricity demand suggests that sustainable growth and efforts to reduce greenhouse gas emissions cannot be achieved simply by becoming efficient in the use of present energy sources. Renewable energy systems also must support this effort. Current production of renewable energy from all sources (biomass, geothermal, wind, and solar) contributes to a mere 2 percent of global production [2]. Even with this small contribution to the overall energy picture, we can see that the

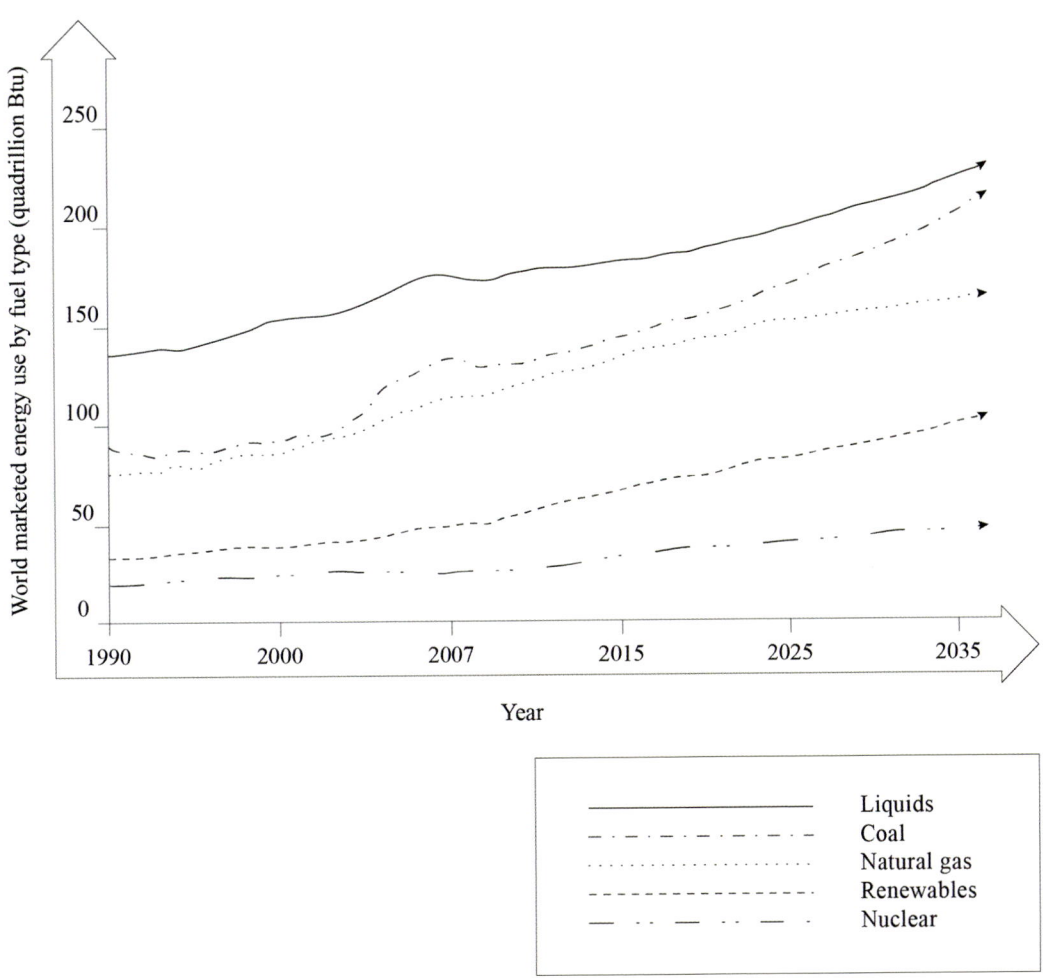

Figure 1.4.5 World marketed energy use by fuel type.
(Source: *International Energy Outlook 2010*.)

renewable energy industry has enormous potential to grow and support sustainable efforts (Figure 1.4.5).

Although renewable energy technologies got a boost in the early 1970s, after the oil embargo in 1973, this has not been sustained. Only in recent years, with dramatic improvements in the performance of solar cells, wind turbines, and biofuels, have renewable energy systems found a decent market niche. Alternative energy systems are also gaining respect due to their promise to reduce the security risk to developed countries such as the USA.

The objective of the building designer should be to combine energy efficiency into both fossil fuel and renewable energy in building systems with the ultimate goal of approaching least energy use in any building. The alternate goal is to create zero-carbon-emitting facilities. Upcoming chapters will address specific ways in which designers can tackle the many challenges presented by current sustainability issues.

Summary

Many encouraging critical perspectives go into today's sustainable designs, yet these innovators face many challenges. Global energy demands are on the rise, with all energy-consuming sectors growing at the same alarming rate. Electric consumption will more than double by 2030. Renewable energy is still in its infancy and has enormous potential to support sustainable best practices.

References

[1] Jerry Yudelson and Ulf Meyer, *The World's Greenest Buildings* (Abingdon, UK: Routledge, 2013).

[2] Robert Socolow and Stephen Pacala, Energy's future: beyond carbon – a plan to keep carbon in check, *Scientific American*, September 2006, p. 50.

Further Reading

Lester R. Brown, *Plan B: Mobilizing to Save Civilization* (New York: W.W. Norton & Company, 2009).

Daniel M. Kammen, *The Rise of Renewable Energy* (New York: Scientific American, 2006).

US Department of Energy, *2007 Building Energy Use* (Office of Energy Efficiency and Renewable Energy, 2007).

Web Support

www.ipcc.ch/.../publications_ipcc_fourth_assessment_report_synthes

Exercises

1 Select from your research one building from a list of projects designed or supported by RMI and write about how they achieved Net Zero energy use.

2 What renewable energy resources can save the USA from totally depleting fossil fuels for future generations?

CHAPTER TWO

Passive Sustainable Design Ideas/Tools

2.1 Principal Sustainable Building Design Ideas

This section introduces basic building elements to achieve a good sustainable design, setting the stage for more detailed descriptions in later chapters. Building design technologies fall into two main categories: passive and active. Passive technologies are sustainable in that they take advantage of natural energy flows, and do not require much, if any, use of fossil fuels. In building design, passive technologies must predominate over active ones, which require the use of fuels for operation. For effective passive and active systems, designers need a thorough understanding of thermophysical properties, heat transfer, and climate.

Building Users

Resource use in a building is directly proportional to the demand and the demand is directly under the control of the user of a building. Thus, one sustainable design challenge lies in being preemptive and limiting the demand in an economically sound and psychologically acceptable way. One way to do this is to determine how much space or volume is actually needed for the comfort and psychological well-being of the user. Unnecessary spaces will require additional resources in materials and energy.

Consider how the human body uses energy. Food taken into the body may be thought of as fuel subjected to a low grade "combustion" (metabolic) process to maintain a body temperature of 37°C. Metabolic rates vary widely depending on physical activity. Note that heat given off by the body while running, about 4.75 kBtu/hr, is almost ten times that of the hourly heat loss of a person doing light work such as typing. We can draw two inferences from this example. First, the behavior of building users can have a significant impact on a building's resource utilization. The runner and the typist have widely differing needs. Second, just as a runner has to expend more energy than a typist, a building that has to work hard to maintain comfortable temperatures is going to burn resources at a faster rate, releasing more emissions. A well-designed building should carefully consider the human demand and other activities in a building to optimize these energy impacts.

Why Begin with Passive Design Concepts?

Passive technologies are permanent and, once installed, are hard – if not impossible – to change, requiring considerable expense. To take advantage of passive concepts, designers need to get it right from the beginning. For instance, orientation of a building cannot be changed once the building is placed on a given site.

Response to Climate and Architectural Implications [1]

A designer determines the optimum shape for a building based on responsiveness to site and climate. The Earth's climate is shaped by thermal and gravitational forces, regional pressures, temperature, and topographical differences, all of which must be taken into account when shaping, siting, and orienting buildings. Adjacent existing buildings and their shapes also affect the climatic condition of any locality. Several passive features can be considered in response to climate and solar issues.

The optimum shape for buildings, taking into account both heat loss in winter and heat gain in summer, show that for simple rectangular plans the most effective shapes will be those elongated along the east–west axis. The east and west faces receive the greatest amount of summer radiation and therefore should be reduced in area. The south/west faces receive radiation in the winter.

Methods for controlling light and shading buildings also optimize the use of energy. Ecological benefits occur through the use of awnings for windows, appropriately located trees, the use of existing buildings to shade new construction, and/or changing the building configuration by increasing or decreasing its height. Configurations that resist unwanted heat gains and losses result in less energy and resource use. If energy can be saved by use of natural illumination, the building perimeter should be increased and its interior space proportionately decreased.

Walls and the insulating materials in them and windows contribute significantly to ecological gain by minimizing the use of natural resources and increasing building performance. Heat transmission is much greater through glass than through most opaque walls and therefore modern windows are designed with attention to heat transfer, as well as to functionality for view and daylighting.

It is fair to say that most building forms generated in recent decades have not responded effectively to the physical environment. Statistics on current energy use in US buildings are revealing. According to the US DOE's *Buildings Energy Data Book*, more energy was consumed in the USA than in any other country in 2008, with 99.5 quadrillion Btu (quads) of primary energy consumed – approximately 20 percent of total global demand (see Figure 2.1.1 for a breakdown of US energy consumption). While US consumption grew by less than 0.5 percent between 2002 and 2008, China's energy demand almost doubled over the same period. Major energy savings, if they are to occur in the immediate future, may have to come from retrofitting existing structures as well as from new sustainable design.

While this energy information is true for existing buildings, it is important to note that increases in new constructions at a national level are estimated to be 3 percent annually. This growth gives designers the opportunity to be proactive in applying sustainable passive designs, which can influence the numbers in a positive way.

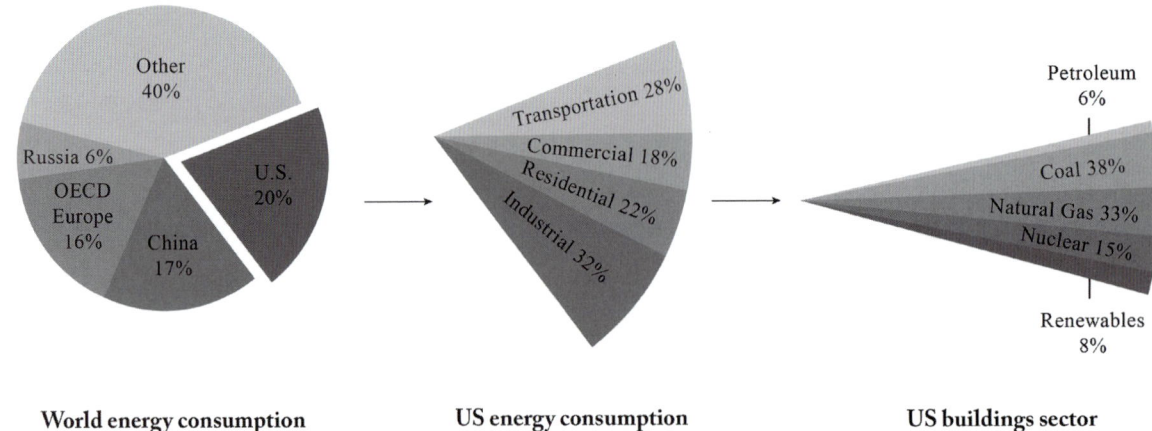

World energy consumption   **US energy consumption**   **US buildings sector**

Figure 2.1.1 US energy consumption. (Source: US Department of Energy.)

Basic Sustainable Design Approach

Passive design techniques allow a designer to create a building that demands the least amount of additional energy to maintain itself while offering comfort to its users. Passive technologies also reduce resource consumption during the entire life of a building. Solar energy is used to naturally heat, cool, ventilate, and light a building without requiring the use of fossil fuels. New construction can and must realize these benefits. Take heat avoidance and passive actions first, and choose technology that minimizes the need for active mechanical systems and equipment later, as illustrated in Figure 2.1.2.

To support sustainable living, architects must balance demands of building users and the local climate and geographical location, and must translate these into sustainable architectural forms. Effectively responding to these demands also requires attention to issues of heat transfer and other physical properties of thermodynamics. These are discussed in later sections.

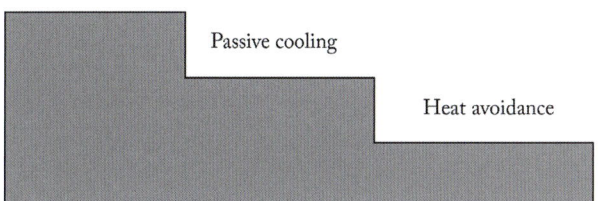

Figure 2.1.2 Basic sustainable design approach. (Source: Kuppaswamy Iyengar.)

Six Sustainable Building Design Ideas

The principal factor used to establish and control energy demand is a well-designed environmental system that relates to heat loss, heat gain, and lighting. Ventilation, air movement, air quality, and humidity will also affect building climate needs. Outdoor environmental conditions influence all of these elements.

1 *Appropriate site selection and/or good use of a site.* It is extremely important to invest adequate time and thought in selecting a facility site to take advantage of natural assets such as sun, wind, contours of the land, availability of water, views, and community

services. In the USA, ensure that proper southern exposure is available for controlling views and light. Look to the site itself for landscaping options, using native trees and plants for shading, cooling, and protection from unwanted wind and for noise prevention.

2 *Understanding climate and geographical location.* Climate is defined as the average condition of weather at a particular location over a period of years. Since weather is the momentary state of the atmospheric environment (temperature, wind velocity, and precipitation) at a particular location, climate can be defined as the sum total of all the weather that occurs at any location. Climates are comparatively constant and, despite short-term but significant and rapid changes, they have weather patterns that repeat themselves at given time intervals.

A building designer is primarily interested in the limits of climate that affect human comfort and the design and use of buildings. Information of value to architects includes temperature changes, the temperature difference between day and night, temperature extremes, wind effects that control infiltration and exfiltration, snowfall and its distribution, sky conditions, hail, hurricanes, and thunderstorms. Climate data are available from the US National Weather Service for numerous locations. In the USA, climate has been broadly divided into four regions according to predominant weather conditions: cool regions, temperate regions, hot and humid regions, and hot and arid regions. Figure 2.1.3 portrays these US regions with brief descriptions of each.

3 *Using appropriate building materials.* A properly designed building envelope uses high-quality wall, floor, and roof material suitable for the location and climate. The heat transfer through the building should be studied with clear understanding of insulation properties of walls, floors, roofs, glazing, and any other materials covering openings. Durable siding materials such as fiber-cement can reduce future maintenance, eliminating painting. Of course, the designer should study the project programming prior to deciding the building envelope to ensure required building footprint and volume.

4 *Designing efficient environmental systems: necessary active technologies.* Artificial lighting, heating, and

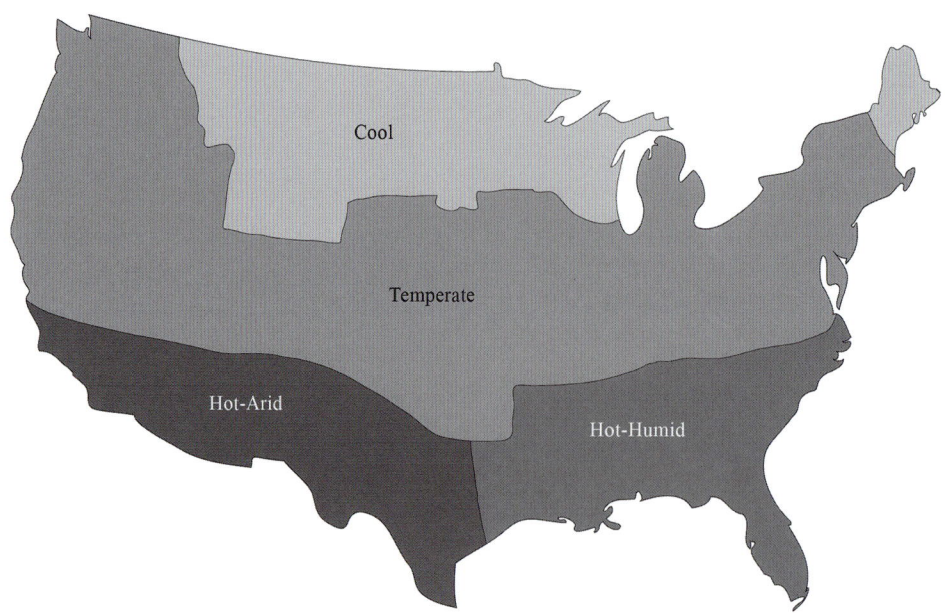

Hot-Humid regions have consistent vapor pressure and high temperatures. Wind velocities and direction vary throughout the day and year and may be accompanied by hurricanes from the E and SE.

Hot-Arid regions have clear skies, dry atmosphere, extended periods of overheating, and large diurnal temperature range. Wind direction is along E-W axis with variations between night and day.

Cool regions have a wide range of temperatures with hot summers and cold winters. Winds are persistent year-round, generally from the NW or SE. Northern locations receive less solar radiation than southern locales.

Temperate regions have equal distributions of overheated and underheated periods. Seasonal winds are from the NW and S. Large amounts of precipitation and high humidity are common as well as clear and sunny days that are followed by extended cloudy, overcast days.

Figure 2.1.3 Climatic regions of the USA. (Source: US Department of Energy.)

cooling through air-conditioning all use electricity or other forms of energy, and all constitute active systems. In sustainable design, downsizing these systems reduces the use of fossil fuels and consequently the levels of pollution released into the atmosphere. Here, a designer can significantly contribute to efforts to reduce carbon dioxide pollution. When final sizing is optimum (no larger than necessary), operating costs during the life of the building for use and maintenance are also minimized.

5 *Maintaining proper indoor air quality (IAQ).* Ventilation is the circulation of air. Outdoor air enters a building by infiltration, and flows out of a building by exfiltration. Ventilation is affected by differences between indoor and outdoor air temperatures and wind. Leaking of hot or cold air takes place particularly through cracks around doors and windows, or infiltration, or through other cracks in the building and through most building materials. Careful design of these minimizes loss of expensive energy and resources.

IAQ concepts and possible design solutions will be discussed in later chapters. The main idea is that designers who approach their projects with awareness of local climate and passive techniques will be more likely to find ways to reduce energy and resource demand and pave the way for additional savings on active technologies and equipment.

6 *Water and waste management.* Water is truly the stuff of life and our dependence on clean water is a common bond we all share, yet society still routinely undervalues it. Since 1980, global water use has more than tripled. Higher water use adds to maintenance and life-cycle costs, and water pollution also continues to be a major problem worldwide. All this means that we should become more prudent in the use of water.

This requires that we purchase water-conserving appliances and plumbing fixtures, use efficient irrigation and pumping systems, and encourage efficient agriculture. Reduce, reuse, and recycle water and many other products to become resource efficient.

How do the sustainable building principles of climate and geography apply in a real-life example? Built in 2011, the Centre for Interactive Research on Sustainability (CIRS), located on the University of British Columbia campus, provides "net positive" benefits to the environment (Figure 2.1.4). CIRS is a "living laboratory" that will help regenerate the environment and advance research and innovation on global sustainability challenges. It reduces the university's carbon emissions, powers itself and a neighboring building with renewable and waste energy, creates drinking water from rain, and treats wastewater on-site.

CIRS is built to exceed LEED® Platinum and Living Building Challenge standards. Situated in a

Figure 2.1.4 CIRS is beyond carbon neutral (no fossil fuels). The surplus energy is used to power a neighboring building which moves an additional 150 tons of GHG emissions annually through reduced natural gas use.
(Source: photo by Xicotencatl; this file is licensed under the Creative Commons Attribution Share Alike 3.0 Unported license.)

wooded area in British Columbia, CIRS is one of the few commercial buildings constructed primarily of certified wood and beetle-killed wood (currently BC's largest source of carbon emissions). Its wood structure locks in more than 500 tons of carbon, offsetting the GHG emissions that resulted from the use of other non-renewable construction materials in the building, such as cement, steel, and aluminum.

Major sustainable features of this 60,000 square-foot, four-story facility include:

- **Site:** thoughtful building location and orientation (southwest).
- **Climate response:** designers had expertise in their geographical location and climate (temperate to cool influenced by mountains and Pacific Ocean).
- **Materials:** beetle-killed wood structure, as described above.
- **Environmental systems:** CIRS utilizes waste heat from the Earth, the sun, and neighboring buildings to heat itself and then return 600 megawatt-hours of surplus energy back to the campus.
- **Indoor environment:** a U-shape design maximizes the amount of natural daylight and fresh air for inhabitants, who control their environment (light levels, temperature) through their computers. The flexible design allows workspaces to be completely reconfigured overnight (no outlets in walls).
- **Rainwater harvesting:** capturing rain and treating it on-site will provide for the water needs of 200 inhabitants, along with hundreds of auditorium and café users. Excess water is used to recharge the local aquifer.
- **Cultural response/users:** CIRS encourages people to adopt sustainability in their lives. The BC Hydro Theatre, which has advanced visualization and interaction technologies, engages audiences in sustainability and climate change scenarios.

Summary

It is best to begin with passive concepts early in the design process, since these elements are relatively permanent and it is expensive to tack them onto existing designs. Maximize the number of passive design components, which in turn can positively reduce the size required for active systems, thereby reducing the need for fossil fuels used in the operation of active systems. Each surface of a building is subjected to different environmental influences, depending upon the geographical location, climate, insolation (the amount of solar radiation received), siting, orientation, and building shape. All of these factors can be manipulated to produce more environmentally and ecologically sound designs that save energy while providing environmental comfort.

Reference

[1] Stephen Dent (James C. Snyder and Anthony J. Catanese, eds.), *Introduction to Architecture* (New York: John Wiley & Sons, 1979).

Further Reading

Bruce Anderson and Michael Riordan, *The Solar Home Book* (Harrisville, NH: Cheshire Books, 1976).

Rocky Mountain Institute, *Technical Briefs* (Winchester, CO: US Department of Energy, 2004).

Craig B. Smith (ed.), *Efficient Electricity Use* (Elmsford, NY: Pergamon Press, 1978).

Web Support

http://buildingsdatabook.eren.doe.gov/Chapter Intro2.aspx

Exercises

1 Using the three-step basic sustainable design approach outlined in this section, briefly list and sketch some strategies you might use for a moderate-size residential building in Phoenix, AZ.
2 Research a sustainable building and write a case study following the six sustainable building principles as defined in this section.

2.2 Passive Heating: Energy from the Sun

The sun's rays cause heat gain in buildings. Passive heating technologies exploit and control the power of the sun in order to harness warmth without having to produce it mechanically. Although the focus of this section is on heating, the subject cannot be isolated from related concepts of cooling, daylighting, and effects of ventilation on thermal conditions. To make use of passive heating methods, designers must understand the sun's impact on buildings, the heating possibilities of direct gain and indirect gain through passive energy storage, and how to control sunlight by shading.

The Impact of the Sun Upon Buildings

The ecological approach to passive solar design is to begin with the big picture, the sun and its existing relationship to the Earth. This requires a quick lesson in solar science, including the role of insolation, sun position, directionality, and the amount and intensity of sunlight striking the Earth's surface in any given location during different times of the year. Once these ideas are understood, designers can turn their attention to building design that makes the best use of the solar conditions for a given site. Designers must learn how to measure the sun's position and find south at any site. They must review principles of direct heat and light gain for buildings, as well as indirect gain through sunrooms or thermal walls. They must also know how to control sunlight through shading technologies.

The sun is the driving force behind all climatic and life forces on Earth. The macro-level transfer of energy and ecological transformations begin when the incoming solar rays strike the outer-level atmosphere. Insolation is the amount of radiation from the sun received by a surface. At any particular point on the Earth, insolation is affected by several factors. Due to the Earth's curvature and the tilt of its axis, incoming radiation reaches particular areas on the Earth's surface at different angles. Radiation received per unit area directly perpendicular to the incoming radiation is greatest. Radiation reaching the Earth's surface is also affected by the atmospheric condition, its purity, and vapor, dust, and smoke content.

Radiation causes heat gain in a building. Heat gain and heat loss in any building are affected by the position of the sun in relation to the Earth, in addition to several other factors. The Earth rotates around its own axis and is tilted at an angle of 23.5° to the plane of the Earth's orbit. The tilt of the Earth's axis remains constant (see Figure 2.2.1).

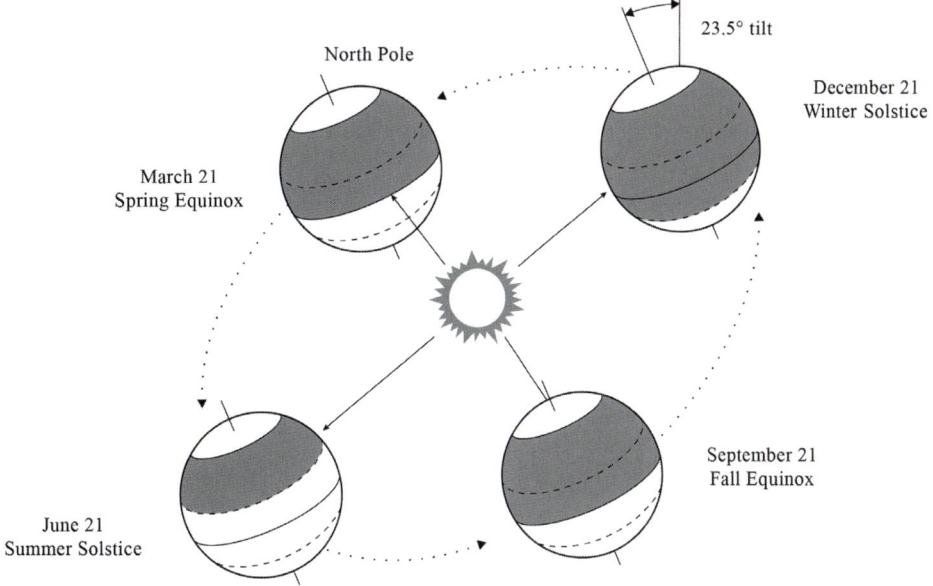

Figure 2.2.1 Diagram of Earth's movement. The tinted areas show different intensities of radiation. (Source: Craig B. Smith (ed.), *Efficient Electricity Use* (Elmsford, NY: Pergamon Press, 1978).)

One obvious factor affecting the amount of radiation striking any particular location is the length of the daylight period, which is dependent upon the day of the year. Maximum intensity of solar radiation is received on a plane perpendicular to the direction of radiation. Due to the tilt of the Earth's axis, the area receiving maximum solar radiation moves north and south between the Tropic of Cancer and Tropic of Capricorn. This is the primary cause of seasonal changes [1].

As shown in Figure 2.2.2, the Northern Hemisphere is slanted toward the sun during summer months, which means it receives more hours of sunshine and incoming radiation is closer and perpendicular to the surface of the Earth. During winter this situation is reversed in the Northern Hemisphere, while in the Southern Hemisphere summer prevails.

Figure 2.2.3 illustrates how to understand and correctly apply radiation information to building design. It is essential to know where the sun is in the sky at any given time. This is measured by the altitude, θ (Theta), and azimuth, φ (Phi), of a place through the sun's position.

A simple method for finding south at any site is helpful for measuring the sun's position. On a sunny day insert a peg, about one foot in height, on the selected site at 10 a.m. and mark the shadow of the peg. Return to the same peg after four hours, i.e. at 2 p.m. (suitable correction should be made for daylight saving time), and again mark the shadow of the peg. Then bisect the angle between the two shadow markings, which will give the direction of south. This essential information allows the designer to plan proper south orientation and southern exposure, and

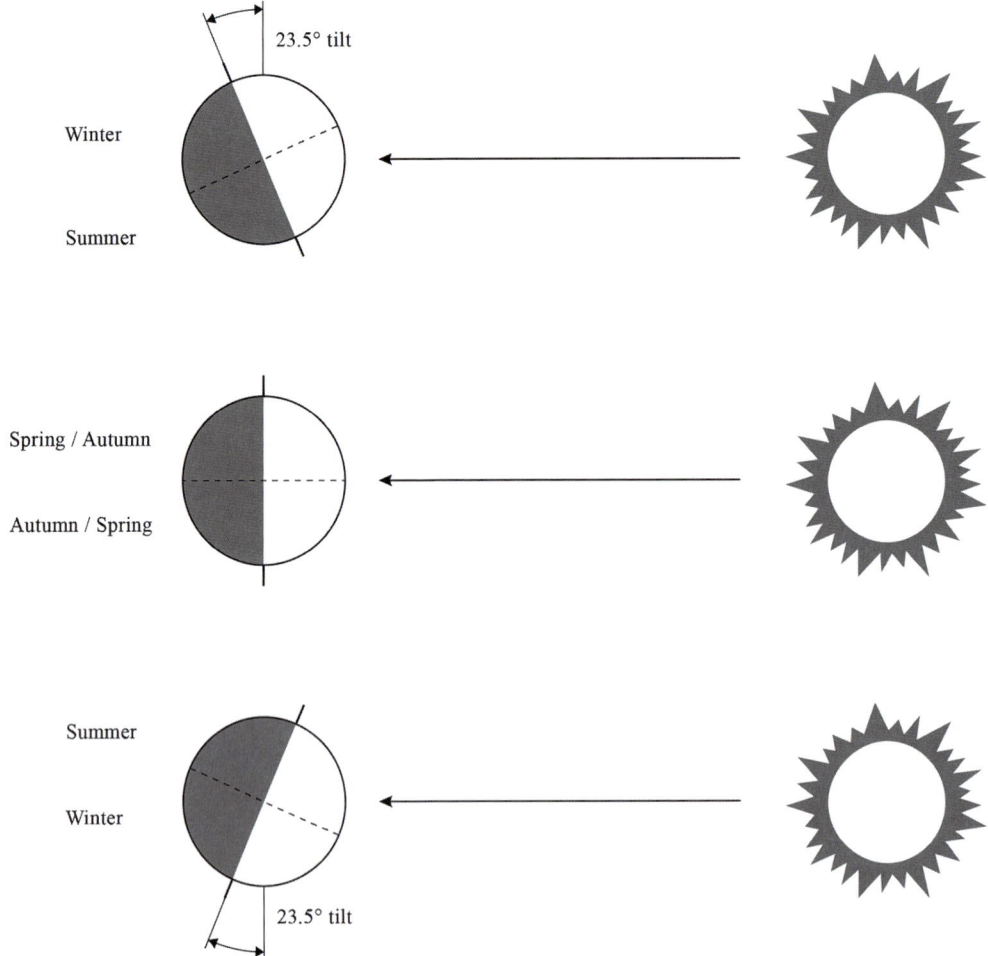

Figure 2.2.2 The Earth's tilt creates seasons.
(Source: adapted from Edward Mazria, *The Passive Solar Energy Book* (Emmaus, PA: Rodale Press, 1979).)

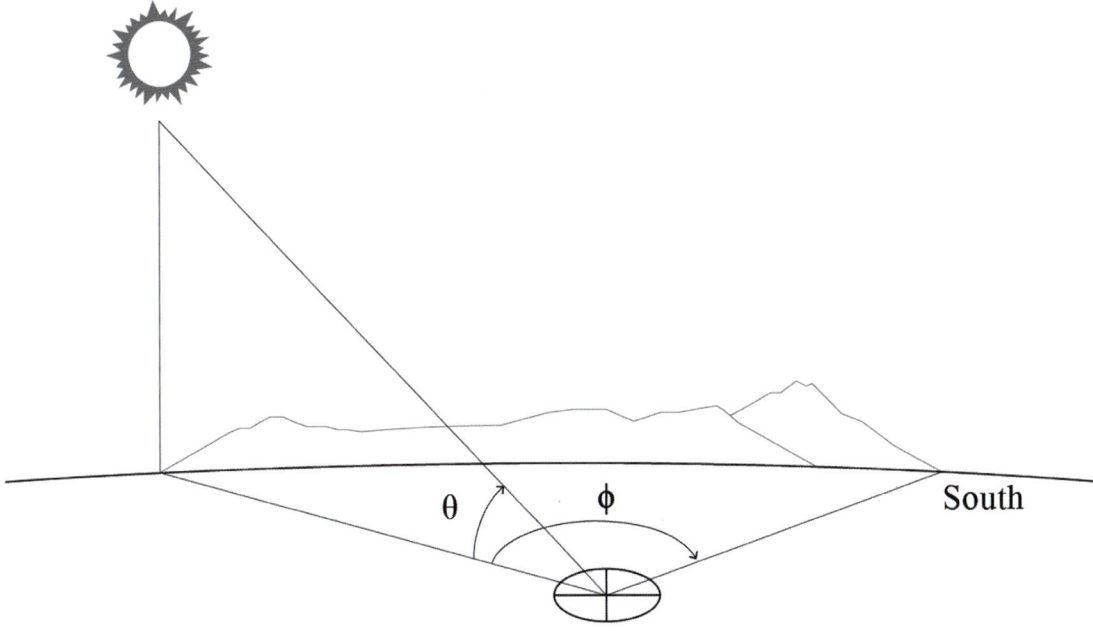

Figure 2.2.3 How to measure altitude and azimuth angles of a location and finding true south. (Source: Kuppaswamy Iyengar.)

to take advantage of direct gain and other passive technologies.

Once solar information is obtained, it is possible to think about how to site and design the building and to make decisions about direct and indirect gain of sunlight. Use *Climate Consultant* software, sponsored by the California Energy Commission and developed by the University of California at Los Angeles (UCLA), for detailed information about the climate of a particular location. Some passive heating techniques for buildings are as follows:

1 Keep the heat in and cold out by adequate insulation and compact forms (see Section 4.1 for heat loss calculations).
2 Protect the building from cold winds and minimize infiltration by tight construction (see Section 4.1 for infiltration calculations).
3 Use sun energy through direct gain systems and *trombe* walls.
4 Take advantage of indirect heating sources such as thermal mass, rock storage, geothermal, etc.

1. **Keep the heat in and cold out.** Cave dwellings and other indigenous buildings from ancient times illustrate how to keep the cold out and the heat in.

Building into the ground against northern slopes will offer exposure to the south (Figure 2.2.4). Building adjacent to other homes and tight construction with additional wall layers can also assist in this effort.

2. **Minimize infiltration.** Providing wind breaks with appropriate trees, berms, and walls, properly caulking around windows and doors and providing airlocks or vestibules all minimize air infiltration.

3. **Direct gain** involves use of radiant heat resulting from sunlight admitted directly to the living spaces through south-facing windows, which warms interior surfaces such as walls, furniture, floors, and other materials. For optimum direct gain, the south-facing window area must be sized for the climate (for example, floor-to-ceiling windows in cold climates), depending on the type of window used and the amount of thermal mass in the home. Masonry, stone, concrete, adobe, water, and other materials are effective as thermal mass for direct gain systems because they absorb and store heat and cool energy and release it slowly. A well-designed passive solar home can hold a constant interior temperature of 68–70 °F with minimal supplemental heating or cooling.

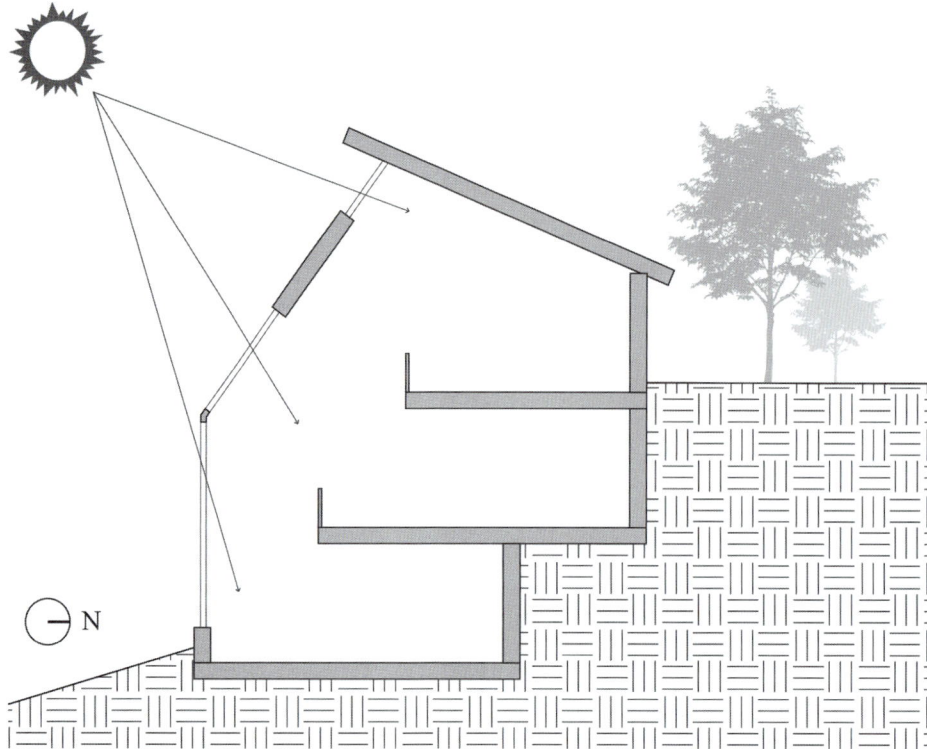

Figure 2.2.4   Keep the heat in and cold out by building into the slope. (Source: US Department of Housing and Urban Development.)

Solar energy storage is yet another option for reducing demand. Energy admitted into the home through south-facing windows can be collected and stored in high-mass walls and floors of masonry, stone, concrete, adobe, water, and other materials. For residential and commercial applications, *trombe walls* used for collecting and storing heat can help offset heating and cooling bills and can significantly reduce or eliminate use of utilities, which is an asset to building users.

A thermal wall, best known as a *trombe wall*, named after Professor Felix Trombe in the 1960s, consists of an 8- to 10-inch thick masonry wall, coated with a dark, heat-absorbing material. These surfaces are then faced with a layer of glazing material separated by one to two inches of air space. The thermal mass of the wall is heated by the sun and warms the air in the air space, causing it to rise due to convection. Openings in the bottom and top of the *trombe* wall (Figure 2.2.5) allow air to circulate and heat the room. Airflow on a building site may be controlled by obstructions, deflectors, filters made by trees, hedges, berms, and/

or different heights within the building. *Trombe* walls should be shaded during summers in hot climates.

A designer should assess the pros and cons of a vented and unvented trombe wall carefully. In a vented system, the amount of heat available for storage in the *trombe* wall is likely to be reduced due to hot air that is constantly circulating. An unvented system does not have this situation and thus has the advantage of storing a greater percentage of the solar energy available to it. This stored heat is, however, not readily available for immediate use. Instead, it is transmitted over time into the living area. The thickness and thermal properties of the wall materials determine the time lag of the heat transmitted from the outside surface of the unvented wall to the interiors. This may vary from several hours to an entire day. Most designers prefer unvented trombe walls for residences, which require heating mainly during the night (Figure 2.2.6). In cold climates, where daytime as well as nighttime heating requirements are high, it is desirable to use a vented wall. In moderate climates where daytime heating is not as important

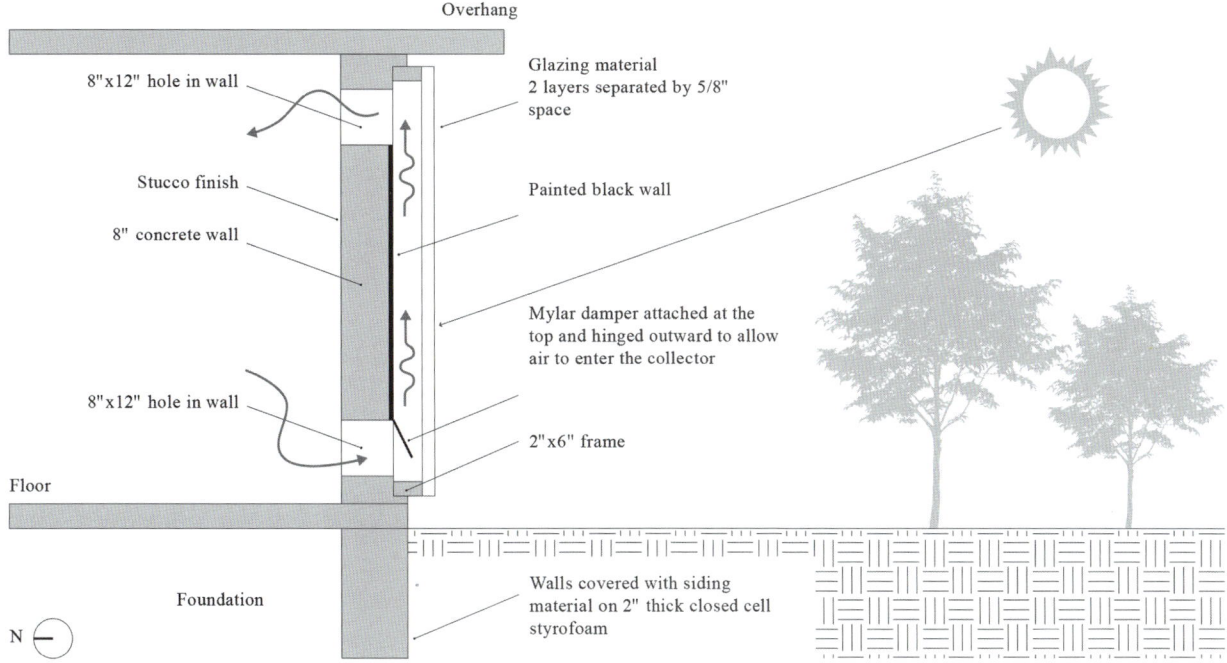

Overhang

8"x12" hole in wall

Stucco finish

8" concrete wall

8"x12" hole in wall

Floor

Foundation

N

Glazing material
2 layers separated by 5/8"
space

Painted black wall

Mylar damper attached at the
top and hinged outward to allow
air to enter the collector

2"x6" frame

Walls covered with siding
material on 2" thick closed cell
styrofoam

Figure 2.2.5 Modified *trombe* wall.
(Source: this file is licensed under the Creative Commons Source Share Alike 3.0 Unported license.)

Figure 2.2.6 *Trombe wall* in Professor Stephen Dent's residence (2001), Cedar Crest, NM *(note the trombe wall including summer shading on the left of the picture).*
(Source: photo by Professor Stephen D. Dent.)

as nighttime heating, an unvented system may be preferable.

A *trombe wall* offers several advantages. Glare and the problem of ultraviolet degradation of materials are eliminated as compared to direct gain systems. There is the potential, however, for a storage wall to block views and daylight.

Approximate Design Methods for Direct Gain and *Trombe* Walls

NREL supplied the theoretical basis for this section (see www.nrel.gov/docs/legosti/old/21217.pdf). The specific example provided here comes from the class notes of Professor Stephen Dent, University of New Mexico.

In 1983 passive solar design guidelines for sizing direct gain and *trombe* walls were developed by Dr. Doug Balcomb at Los Alamos National Laboratories for locations in the USA. The goal was to establish the size of glazing or window openings as a means of receiving the sun's energy, passively heating a building and thus eliminating and/or minimizing the use of fossil fuels. The technique is not a substitute for more rigorous computer-simulated thermal analysis by a professional engineer, but it gives a designer a solid basis for schematic design decisions. This research, funded by the US government in the late 1970s, includes information on infiltration rates and selecting insulation R-values for the walls, ceiling, perimeter, and basement. Following is an example showing how design guidelines would work for a building in Denver, Colorado.

Step A: Project Data

- Name and location
- annual heating and cooling degree days – From *Mechanical, Electrical, and Equipment for Builders* (MEEB), by Stein *et al.* [2]
- size of the residential building is 3,000 square feet
- any other required data, such as number of stories.

Step B: Calculation of Recommended Energy Efficiency guidelines

From Figure 2.2.7 select the conservation factor (CF). For the chosen building it is 1.8. (Selected R-values are determined by the designer and are typically more than code requirements. For discussion of R-values see Chapter 4.) For the selected building, R-values should be:

Walls	R × CF = 14 × 1.8	= 25.2
Roof	R × CF = 22 × 1.8	= 39.6
Perimeter (slab)	(R − CF) − 5 = (13 − 1.8) − 5	= 18.4
Floor over vented space	R × CF = 14 × 1.8	= 25.2
Basement wall insulation	(R − CF) − 8 = (16 − 1.8) − 8	= 20.8
Windows with glazing layers	R × CF = 1.7 × 1.8	= 03.0
Number of air changes	ACH/CF = 0.42/1.8	= 0.23

Step C: Preliminary Estimate of Net Load Coefficient (NLC), Load Collector Ratio (LCR) and Passive Solar Collection Area (Ap)

If the above guidelines are followed, then

$$NLC = \frac{GF \text{ (Figure 2.2.8)} \times Af \text{ (building area)}}{CF}$$

$$= \frac{5.4 \times 3000}{1.8} = 9,000$$

Suggested area of solar collector for direct gain and *trombe* wall:

$$Ap = \frac{NLC}{LCR \text{ (LCR from Figure 2.2.9)}}$$

$$Ap = \frac{9,000}{20} = 450 \text{ sq.ft of glass area}$$

This glass area can be between direct gain, 50 percent, and the rest in *trombe* wall. Avoid placing obstructions such as furniture, carpet, or drapes in front of a direct gain system.

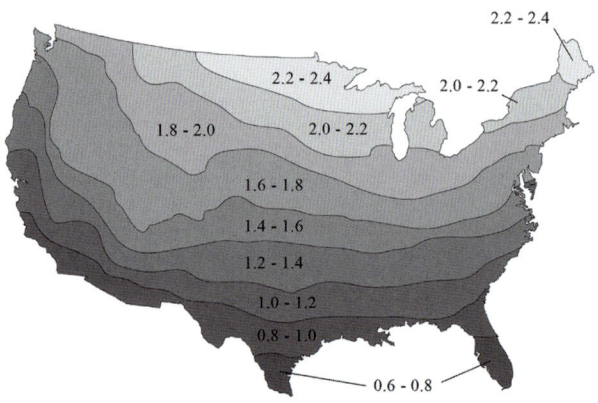

Figure 2.2.7 Conservation factor map for the USA. (Source: US National Renewable Energy Lab, Golden, CO.)

GEOMETRY FACTOR (GF)				
Floor Area (sq. ft.)	Number of Stories			
	1	2	3	4
1,000	7.3	-	-	-
1,500	6.5	6.7	-	-
3,000	5.4	5.4	5.7	-
5,000	4.9	4.7	4.9	5.1
10,000	4.3	4.0	4.0	4.2

Figure 2.2.8 Geometry factor. (Source: Courtesy of US National Renewable Energy Lab, Golden, CO.)

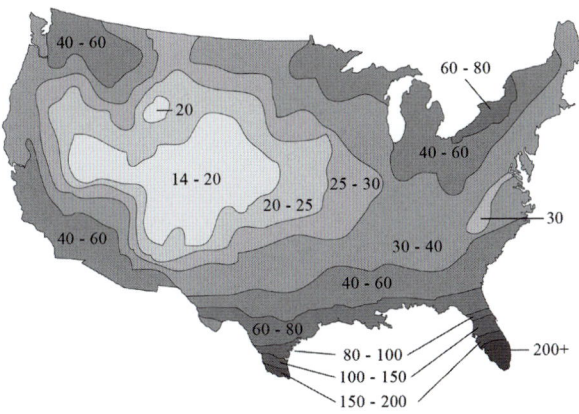

Figure 2.2.9 Map to find load collector ratio. In MEEB there are definitions of the various system types and LCRs for a number of cities. Designers selecting from among the passive system types make basic decisions about: amount of mass, number of glazings for a passive collector, whether or not there is selective coating for the *trombe* wall or if there is a system of night insulation (to prevent back-flow of energy). In general, more mass is better, double glazing is preferred, and selective glass surfaces can be substituted for night insulation at less cost.
(Source: US National Renewable Energy Lab, Golden, Colorado.)

4. There are several **indirect gain** systems that employ an attached sunspace or wall designed to collect the sun's energy before transferring it to other spaces in the building.

In the *first* example (Figure 2.2.10), the air heated in a sunspace circulates to other rooms naturally or with the aid of fans.

Indirect gain systems are similar to direct gain systems in terms of materials and design principles. An indirect gain system positions the thermal mass – rock or contained liquid such as water in a wall – between the sun and the space to be heated.

The sun's heat is collected and trapped in a narrow space between the glazing and the thermal mass after it passes through the windows/glazing. This heats the air, which rises and travels into the room through vents at the top of the wall. Due to stratification, the cooled air then settles down near the bottom vents of the wall. The heated air circulates throughout the room by convection. Also, the thermal mass continues to absorb and the heat to radiate back into the room even after the sun sets. Dampers can be used to close the vents to prevent warm air from escaping at night.

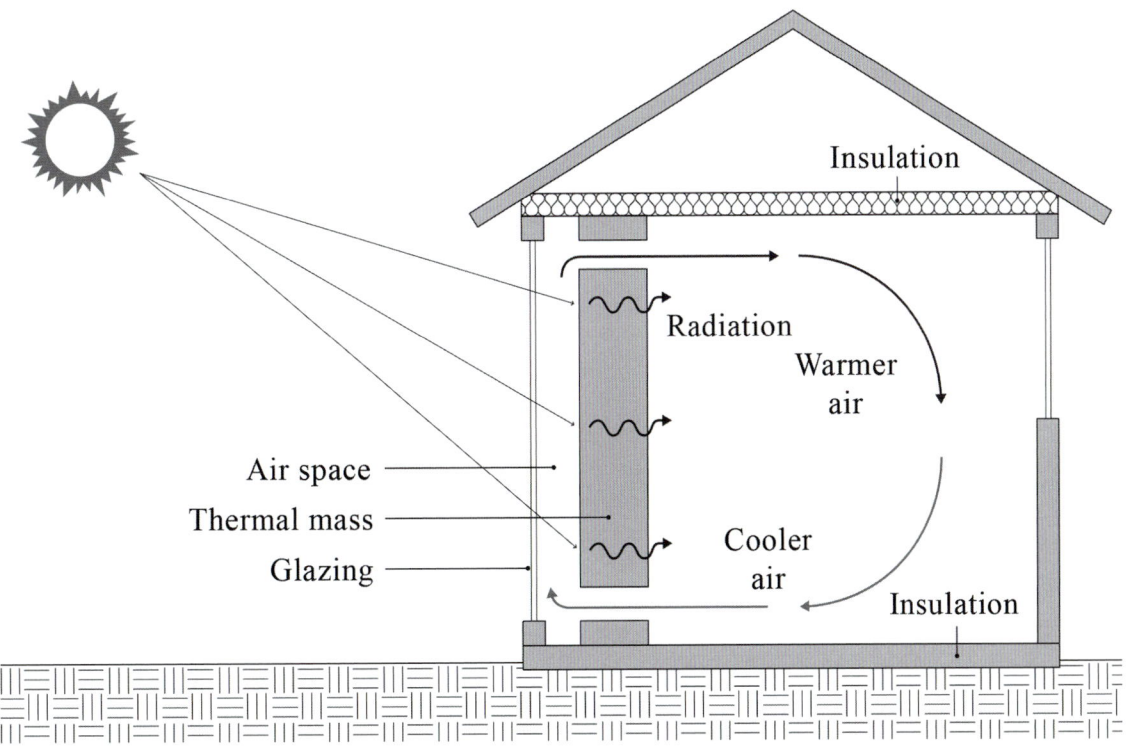

Figure 2.2.10 Indirect gain system 1.
(Source: Kuppaswamy Iyengar.)

During the summer the process is reversed. The thermal mass is prevented from receiving direct sunlight while absorbing the room heat, to keep the temperature comfortable by shading the glass in front of the glazing.

The *second* indirect gain system (Figure 2.2.11) can also be used in conjunction with active *solar systems such as flat-plate collectors* (see Section 2.6 for details of flat-plate collectors). The collectors are always located below the thermal mass storage tanks or bins to take advantage of the natural movement of convection currents.

The *third* type of isolated indirect gain system utilizes solar energy to passively move heat from or to the living space using a fluid, such as water in *roof ponds* or air by natural or forced convection. Heat gain can also occur through a sunspace, solarium, or solar closet. These areas can double as a greenhouse or drying space. An equator-side sunroom can have exterior windows higher than the windows between the sunroom and the interior living space, to allow the low winter sun to enter the cold side of adjacent rooms. Placements of overhangs prevent solar gain during the summer. Earth cooling tubes (cool energy collected from constant cool temperatures below the earth's surface) or other passive cooling techniques can be utilized to cool a sunspace in the summer.

The *fourth* indirect system, *roof ponds* such as Harold Hay's SKYTHERM® seen in Figure 2.5.5, are isolated systems used in the hot dry climates of Arizona and New Mexico and along the California coast. The roof pond places the thermal mass in the roof structure to regulate heat transfer.

A *fifth* indirect gain system through sunspaces has become one of the most popular passive methods for harnessing the sun's energy in recent years. Sunspaces can be particularly effective in areas that have year-round sunshine. In terms of retrofit, it is easy to add a greenhouse (sunspace). The space can function as a solar heat collector while also being used as a conservatory, sunroom, solarium, breakfast room, or lobby. As Figure 2.2.12 indicates, a greenhouse or sunspace is a tightly constructed enclosure facing south that provides heat, light, and controlled ventilation. Sunspaces are especially efficient when combined with thermal mass using a thick floor and a high-mass northern wall. The most effective sunspaces integrate natural and forced convection to distribute

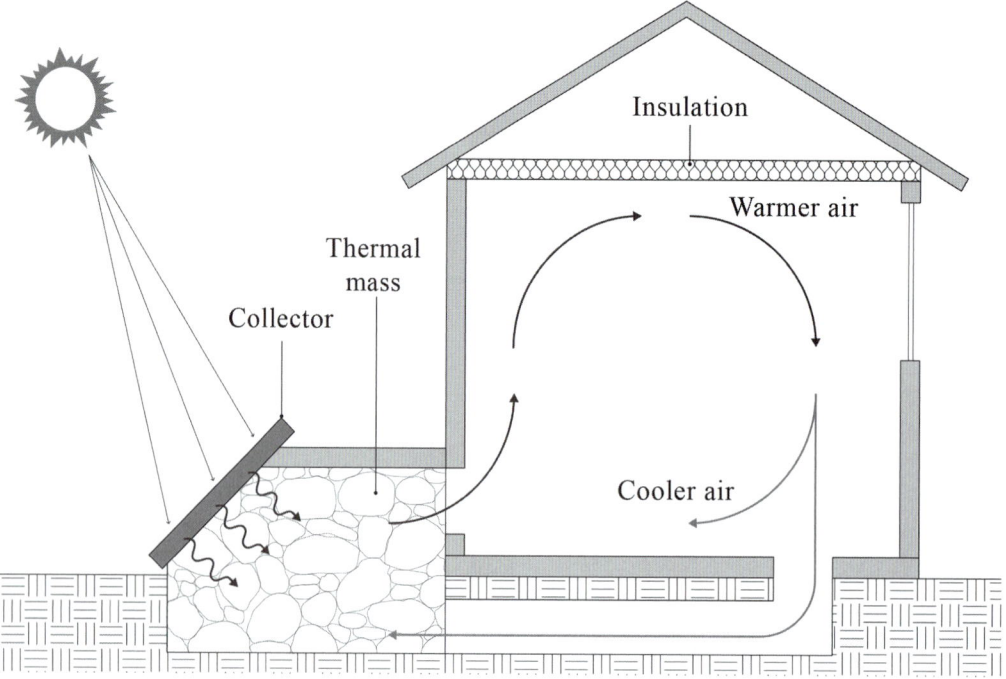

Figure 2.2.11   Indirect gain system 2.
(Source: Kuppaswamy Iyengar.)

heat energy throughout a home or a large commercial space. The heat generated by these spaces can be ventilated to different rooms. Often with overhead glazing, one must watch for overheating. Even so, sunspaces offer the greatest architectural possibilities of all passive systems.

Again, knowledge about the sun and its relationship to the Earth also has implications for related design systems for cooling and daylighting. What are some variations on the theme of passive heating? How do shading, daylighting systems, ventilation and wind, and more operate in conjunction with passive heating technologies?

Use Wind to Appropriately Ventilate Buildings When the Sun is Too Hot

There are a few months even in cold climates when sun can be severe. In those situations wind can be directed to ventilate the building to reduce the effects of hot sun. Ventilation is discussed in Section 2.3.

Shading Devices to Keep the Sun Out

The flip side of heating is cooling. Since seasons, times of day, and days of the year are all changing cycles, it becomes necessary to regulate and balance passive heating technologies with shading devices. Knowing the latitude of a particular location allows designers to predict exactly how the sun will impinge on a building at a given time. With this information it is possible to calculate precisely the optimal length of overhang of a sun shade (usually a horizontal building element), the depth of a fin (usually a vertical element), the location of an inside courtyard, or the size of shadows cast by trees and adjacent structures. It is important to study the shading effect of sun control devices for winter solstice, equinox, and summer solstice. Knowledge of the sun's motion also is important in designing a building envelope efficiently. Olgyay and Olgyay have completed some useful work in designing horizontal and vertical sun controls that take these elements into account [3]. Figure 2.2.13 illustrates the design method for these shading devices.

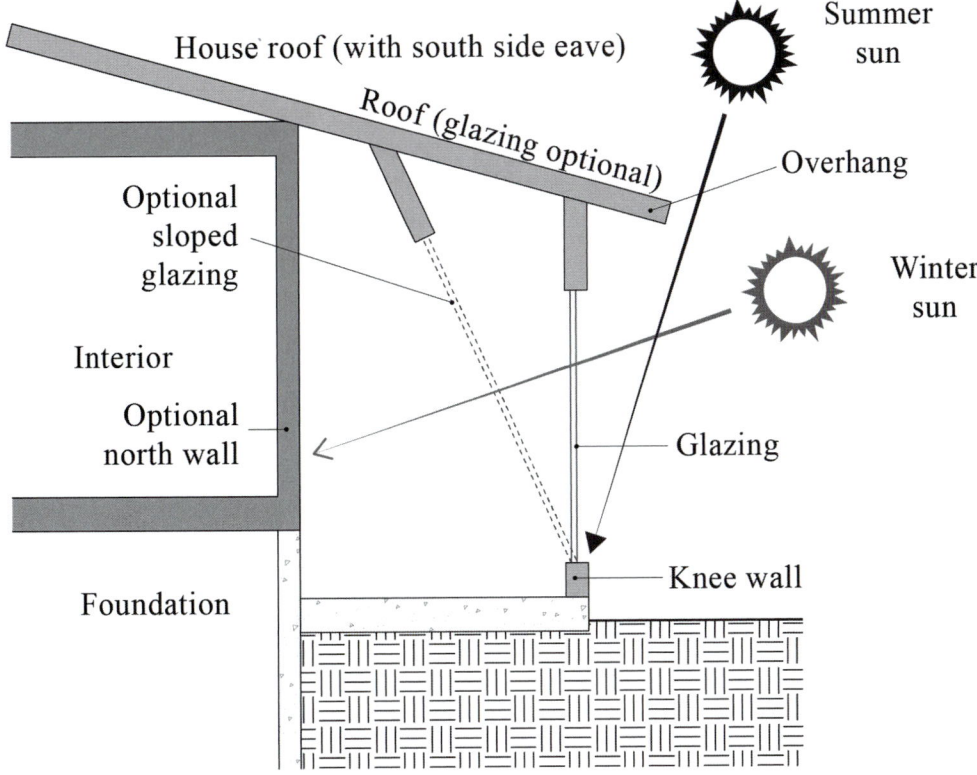

Figure 2.2.12 Sunspaces.
(Source: US Department of Energy, Rocky Mountain Institute, USARMI Briefs.)

Figure 2.2.13   South-side solar shades for Keystone Office Buildings, designed by Professor Stephen D. Dent and Richard Nordhaus in Santa Fe, NM.
(Source: photo by Professor Stephen D. Dent.)

External shading devices should keep the solar radiation off the opaque solid elements of the building's envelope where possible. Special care should be taken to shade windows to reduce the incoming heat and the risk of overheating.

Computer software programs can be used to accurately design and shape shades for very specific purposes. With basic understanding of the mechanics of sun position and sun-path diagrams, manual methods can also be used. External shading devices, which prevent the sun's energy from entering the building in the first place, are preferable and more effective than internal ones. These devices are fixed to the outside of the window or attached to the building exterior. Some operable units include louvers made of wood or metal, exterior Venetian blinds, shutters, awnings, and fixed or movable overhangs (Figure 2.2.14).

A most important characteristic of solar position is its seasonal variation. At the height of summer in the Southern Hemisphere the sun rises slightly southeast and sets slightly southwest. In winter sun rises slightly northeast and sets slightly northwest. Sunlight is available for a greater number of hours in summer than in winter. In the Northern Hemisphere, due to seasonal variations, north and south are reversed. The goal of good shading design is to use these characteristics to best advantage, usually aiming for complete exclusion in summer and maximum exposure in winter.

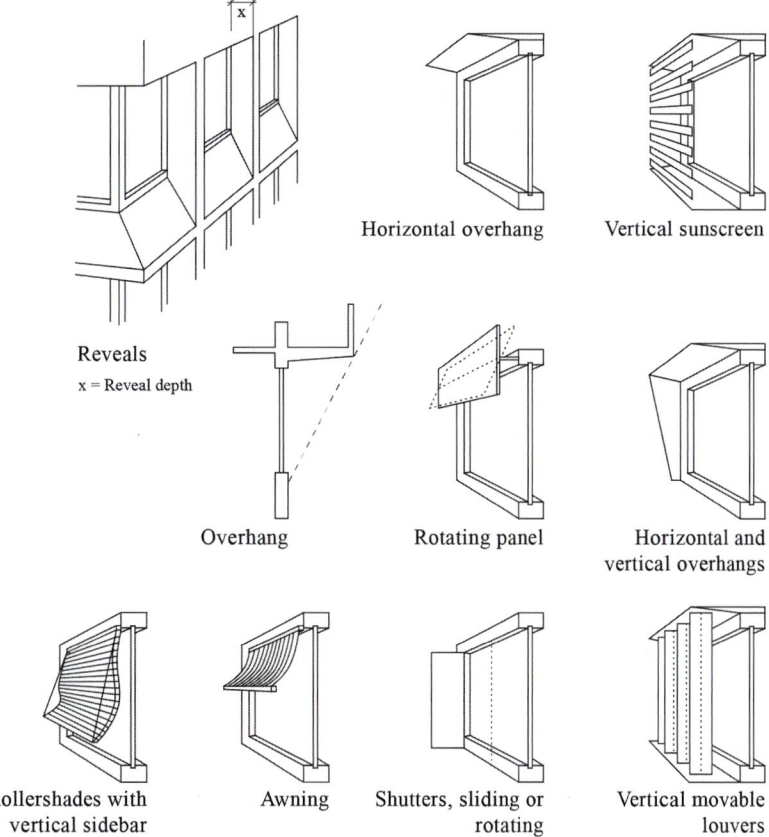

Horizontal overhang   Vertical sunscreen

Reveals
x = Reveal depth

Overhang   Rotating panel   Horizontal and vertical overhangs

Rollershades with vertical sidebar   Awning   Shutters, sliding or rotating   Vertical movable louvers

Figure 2.2.14 External shading devices.
(Source: Gaia Research Report "Understanding Daylighting of Sports Halls".)

Rules of Thumb

Orientation of the window determines the appropriate shading devices. Some orientations are easy to shade, while others are much more difficult as the sun can shine in almost horizontally at times. Typical shading methods are shown below. These are guidelines only and it should be understood that there are many variations to these basic types.

- north orientation (equator-facing)   horizontal louvers
- east or west orientation   vertical louvers (movable devices)

The horizontal and vertical shadow angles relative to the window plane are important. These can be calculated for any time if the azimuth and altitude of the sun are known, as well as the direction of the window facing the sun.

The Effects of Shading

A sun-path diagram and a percentage overshadowing graph are of immense use to understanding effects of shading. Although we typically want 100 percent shading throughout most of the summer, we could probably live with only 80–85 percent shading in early autumn in order to benefit from extra solar gains in winter. You will notice the shading patterns displayed in Figure 2.2.15.

In winter, judiciously placed deciduous trees on south-facing building exposures can be a good passive energy-saving technique. Buildings can also be shaded to prevent solar radiation from reaching different surfaces, particularly windows. Masonry or hard top surfaces surrounding a building may act to re-radiate the heat received onto the building itself. This effect can be avoided by the use of shrubs and plants. The absorption or reflection of heat is also affected by the colors of the buildings; for

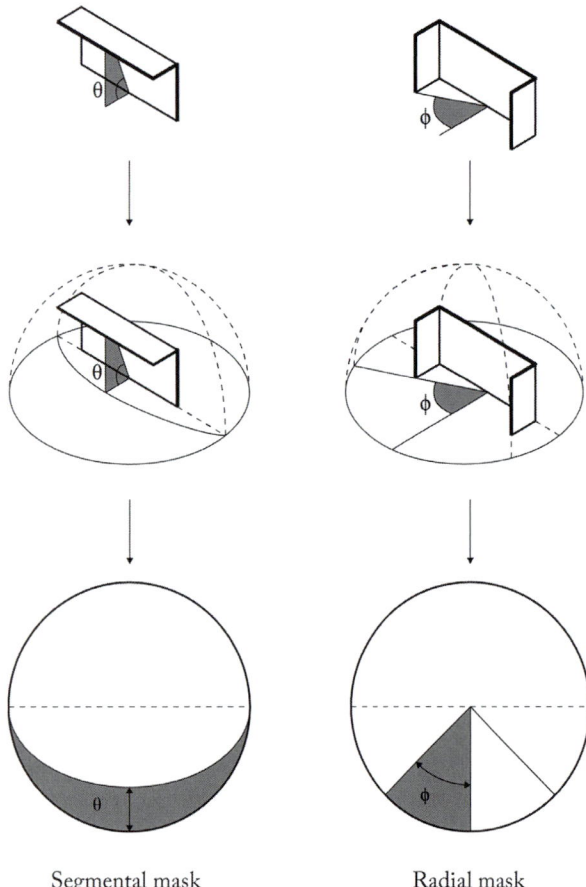

Figure 2.2.15 Generic sun control elements. Sun shading masks show shadows by vertical and horizontal louvers. (Source: Craig B. Smith (ed.), *Efficient Electricity Use*, Elmsford, NY: Pergamon Press, 1978.)

example, light colors, particularly roofs, are effective in reducing heat gain.

Value of Daylight in Building Design

Daylighting is the controlled admission of natural light into a space. The performance of daylighting depends on availability, type of windows, and properties of the space. As such, daylighting is inseparably linked to solar gain. In general, the goal of building design is to reduce heating and cooling loads. The aims of daylighting design are not only to illuminate visual tasks and to create an attractive visual environment, but to support sustainability, balance heat gain and loss, and address variations in daylight availability. To achieve this, the simplest method is the direct

gain approach, where a shading device simultaneously controls the visual and thermal environment. Building orientation and the application of shading systems as a function of the sun's position are both essential to passive architectural design.

Daylighting provides an opportunity to reduce the use of artificial lighting. About 50 percent of the energy used in commercial offices and other similar building types goes to artificial lighting. It is possible to use daylighting in combination with controlled artificial lighting to reduce energy use by 30–60 percent or more due to reductions in electric lighting and air-conditioning system size. Another benefit is that productivity increases and student test scores rise in daylit spaces [4].

Some daylighting systems help redirect sunlight to areas where it is required without glare. Other than plain windows, many of these systems use optical devices such as light shelves, which initiate reflection, refraction, and total internal diffusion of sunlight and/or skylight (Figure 2.2.16). While many advanced actively managed tracking systems are available, discussion here is limited to passive use of daylight. The use of natural light in non-residential and residential buildings has become an important strategy to improve energy efficiency by minimizing lighting, heating, and cooling loads. Also, natural light significantly improves the indoor environment and reduces health problems associated with artificial lighting [5]. Early office buildings used C-, E-, and square-shaped plans to minimize the cross-section for light penetration.

The form, position, and dimensions of openings for atria and windows are discussed, including examples, in Chapter 5.

Atria

In some Eastern countries, before the invention of air-conditioning, designers extensively used atria (large, open central halls) to take advantage of the property of air stratification (hot air rises to the top since it is lighter). When an atrium faces the wind direction, the prevailing wind carries away the hot air at the top of the structure, thus allowing colder air to enter the space at lower levels, which results in comfortable indoor air temperatures.

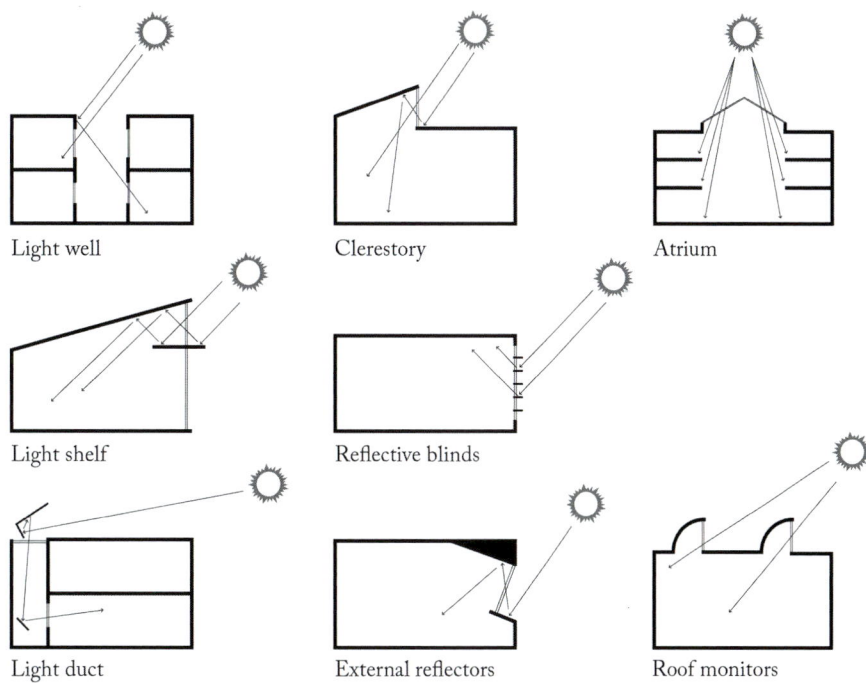

Figure 2.2.16 Daylight concepts for the design of building envelopes.
(Source: Owen J. Lewis, *A Green Vitruvius* (London: Architects Council of Europe, 1999, p. 91).)

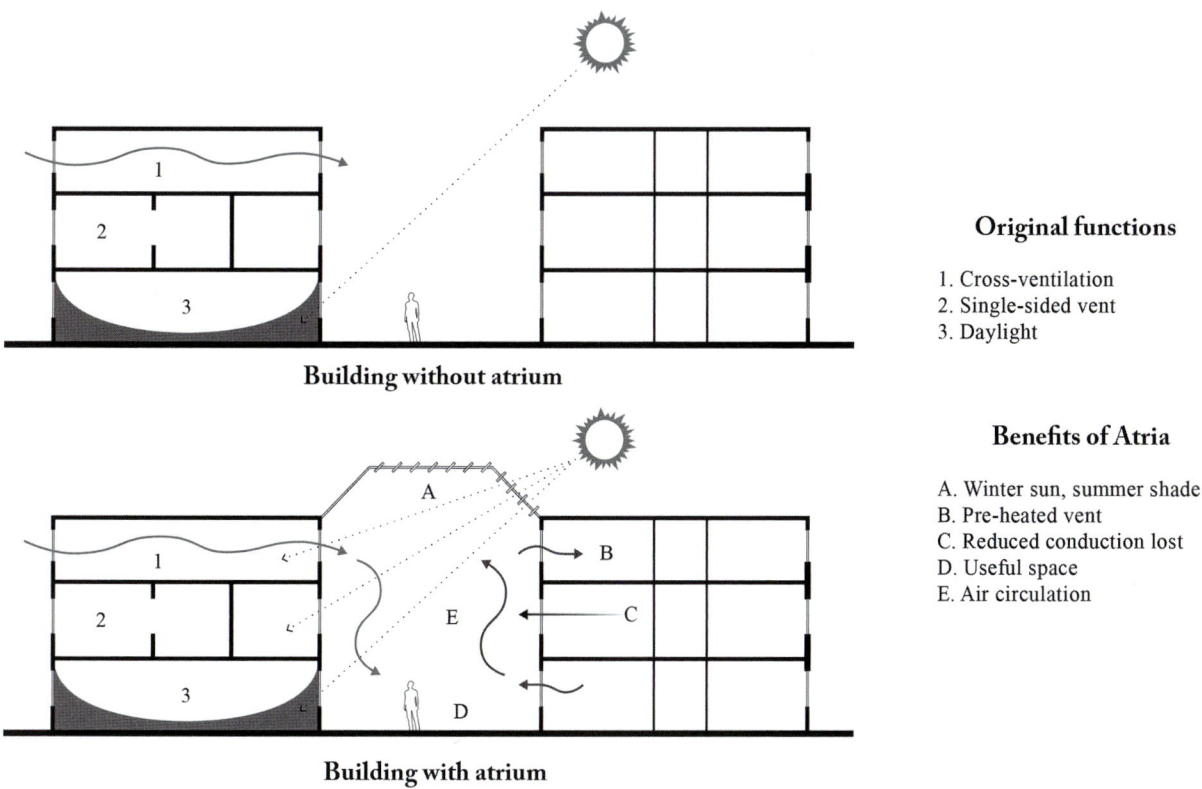

Original functions

1. Cross-ventilation
2. Single-sided vent
3. Daylight

Benefits of Atria

A. Winter sun, summer shade
B. Pre-heated vent
C. Reduced conduction lost
D. Useful space
E. Air circulation

Building without atrium

Building with atrium

Figure 2.2.17 Atrium for heating a structure.
(Source: Owen J. Lewis, *A Green Vitruvius*. (Source: London: Architects Council of Europe, 1999, p. 74).)

By enclosing the atrium, as shown in the following diagram, the sun's energy can be harnessed in winter to heat the building. Due to stratification of air, colder air coming in from lower levels moves up to heat upper levels naturally. The effect of the sun's heat can be diverted by providing shading devices in summer (Figure 2.2.17).

Summary

Sunlight can be used effectively as a passive energy source for heating and providing daylight to a facility. Use of fossil fuels is minimized and buildings that use sun energy can significantly reduce the size of their electric and natural gas bills by using passive solar heating technologies. Issues of direct gain, *trombe* walls, shading buildings, sunspaces, overhangs, atria, and daylighting design, and the effects of ventilation on thermal states, are embedded in the discussion of passive heating design.

References

[1] Edward Mazria, *The Passive Solar Energy Book* (Emmaus, PA: Rodale Press, 1979).

[2] Benjamin Stein, John Reynolds, and William J. McGuinness, *Mechanical and Electrical Equipment for Buildings* (New York: John Wiley & Sons, 1992).

[3] Victor Olgyay and Aladar Olgyay, *Design with Climate* (Princeton, NJ: Princeton University Press, 1963).

[4] Heschong Mahone Group, Inc., Daylighting in Schools, 1999. www.daylighting.com/pdf/product_testing/Heschong_Mahone_Daylight_%26_Schools_1999.pdf.

[5] P. Boyce, C. Hunter, and O. Howlett, *The Benefits of Daylight Through Windows* (Troy, NY: Rensselaer Polytechnic Institute, 2003).

Further Reading

Bruce Anderson and Michael Riordan, *The Solar Home Book* (Harrisville, NH: Cheshire Books, 1976).

G.Z. Brown and Mark DeKay, *Sun, Wind & Light* (New York: John Wiley & Sons, Inc., 2001).

International Energy Agency, *Day Light in Buildings* (July 2000).

Owen J. Lewis, *A Green Vitruvius* (London: European Commission, 1999, pp. 35–37).

US Department of Housing and Urban Development, *Regional Guidelines for Building Passive Energy Conserving Homes* (July 1980).

Web Support

www.energysavers.gov/your_home/designing.../related.../mytopic=10310

http://newlearn.info/learn/packages/clear/thermal/buildings/passive_system/solor_acess_control/external_shading.html

Exercises

1 Design an approximate solar direct gain heating system, using a *trombe* wall and brick flooring, for a 25' × 60' building located in Phoenix. State your references and assumptions.

2 For sustainable living, what considerations must a designer adopt for a moderate-size residential building in Houston, Texas? How will you adopt "six sustainable design ideas" for this project and explain them in brief explanations and sketches?

3 How might you take advantage of a steep slope for a small commercial facility to minimize the impact of cold in Minnesota? Show design sketches along with your reasoning.

2.3 Passive Cooling: Sun Control, Orientation, and Ventilation

Effective use of passive cooling techniques requires understanding climate. The USA has hundreds of localized design climates. For detailed information on weather for the entire USA, refer to the National Climatic Center of the National Oceanic and Atmospheric Administration (NOAA).

Although the principles of passive cooling can be applied anywhere they are needed, they are most often used in two distinct climate zones:

1 hot and arid
2 hot and humid.

In both climates summers can have maximum average temperatures exceeding 100 °F, with low humidity and precipitation in arid zones and high humidity in hot and humid zones.

A hot and arid climate is primarily desert-like, characterized by extremely hot summers and moderately cold winters. The Middle East, India, China, and several other countries experience this type of climate, which is also predominant in New Mexico, Arizona, Nevada, and California. Features common to buildings in hot and arid regions, dating back to ancient times, include shaded windows, dugouts and caves, the building being embedded into the ground, light-colored roofs and walls, heavy insulation, and massive construction materials.

Hot and humid weather dominates in parts of Texas, Louisiana, and Florida in the USA; parts of South America, Greece, and Italy experience similar climate. In hot and humid climates buildings should keep the sun out by use of common walls, heavy insulation, light colors, massive walls, and by preventing direct sun in summer, admitting sun in winter, and providing for natural night ventilation.

Some of the passive cooling techniques for buildings in *hot and arid (dry)* zones are:

1 employ massive construction to even out night- and daytime temperatures (Figure 2.3.1);

2 keep the summer sun out by engaging common walls to reduce exposed exterior walls and use sun shades (Figure 2.3.2);
3 use light colors on roofs and walls;
4 admit sun in winter to minimize heating requirements (understand sun angles, see Figure 2.3.3);
5 use double glazing and sufficient insulation (see Chapter 4 for design details);
6 take full advantage of natural ventilation and air movement (Figure 2.3.4 and see Chapter 5 for details);
7 use evaporative cooling with natural ventilation when the air is dry (see Chapter 4).

Passive cooling principles to follow in *hot and humid* zones are:

1 take advantage of *air movement* to ventilate and maximize the air flow through the building (Figures 2.3.4 and 2.3.5);
2 keep the sunshine out by providing sun shades and proper vegetation (Figure 2.3.2);
3 use winter sun for heating and avoid cold air in winter by proper building shape;
4 prevent more humidity by not placing plants, pools, etc., close to the building and by using natural ventilation to avoid additional interior humidity (Figure 2.3.8);

Figure 2.3.1 Historical passive cooling techniques adopted with high-mass construction in hot and dry climates with small windows, light colors, and massive construction. Thera, Santorini, Greece.
(Source: *Proceedings of the International Passive and Hybrid Cooling Conference*, Miami Beach, FL, November 16, © American Solar Energy Society, 1981.)

Figure 2.3.2 Buildings suitable for *hot and humid* climates (light and airy), typical of the southeast and south USA (Manor house in Louisiana). Sun shading also has uses in hot and arid climates.
(Source: photo by Destrehan Manor House, Michael Overton; this file is licensed under the Creative Commons Source Share Alike 2.0 Generic license.)

5 use massive construction to even out night- and daytime temperatures (Figure 2.3.1).

Use Air Movement for Building Comfort

Passive cooling requires attention to prevailing wind characteristics and microclimates (small areas with climates that may vary from that of the overall region), and also can affect the design of HVAC systems. The three main features of wind are air temperature, speed, and direction, all of which have implications for building orientation, use of natural ventilation, and for controlling airflow on building sites. Unwanted winter winds can be guided away from a building while cooling summer winds can be guided into a structure for thermal advantage. An understanding of how air moves is fundamental to passive cooling design.

A designer should pay more attention to the microclimate(s) of a particular building site than to the overall climate of the region. By studying a full year of site climate data, including wind, a designer can determine the appropriate responses to the landscape, the urban context, and the building form. Wind direction and velocity by monthly averages can be obtained from the local weather station from a nearby city or an airport for any site. Usually the gradient wind velocities are indicated in miles per hour (mph).

Typically, on large projects wind tunnel tests are conducted to study airflow patterns, not only for ventilation but also for structural wind loading and occupant comfort. In the absence of wind tunnel studies and for small projects, the following air movement principles can be used to approximate wind flows on a site to improve designs (see Figures 2.3.4 and 2.3.5). Not only is wind velocity affected by terrain, but it also increases with altitude.

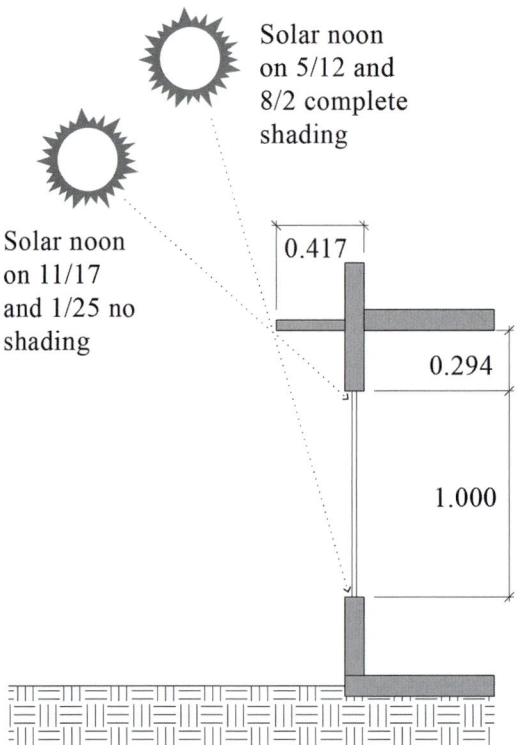

Solar noon on 5/12 and 8/2 complete shading

Solar noon on 11/17 and 1/25 no shading

0.417

0.294

1.000

Shading geometry (in dimensionless units) and sun positions for south-facing windows at 36° north latitude.

Figure 2.3.3 Approximate solar shading guidelines. (Source: Kuppaswamy Iyengar.)

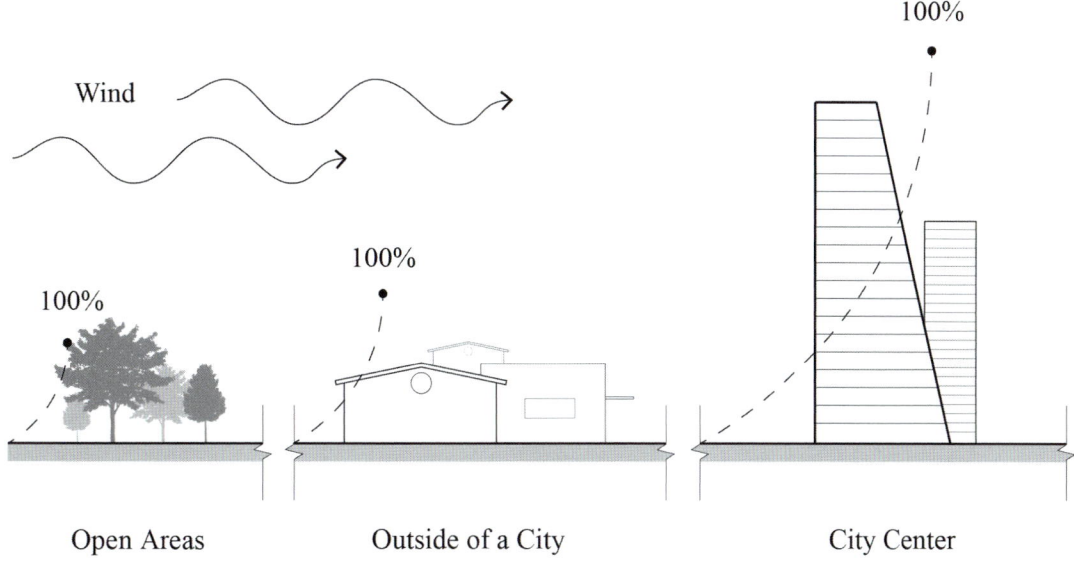

Figure 2.3.4 Changes to wind speed due to ground friction in urban, suburban, and open areas. (Source: http://sustainabilityworkshop.autodesk.com/buildings/wind.)

Three General Principles Apply for Air Movements with Respect to Buildings

1 Due to ground friction, air velocity is slower near the surface of the earth than higher in the atmosphere. As weather experts and pilots know, for example, wind speeds are higher at 30,000 feet than they are on the ground. The higher portions of a building experience greater wind speed effects than lower floors.

2 Following Newton's law, due to inertia (a body in motion tends to stay in motion), air tends to continue to move in the same direction until it confronts an obstruction. This results in air going around objects such as walls, trees, and rocks.

3 Air flows from areas of high pressure to areas of low pressure. When dense air at lower altitudes warms up due to solar radiation, its pressure drops and the air rises, making room for denser air from surroundings areas to move in, or for heavier top layers to sink.

Many design implications arise from these three general principles. For example, *the first principle* suggests that in a tall building lighter load spaces and spaces requiring greater ventilation can be designed into the top floors, while heavy load spaces such as libraries can be located on lower floors.

One of the implications of the *second principle* is that airflow [1, 2] on a building site may be controlled by obstructions, deflectors, filters made by trees, hedges, berms, and/or different heights within the building (Figure 2.3.5). In humid climates any unwanted air can also be made to move around the building by landscaping, berms, and walls or ornamental grilles (typical of Far Eastern architecture).

Also, wind patterns are altered around built and natural forms in complex ways that must be taken into account in designs. Figure 2.3.6 indicates the approximate flow of wind around a building showing increased speed and eddies. These patterns were studied by Evans [3] and are useful for understanding the aerodynamics of building forms. This knowledge could, for example, help a designer locate a building in front of an obstruction without putting the building through turbulent flow, which can be energy inefficient.

Wind flows around different building configurations and orientations are graphically represented in plan view in Figure 2.3.7 to help designers develop site and building designs. For more detailed building shapes, refer to *Sun, Wind & Light* [4], p. 20.

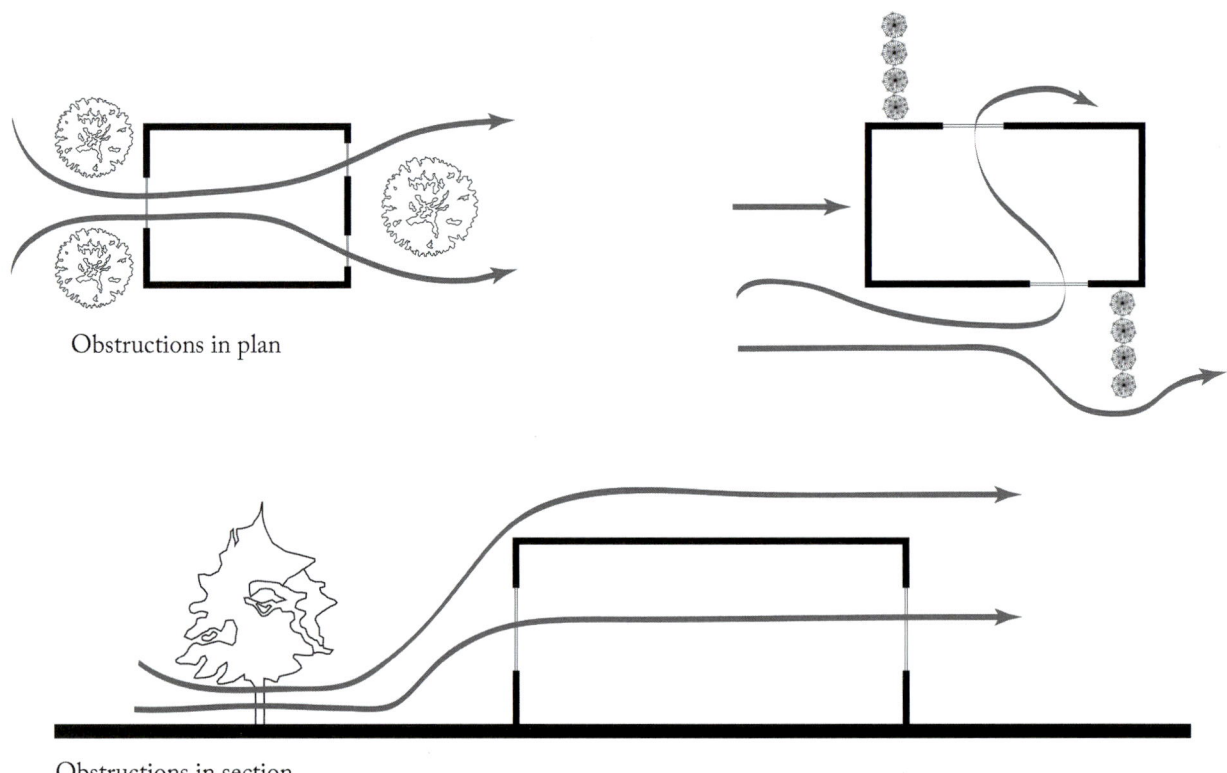

Obstructions in plan

Obstructions in section

Figure 2.3.5 Using obstructions to control airflow in a building. Deflectors and filters made by trees, hedges, berms, and different heights within the building.
(Source: Owen J. Lewis, *A Green Vitruvius* (London: Architects Council of Europe, 1999, p. 39).)

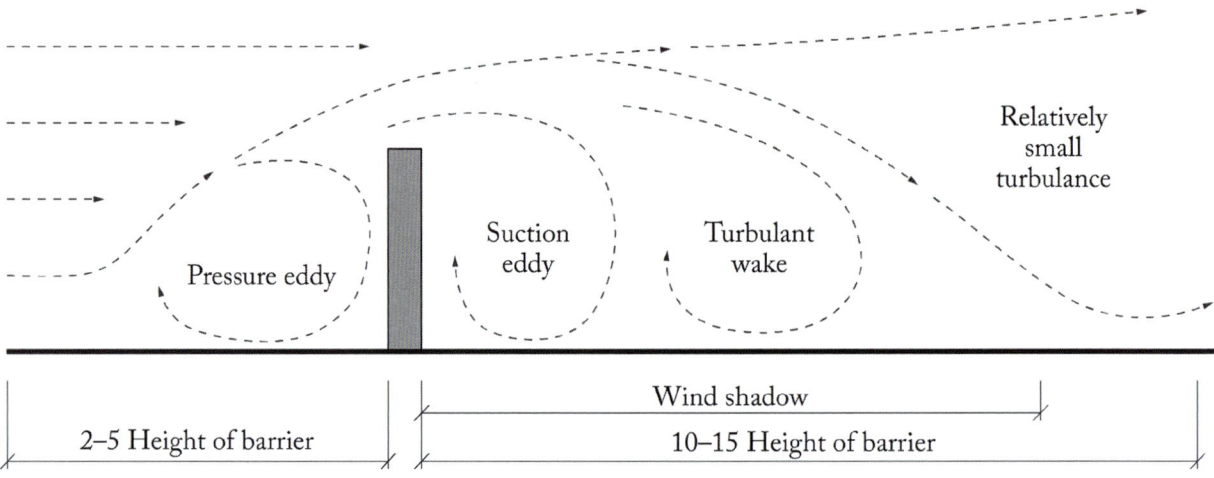

Figure 2.3.6 Approximate wind patterns around a built form showing increased speed and eddies.
(Source: Professor Stephen D. Dent, University of New Mexico, School of Architecture and Planning.)

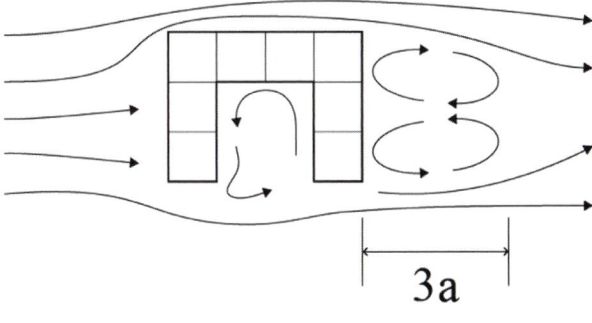

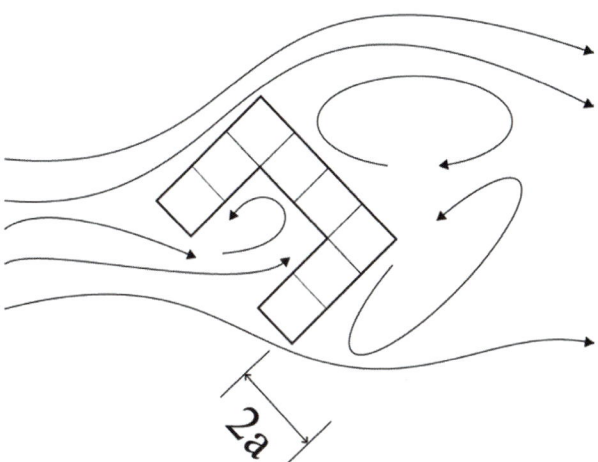

Figure 2.3.7 Example of wind flow around different building configurations. a = the height of the building. (Source: Regional Guidelines for Building Passive Energy Conserving Homes by AIA Research Corporation, US Department of Housing and Urban Development.)

Airflow resulting from pressure differences, the *third basic air movement principle* affecting buildings, is discussed in more detail in Section 2.4 on *cooling towers* and the *stack effect*. To naturally ventilate a room and take advantage of pressure differences caused by outdoor winds, there should be openings on both opposite walls of the room. The opening on the windward side is larger than the leeward side to optimize the airflow. It is also preferable to keep the room free of obstructions as much as practicable. See Figure 2.3.5 for openings on adjacent walls to direct the air to flow through the room perpendicular to the direction of the wind flow, when necessary. In hot and humid climates a designer should avoid adding additional moisture into the building [5]

by ventilating kitchens, baths, and laundries (Figure 2.3.8). Any water bodies, such as ponds and swimming pools, should be on the leeward side of the building.

Passive Ventilation Techniques

Ventilation is the intentional movement of air into and out of a building. Architects may alter the building envelope to take advantage of the three principles discussed above, in order to use natural forces of wind and airflow to cool interior spaces. Natural ventilation systems rely on air pressure differences to circulate fresh air throughout buildings. Pressure differences can be caused by wind, by the buoyancy effect created by temperature differences, or by differences in humidity. Designers can manipulate these properties to create systems that move air through buildings in desired ways. Simply speaking, pressure is positive on the windward side of a building and negative on the leeward side, creating an imbalance that can be used to drive air through a building. As with solar design, location, orientation, and form and dimensions of buildings can aid in passive ventilation.

Passive ventilation [4] often makes use of outdoor spaces that are carefully situated for maximum comfort. Observe closely the different outdoor room locations for different wind and sun directions in different climatic conditions. Obstructions in front of a building can block the sun and alter the wind direction, resulting in different microclimates for that land. This condition has implications for locating outdoor living spaces as part of building designs. For example, in a temperate climate when the summer wind and sun directions are coincident, it is best not to place outdoor rooms on the north side of the building (Figure 2.3.9). This might block wind access to the rest of the building, which is needed to cool interior spaces.

Passive ventilation techniques are found at the Wallen Maybeck house in the cool Berkeley Hills of California (Figure 2.3.9). The south-facing outdoor space is surrounded on two sides by the house, on a third side by the garage, and is sheltered by a low wall to ensure a good view. This orientation guarantees protection from north-northwest winter winds.

Another example of a low-energy and passive ventilated building is De Montfort University's Queen's

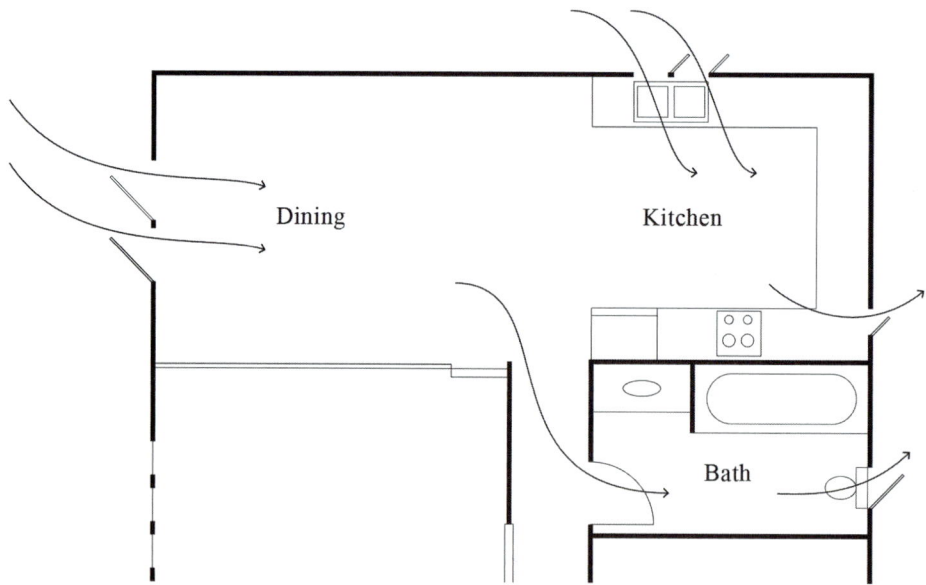

Ventilate kitchens, baths, and laundry
rooms in order to exhaust humid air.

Figure 2.3.8 Avoid creating additional humidity by natural ventilation in a building (ventilate kitchens, bath, and laundry rooms to exhaust humid air).
(Source: *Regional Guidelines for Building Passive Energy Conserving Homes* by AIA Research Corporation, US Department of Housing and Urban Development.)

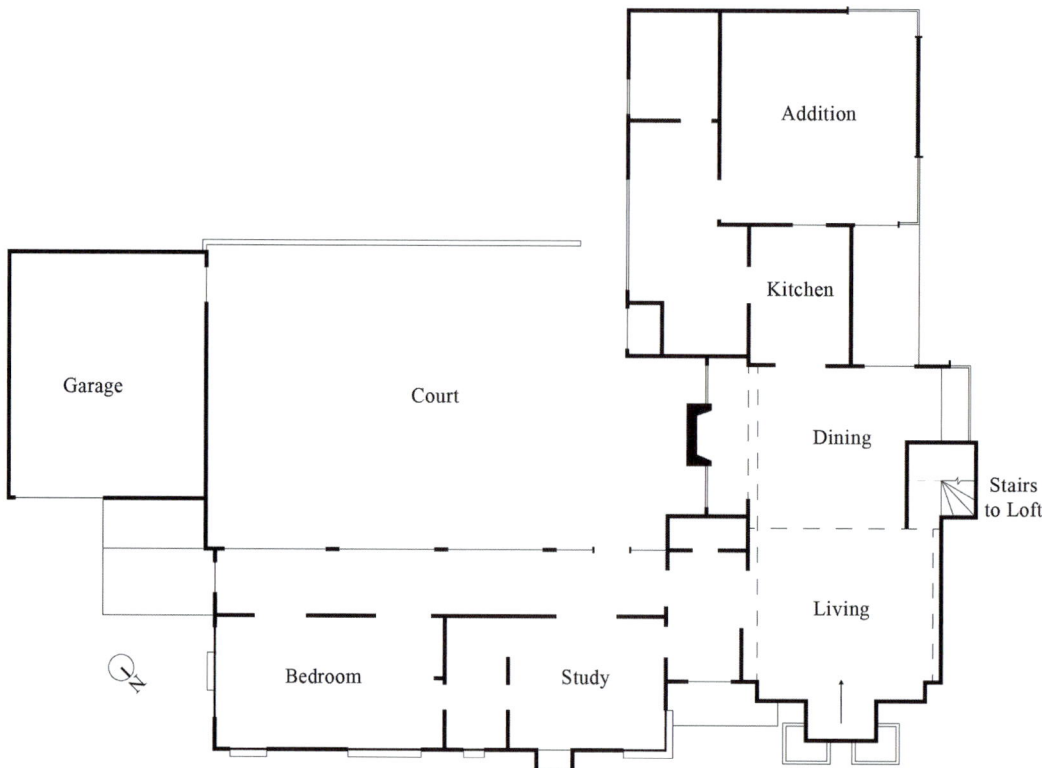

Figure 2.3.9 Wallen Maybeck House, Berkeley Hills, California.

Building in the UK [6], built in 1993 (Figures 2.3.10 and 2.3.11). The university's aim was to be innovative and creative in terms of passive environmental design. Designers used natural ventilation and thermal mass to maintain occupant comfort. An evaluation of the building after 15 years of use revealed most parts work well in terms of ventilation. The flagship space of the Queen's Building is the auditorium. The natural ventilation system of this popular space works very well, with heat accumulating at a high level and exhausting through two chimney stacks behind the screen. The incoming outside air, which can be heated if required, traverses through concrete ducts below the seats, and the buoyant exhaust air is expelled through the stacks. The quantity of incoming air is controlled by louvers which have motorized as well as manual controls. The arrows in Figure 2.3.10a indicate the air movement.

The Building Services Research and Information Association (BSRIA) in the UK, which conducted post-occupancy research on this building, concluded that the auditorium functions well with passive ventilation. Although the main laboratory building has

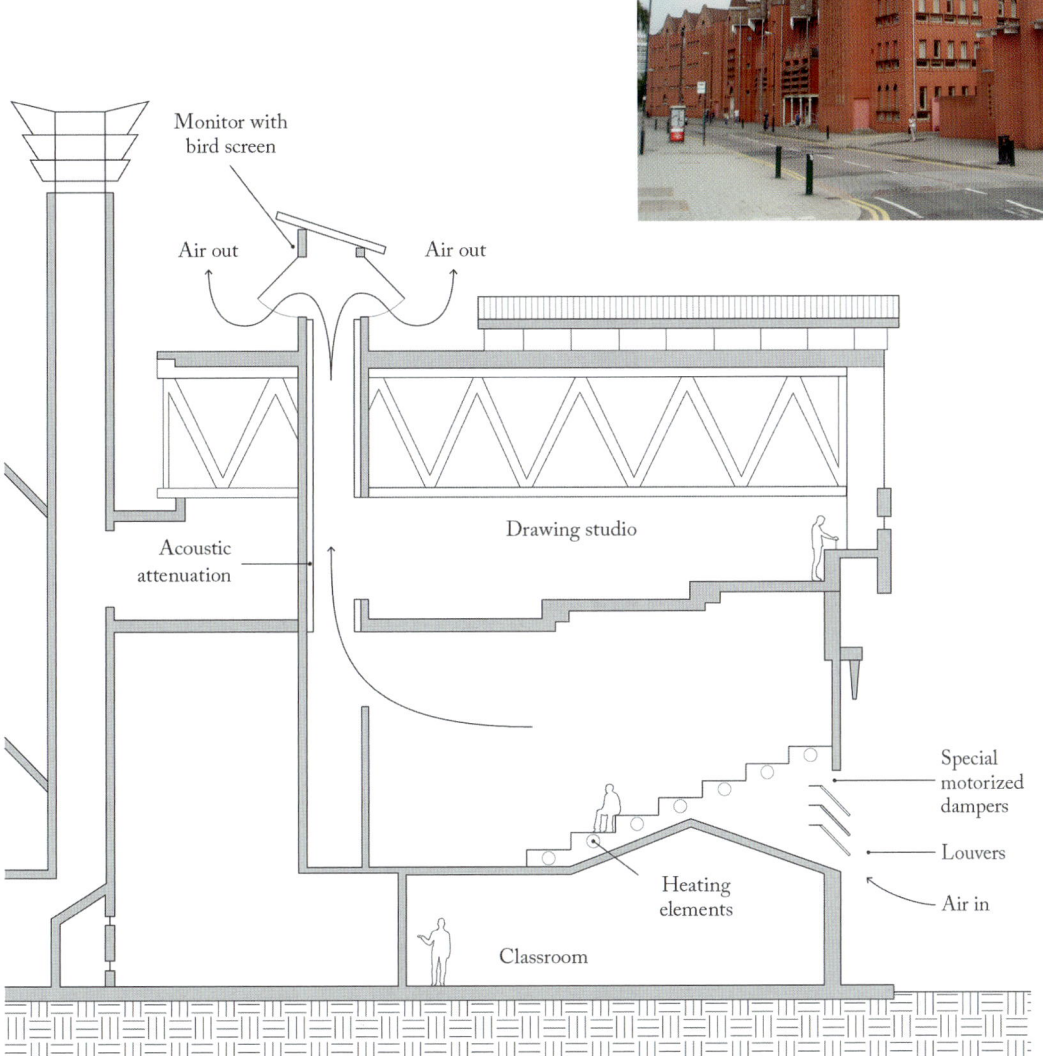

Figure 2.3.10 Section and street view of the auditorium building. (Source: https://commons.wikimedia.org.)

Figure 2.3.11 The interior view of the auditorium illustrates well-integrated, inconspicuous ventilation and heating systems under the seats – see Figure 2.3.10a.
(Source: Courtesy of DeMontfort University.)

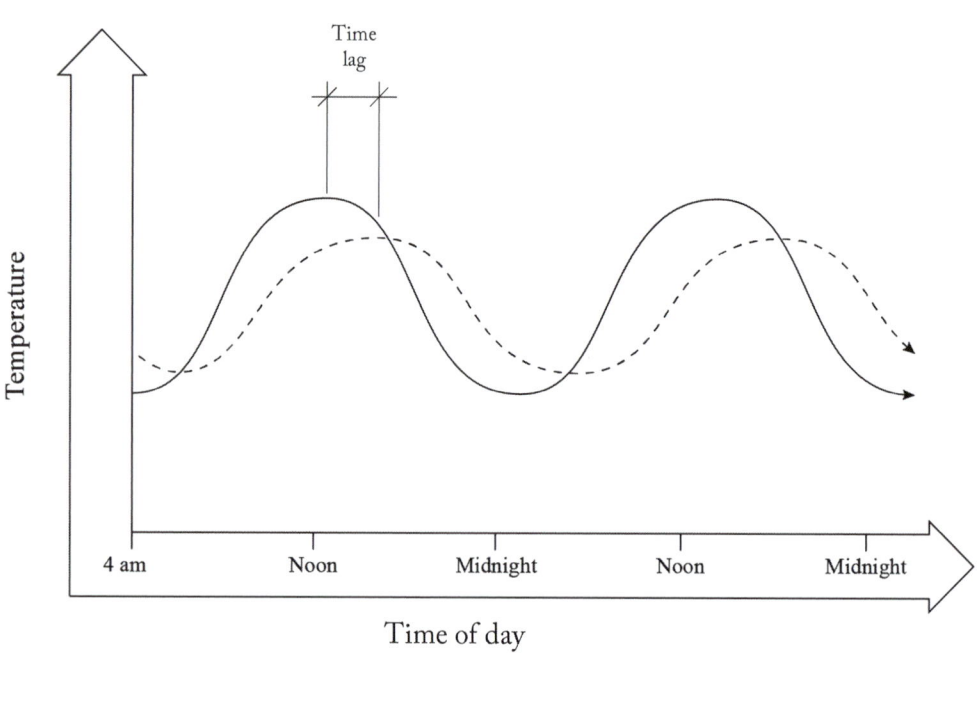

Figure 2.3.12 Effect of external building thermal mass on inside temperature.
(Source: Kuppaswamy Iyengar.)

some minor problems, the Queen's Building project provides a successful example for the incorporation of passive ventilation systems into sustainable designs. A thorough understanding of airflow contributes to the success of such passive cooling designs.

Challenges of Natural Ventilation

Natural ventilation for cooling is not a new idea. As early as the tenth century builders used ventilation in extreme weather conditions to keep the occupants of a building reasonably comfortable. Structures known as wind vanes directed the wind toward a building and through it to improve ventilation. These wind vanes, also known as *"Badgirs"* are discussed in more detail in Section 2.4. However, after the advent of affordable air-conditioning, natural ventilation has been largely ignored. Using natural ventilation as the sole system for cooling in a building requires architects to provide adequate insulation for the winter months and to ensure the building is shaded properly to minimize the effects of the summer sun.

Not all types of natural cooling are effective in all climates. Those dependent on evaporative principles will not be as effective in low-humidity and high-temperature regions, since the benefit of evaporation already exists. A designer should be aware that natural cooling is effective only in moderate climates. In high humidity very high air speed is required to remove the moisture from air and therefore natural methods may not work. Indoor air speeds of more than 2.6 mph (228 feet per second) are considered too drafty and therefore unacceptable, which limits the use of natural ventilation (see Table 4.4 in Stein *et al.*'s *Mechanical and Electrical Equipment for Buildings* [7]).

It is easy to make a building comfortable in winter if it can be built with a tight envelope and vulnerable areas are sealed, making air penetration impossible through weather stripping, caulking, protected entryways (double doors), and so on. However, studies have shown that very tight buildings pose other problems, such as build-up of mold and poor indoor air quality. Tight buildings often do not have operable windows, which can mean over-reliance on mechanical systems for cooling.

HVAC systems, whether they are passive or mechanical, must also be designed with properly located venting to avoid intake or accidental recycling of exhaust or other pollutants. Winds also influence intake and output of air, and thus must be evaluated as part of the design.

Effect of Building Mass

Finally, the type of construction will determine whether a building can be comfortable for natural ventilation. Figure 2.3.12 shows temperature fluctuations based on the mass of a building. As shown in the graph, the interior temperature of a massive construction will fluctuate much less than a light-frame construction. In warm, humid climates a high-mass construction will hold the interior temperature fairly constant at an undesirable level, absorb moisture, prevent air movement, and maintain high humidity. Therefore buildings in these climates are airy and light. But in a dry climate with large diurnal temperature swings, a high-mass wall predominantly acts to retard heat transfer from the exterior to the interior during the day. Massive walls prevent thermal energy from reaching the inner surface. When temperatures fall at night, the walls re-radiate the thermal energy back into the night sky. It is critical that such walls be massive to prevent heat transfer into the interior.

Additional key points on passive cooling are:

1 Make full use of heat avoidance before applying any passive cooling strategies.
2 Comfort ventilation is used day and night to cool people and to keep the indoor temperature close to the outdoor temperature. This type of ventilation is used mainly in very humid climates and in temperate climates when the humidity is high.
3 Night-flush cooling uses night ventilation to cool the mass of the building. During the day, the windows are closed and the mass acts as a heat sink. This passive cooling strategy is used in both dry climates and temperate climates whenever the humidity is low.
4 Air flows from positive- to negative-pressure areas.
5 There is a positive pressure on the windward side, and a negative pressure on both the leeward side and the sides of the building parallel to the wind.
6 Hot air can be exhausted from the top of a building by stratification, the stack effect, the shape of the

roof (the Venturi effect), and the increased wind velocity found at higher elevations (the Bernoulli effect).

7 Use cross-ventilation whenever possible.

8 Have air flow across people for comfort ventilation and across the building mass for night-flush cooling.

9 Radiant cooling from the roof works well in climates in which the humidity is low and clouds are few.

10 Use direct evaporative cooling when the relative humidity is low.

11 Use indirect evaporative cooling when the relative humidity is high.

12 Use earth cooling mainly in the north and west. Condensation can be a problem in the humid southeast.

Summary

The principle characteristics of air movement both outside and inside buildings govern possibilities for passive cooling. Ventilation is the intentional movement of air into and out of a building, and natural ventilation accomplishes this without tapping into the power grid. Architects can accomplish passive cooling through careful research into local wind and microclimate patterns, siting, orientation, and form and dimensions of openings within the building. The following sections give examples of specific passive cooling technologies that take advantage of the natural physical properties of air and sun.

References

[1] Owen J. Lewis, *A Green Vitruvius* (London: European Commission, 1999, pp. 35–37).

[2] Stephen Dent (James C. Snyder and Anthony J. Catanese, eds.), *Introduction to Architecture* (New York: John Wiley & Sons, 1979).

[3] B.H. Evans, *Natural Air Flow Around Buildings* (College Station, TX: Texas A. & M. College, 1957).

[4] G.Z. Brown and Mark DeKay, *Sun, Wind & Light* (New York: John Wiley & Sons, Inc. 2001).

[5] The AIA Research Corporation, *Regional Guidelines for Building Passive Energy Conserving Homes* (Washington, DC: US Department of Housing and Urban Development, 1980).

[6] Battle McCarthy, *Wind Towers* (Chichester: Academy Editions, 1999).

[7] Benjamin Stein, John Reynolds, and William J. McGuinness, *Mechanical and Electrical Equipment for Buildings* (New York: John Wiley & Sons, 1992).

Further Reading

Victor Olgyay and Aladar Olgyay, *Design with Climate* (Princeton, NJ: Princeton University Press, 1963).

Exercises

1 Suggest some overall passive concept ideas to design a small summer residence of 1,800 square feet in Mumbai, India. Your sustainable and environmental design ideas should be in the form of a brief narrative and clear sketches. Research your concepts from *Sun, Wind and Light* [4].

2 What passive cooling technologies would you use for buildings in Albuquerque, New Mexico?

3 Explain how you could use thermal mass in designing a school building in a hot and arid zone.

2.4   Passive Cooling: Air and Water Systems

How do architects use knowledge of air movement principles to design passive cooling systems for buildings? It is useful to think of a natural ventilation system as a pathway, with equal consideration given to supply and exhaust. Certain systems such as towers and scoops or chimneys have a long history as efficient tools for capitalizing on wind, airflow, temperature, and/or differences in air density. These systems are designed to bring cool air into a building and vent warm air out of the building. Openings between rooms such as transom windows, louvers, grills, or open plans are techniques to complete the airflow through a building. Certain systems work better than others in certain climates. Always keep in mind that orientation, appropriate building mass, insulation, glazing, color, reflectivity, vegetation, and shading reduce initial solar impact.

Following is a list of different passive cooling systems [1].

Cooling with Ventilation

1 *Comfort ventilation:* ventilation during the day and night to increase evaporation from the skin and thereby increasing thermal comfort.
2. *Night-flush cooling:* ventilation to pre-cool the building for the next day.

Radiant Cooling

1 *Direct radiant cooling:* a building's roof structure cools by radiation to the night sky.
2 *Indirect radiant cooling:* radiation to the night sky cools a heat-transfer fluid, which then cools the building.

Evaporative Cooling

1 *Direct evaporation:* water is sprayed into the air entering a building. This lowers the air's temperature but raises its humidity.

2 *Indirect evaporative cooling:* evaporation cools the incoming air or the building without raising the indoor humidity.

Earth Cooling

1 *Direct coupling:* an earth-sheltered building loses heat directly to the earth.
2 *Indirect coupling:* air enters the building by way of earth tubes.

A combination of these techniques is necessary, depending on site-specific situations.

Natural Ventilation

An obstruction such as a building in a wind path reduces wind speed, causing an increase in static wind pressure. On the other side and top of this building, due to reduction of area of cross-section surrounding the building, the wind speed is accelerated. This increase in wind speed reduces static pressure, resulting

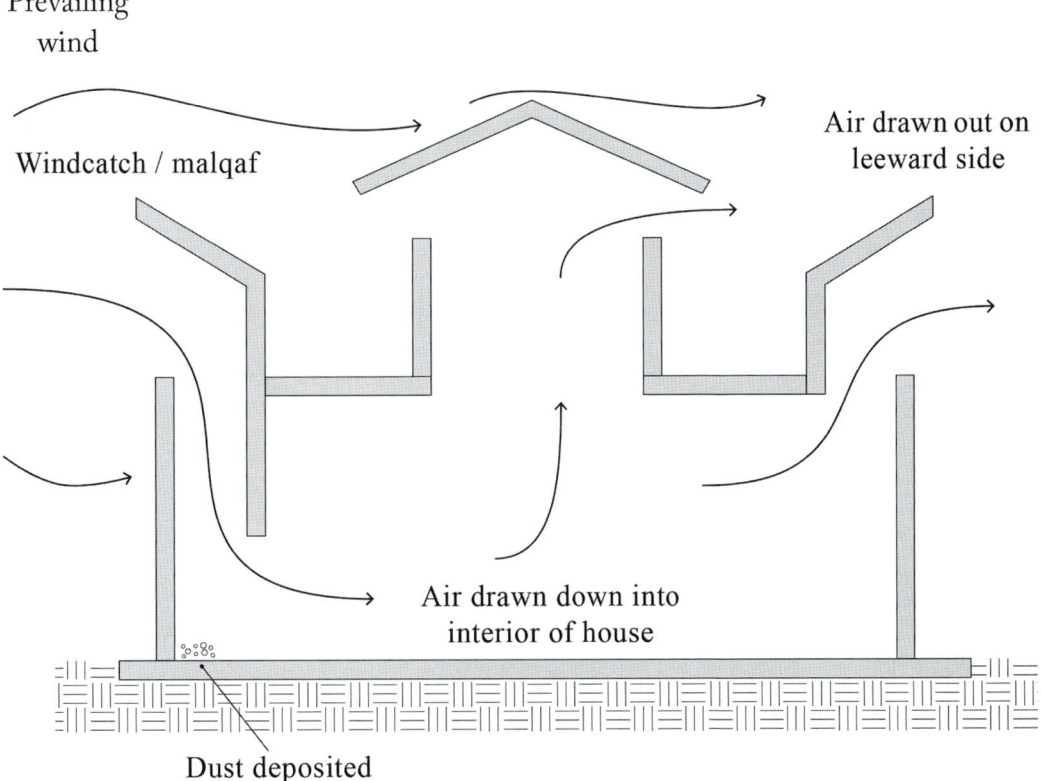

Figure 2.4.1 Behavior of wind on a building.
(Source: this file is from the Wikimedia Commons and is in the public domain.)

in suction on the leeward side (Figure 2.4.1). Using this principle, wind towers optimize pressure differences caused by wind to move the air. The opening or window area on the leeward side, typically, is smaller to create the suction to move air. It is important to avoid placing obstructions in front of windward and leeward windows.

Natural ventilation is dependent on three climatic conditions:

1 *Wind velocity*. A designer should position the wind tower to maximize the inlet and exhaust openings to improve the efficiency of the ventilation system. Pressure differences between inside and the surrounding area of a building will have great influence on the ventilation effect.

2 *Wind direction*. Wind direction will not remain constant throughout the season and it is likely to vary even on a daily basis. Openings for ventilation should be designed keeping in mind this reality.

3 *Temperature differential*. When air temperature increases, the density of air reduces, making it lighter and causing it to rise. The temperature differences between different parts of a building and different areas around the building create pressure differences, causing air to move in a process known as the "stack effect" (Figure 2.4.2).

Natural ventilation uses wind and buoyancy to deliver fresh air into buildings. Fresh air in buildings is necessary to alleviate odors, to provide oxygen for breathing, and to increase thermal comfort. Interior temperature can be reduced as much as 5 °F if interior air velocities reach 160 feet per minute. Natural ventilation is not very effective in reducing the humidity of air, which is a problem for hot and humid zones. This limits the use of natural ventilation in all climatic zones.

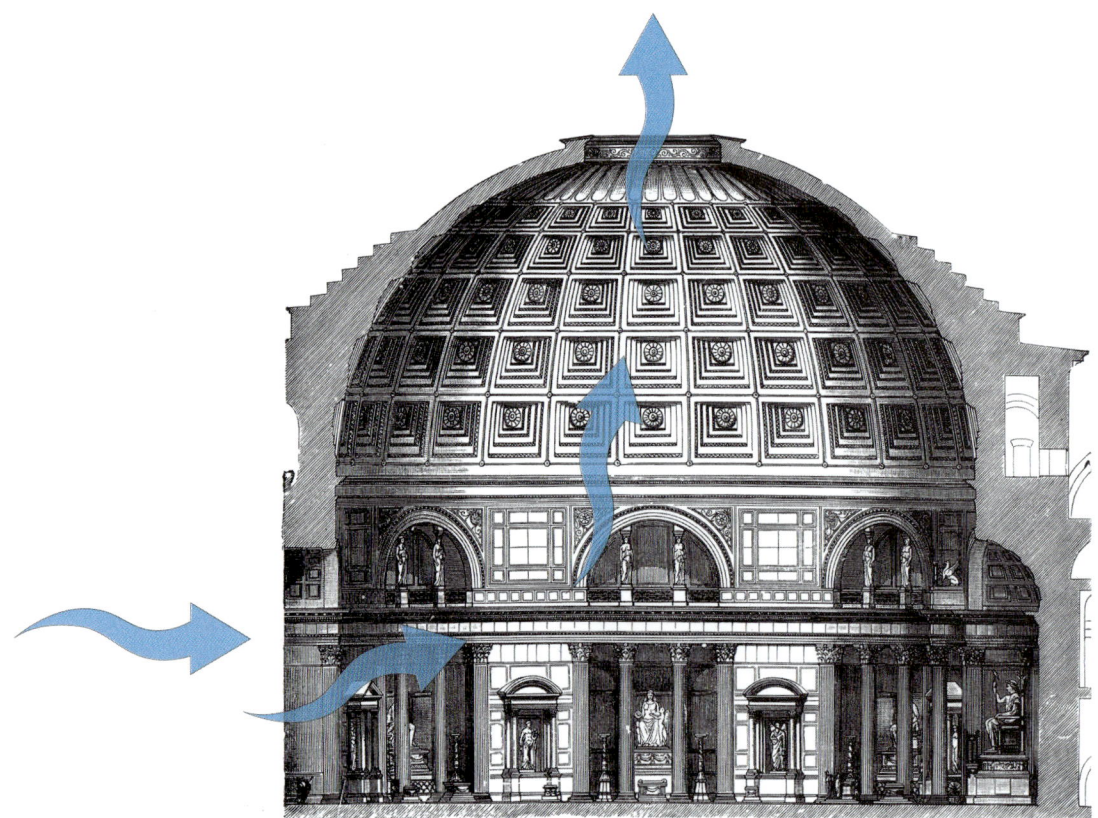

Figure 2.4.2 The Pantheon in Rome, Italy (AD 126) uses wind-driven ventilation. (Source: https://cs.wikipedia.org/wiki/Pantheon.)

Hot and Arid Zones

Egyptians from as long ago as 1300 BC used the *malqaf* (meaning wind catcher) for natural ventilation of buildings. These ancient designs still have value today. Well-known Egyptian architect Haasan Fathy recommends that traditional solutions in vernacular architecture should be evaluated to make them compatible with modern requirements [2].

Wind Towers and Wind Scoops

Wind scoops (Figure 2.4.1) are the structures designed to catch the wind and redirect fresh air into the building. For them to be effective they must be able to catch the wind from all directions. They are excellent design elements when large quantities of air need to be moved into large building spaces, such as atriums.

For natural ventilation it is advisable to use wind towers and scoops in combination to address the problem of changing wind direction when redirecting the wind into buildings. To receive wind from any direction, wind towers in the Middle East were conceived with four vertical shafts to catch the breeze. These are known as *badgirs*.

History of the *Badgir* or Wind Tower

In the Middle East and in certain parts of India and Pakistan the wind tower or *badgir* has been used since at least AD 900 as a means to cool and ventilate buildings (Figure 2.4.3). These vertical structures are used to capture prevailing summer winds and direct them into the interior or basement of a building. A *badgir* functions by altering the temperature and consequently the density of the air in and around the tower, which creates drafts that pull air up or down the passage.

Wind Towers in Dubai, UAE (Figure 2.4.4), are designed to catch the wind from any direction, making them truly a combination wind tower and wind scoop.

The wind tower site should experience winds with a fairly good and consistent velocity. A successful wind tower operates in different ways, based on the time of day and the presence of wind. Its operation relies on the changing temperature of the structure and thereby on the density of the air in and around the tower. The difference in density creates a draft, pulling air either upwards or downwards through the tower.

The tower area is designed with a large heat storage capacity at the top and a large surface area for heat

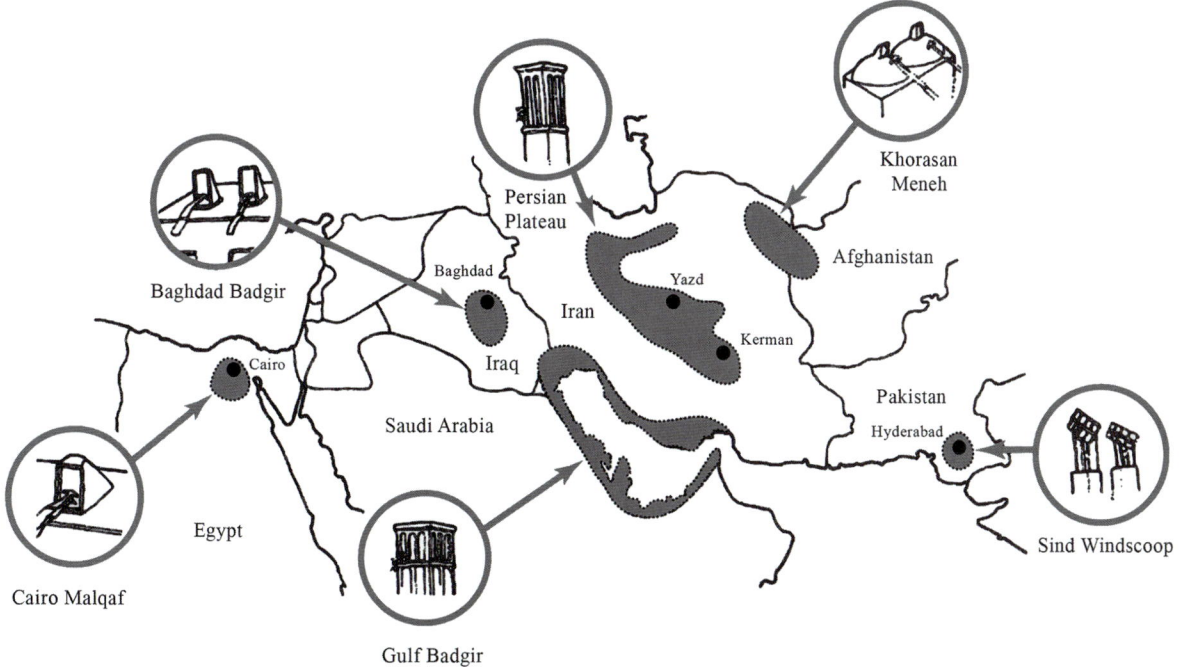

Figure 2.4.3 Location of wind catchers in the Middle East. Wind catching systems are designed to bring cool air into the building and vent warm air out. (Source: drawing by Mustafa Howeedy, American Solar Society Conference, 1981.)

Figure 2.4.4   Wind towers designed for passive cooling in Dubai, UAE.
(Source: this file is from the Wikimedia Commons and is in the public domain.)

transfer. The tower walls and the internal walls of the airflow passages absorb heat during the day and release it at night, warming the cool night air in the tower. Due to convection, the warm air moves up, creating a draft that is exhausted through the openings. The pressure difference thus created pulls the cool night air though the doors and windows into the building. The night radiation through the roof and the external walls brings about additional cooling. The tower acts as a chimney when there is no wind. The cool night air can enter the tower when wind is present, and forces itself down into the structure. Sufficient cooling can be achieved due to forced circulation.

Wind scoops have some different characteristics from wind towers and are well-suited for large-volume spaces. A wind scoop consists of a vane or a thick plate placed on top of a roof of a building to redirect wind into the building. This permits clean outside air to mix within the interior space. The assumption is that the air at higher levels is cleaner than the air at lower levels. Another wind scoop design works by bringing the outside air from a remote place via underground tubes and ducts and then mixing it with the building air. This design takes advantage of cooler air some distance away from the building.

When the façade of a building cannot be punctured for ventilation due to some urban conditions such as noise, pollution, or non-availability of appropriate air, wind scoops offer an alternative solution. Also, when adjacent spaces of an atrium are mechanically air-conditioned, wind scoops provide an economical alternative for creating comfort inside an atrium.

In shopping malls, the open mall area typically is not required to meet strict air-conditioning standards.

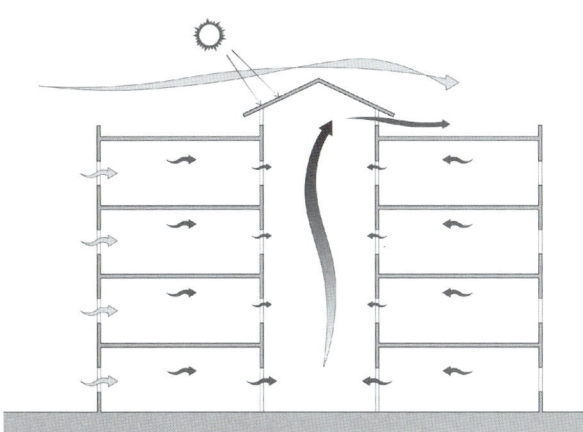

Figure 2.4.5 Hot air is pulled from the atrium. (Source: Kuppaswamy Iyengar.)

Natural ventilation offers an opportunity to provide a clean, fresh environment and to create a sense of being outside. Wind scoops bring in outside air, plenty of light, and on occasion the calming sounds of nature.

In Figure 2.4.5, hot air is expelled at the top of the atrium, which attracts cooler air to enter at the lower levels.

Hot and Humid Climates (Tropical Areas)

As noted in Figure 2.4.6, traditional buildings in hot and humid regions (for example, Malaysia or Louisiana) are designed to encourage ventilation by adopting a number of devices. The building is raised on stilts to catch higher-velocity winds and allow lower-level cooler winds to cool the floors. Vents are built into the top level of external walls to take advantage of stratified hot air, which escapes from the top level.

Figure 2.4.7 illustrates features of a typical historic southern Louisiana building: (1) generous galleries, (2) a broad spreading roofline, (3) gallery roofs supported by light wooden colonnades, (4) placement of the principal rooms well above grade (sometimes a full story), (5) a form of construction utilizing a heavy timber frame combined with an infill made of brick or a mixture of mud, moss, and animal hair called bousillage, (6) multiple French doors, and (7) French wraparound mantels. Some modern architects have adopted these principles in their sustainable architectural designs.

Wind

Figure 2.4.6 Response to tropical climate, Malaysian Vernacular House. (Source: Courtesy of Professor A. Ghafar Bin Ahmad.)

Contemporary Applications of Cool Towers

The contemporary use of the cool tower utilizes the historic *badgir* system with modern materials and equipment. Two variations of the technology are balanced stack ventilation (BSV) or passive downdraft evaporative cooling (PDEC) (see Figure 2.4.8).

In a *BSV system*, air is supplied in a cold stack where the temperature is maintained close to outdoor conditions by insulation of the unit. Air is vented through a warm stack. The pressure within the stack is determined by the indoor–outdoor air density difference and the height difference from the stack exhaust and the floor-level inlet locations. Examples of this system include the Monodraught *Windcatcher* models from the UK. The *Windcatcher* uses compartmentalized vertical vents to bring fresh air into a room, while venting warm air out. As warm air rises and decreases the air pressure within a room, the cooler air descends

Figure 2.4.7   Parlange Plantation, an example of the French Creole style, Louisiana, USA.
(Source: image courtesy of the Louisiana Division of Historic Preservation.)

Figure 2.4.9   A Market in Bridgetown, Barbados using a BSV system.
(Source: Monodraught.)

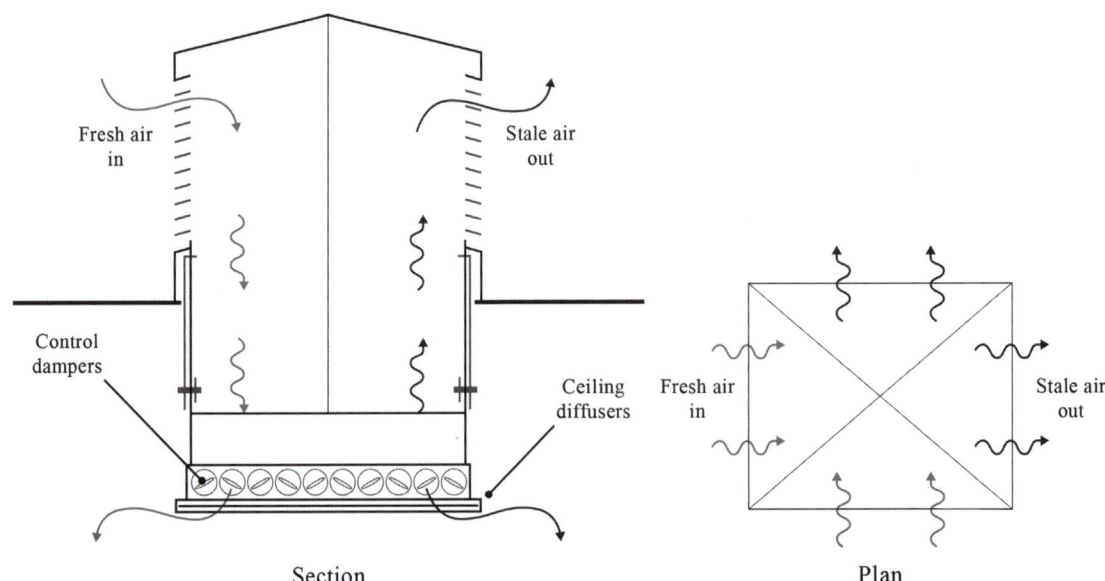

Figure 2.4.8   Balanced stack ventilation (BSV). The pressure within the stack is determined by the indoor–outdoor air density difference and the height difference from the stack exhaust and the floor-level inlet locations.
(Source: Monodraught.)

(Figure 2.4.9). Stack effect is achieved as a result of temperature difference between inside and outside the building, and the subsequent imbalance in air densities and pressure give rise to the hot air rising up inside the building, making room for the cold air to enter at the lower levels and windows. Prevailing winds remove the stale and warm air away from the building.

Cool Tower Basics

In climates where the temperatures and humidity are moderate, evaporative cooling works well (for a detailed description of evaporative cooling, see Section 5.2). Based on the concept of the *badgir*, PDEC towers can also be used to supply cool air to rooms in a building. PDEC systems add evaporative cooling to the BSV system. Examples of this technology include the Torrent Research Laboratory in Ahmedabad, India, designed by Nimish Patel and Parul Zavei, and the Zion National Park Visitor Center in Utah.

The *Torrent Complex* (Figure 2.4.10) contains 20 air-intake towers and 58 taller exhaust air outlets. Pressurized nozzles at the top of the towers produce a fine mist that cools the air through evaporation. The cool air descends into corridors which contain openings that provide ventilation for adjacent spaces.

Other openings move warm air to the exhaust towers. Airlocks on each level of the laboratory maintain the proper functioning of the system. During the humid monsoon season, the misting system is turned off and ventilation is assisted by fans. Electric energy is needed to run the fans; however, that energy in most cases can be derived from photovoltaic systems, thus avoiding the use of fossil fuels.

At the 7,600 square foot *Zion National Park Visitor Center* (Figure 2.4.11), a one-third horsepower pump is used to circulate water over pads at the top of the cooling towers. The cooled air descends to

Figure 2.4.10 Torrent Research Laboratory, Ahmedabad, India. The Torrent Research Laboratory Complex contains 20 air-intake towers and 58 taller exhaust air outlets.
(Source: photo by Abhikram.)

large openings at the base of the tower. An energy management computer controls these openings and can direct cool air into the building or out to the patio. Measured flows from the tower are approximately 8,000 cubic feet per minute for each tower. Again, these systems can be made totally free from the electrical grid system by using a simple photovoltaic (PV) array to supply the necessary power to the required small pumps that move the air.

In other options, the cool tower provides cool air by taking in hot, dry outdoor air through high inlets wrapped with a wetted evaporative pad. A slow trickle of water is supplied by a water pump, powered by a PV system. The hot air passing through the pads will pick up moisture, which lowers the air temperature and increases its humidity. This dense air drops to the lower levels, moves into spaces at the lower level, and exits through the operable windows. Buildings with cooling towers have their own unique configurations since the rooms requiring cool temperatures tend to be bunched around these towers.

In *stack ventilation*, air movement depends on temperature, and in *cool towers* humidity guides the system design. Buoyancy results from the difference in air density. A cool tower can deliver cooled air to the space. When the temperature of the room air increases it will rise and the stack ventilation effect helps in exhausting that air to the outside. It is possible to combine both systems.

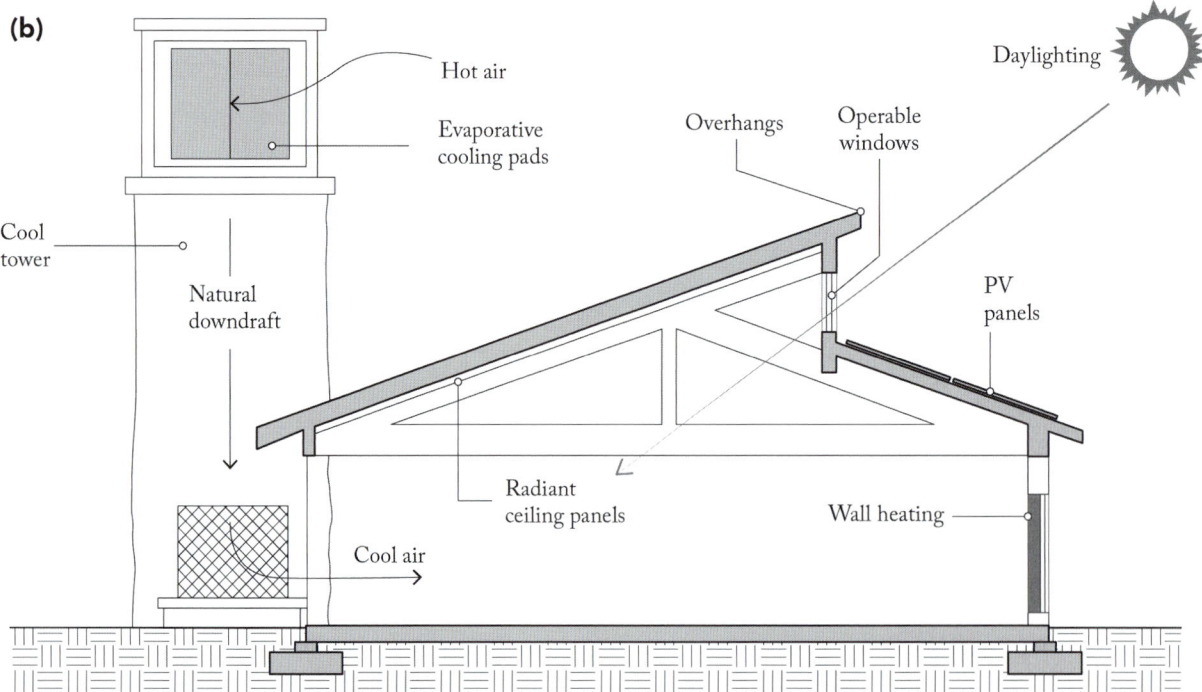

Figure 2.4.11   (a) Zion National Park Visitor Center in Utah, USA. (Source: photo by flickr user Bryan Ungard); (b) Zion National Park Visitor Center in Utah, USA. A one-third horsepower pump is used to circulate water over pads at the top of the cool towers. The cooled air descends to large openings at the base of the tower.
(Source: https://commons.wikimedia.org.)

Calculating Airflow for Cool Towers

Designers must not only understand the general principles behind the operation of cool towers, but must also know how to precisely calculate airflow for their designs. There are several equations that are relevant to the discussion of cooling towers. An expression for the volume of airflow induced by wind is:

$$Q\,wind = KAV$$

where:
Q wind = volume of airflow (m³/h)
K = coefficient of effectiveness (a constant)
A = area of smaller opening (m²)
V = outdoor wind speed (mph).

The coefficient of effectiveness depends on the angle of the wind and the relative size of entry and exit openings. It ranges from about 0.4 for wind hitting an opening at a 45° angle of incidence to 0.8 for wind hitting directly at a 90° angle.

An expression for the airflow induced by the *stack effect* is:

$$Q\,stack = Cd \times A \times [2gh\,(T_i - T_o)/T_i]^{1/2}$$

where,
Q stack = volume of ventilation rate (m³/s)
Cd = 0.65, a discharge coefficient
A = free area of inlet opening (m²), which equals area of outlet opening
g = 9.8 (m/s²), the acceleration due to gravity,
h = vertical distance between inlet and outlet midpoints (m)
T_i = average temperature of indoor air (K), noting that 27°C = 300 K
T_o = average temperature of outdoor air (K).

The following expression for the airflow induced by the column of cold air pressurizing an air supply is based on a formula developed by NREL, with the coefficient from data measured at Zion National Park Visitor Center. This tower is 7.4 m tall, 2.4 m square in cross-section, and has a 3.1 m² opening.

$$Q\,cooltower = 0.49 \times A \times [2gh\,(T_{db} - T_{wb})/T_{db}]^{1/2}$$

where,
Q cooltower = volume of ventilation rate (m³/s)
Cd = 0.49 is an empirical coefficient calculated with data from Zion Visitor Center, UT, which includes humidity, density correction, friction effects, and evaporative pad/effectiveness
A = free area of inlet opening (m²), which equals area of outlet opening
g = 9.8 (m/s²), the acceleration due to gravity
h = vertical distance between inlet and outlet midpoints (m)
T_{db} = dry bulb temperature of outdoor air (K), noting that 27°C = 300 K
T_{wb} = wet bulb temperature of outdoor air (K).

For design standards refer to ASHRAE for air change guidelines [3].

Approximate Method for Sizing of Evaporative Cool Towers

An approximate size for Down Draft Evaporative Cool Towers can be determined through the use of nomograms in *The Green Studio Handbook* by Kwok and Grondzik, pg. 181.

How Location Affects Effectiveness

Evaporation, as a passive cooling method, works best when relative humidity is lower than 70 percent during the hottest periods and the air has a greater capacity to take up water vapor. Thus, cooling towers are best suited to warm and drier climates as well as those areas that experience a larger variation between day and evening temperatures. Various studies present cooling data, but the following case from Arizona seems pertinent to many southwest regions of the USA.

Research was conducted for two days on a passive evaporative air cooling tower attached to a building in Tucson, Arizona, in 1986. The system consisted of a downdraft tower with pump-wetted pads at its top, as well as a solar chimney to enhance the airflow rate through the tower and building (Figure 2.4.12). The results showed that when the outside maximum temperature was 105°F and the wet bulb temperature (measures the lowest temperature that can be reached

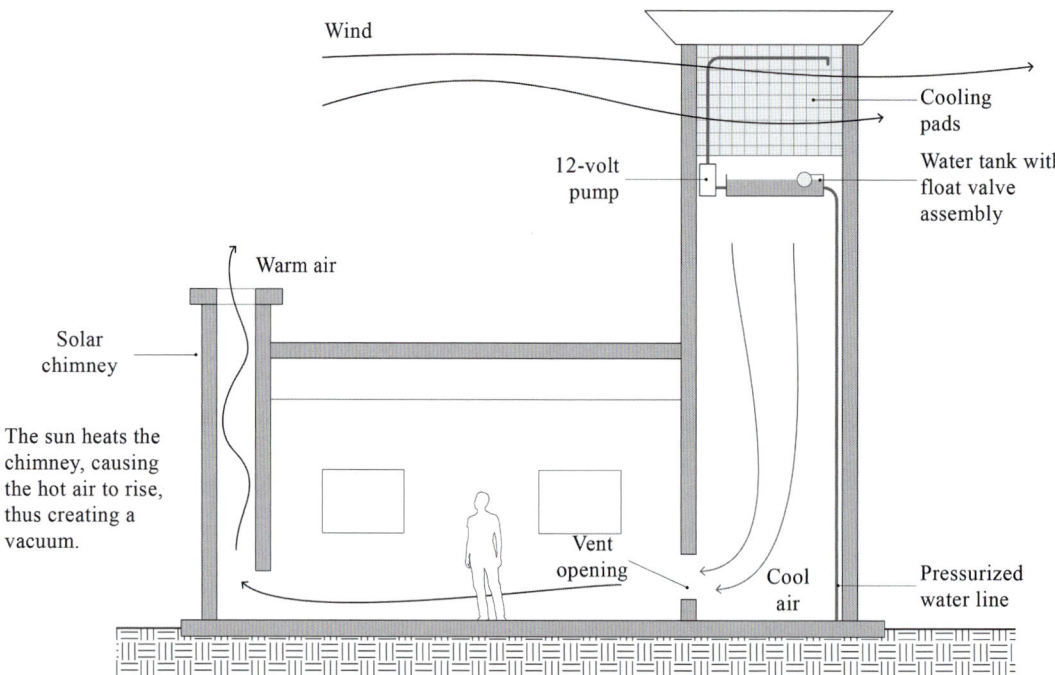

Figure 2.4.12 Evaporative cool tower basics.
(Source: Global Village Institute.)

under current ambient conditions by the evaporation of water) was 71 °F, the tower exit air temperature was 75 °F. The corresponding speed of the exiting air was 150 fpm. The efficiency of the system is clear. Air temperature was reduced by 30 °F, inside temperatures remained a comfortable 71 °F, and additional heat was released with exiting air of 75 °F.

Sustainability Claim by Cool Towers

Cool towers are proven successes in terms of sustainability. They can operate as passive devices without the use of electricity or with a minimum input of electricity to power small circulation pumps to induce evaporation. The following analysis data from the Zion project displays such energy savings. The total cooling energy (both cooling tower pumps and circulation fans) for the visitor center complex during 2001 was 4,940 kWh or 8.4 percent of the total energy consumed.

The cooling energy intensity was 1.28 kBtu/sq.ft-yr, which was 77 percent less than a typical building in the western USA, which uses 5.5 kBtu/sq.ft-yr. In addition to electricity, the two cooling towers did use

111, 200 gallons of water in 2002, which is a minor drawback that can be alleviated by a water-harvesting system. Another example is in Figure 2.4.13.

Atria, Roof Ponds, and Green Roofs as Passive Cooling Systems

As further proof of quality and effectiveness, the Godrej building in India (Figure 2.4.14) has used a cooling tower system combined with green roofs and photovoltaics to environmentally condition this building. It received the USGBC highest award for sustainability outside of the USA, the LEED®-India Platinum.

Atria can serve more than one purpose. Atria are used to bring daylight into interior spaces when the room width exceeds five times the height of the window. Natural light typically can only penetrate interior spaces to an extent of 2.5 times the height of the window. (Atria design for daylighting is discussed in detail in Section 5.1.) As well as facilitating the entry of daylight into a building, atria can also assist in evacuating unwanted hot air to the outside using the "stack effect" or principle that cold,

Figure 2.4.13   Evaporative cool tower at Nitzana Youth Village in Israel. (Photographer, Azri Samin.)

Figure 2.4.14   Sohrabji Godrej Green Business Centre (CII) building in Hyderabad, India.
(Source: image courtesy of CII-Godrej GBC, Hyderabad, India.)

dense air sinks and warmer, less dense air rises. By serving as passive ventilation stacks they reduce the heat loss and heat gain in large buildings. A recent example of such an atrium is the Eastgate building in Harare, Zimbabwe, designed by Mick Pearce in association with Arup Associates (Figure 2.4.15).

Atria also support plant life, thus increasing sustainability efforts, adding to the marketability of the building and the comfort of its occupants (see also Figure 3.3.1).

Summary

Natural ventilation is a kind of open loop, taking into account supply and exhaust, as air cycles into and out of buildings with little, if any, reliance on mechanical systems. Wind towers, cool towers, and atria all take advantage of air stratification, also known as the "stack effect," to move cool air into buildings at lower levels and to vent warm air out of buildings through the manipulation of factors such as wind and airflow, air pressure differences, air suction, temperature differences, and evaporation and humidity. Passive cooling systems are sustainable designs because they reduce the need for active cooling systems while still meeting needs of thermal comfort for building users.

References

[1] Norbert Lechner, *Heating, Cooling and Lighting* (New York: John Wiley & Sons, Inc. 2009).

[2] Battle McCarthy, *Wind Towers* (Chichester: Academy Editions, 1999, p. 23).

[3] ASHRAE, *ASHRAE Handbook of Fundamentals* (New York: ASHRAE, 2009).

[4] A. Kwok and W. Grondzik, *The Green Studio Handbook* (London: Routledge, 2011, p. 181).

Further Reading

M.N. Bahadori, "Passive Cooling in Iranian Architecture," *Scientific American* Vol. 238, No. 2, February 1978.

George Baird, *The Architectural Expression of Environmental Control Systems* (London: Spon Press, 2001).

Baruch Givoni, *Climate Considerations in Building and*

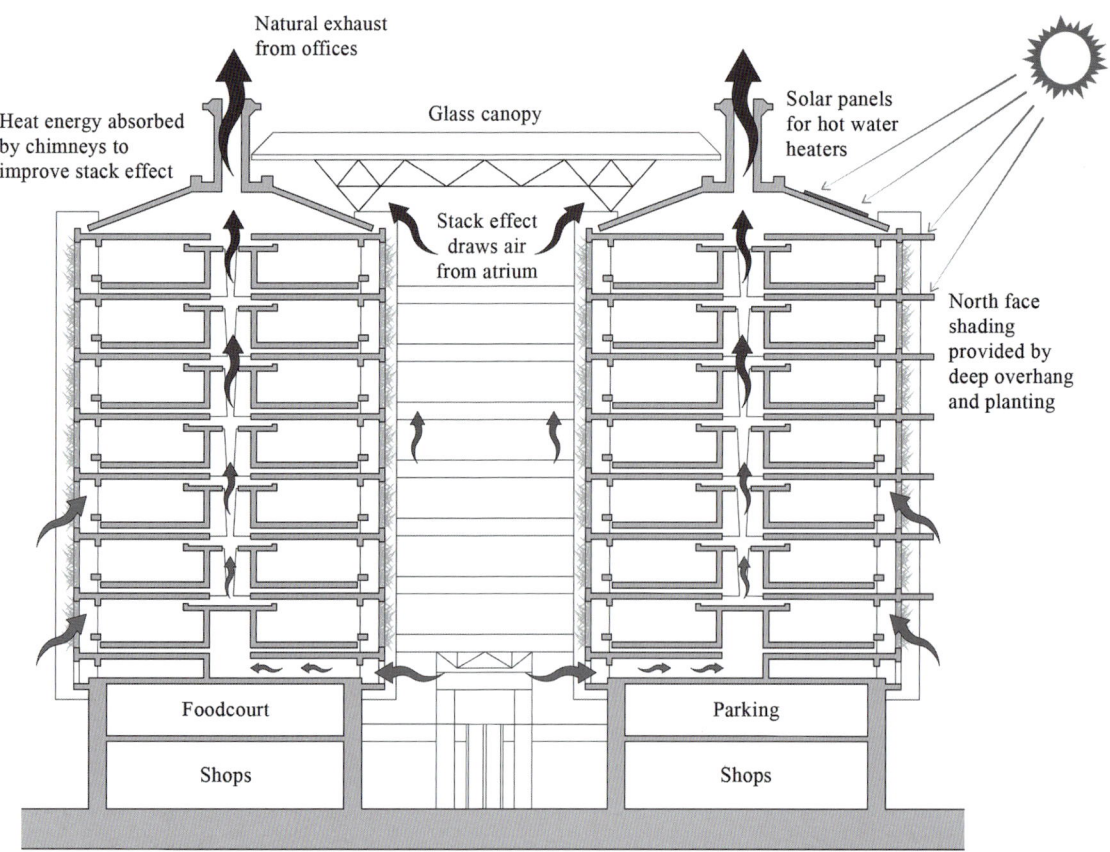

Figure 2.4.15 Atria in the Eastgate building, Harare, Zimbabwe, use building concrete for night-cooling purposes. (Source: US Environmental Health Perspectives.)

Urban Design (New York: Van Nostrand, Reinhold, 1998).

National Renewable Energy Laboratory, *High Performance Building Research* (Golden, CO: NREL, 2005).

Santamouris, M. (ed.) *Solar Thermal Technologies for Buildings: The State of the Art* (London: James & James Ltd., 2003).

P. Torcellini, N. Long, S. Pless, and R. Judkoff, *Evaluation of the Low-Energy Design and Energy Performance of the Zion National Park Visitor Center* (Golden, CO: NREL, 2005).

Andrew Werth, "Cooling Towers," a paper presented in a Sustainable Design class at the University of New Mexico, 2006.

Web Support

www.i4at.org/lib2/aircool.htm

www.flonnet.com/fl2208/stories/20050422000106500.htm

www.sunpipe.co.uk

www.archnet.org

www.nrel.gov/buildings/highperformance/zion.html

www.environmentcity.org.uk/article.asp?ParentID=105&ArticleID=123

http://sustainability.stanford.edu/greendorm/involvement/coursework/mini_reports/3-10%20Cool%20Tower.pdf

www.yazd.com/album/0171.htm

www.wrcc.dri.edu/

www.weatheranalytics.com/get-weather-data

www.nrel.gov/buildings/highperformance/zion.html

www.nrel.gov

www.nps.gov/zion/naturescience/upload/DOE%20Brochure.pdf

Exercises

1 Research and describe your understanding of five natural cooling systems.

2 Sketch essential building features of a retail commercial building in a hot and humid climate such as New Orleans.

3 Describe a balanced stack ventilation (BSV) system and how you would adopt it for a building

in a hot and arid zone, anywhere from California to Arizona.

4 Design a down-draft cool tower, using the nomogram in this chapter, for a single-story 5,000 sq.ft retail building in a hot and arid zone. Clearly indicate the cool tower inlet and outlet opening sizes.

2.5 Ground Source and Other Heating and Cooling

Geothermal power is a renewable energy source found in natural heat beneath the earth's surface. The same basic principles apply to different geothermal technologies. One method is to tap into natural heat reservoirs created by the heat of the earth's core. The other is to take advantage of stable temperatures near the earth's surface to either heat or cool spaces above ground. Geothermal energy can be used directly from sources near the earth's surface, indirectly through pump systems, and for both small- and large-scale operations. Other passive heating and cooling concepts include ground source heat pumps and solar cooling based on principles of radiation and the heating and cooling of water.

A Brief Review of Geothermal Energy

The core of the earth is very hot – hot enough to melt rock. Earth's geothermal energy comes from the formation of the planet (20 percent) and the radioactive decay of minerals (80 percent). Geothermal energy is derived from a continuous conduction of heat from the core to the surface. Scientists claim, theoretically, the Earth's geothermal resources are more than adequate to supply humanity's energy needs. Also, scientists estimate that for every 100 feet we go down from ground level the temperature rises 1 °C. The earth's heat is a source of energy that can be tapped to generate electricity and to control building temperatures above ground. (These active systems are discussed in Chapter 4.) By installing pipes filled with water, the underground temperature can be transferred to fluid and brought to the surface for many uses. Almost everywhere ground temperature within the top 10–12 feet of the earth's surface can be fairly constant at about 50–60°F. This range is generally above winter low temperatures and below summer highs, allowing for the transfer of heat in winter and cooling in summer. These types of energy exchange, either hot or cold, can be useful in maintaining the internal temperature of small buildings. The same geothermal principles can be used to preheat water for hot water purposes. Direct geothermal energy has been used for thousands of years in some countries for cooking and heating. In volcanically active places such as New Zealand and Iceland geothermal energy is a renewable resource for electric power production and hot water use. The electricity generated can be utilized for many purposes, including air-conditioning, thereby reducing reliance on fossil fuels.

Figure 2.5.1 identifies the potential for *geothermal energy in the USA*. Large-scale geothermal energy sources are mainly located in the western part of the country. These energy sources can be used to develop large power plants to produce electric energy without use of any non-renewable energy sources. The power generated by the system can be utilized to operate all pumps, generators, and other systems needed for plant operation, making the geothermal systems truly renewable energy sources. Geothermal projects are planned in Alaska, Nevada, Idaho, and Arizona. Geothermal plants can be expensive when compared with traditional fossil fuel power plants; however, greenhouse gas (GHG) emissions from geothermal plants are minimal.

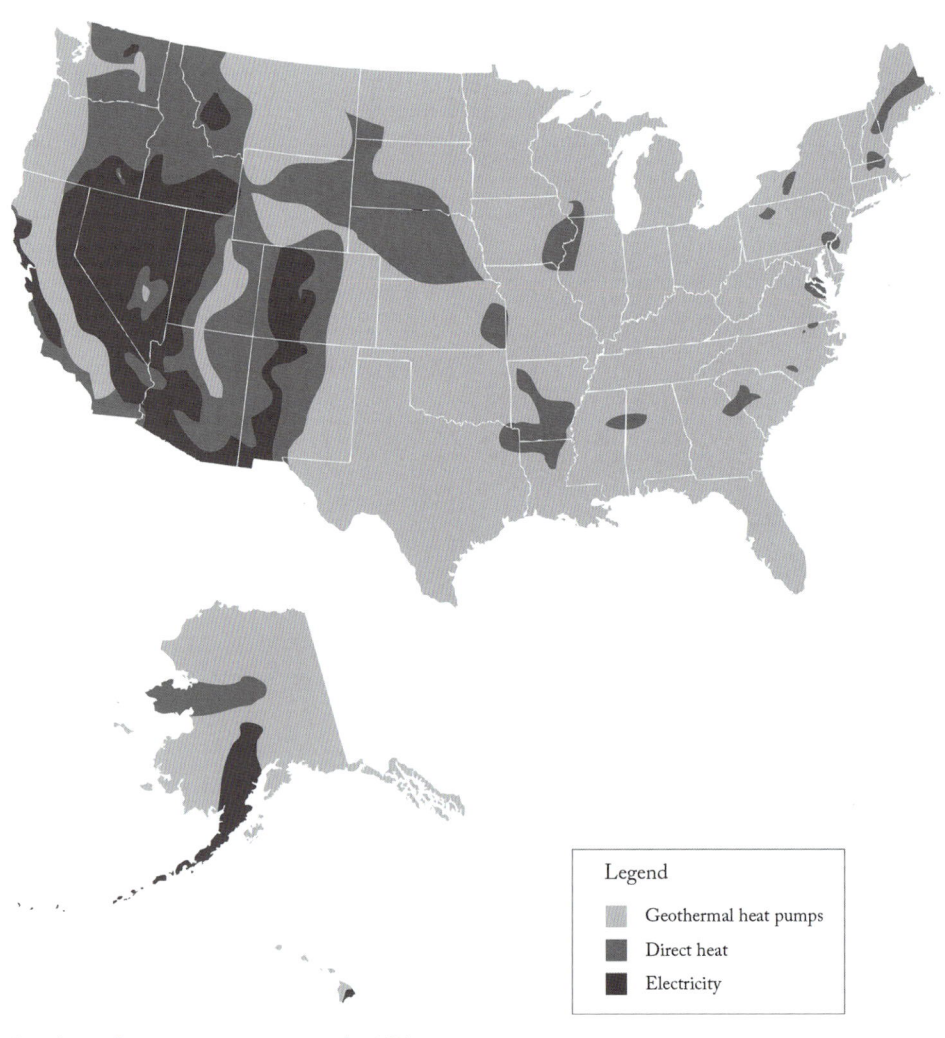

Legend
- Geothermal heat pumps
- Direct heat
- Electricity

Figure 2.5.1 Geothermal energy source sites in the USA. (Source: US Department of Energy.)

Large-scale Electricity Production

Figure 2.5.2 explains how geothermal energy works for large-scale power production. Typically, cold water is pumped to the natural hot reservoir or hot rocks. This heated water can be pumped back and then converted to steam by passing through heat exchangers. The purified steam is then sent through turbines to produce electricity. The condensed steam can be reused or sent back to the geothermal reservoir for further heating.

Passive Ground Source Heating and Cooling

Closed-loop ground-coupled heat pumps (GCHP) utilize ground temperatures to heat or cool a building. Even though this system's name implies it is used for heating, it is also reversible and can be used for cooling (Figure 2.5.3). This type of heat pump consists of a vapor compression cycle linked to a heat exchanger buried in the ground. Most of these systems are known as indirect systems, with or without antifreeze solution circulating through sealed underground loops. The energy is transferred to or from the heat pump refrigerant circuit through a separate heat exchanger.

When heat is required in a residence, the system collects the heat from the ground and passes it on to the heat exchanger for proper control before pumping it into the residence. Piping for this type of system consists of vertical or horizontal pipe loops, typically located 5–6 feet below ground, depending on the ground temperature and the availability of land. When the land area is small it makes sense to use vertical pipes (Figure 2.5.3b).

Since earth temperatures in the ground are often more uniform than the air temperatures above ground year-round, GCHP can operate with higher efficiency when compared to conventional electric systems. They can save 50–70 percent of heating energy, depending on the climatic conditions, when compared to electric resistance heating. When cooling is required the system will experience similar efficiencies. Careful installation of the ground coil is necessary to ensure that continuous and reliable heat transfer is maintained between the earth and the coil. A rule of thumb while designing GCHP is that the soil temperature 10–12 feet below the surface is equal to the average annual temperature.

Maintenance required for this system is less than for a typical electric system since most of the parts are not exposed to deterioration by the weather. With

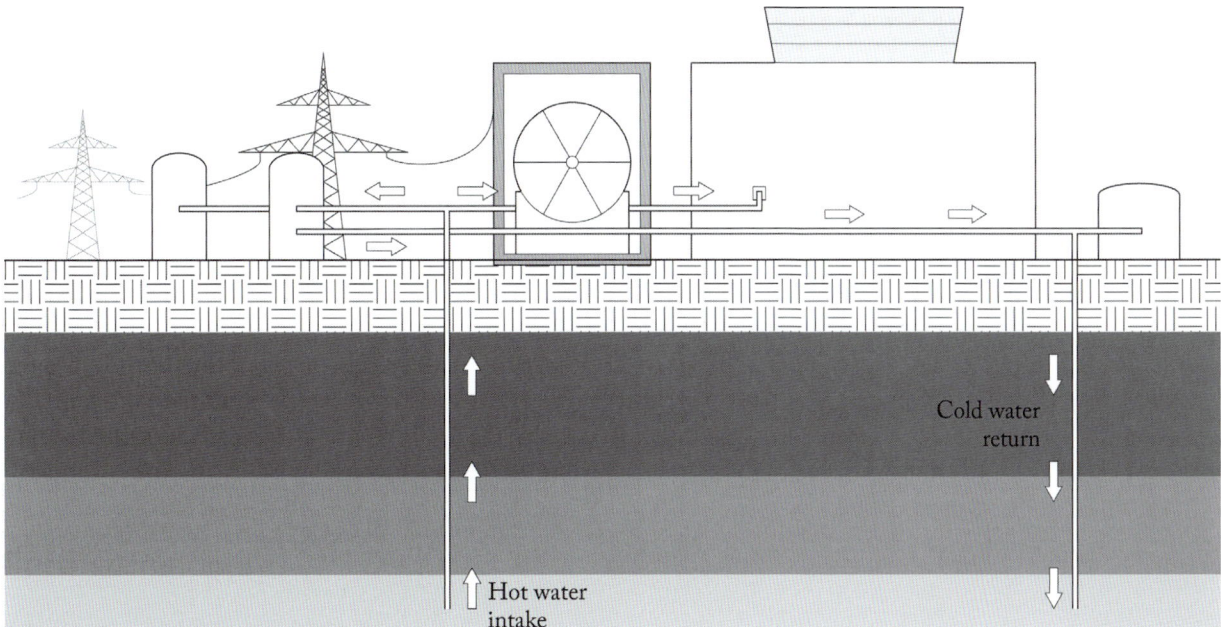

Figure 2.5.2 Geothermal for large-scale power production. (Source: Geothermal Education Office, Tiburon, CA.)

good periodic maintenance these systems can last 20–25 years. Since GCHP reduces the use of fossil fuels it also contributes to the reduction of GHG emissions.

Figure 2.5.3 illustrates how two types of closed-loop heat pumps, horizontal and vertical, can be configured, depending on the land availability. Also,

Closed loop systems horizontal

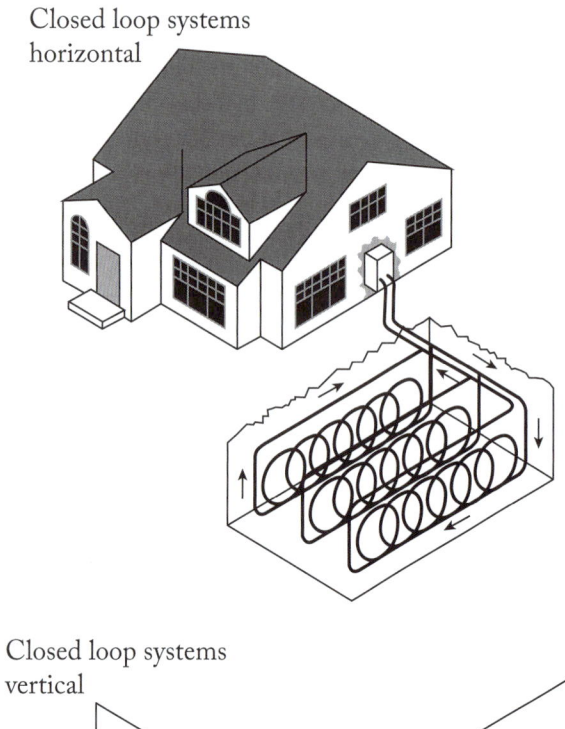

Closed loop systems vertical

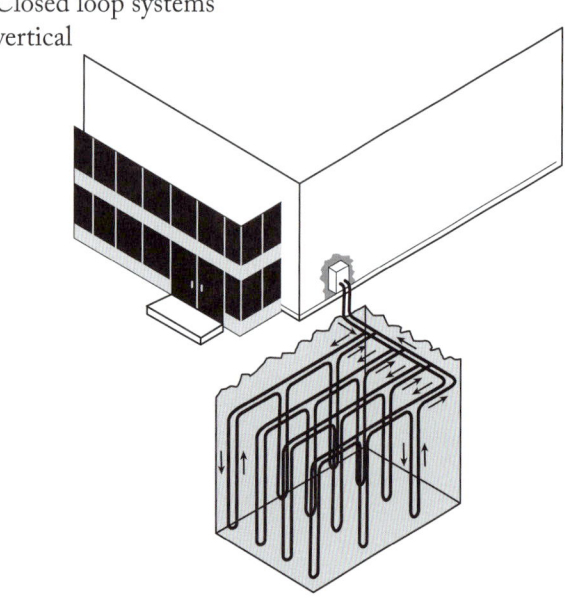

Figure 2.5.3 Horizontal and vertical loop systems for GCHP. (a) The slinky loops allow longer length tubes, good for shallow depths and cost-effective systems; (b) Useful when the land is expensive and the bore depth varies 100–400 feet. (Source: US Department of Energy.)

if a building is close to a water body such as a lake, a slinky loop system (Figure 2.5.3a) can be quite effective and inexpensive.

Earth Cooling

1 *The earth sheltered building* (loses heat directly to the earth) is the oldest method of building to take advantage of the properties of insulation, helping to provide ambient and constant temperatures in the building. The method involves piling earth around the exterior walls of the building or building into the earth (Figure 2.5.4) so that the earth provides protection from heat and wind, thus saving energy costs. The disadvantage for such buildings is that the exits and location of windows become restrictive and need careful design attention. Buildings set into hills and underground buildings demand care in technical design to avoid water seepage in and around the site.

2 *Earth tubes* (air enters the building by way of earth tubes) are a passive heating and cooling technique used for thousands of years. The method takes advantage of constant ground temperatures of 50–60°F to pre-heat incoming air in the winter and pre-cool incoming air in the summer through tubes buried under the earth, before bringing the air into the building. It works well in climates that have extreme weather conditions. For actual design specifications, use the software program *Energy-Plus* from the US Department of Energy (DOE).

Solar Heating and Cooling Concepts (Skytherm)

Harold Hay, a pioneer in the use of solar energy, designed a house in Atascadero, CA, to test cooling concepts. Hay's "Skytherm" project (the patented name for the system) achieves constant comfort conditions through radiant cooling and heating.

The roof pond places the thermal mass in the roof structure. It depends on a changeable, exterior insulation scheme to make it effective for both heating and cooling. In winter in the heating mode, the insulation is moved to allow the sun's rays to heat water in plastic bags or water mass, about six inches in

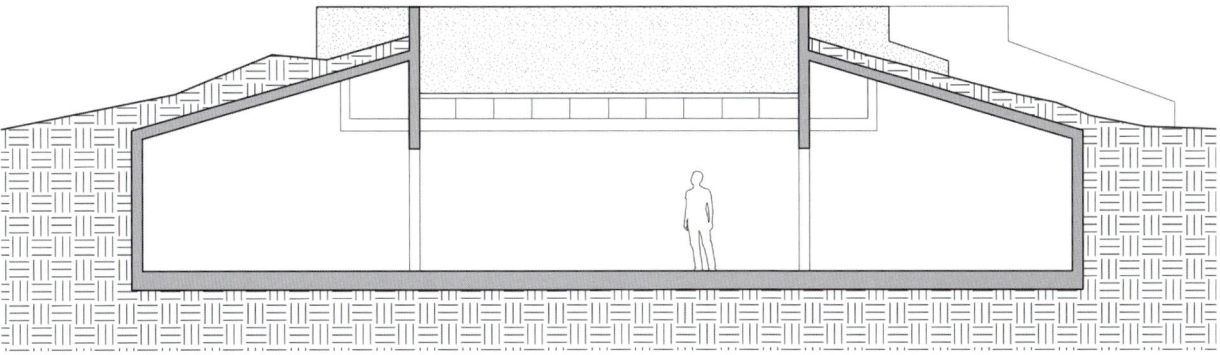

Figure 2.5.4 Earth sheltered building.
(Source: Odyman at en.wikipedia.)

depth, above the metal ceiling, which in turn radiates heat into the room below. In the night the insulation is deployed to retain the heat.

In summer in the cooling mode, the insulation is deployed by day. The thermal mass, such as water in containers or otherwise, must remain in direct thermal contact with the interior of the building, usually through the use of a structural steel deck. The concept consists of a large mass of water contained in a plastic bladder and liner, lying on a metal ceiling deck, which should be corrugated to increase the thermal coupling with the house below. A movable insulation panel is installed above the water level. This stores and dissipates heat energy to maintain constant comfort conditions inside the building.

On days with clear skies and low humidity the night sky gets cold, well below freezing. The "sky cooling" effect is achieved by exposing a warm mass to the night sky and preventing the daytime sunshine from reheating it by using a movable insulating panel. The primary cooling mode for a roof pond system is radiation, which can cool the water significantly below wet bulb temperature. The Skytherm (Figure 2.5.5) concept is best suited for areas of low humidity and clear nights because of its reliance on radiative cooling.

Roof ponds

For residential-scale projects, containers of water on the roof can also be used to collect and store cool

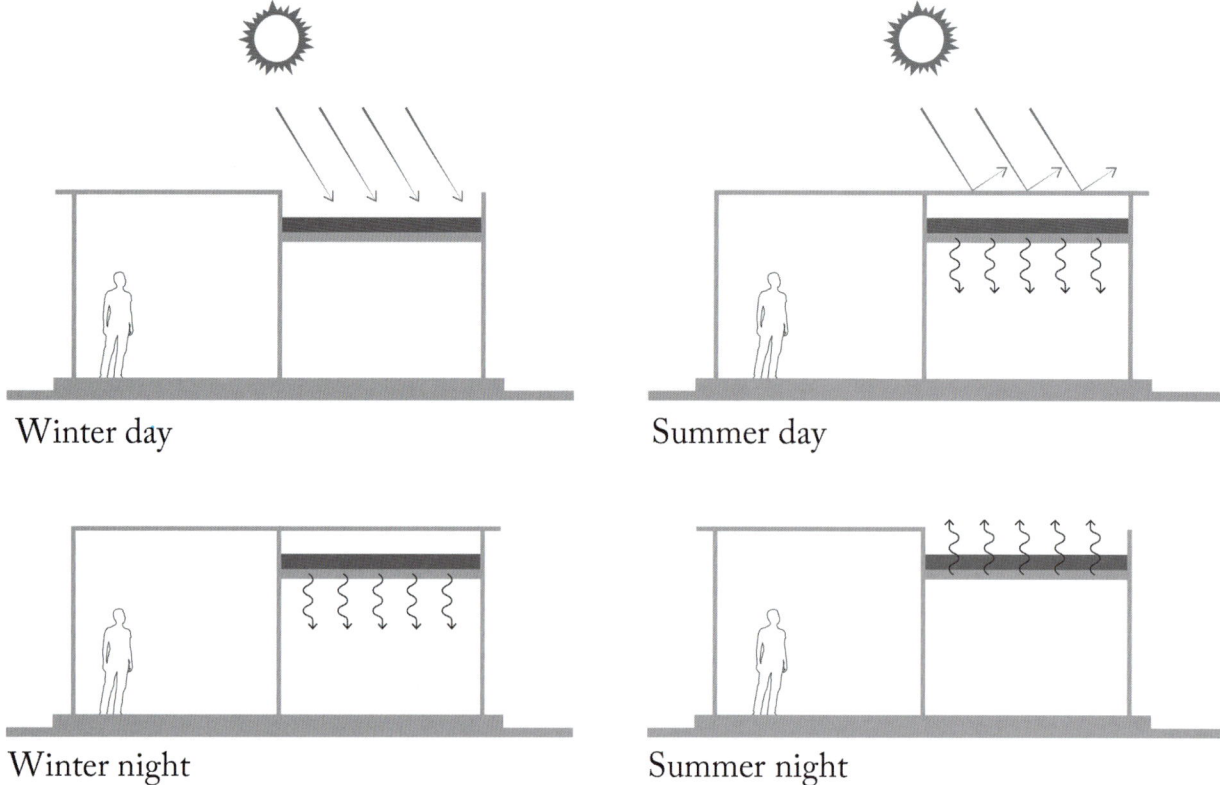

Figure 2.5.5   Roof pond or Harold Hay's SKYTHERM – solar heating/cooling concepts. (Source: David Lord, Cal Poly.)

energy from the night sky. The water can be kept in shallow troughs confined by concrete edge walls (for strength). During the day, these troughs filled with water can be covered with movable insulation. Heat from the room below is usually absorbed by the water in the trough and radiated back to the night sky. For winter heating, when the insulation is removed, the solar radiation absorbed by the water can be radiated into the room below. In particular, roof pond collectors are well suited for lower latitudes – those between 35°S and 35°N. At these latitudes the sun is at higher altitudes in winter, thus providing sun energy for an extended period of time. In climates with substantial cooling requirements, the roof pond area approaches the floor area of the building, requiring sophisticated roof design. For information regarding heating and cooling designs, refer to the Heat Pump Centre's *Annual Review of Energy* [1], and also to Givoni's *Climate Consideration in Buildings and Urban Design* [2]. Steve Baer of Zomeworks in Albuquerque, New Mexico and Professor Jeff Cook of Arizona State

University (ASU) have pioneered similar cooling concepts. Their project details can be seen in ASU Environmental Resources and University of Arizona Environmental Laboratories publications.

Summary

The earth's natural stores of heat can be used by designers to generate electricity and to heat homes, reducing reliance on the use of fossil fuels. The constant temperature at certain underground levels can also be used for both heating and cooling of buildings in different seasons. Ground coupled heat pumps are efficient systems that collect the heat from the ground and pass it on to a heat exchanger for proper control before pumping it into a residence. These systems can also be reversed to remove heat from a building. Hay's "Skytherm" is a solar cooling and heating concept using a roof pond system based on principles of radiation and insulation to maintain comfortable indoor temperatures.

References

[1] Heat Pump Centre, *Annual Review of Energy* (Netherlands: International Energy Agency, 1978, pp. 176–177).

[2] Baruch Givoni, *Climate Consideration in Buildings and Urban Design* (New York: John Wiley & Sons, 1998).

Further Reading

Electric Power Research Institute, *Technology Guide: A Guide to Renewable Energy Technology* (Palo Alto, CA: Electric Power Research Institute, 2007).

Web Support

iga.igg.cnr.it/geo/geoenergy.php

www1.eere.energy.gov/geothermal/powerplants.html

http://geo energy.org/Basics.aspx

http://renewableenergyworld.com

http://greenlaurier.ca/geothermal drilling

http://newsroom 1.net/newsroom/wpcontent

Exercises

1 Conduct a detailed research to select an ideal site and building conditions that encourage use of horizontal loop pipes for geothermal energy system design.

2 Is geothermal a viable option for future energy supply? Support your argument with current research data.

2.6 Sustainable Technologies: Works in Progress

Designers are now seeking ways to make better use of renewable resources and principles of passive energy use through technology. These emerging systems help close the gap between outdated designs and those that are sustainably aware. This section surveys some of the sustainable technologies that are emerging today in response to our ever-increasing demand for power and electricity. These technologies have tremendous potential for energy production but are underused today due to cost considerations. Direct solar, solar thermal, photovoltaics (solar cells), wind energy, biomass, and biogas all make use of renewable sources of energy. In addition, many small sources of energy such as fuel cells, light emitting diodes (LED), micro-turbines, and small-scale hydroelectric systems (hydros) provide a range of energy solutions, reduce reliance on fossil fuels, and offer the opportunity to locate power sources near the user, thus increasing energy efficiency.

Direct Solar: Flat-plate Collectors

The most common kind of solar collector used for producing domestic hot water is the flat-plate collector, developed in the 1950s (Figure 2.6.1). It consists of (1) a dark flat-plate absorber of solar energy made up of aluminum, steel, or copper, to which a matte black or selective coating is applied; (2) a transparent cover that allows solar energy to pass through but reduces heat losses, acting like a greenhouse; (3) a heat-transport fluid (air, antifreeze, or water) to remove heat from the absorber; and (4) a heat-insulating

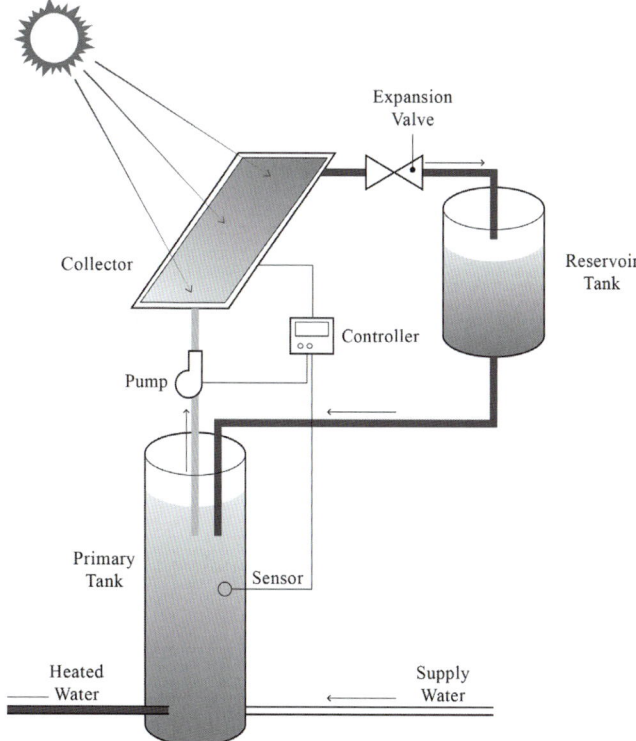

Figure 2.6.1 Flat-plate collector for domestic hot water. (Source: https://en.wikipedia.org.)

Approximate Sizing of a Domestic Solar Hot-Water System				
Number of People per Household	Tank Capacity (gallons)	Collector Size (ft²) Region 1	Collector Size (ft²) Region 2	Collector Size (ft²) Region 3
2	60	20	24	28
3	80	28	36	42
4	100	36	48	56
5	120	44	60	70
6	140	52	72	84

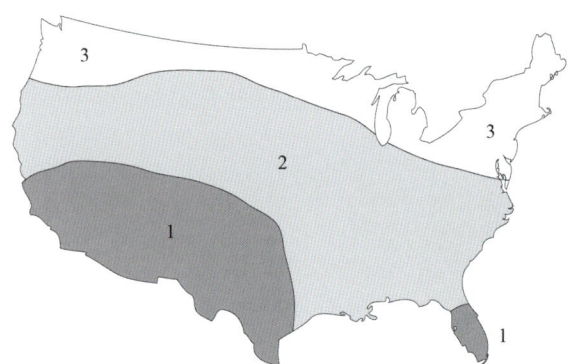

Figure 2.6.2 Approximate sizing of a solar domestic hot water system. (Source: US Department of Energy, National Renewable Energy Laboratory.)

backing. It is extremely important that an expansion valve is located at the top of the collector to release the excessive pressure build-up due to uncontrolled temperature rise. In water heat panels, fluid is usually circulated through tubing to transfer heat from the absorber to an insulated water tank. This may be achieved directly or through a heat exchanger.

The optimum collector tilt is the latitude of the location plus or minus 15°, and the orientation should be true south. For the approximate collector sizing use the table in Figure 2.6.2. For location, roof loading considerations, and installation requirements, refer to the local building codes.

When very hot water is required, concentrating collectors are employed. However, they can be complicated in structure since they should track the sun. A universally used solution, instead of concentrating collectors, is the *vacuum tube*, 2–4 inches in diameter. These tubes need not track the sun yet have decent efficiency, and it is easy to mass produce them. When water is circulated in the tube, it can be in any position. There are several manufacturers who can design and install this system.

Solar Thermal to Generate Electricity and Heat

Larger systems called solar thermal plants have made a resurgence. These systems have long been used to generate electricity by producing very high temperature hot water and steam to power generators. In this system, molten salt is heated to high temperatures

using sunlight to produce steam to run a turbine to generate electricity.

In another system, a photovoltaic array is used to produce high-temperature steam to produce 18 MW of direct current power, which can then be converted to AC current.

In 2005, *Stirling Energy Systems* signed contracts with two California utilities to produce one 300 MW and two 500 MW plants using 12,000 and 20,000 curved dish mirrors, respectively, as concentrators to harness the sun's energy. The company intends to use high-performance Stirling Engine Technology, which shuttles a working fluid such as hydrogen gas between two chambers to run an electric generator [1].

All solar power plants improve air quality by avoiding millions of metric tons of carbon dioxide (CO_2) emissions over the plant's life, along with reduced air pollutants such as nitrogen oxides (NO_X) and sulfur oxides (SO_X) when compared to gas-fired power plants. Electricity produced by today's solar-thermal technology costs around 5–13 cents per kwh, which is about three times the current cost of coal-powered operations. The hope is that solar-thermal plants will become competitive with fossil fuel power plants as the technology matures in the near future.

Photovoltaics

Scientists estimate that the sun's energy can produce about 5000 times the energy the world needs in a year. Yet solar energy produced now is only a tiny fraction of the overall energy production worldwide, about 0.15 percent. Recent design improvements and encouragement from many governments have boosted production and efficiency of photovoltaics (PV) to become more cost competitive. There are two main kinds of PV or solar cells. The first, *monocrystalline solar cells*, are created from melted purified silicon fused into a highly structured mold. The silicon atoms are arranged in a continuous lattice structure, the same arrangement as seen in a diamond, with silicon instead of carbon. Wafers are then cut from the silicon, chemically treated, and printed with electrical contacts to make a functional solar cell.

The uniform structure of the silicon in a monocrystalline solar cell creates a high-efficiency solar cell, reaching up to 30 percent in the laboratory. This cell architecture is favored most in the production of high-efficiency commercial solar products. Monocrystalline PV cells are more complicated to manufacture, and thus expensive.

The second type, the *polycrystalline solar cell*, is created by casting molten silicon into a simple mold and allowing the silicon to gradually cool and solidify. The result is a solid block of crystalline silicon composed of multiple grains of silicon crystals. The PV cells are created by cutting the rectangular polycrystalline block into wafers of the appropriate thickness, treating the cell surfaces, and printing electrical contacts onto the surface. Polycrystalline cells are less efficient (about 15 percent) and less expensive than monocrystalline cells.

The *thick-film silicon* solar cell, a variation on multicrystalline technology, has a fine-grained sparkling appearance, where the silicon is deposited in a continuous process onto a base material. It is normally encapsulated in a transparent insulating polymer with a tempered glass cover and bonded to a metal-framed module.

There is an increase in the commercialization of PV cells that use thin layers of various semiconductor materials to create functional solar cells. These cells are commonly referred to as *thin-film photovoltaics*. In general, thin-film PV modules are less efficient than most crystalline silicon modules, but the manufacturing techniques employed allow for lower fabrication costs. Three current thin-film technologies are:

1 *Amorphous silicon.* A very thin layer of silicon and other elements is deposited in gaseous form onto a substrate, typically glass or a thin metal, and then etched into individual cells.
2 *Copper indium gallium diselenide (CIGS).* CIGS modules are an emerging technology. They use several semiconducting layers deposited onto a substrate to create a low-cost PV module.
3 *Cadmium telluride (CdTe).* Thin layers of cadmium sulfide and zinc telluride sandwich a layer of cadmium telluride that absorbs light.

With further research these efficiencies and costs can be improved. Other PV considerations include sizing of PV arrays, integration with the roof, worldwide use of PV, and larger solar-thermal technologies.

Off-grid or On-grid Systems

Grid-tied homes are connected to power lines operated by the utility company, while off-grid homes rely solely on a renewable energy system and batteries.

Most homeowners go with the standard, grid-tied solar energy system to receive reliable power in their homes at all times. Batteries used in off-grid systems can only store so much energy, making power less reliable during temperature extremes and periods with extended cloud cover.

Being on-grid includes zero maintenance, low monthly payments to maintain the connection, and smaller up-front costs. Connecting the system to the grid is a basic installation requirement. Grid-tied homes can also take advantage of net metering, or generating credits when energy production exceeds use (Figure 2.6.3).

Typically, owners who select to be off the grid include those who live in remote areas located far away from power lines and those who would like to have a sense of independence and self-sufficiency. It can be a source of pride to lose reliance on conventional electricity generated by burning coal and natural gas.

Off-grid system owners must keep in mind that battery life is shorter than the life of most solar panels. Battery replacement and maintenance is a big consideration, especially since they contain toxic elements. Of course, homes connected to the grid

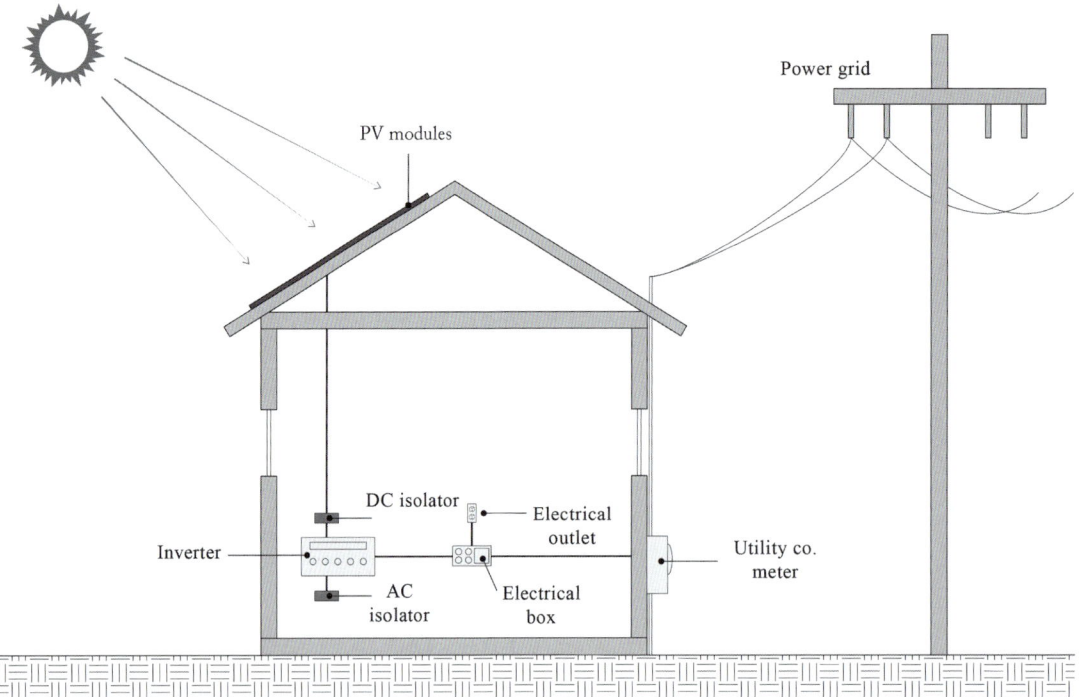

Figure 2.6.3 A grid-connected system.
(Source: Kuppaswamy Iyengar.)

can use back-up batteries as well. These are the most expensive systems to install, but they give access to the best of both worlds.

Sizing PV Systems

Photovoltaics can be sized to match the building's electric load. All loads such as lighting, some heating, and yard lighting can be hooked up to solar systems. Most utility companies in the USA offer rebates to install PV systems and also buy back electric energy from customers who produce enough of their own power to be off the grid during the day. A reverse meter that measures the electric energy produced by the customer is usually installed at the customer's site.

The average December solar radiation in sun hours for a surface with a tilt is equal to altitude plus 15° (see Figure 2.6.4 for typical sun hours). Because December has the least sunshine, it is usually used for sizing PV systems.

Following is a simple example of how to size a PV array. The electrical load can be ascertained from the residence's utility bills for an existing building or

from an energy audit (detailed electric load and use calculations).

An Example of Residential PV Design

A residence in a remote location near Albuquerque, New Mexico cannot connect to the utility grid. An energy use assessment has determined that the home requires approximately 3,200 watt-hours (WH) per day. The following calculations illustrate how to determine the required south-facing single crystal or standing seam PV array size. Assumptions are indicated.

- Electric load (typical for a 1,800 sq.ft residence) = 3,200 WH/day
- Adjusted load with a factor of safety of 50 percent 3200 × 1.5 = 4800 WH/day
- Sun-hours for Albuquerque from the map = 5 hours
- Peak Watts (Wp) = 4800/5 = 960 Wp
- Area of PV array, using *single crystal PV* (12 W/sq.ft) 960/12 = 80 sq.ft

    Or *standing seam PV* area (less efficient) = 960/5 W/sq.ft = 192 sq.ft

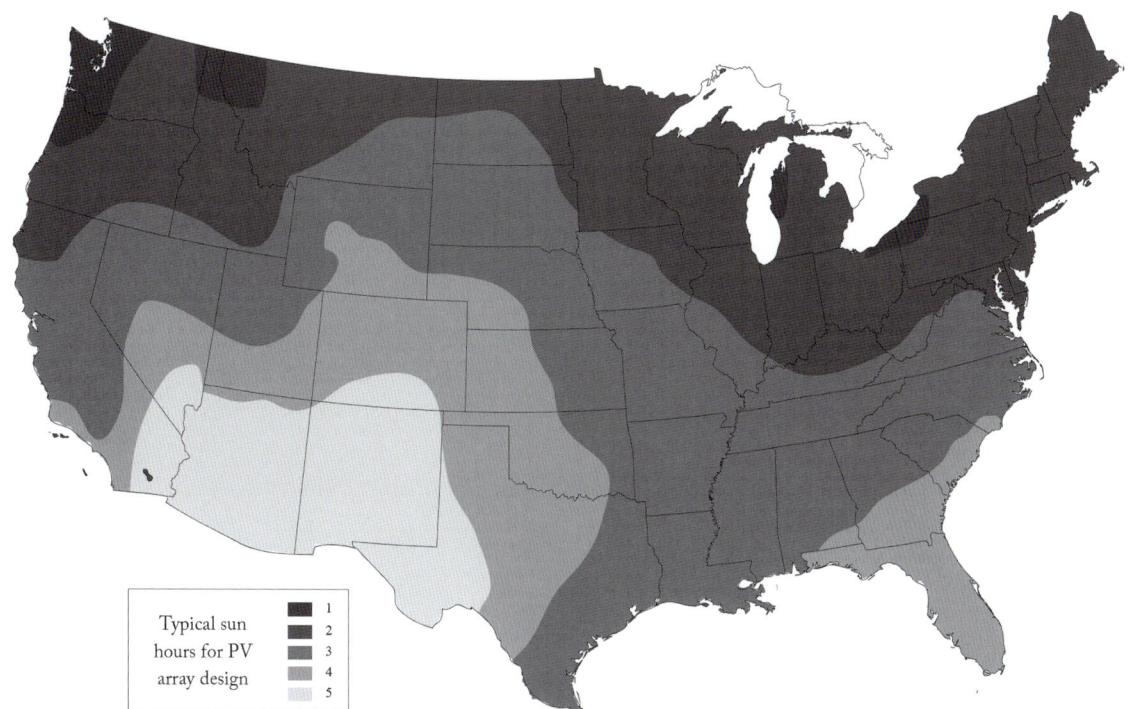

Figure 2.6.4 Typical sun hours for PV array design (December). (Source: www.nrel.gov/gis/solar.html.)

PV arrays may be integrated with the roof in several different ways. They may be mounted on racks as an attachment to the roof, integrally built into the structure, and/or fused into the roofing tiles, shading devices, or glazing. In general, fixed PV systems face south and are placed at an angle equal to the latitude of the place, plus or minus 15°. Many large arrays are almost flat on large flat roofs for summer collection and reduction of demand charges.

There is a push for PV systems in California (see Figure 2.6.5) which has joined solar leaders Japan and Germany to take advantage of this technology. The "Million Solar Roof" commitment by the state of California is intended to install 3,000 MW of generating capacity by 2018. With this type of commitment the USA alone can reach accumulations of 10,000 MW in solar PV power in 20 years.

Solar cells can be installed in many places, making them an easy product to exploit for energy advantage in many parts of the world. Per capita, the developing nation of Kenya has become a leader in the use of solar cells. It is estimated that over 30,000 small solar panels are sold in this country annually. These panels, made from amorphous silicon and ranging in size from 12 to 30 watts, are used for lighting a few lamps, operating a TV, or charging a car battery. Similar stories come from small villages in India. Nearly 1.2 billion people, one-fifth of the world's population, avail themselves of these systems since they do not have access to grid electricity. Manufacturers are improving performance (efficiency) and installation practices, which will allow future PV panels to be smaller.

Figure 2.6.5 Example of a residential solar installation. (Source: photo by Gray Watson; this file is licensed under the Creative Commons Source Share Alike 2.0 Generic license.)

Wind Power

Human beings have been harnessing the wind's energy for hundreds of years. From traditional Holland to farms in the USA, windmills have been used for pumping water or grinding grain. At present, a *wind turbine* can use the wind's energy to generate electricity.

Wind turbines, like windmills, are mounted on a tower to capture the most energy. At 100 feet or more above ground, they can take advantage of faster and less turbulent wind. Turbines catch the wind's energy with their propeller-like blades. Usually, two or three blades are mounted on a shaft to form a *rotor* (Figure 2.6.6).

A blade acts much like an airplane wing. When wind blows, a pocket of low-pressure air forms on the downwind side of the blade. The low-pressure air pocket then pulls the blade toward it, causing the rotor to turn. This is called *lift*. The force of the lift is actually much stronger than the wind's force against the front side of the blade, which is called *drag*. The combination of lift and drag causes the rotor to spin like a propeller, and the turning shaft spins a generator to make electricity.

For utility-scale (megawatt-sized) sources of wind energy, a large number of wind turbines are usually built close together to form a *wind plant*. Several electricity power producers use wind plants to supply power to their customers. Stand-alone wind turbines are typically used for water pumping, communications, and to lower electrical bills for farmers and ranchers in windy areas.

Small wind systems also have potential as distributed energy resources. Distributed energy resources refer to a variety of small, modular power-generating technologies that can be combined to improve the operation of the electricity delivery system.

European nations have reached over 50,000 MW of capacity from wind power. Germany alone has 31,000 MW while Spain has 21,000 MW.

Figure 2.6.6 These wind turbines near Lamar, Colorado, are part of the 162 MW Colorado Green Wind Farm. Each turbine produces 1.5 MW of electricity.
(Source: US Department of Energy, National Renewable Energy Laboratory.)

China (76,000 MW), India (19,000 MW), Great Britain (8,000 MW), Italy (8,100 MW), Portugal (4,500 MW), and the rest of the world (40,000 MW) also use significant amounts of wind power. The USA generated over 60,000 MW in 2012 (Figure 2.6.7), which is about 2.0 percent of the nation's electricity use.

The potential for wind power is enormous in the USA, especially in the Great Plains states (Figure 2.6.7). It is estimated that if all potential US wind power were harnessed, this would produce three times the energy produced by all sources in 2006. As shown in Figure 2.6.8, wind turbines ranging from 4 to 6 MW can produce electricity cost-effectively, between 4 to 7 cents/kwh. One of the main objections to wind power is that it affects the landscape view (Figure 2.6.9). Society must weigh the social cost of expanding fossil fuel power plants against appearance and other effects on the landscape.

Although wind power produced worldwide is a little more than 1 percent, it is also competing nicely with other renewable energy systems. Worldwide wind capacity reached 254 GW in 2012.

Combined Wind and Solar Systems

One of the latest developments in renewable technology is to combine wind and solar systems (Figures 2.6.10 and 2.6.11) to offset the problem of the lack of sunlight during nighttime hours. Wind energy produces electricity day and night, augmented by solar photovoltaics during the day. These systems are small and can be easily installed in suburban areas on a residential scale. These combined hybrid

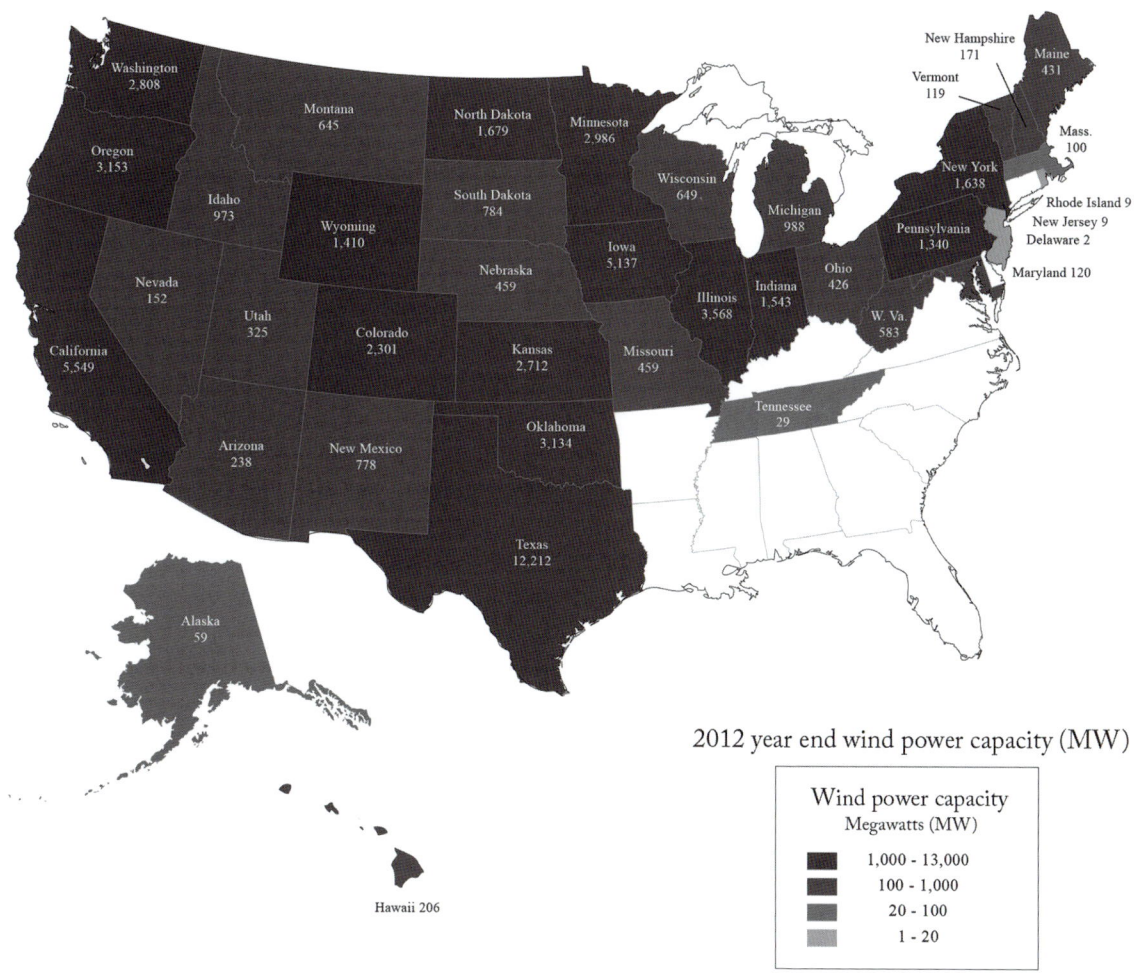

Figure 2.6.7 2012 Wind power capacity (MW) in the USA.
(Source: Courtesy of the US National Renewable Energy Laboratory, Golden, CO.)

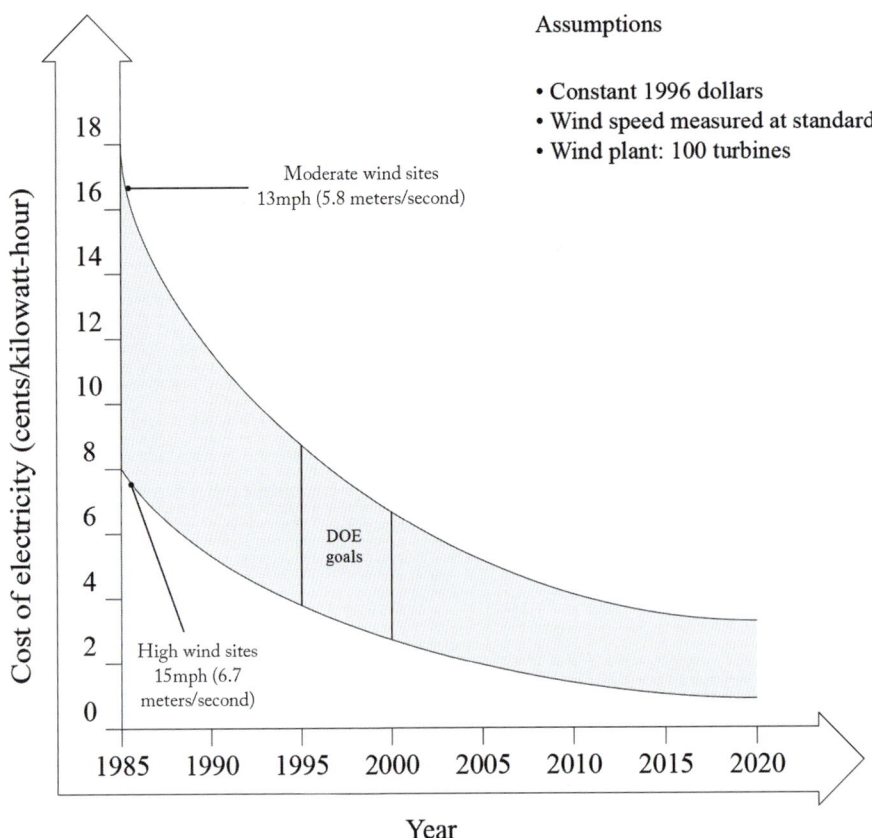

Figure 2.6.8   Cost of wind energy.
(Source: US Department of Energy, National Renewable Energy Laboratory.)

Figure 2.6.9   Wind power landscape. A new generation of wind turbines will make wind generation competitive with power from existing natural gas or coal plants.
(Source: photo by Brian Robert Marshall; this file is licensed under the Creative Commons Source Share Alike 2.0 Generic license.)

systems are stand-alone units that operate off-grid. For the times when neither the wind nor the solar system is producing, most hybrid systems provide power through batteries. This set-up could be ideal for various remote applications including military, government, disaster relief, and telecommunications.

Biomass: Waste to Energy

In the USA several biomass plants exist not only to generate power but to make use of, and thereby reduce, waste.

It is estimated that 500 facilities, mostly industries, are using forest products and municipal solid waste to produce about 10 GW of electricity. For their own use, many pulp and paper industries install biomass power plants with an average size of 20 MW. The cost of electricity using this process is around 8–13 cents per kwh, and the contribution of biomass energy is about 1 percent of the total electricity produced in

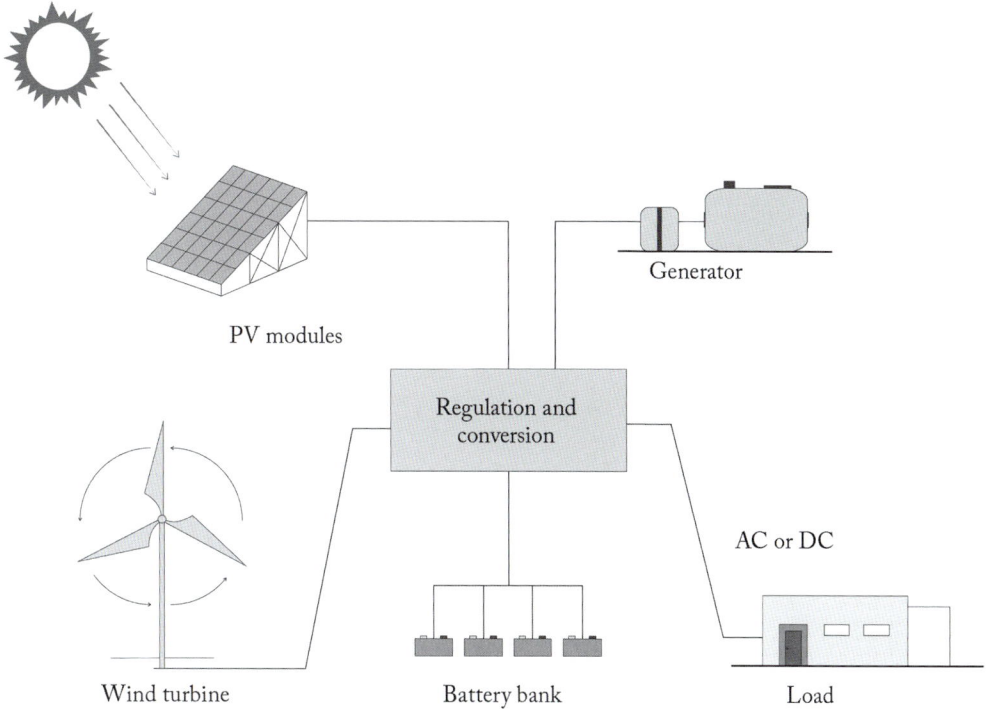

Figure 2.6.10 Hybrid solar and wind system combines multiple sources. (Source: US Department of Energy.)

Figure 2.6.11 Combined solar and wind system by Reiner Lemoine Institut and Solarpraxis AG, Germany.
(Source: photo by Armin Kübelbeck; this file is licensed under the Creative Commons Source-Share Alike 3.0 Unported license.)

the USA. These systems have to be carefully designed to minimize or eliminate CO_2 production to be truly sustainable. Of the estimated total resource of 590 million wet tons, only 20 million wet tons (equivalent to 14 million dry tons, or enough to supply about 3 GW of capacity) is currently available for use. In the USA energy from biomass is not anticipated to increase substantially by 2020.

Generally, gasification-based biomass, direct-fired biomass, and biomass co-firing are the main types of plants used to produce electricity. Figure 2.6.12 illustrates one of the three electricity-producing concepts using biomass. These different types exist based on the way the biomass is utilized to produce steam to turn the turbine.

Landfill Gas and Biogas (Renewable Natural Gas)

Landfills have produced abundant quantities of methane gas, which has been used as an energy source to produce electricity (Figure 2.6.13). Landfills decompose organic waste to produce biogas, which

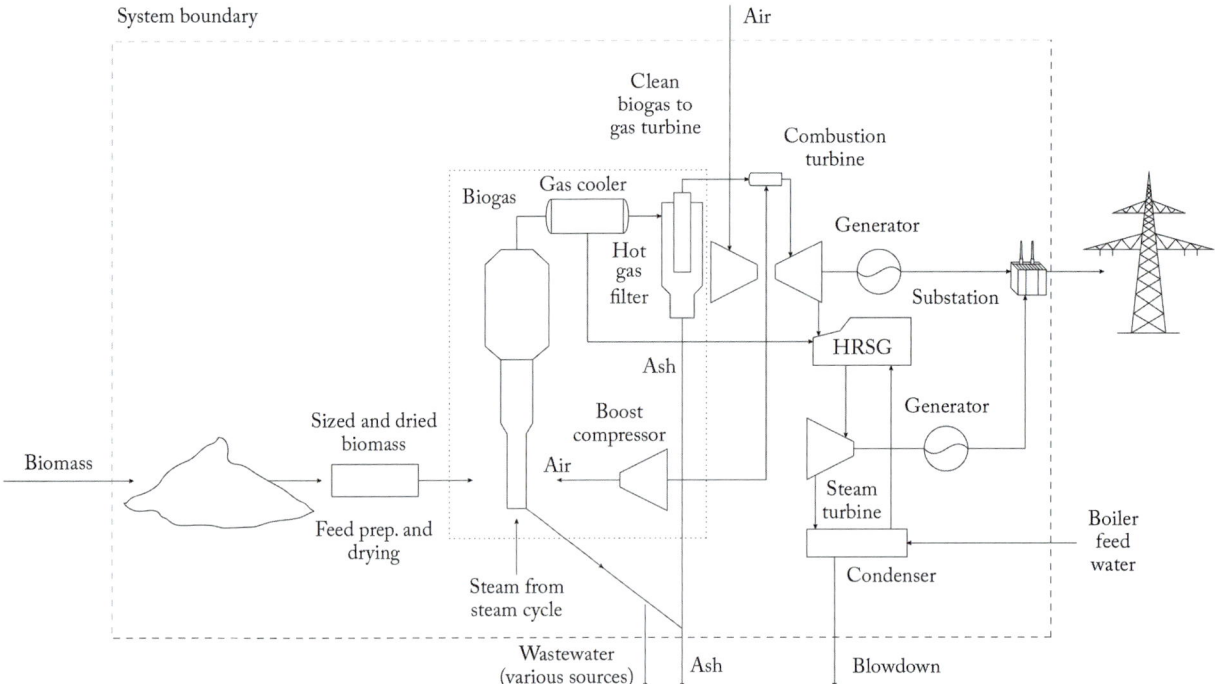

Figure 2.6.12 Biomass gasification combined cycle (BGCC) system schematic.
(Source: US Department of Energy, Electric Power Research Institute, 1997.)

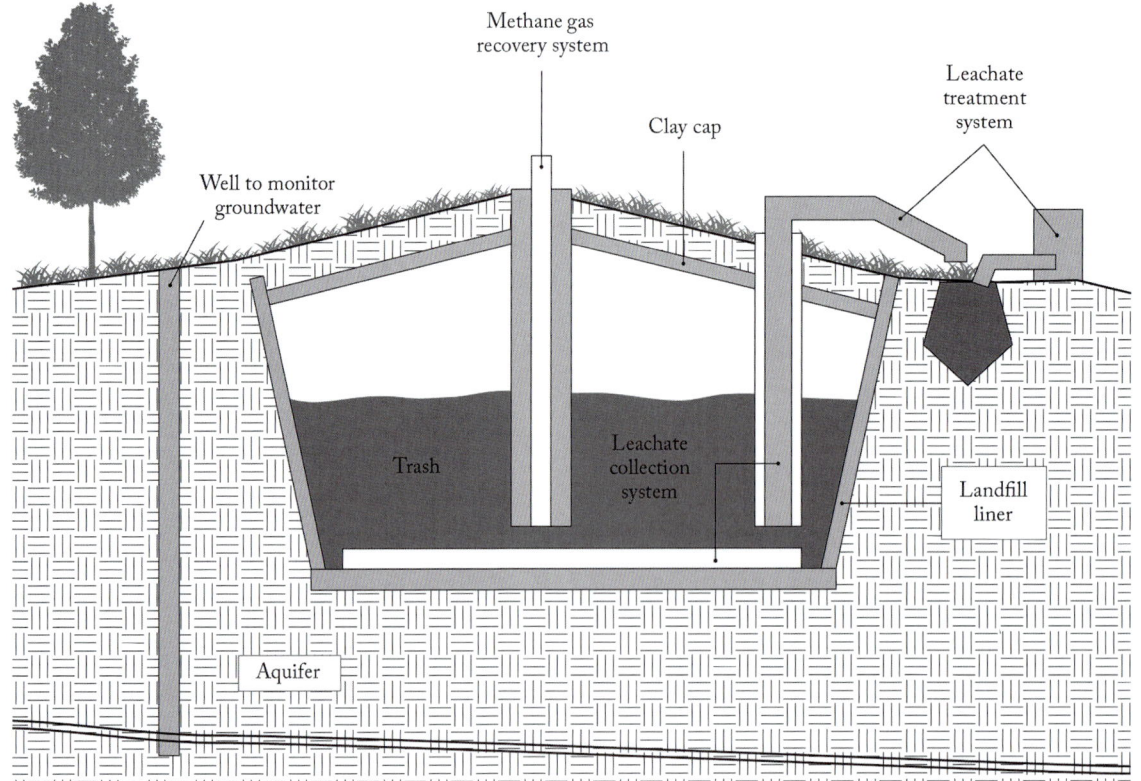

Figure 2.6.13 Diagram of a landfill.
(Source: US Department of Energy.)

contains methane. Methane, a very strong greenhouse gas, is colorless and odorless, which can be dangerous to people or the environment. When it is used for domestic consumption natural gas utilities add an odorant so people can detect natural gas leaks from pipelines. New rules require landfills to collect methane gas for safety and pollution control. Biogas (bio-methane, swamp gas, landfill gas, or digester gas) is an outcome of anaerobic digestion (decomposition without oxygen) of organic matter. This natural gas can be used in power plants to provide electricity and heat, as well as fuel for vehicles.

As of 2012, there were 594 operating landfill gas energy projects in the USA. The largest gas-to-energy facility of the three constructed by the Sanitation Districts of Los Angeles, located at the Puente Hills Landfill, has been in full commercial operation since January 1987 and has remained online 95 percent of the time. The facility produces 50 MW (gross) of power, equivalent to the energy requirements of approximately 70,000 homes. The downside to such plants is that the production of methane is not at a constant rate. There also is uncertainty that the landfill will consistently yield clean, quality methane that will not hurt the metal components of a power plant (Figure 2.6.13).

Fuel Cells

On-site small power systems. Well-designed fuel cell power systems can be small and compact, requiring very little space, which makes them useful as power sources in remote locations, such as spacecraft, remote weather stations, large parks, communications centers, rural locations including research stations, and in certain military applications. Unit sizes vary from 1 KW to 100 KW. There are several different types, depending on the type of fuel used. Essentially, a fuel is made up of an anode and a cathode separated by an electrolyte (Figure 2.6.14). Fuel cells generate electricity from a catalyst-facilitated chemical reaction between hydrogen and oxygen ions in a cell.

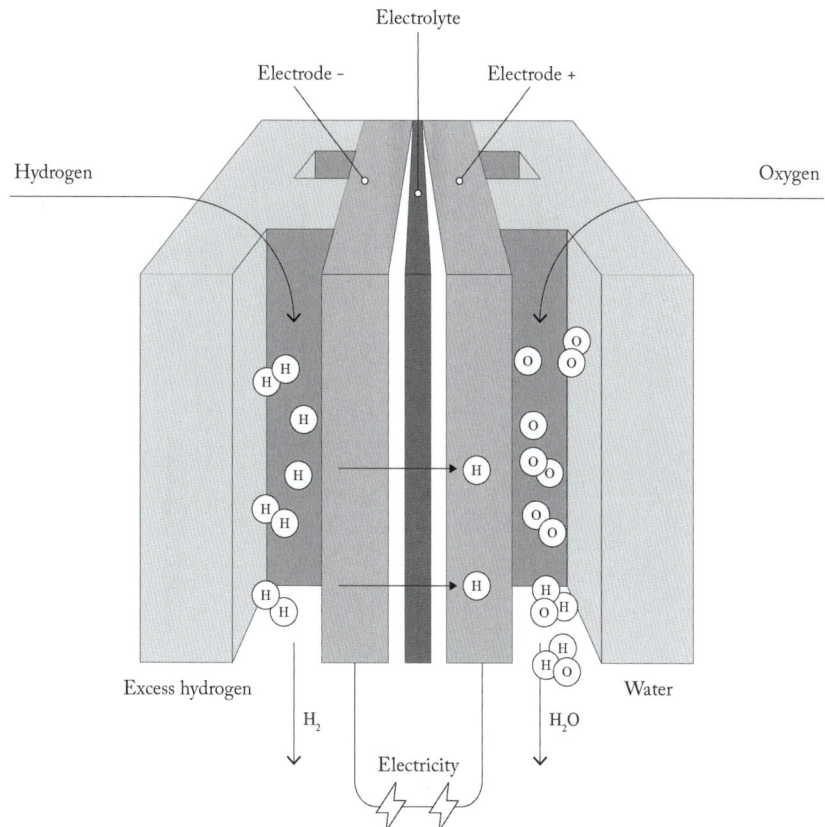

Figure 2.6.14 Proton exchange membrane fuel cell. (Source: California Fuel Cell Partners.)

There are seven types of fuel cells currently at different stages of development. *Photon exchange membrane (PEM)* and *solid oxide fuel cell (SOFC)* fuel cells are commercially viable; the remaining five types are undergoing further development and refinement before entering the market.

Micro-turbines

Micro-turbines are small machines with rotating blades to produce power, well suited for moderate-size apartments, retail stores, and small medical facilities. These systems, ranging from 1.5 to 20 kW, are located close to the facility and do not require distribution systems. They are capable of producing electricity and heat for the facility and are usually immune to price volatility since they use any type of gas, including methane. Some of the systems, such as the Capstone system made in California (Figure 2.6.15), claim 40,000 hours of useful life. Once again, potential has yet to be fully realized. There are several new systems under various stages of development.

Small-scale Hydro

An old technology but still a valuable feature in a renewable portfolio is the small-scale hydro, capable of producing up to 200 KW. Small-scale hydro (Figure 2.6.16) can be operated without the use of fossil fuels. This type of system is especially effective for use in mountainous country with river valleys. Its CO_2 emissions are about 3.6–11 g/kwh, while a coal plant produces 1,026 g/kwh of CO_2.

Design considerations for small scale hydro are as follows. To *estimate available power* in a particular location, in kilowatts (kW), use the following formula:

$$\text{Gross Head} \times \text{Flow} \times \text{System Efficiency (in decimal equivalent)} \times C = \text{Power (kW)}$$

C is a constant (the value is different in English and metric units).

Figure 2.6.15 Capstone's micro-turbine.
(Source: image courtesy of Capstone Turbine Corporation.)

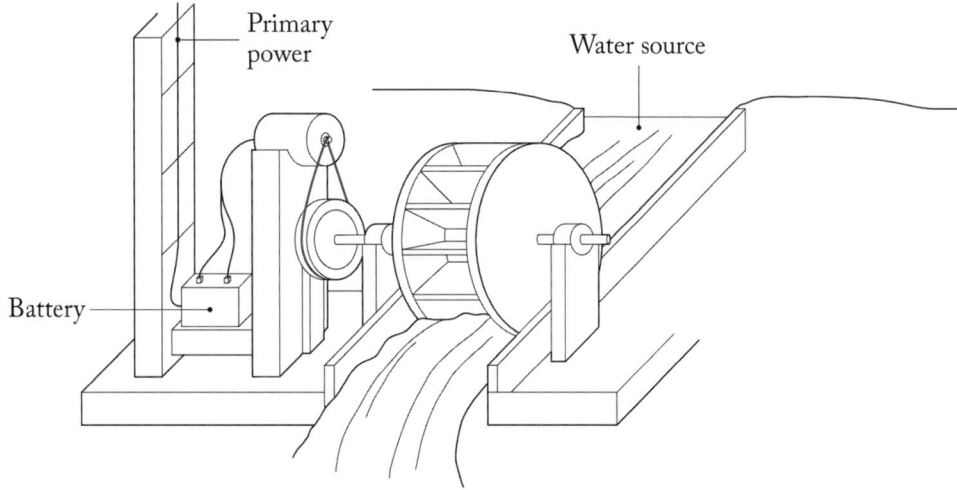

Figure 2.6.16 Small-scale hydro power plant.
(Source: Kuppaswamy Iyengar.)

Examples:

1   20 feet × 2 cfs × 0.55 × 0.085 = 1.9 kW; or
2   50 feet × 0.8 cfs × 0.55 × 0.085 = 1.9 kW.

Note that net head and flow rate can be manipulated
to arrive at the same power output.

Summary

Sustainable technology is a rapidly emerging field
with new developments in photovoltaics (solar cells),
solar-thermal technologies, wind power, biomass,
biogas, and combined wind and solar systems. Other
technologies such as fuel cells, light emitting diodes,
micro-turbines, and small-scale hydros are all helping
to increase sources of power and reduce reliance on
fossil fuels in order to meet energy demands.

Reference

[1] Daniel M. Kammen, The rise of renewable energy,
Scientific American, September 2006, p. 88.

Further Reading

Electric Power Research Institute, *Technology
Applications* (Palo Alto, CA: Electric Power
Research Institute, 2000)

Daniel M. Kammen, *The Rise of Renewable Energy*
(New York: Scientific American, 2006).
Norbert Lechner, *Heating, Cooling, Lighting*, 3rd
edition (New York: John Wiley & Sons, Inc. 2009).
Richard Newell (administrator), Biomass in the
United States Energy Economy: International
Biomass Conference & Expo, May 3, 2011, St.
Louis, MO. www.eia.gov/pressroom/presentations/
newell_05032011.pdf
Peter F. Smith, *Sustainability at the Cutting Edge*
(Oxford: Architectural Press, 2003).
Union of Concerned Scientists, *Biomass Resources in
the US* (2012). www.ucsusa.org/clean_vehicles/
smart-transportation-solutions/cleaner_fuels/eth
anol-and-other-biofuels/biomass-energy-resour
ces.html#.VEQQIijgWG4

Web Support

www.nrel.gov/docs/fy
www1.eere.energy.gov/buildings/ssl/sslbasics_
ledbasics.html
www.oregon.gov/ENERGY/RENEW/Hydro/
Hydro_index.shtml
http://en.wikipedia.org/wiki/Stirling_engine
www.nrel.gov/learning/re_wind.html
www.nrel.gov/wind/publications.html

Exercises

1 Size a domestic hot-water system, in Kansas City, for a family of four. Sketch the basic system description.
2 Write a research report on current development in LED use and its future for commercial and industrial applications.
3 What are your thoughts on landfill gas power plant development? Are these plants environmentally sound propositions?
4 Should society invest in the development of combined solar and wind systems? Why?

CHAPTER THREE

Site Issues

3.1 Site: Selection and Analysis

There is no perfect site. In terms of sustainability, a good site should have clean air, access to water, good soil conditions, solar access, and appropriate landforms for building purposes. In this section the emphasis is on site selection for new projects, since it is sometimes difficult or impossible to retrofit buildings on old sites. In sustainable design, characteristics of a particular site inform choices made about building orientation, location, configuration, and landscaping.

Inappropriate Sites

The first intent of site selection is to avoid development of inappropriate sites. In order to achieve this objective according to the USGBC's LEED® Green Building certification process, buildings, roads, or parking should not be developed on the following: (1) prime farmland; (2) elevations lower than five feet above the elevation of a 100-year flood; (3) habitat of federal or state threatened or endangered species; (4) within 100 feet of any wetland; or (5) on public parkland (unless replaced).

Considerations in Site Selection

A second major goal of careful site selection is to reduce the environmental impact of building on a site and its surroundings. Following are some of the essential items that should be considered for making a site sustainable:

- Prevent any kind of environmental damage (do not cut down old-growth trees).
- Make every effort to bring back a degraded site to environmental productivity and biological diversity.
- Preserve historical landmarks (an old house, for instance), windmills, bridges, and barns.
- Understand conditions for maximum solar benefit.
- Understand how the wind can be utilized for passive energy uses and ventilation.

For a new construction, determine whether the site has access to public transportation and is near a school and other social facilities. If the site can make use of existing infrastructure such as roads and utilities, it will have less impact on the natural landscape and minimize use of natural resources.

Development of the land should be based on an understanding of a "land ethic" taken from author, teacher, and naturalist Aldo Leopold (1887–1948), who reminded us there is no truly vacant land since there are many living things already residing there. To show respect, we should cultivate the belief that the existing living things have as much right to exist on a site as we have. We should not thoughtlessly bulldoze the land but rather we should plan to work with the land to minimize the environmental damage. Animals and plants in a place are not expendable, but instead are a vital natural resource that can enhance environmentally productive site development. In the end, a question that is not technical but still should be asked is: Does it feel right to build on this site?

Site Analysis

Site analysis is used to examine the location for its physical properties, such as topography, soil quality, water, wetlands, native life forms, microclimates, etc. (Figure 3.1.1). Site analysis that takes sustainability into account will relate these features to the potential for passive system designs and sustainable technologies, and will result in schematic drawings that map landforms, water and wetlands, slopes, prevailing winds, soil quality, views, and other major features of

the site. These schematic plans can be embellished with sustainable design ideas for recycling or solar access.

Prepare for building placement concepts discussed earlier in Chapter 2 by studying the site for ways to maximize benefits of solar orientation and access to daylighting and natural cooling. For optimal performance pay attention to the prevailing breezes and local landforms. A well-designed site/building takes advantage of breezes to cool the building in summer and to avoid cold wind in winter (Figure 3.1.2).

Plan how to use existing slopes for greatest building form advantage and energy performance by terracing the building and the site. Terracing can help control light and wind and also offers interesting landscape opportunities. Imagine how one might cluster groups

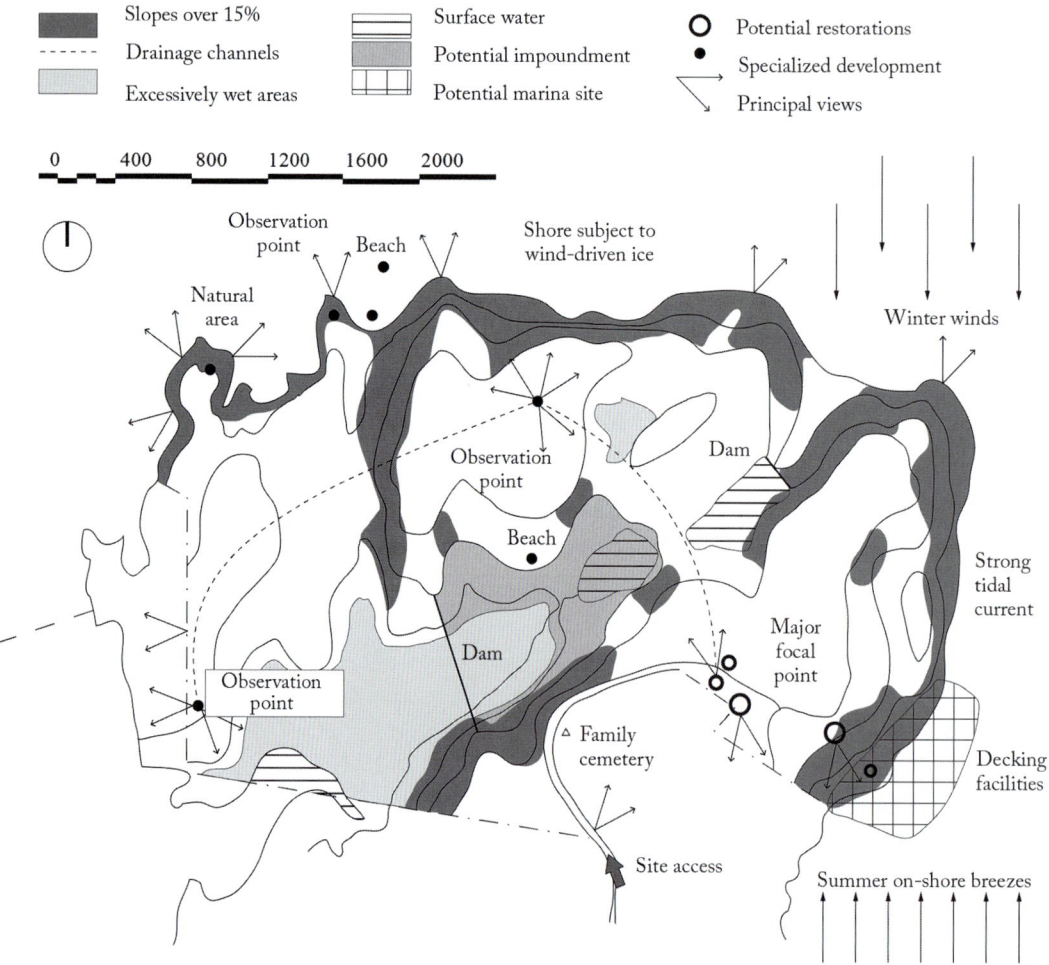

Figure 3.1.1 A preliminary site analysis with essential items for site design.
(Source: Kevin Lynch and Gary Hack, *Site Planning*, 2nd edition, Figure: Site Analysis, page 20, © 1971 Massachusetts Institute of Technology, by permission of The MIT Press.)

of buildings so that they are tightly knit, making room for larger surrounding green spaces that are comfortable and not wasteful. Also, the orientation of building in an urban setting should reflect understanding of the shadows cast by adjacent buildings (see Section 3.5). Remember that a well-placed building on a site can reduce energy use by 25–30 percent.

Finally, keep beauty in mind. Most experts agree that if there is a beautiful and wonderful spot on a site, then that is the place to preserve untouched.

The Solar Envelope

According to Professor Emeritus Ralph Knowles of the University of Southern California, the solar envelope (Figure 3.1.4) is a way to assure urban solar access for both energy and life quality. The solar envelope regulates development within imaginary boundaries derived from the sun's relative motion. Buildings within this container will not overshadow their surroundings during critical periods of the day and year.

The idea of solar access is ancient and has been practiced in many parts of the world. It is evident in the patterns of such early settlements as Acoma Pueblo (Figures 3.1.5 and 3.1.6). Located on a plateau about 50 miles west of modern Albuquerque, New Mexico, Acoma appears to have been continuously occupied for over 1,000 years. Its rows of houses are stepped down to the south. Walls are of thick masonry. Roofs and terraces are of timber and reeds, overlaid with a mixture of clay and grass [1].

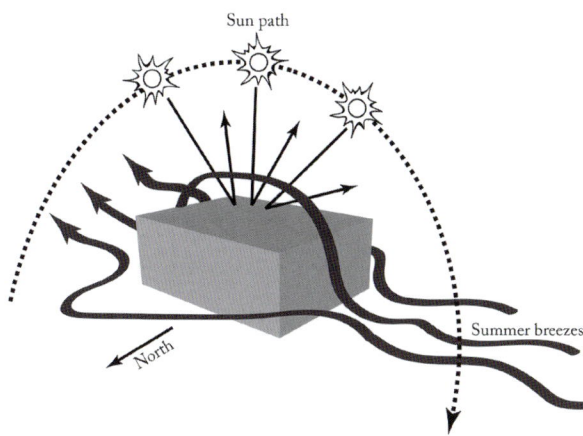

Figure 3.1.2 Taking advantage of sun position and wind movement.
(Source: adapted from Edward Mazria, *The Passive Solar Energy Book*. Emmaus, PA: Rodale Press, 1979.)

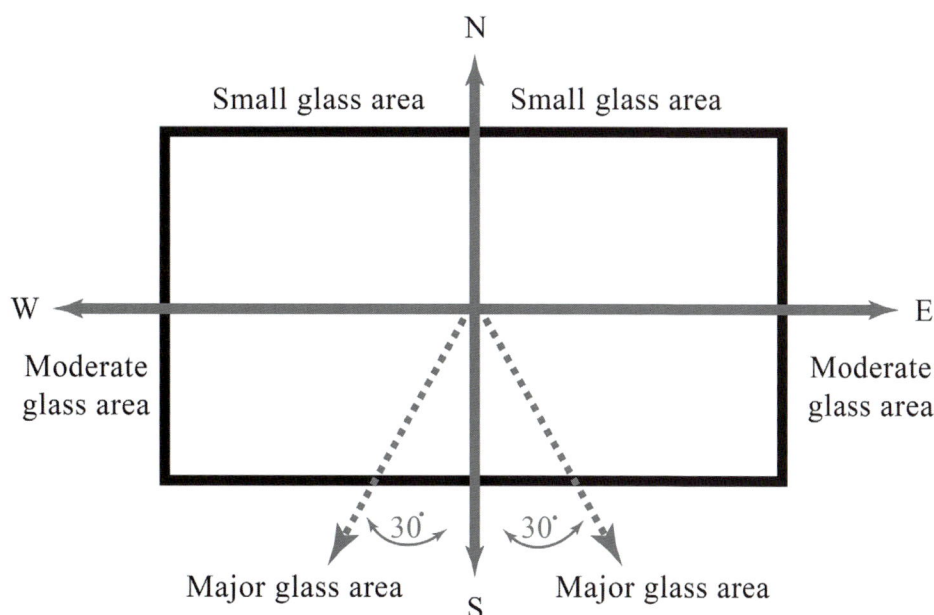

Figure 3.1.3 Optimum building orientation in the Northern Hemisphere.
(Source: adapted from Edward Mazria, *The Passive Solar Energy Book*, Emmaus, PA: Rodale Press, 1979.)

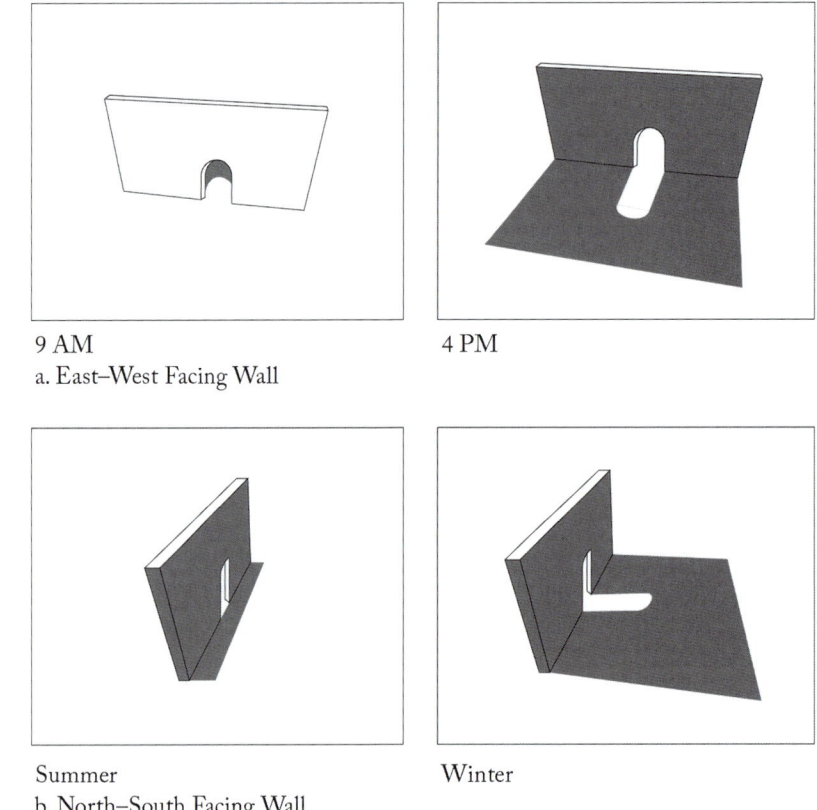

9 AM   4 PM
a. East–West Facing Wall

Summer   Winter
b. North–South Facing Wall

Figure 3.1.4 Solar envelope.
(Source: Ralph Knowles, *Energy and Form: An Ecological Approach to Urban Growth*, Figures: Solar Envelope, © 1975 Massachusetts Institute of Technology, by permission of The MIT Press.)

Figure 3.1.5 Acoma Pueblo, New Mexico.
(Source: Ralph Knowles, *Energy and Form: An Ecological Approach to Urban Growth*, Figures: Acoma Pueblo Drawing, © 1975 Massachusetts Institute of Technology, by permission of The MIT Press.)

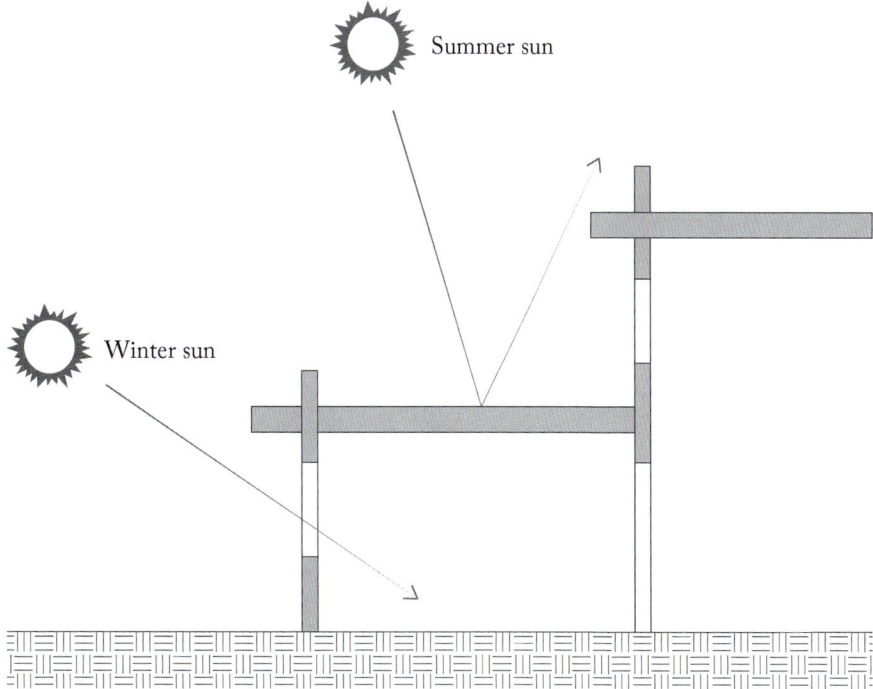

Figure 3.1.6   The houses of Acoma are well-suited for the high desert climate.
(Source: Ralph Knowles, *Energy and Form: An Ecological Approach to Urban Growth*, Figures: Diagram of Acoma Houses, ©
1975 Massachusetts Institute of Technology, by permission of The MIT Press.)

The solar envelope is conditioned in space and time, assuring solar access to the properties surrounding a given site. A concept known as *shadow fences* accomplishes solar access by limiting the size of on-site buildings, thus avoiding unacceptable shadows above a boundary along neighboring property lines. This also is of special importance in planning urban areas, where clustered buildings impact on each other and can alter the microclimate, as discussed later in this chapter.

Balance of Built and Open Spaces

Look at the site with an eye toward how open and built spaces in a site can complement each other. If the open space or landscaping is planned after the building is built, the final landscaping can become an afterthought and end up being expensive. Plan the landscape and the building together to avoid costly site improvements. See more on landscape design in the next section.

Consider how well a site can support systems that operate across indoor and outdoor needs. Water is becoming expensive in many parts of the world.

Consider installing a gray water system for reuse in the landscape and for cleaning in the building where non-potable water can be used. Rain harvesting can supplement needed water in any site and, if it is planned right from the beginning, it will add to the sustainability of that site. According to LEED®, stormwater management and treatment should limit disruption of natural water flows by eliminating stormwater run-off, increasing on-site infiltration and eliminating contaminants (see Section 3.2, Figure 3.2.5). If possible, develop a planting system that can provide shade to a building and at the same time create an outdoor microclimate that can lower the temperature by 10–15 °F. The shedding of leaves in the fall can provide compost for developing an edible garden in the same location.

Soil Issues

Soil issues come into play when examining a site for suitability and usage. The US Green Building Council's LEED® program evaluates site use by how sensitive designers have been in terms of environmental issues such as planning for site erosion control. Each project must include a sediment and erosion control plan that has been designed specific to its site and that conforms to the local State Storm Water Construction Permit. As required by LEED®, the local erosion and sedimentation control standard is more stringent than that of the EPA and should therefore be the measure used. The plan should cover prevention of soil loss by stormwater run-off and/or wind erosion, sedimentation, and/or dust/particulate matter air pollution, to meet the following objectives:

- prevent loss of soil during construction by stormwater run-off and/or wind erosion, including protecting topsoil by stockpiling for reuse;
- prevent sedimentation of storm sewers or receiving streams;
- prevent polluting the air with dust and particulate matter;
- control erosion to reduce negative impacts on water and air quality.

This is yet another example of the broad view taken by sustainable thinkers. The site is not seen in isolation, but as an integral part of its larger surroundings.

Other Site Issues

Some of the following sustainable site selection issues concern existing sites and others address new projects. Best practices and USGBC LEED® requirements relevant to site selection and usage include the following:

- Encourage development and increase density in urban areas with existing infrastructure, thus protecting green fields and preserving habitat and natural resources. Other measures include to reduce site disturbances, protect or restore open space to conserve existing natural areas, restore damaged areas, provide habitat, and promote biodiversity.
- Take advantage of public transportation access to reduce pollution and land development impacts from automobile use. Providing suitable means for securing bicycles, with changing/shower facilities for use by cyclists, can also reduce pollution and land development impacts from automobile use.

- Encourage the use of bicycles, vehicles with alternative fuels and preferred parking for carpools/vanpools to actually reduce parking spaces to increase green spaces.
- Design stormwater management and treatment to limit disruption (rate and quantity) of natural water flows by eliminating storm water run-off, increasing on-site infiltration and eliminating contaminants.
- To minimize the heat island effect, implement recommended landscape and external design ideas for non-roof and roof areas (thermal gradient differences between developed and undeveloped areas) to minimize impact on microclimate and human and wildlife habitat.
- For roof design, use Energy Star Roof compliant, high-reflectance, and low emissivity roofing.

Light pollution has an impact on nocturnal environments. Site and building design should avoid light trespass from the building and site, and improve night sky access.

Summary

Begin site selection for projects with sustainability in mind. Examine the site for suitability in terms of the impact on the existing habitat, the need for any additional infrastructure, access to sunlight and natural ventilation, erosion management, and other environmental issues such as developing urban areas, encouraging public transportation, stormwater management, and minimizing or reducing heat island effects. Balance open space and building footprints to reduce site disturbances and ensure quality of life.

Reference

[1] Ralph Knowles, *Energy and Form* (Cambridge, MA and London: MIT Press, 1975).

Further Reading

Kevin Lynch, *Site Planning*, 2nd edition (Cambridge, MA and London: MIT Press, 1971).
Edward Mazria, *The Passive Solar Energy Book* (Emmaus, PA: Rodale Press, 1979).

Web Support

www.usgbc.org

Exercises

1 Describe details of an inappropriate school building site in your town and state remedial actions you would suggest to make it sustainable property for development.
2 Review *Site Planning* by Kevin Lynch and summarize all the essential elements a designer should consider in developing a sustainable site.
3 How does understanding of the solar envelope mitigate abuse of site and building development?

3.2   Site: Landscape Design

The purpose of a sustainable landscape design is to conserve existing resources and to require little or no additional water, fertilizer, pesticides, or significant maintenance. It is crucial that developers respect the landscape needs of a development. A landscape is more than decoration. It can serve several sustainable functions, as a result making developments more habitable, reducing energy use, saving and recycling water, reducing pollution, minimizing the heat island effect in cities, and ultimately having an impact on carbon dioxide emissions. This section examines several ways in which thoughtful developers create sustainable designs using landscaping.

Respect for Local Landscape

The High Line Park (also known as "the viaduct"), inspired by a project in Paris completed in 1993, is a one-mile long New York City linear park built on a 1.45-mile section of a disused New York Central Railroad, which illustrates the power of deep respect for the local landscape (Figure 3.2.1). The High Line Park is on the southern portion of the West Side Line, running to the Lower West Side of Manhattan. It currently runs from Gansevoort Street in the Meatpacking District, to 30th Street, through Chelsea. The railroad line was redesigned and planted as an aerial greenway and rails-to-trails park in 2006 through 2014.

Figure 3.2.1   The High Line in New York City, New York by James Corner Field Operations and Diller Scofidio + Renfro. (Source: flickr user David Berkowitz.)

The revitalization of High Line has spurred real estate development in the neighborhoods which lie along the line and has also improved the quality of life. The recycling of the railway into an urban park has brought on other development in the neighborhoods that lie along the line while reducing crime in the park.

Ratio of Building to Land Area

The amount of landscape required depends on the knowledge of onsite existing resources such as the ecology of the area, soil, sun, wind, and topography. Wise choices require that the right plants be placed at the proper location to remove any plant stress. USGBC LEED® criteria recommend that the ratio of landscape to built area should be about 50 percent.

A balance between structures and surrounding landscape must be encouraged, especially in urban development projects. When land becomes expensive it is the attitude of most builders, especially in developing countries, to exploit every inch of it for built space. This shortsighted approach demands higher energy use, in part by increasing local temperatures significantly through a heat island effect.

Impact of the Urban Heat Island Effect

When natural land cover is modified by buildings and pavement, and when waste heat is generated by building use, the surrounding temperature rises. This situation is called the "heat island effect." Typically, in urban centers, the heat island effect is responsible for the rise of ambient temperature by about 6–7 °F (Figure 3.2.2).

In urban settings, heat loss occurs by radiation to deep space and by conduction at lower night temperatures. Mass in roads and buildings holds heat. Also, surface properties of buildings including heat capacity in urban centers lack evapotranspiration (evaporation plus plant transpiration). This situation alters the energy balance of urban areas, leading to higher temperatures. Cities like Tokyo have experienced significant temperature increases in their microclimates (see more in Section 3.3).

As a consequence, buildings in these regions require greater amounts of energy to cool. More energy causes more environmental degradation. Extensive research in the USA reveals impacts of climate change on health, water, energy, transportation, agriculture, forests and ecosystems [1].

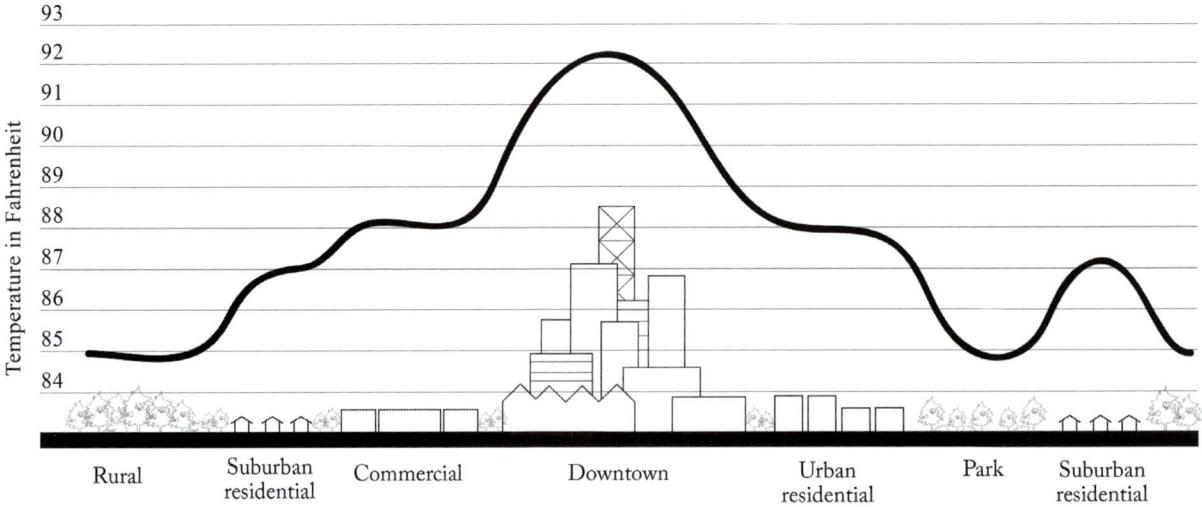

Figure 3.2.2   US EPA's urban heat island (UHI) profile on a summer day.
(Source: Lawrence Berkeley Laboratory.)

Providing green spaces, public gardens, and landscaping for individual buildings will reduce the heat island effect. Planting trees is an inexpensive way to have a significant impact on the quality of life. Cities benefit indirectly from trees through reduced energy consumption, lowered cooling costs, enhanced aesthetic value of the city, improved air quality, and decreased related health problems. Currently, ordinances and guidelines for vegetation and lighter-colored roofing are being developed at the Lawrence Berkeley Lab in California for existing and new construction. Urban planners can use these guidelines to mitigate the heat island effect across the country.

Although research on urban conditions suggests the heat island effect has a negative local impact, some NASA researchers believe, based on their satellite imaging, that the effect is not a significant cause of global climate change compared to other factors.

Effect of Water and Waste Water on Landscape

Severe environmental impacts can also result when designers fail to consider the effect of stormwater drainage on sewage systems. In a big storm, run-off can overload drainage systems and sewage plants, causing raw sewage to flow into rivers or the ocean. The damage to health and pollution clean-up can both be costly. Imagine, instead, a thoughtfully designed landscape, a development with fewer concrete surfaces, allowing the water to percolate into the soil, with small retention ponds to hold rainwater temporarily, and surface swales to slow down the flow of water and reduce run-off. This beautiful landscape could also minimize the heat island effect.

In many parts of the world expensive water is misused. For more detail, and to appreciate the problems we are facing in managing water resources in the USA, read Marc Reisner's *Cadillac Desert* [2]. *World Watch Institute* reports give readers an understanding of the problems of water the world over. Briefly, the groundwater table is dropping at an alarming rate in India, China, and the USA. All societies must educate their citizens to conserve precious water. In landscape design, using local plants appropriate to the region and minimizing the use

of watering is a responsibility of developers and landscape designers.

Collecting rainwater and using gray water are smart ways to manage water resources, but they are often underused. For example, in Albuquerque, New Mexico, 40 percent of the water treated to drinking water standards is used for irrigation.

Fortunately, there are several examples from around the world from communities that recycle their water expertly. Several South American countries and many cities have designed and built water reclamation and biologic treatment systems where sewage enters the plant at one end and clean water emerges at the other end. In landscape design use of these concepts respects sustainable goals and can be cost-effective at the same time.

Understand Local Plants and Ecology

For landscaping it is important to select plants for their toughness, adaptability, and enduring beauty appropriate to the climate. It is also important to understand every region has its own peculiarities regarding soil properties, climate, and the plants that are suitable to that area. For example, in New Mexico there are over 4,400 native species and many hundreds of exotic species. In the southwest, xeriscaping, or landscaping for areas that experience drought using plants that require little watering, is a popular replacement for eastern-style lawns. It is important to choose plants that can survive changes in topographic features. The desert can be dry and arid. It is extremely hot in the day and experiences low, cool temperatures at night. Local horticulturists have competencies to advise on the appropriate species for any sustainable landscape design (Figure 3.2.3).

Examples of Sustainable Landscapes

There are many good examples of developments that address needs for sustainability. At the *ING Bank, Amsterdam* (Figure 3.2.4), half a million square feet of bank in over five floors rests on a plinth of garage and parking of 300,000 square feet. The gardens on this site are watered entirely by rainwater harvesting. Not only do taller buildings gain valuable land space, but gardens filling that space can help with run-off.

Figure 3.2.3   Appropriate plants for local climates.
(Source: photo by Stan Shebs; this file is licensed under the Creative Commons Source-Share Alike 2.5 Generic License (a & c); Mark Byzewski; this file is licensed under the Creative Commons Source 2.0 Generic License (b).)

The architect of this project sought input from the bank employees for design decisions starting from the site selection, building layout, and sustainable design ideas. This organic architecture, built in 1979–1982, remains a model of energy efficiency today. It saved $2.9 million per year in operating costs and saw a 15 percent drop in absenteeism.

Years ago at the *White House in Washington, DC*, President Roosevelt encouraged the development of a habitat which is home to nearly 85 species of birds. This habitat has flourished in the middle of the busy metropolitan city, creating an oasis for birds and animals even today.

Village Homes in Davis, California, conceived and built in 1975, provides a fine example of planned ecological development. This development has parks, vineyards, orchards, community gardens, community buildings, and residential facilities. Every building has solar access for passive design. The streets are only 24 feet wide instead of the traditional 32 feet, enough for two fire trucks to pass each other. The additional land acquired by narrowing the streets allows for landscaping and plantings that reduce the ambient site temperature by 10–15 °F. The stormwater drainage system provides for six-day retention, where the water is retained in the ground without dumping into the drainage system. Initially the public works did not believe that this would work and demanded a performance bond to be posted by the developers. Three years after the project was completed a 100-year storm

Figure 3.2.4 Healthy and sustainable building; ING bank in Amsterdam, the Netherlands.
(Sources: (a) This file is from the Wikimedia Commons and is in the public domain; (b) this file is licensed under a Creative Commons License, Attribution 2.0 Generic; photo by flickr user Husky.)

Figure 3.2.5 Village Homes: section through a commons. Rainwater is collected in shallow swales where it can slowly percolate into the soil.
(Source: illustration courtesy of Village Homes Board of Directors.)

Figure 3.2.6 Village Homes: planned ecological developments (narrow streets for plant growth, good solar access community gardens, vineyards, and parks).
(Source: © 2014 Kathy West Studios, Davis, California, All Rights Reserved.)

hit the area and the stormwater management system worked perfectly by retaining the water for six days as designed (Figures 3.2.5 and 3.2.6).

For sustainable design, developers should seriously consider the environmental approach to their projects, including respect for and use of what is already there. Resource efficiency embodies doing more with less. In landscape and building design, sensitivity to the local environment plays a crucial role in managing resources. With modern equipment it is possible to transform any site to fit the desires of a designer; however, respect for the existing land and its topography should not be ignored.

Minack Greek Amphitheatre, UK, is a fine example of respecting what is already there (Figure 3.2.7). This modern-day copy of the Greek Amphitheatre honors

Figure 3.2.7   Responding to natural landscape in the Minack Greek Amphitheatre, Cornwall, UK. (Source: https://commons.wikimedia.org.)

the sculptural qualities of the rock at the site and celebrates architectural opportunity and sensitivity. The combined landscape design and architectural project highlights minimal disturbance to the site.

Summary

Landscapes serve many sustainable functions and are an integral part of any development project. Carefully placed and selected vegetation can reduce urban heat island effects while also addressing environmental issues caused by uncontrolled run-off, thereby reducing pollution. These landscapes also reduce the strain on built infrastructure such as drainage, sewage, and cooling systems. Developers and designers can use properties of natural local landscapes and plants to improve the quality of life and sustainability of urban communities.

References

[1] Global Change Research Program, *National Climate Assessment Report* (Washington, DC: Global Change Research Program, 2014).

[2] Marc Reisner, *Cadillac Desert* (New York: Viking, 1986).

Further Reading

Thomas Derek, *Architecture and the Urban Environment* (Oxford: Architectural Press, 2002).

Baker H. Morrow, *Best Plants for New Mexico Gardens and Landscapes* (Albuquerque, NM: University of New Mexico Press, 1995).

Rocky Mountain Institute, *Green Developments* (Golden, CO: 2001).

Web Support

www.epa.gov/hiri

Exercises

1 Draw one landscape solution to the problem of water run-off in a city.
2 Explain the successes of landscape design in Village Homes in Davis, California, and how one can learn from it to make other communities sustainable.
3 What are the benefits of using native plants in landscapes? Describe with photographs a landscape with native plants that you admire.

3.3 Thermal Impact of Urban Infrastructure – Droplets of Water Can Create a Lake

Cities pose special challenges to designers who seek to mitigate the heat island effect in the interests of sustainability. Impervious surfaces in urban areas such as building rooftops, roads, parking lots, sidewalks, and other constructed surfaces inhibit the infiltration of stormwater run-off and also absorb and emit heat, creating air and surface temperatures that are significantly higher than those of rural areas. As urbanization and build-out occurs, the thermal properties of the surrounding environment are altered. Heated built surfaces not only alter the temperature of the surrounding areas, but can also thermally alter stormwater run-off which flows into receiving water bodies and potentially increases the base temperature of the surface water in lakes, streams, and estuaries. The amount of heat transferred and the degree of thermal pollution affects cold water fisheries and the ecological integrity of receiving waters.

Heat Island Effects in Cities

According to the US EPA, cities with more than a million people often experience the heat island effect. The annual mean air temperature of a city can be 1.8–5.4 °F (1–3 °C) warmer than its surroundings. In the evening, the difference can be as high as 22 °F (12 °C). Heat island effect in a city can cause increases

in summertime peak energy demand, air-conditioning costs, air pollution and GHG emissions, heat-related illness and mortality, and water quality issues.

Urban areas can mitigate these effects by adopting energy-saving strategies suggested by the EPA (www. epa.gov/hiri/mitigation/index.htm):

*   *Trees, vegetation, and green roofs* can reduce heating and cooling energy use and associated air pollution and GHGs, remove air pollutants, sequester and store carbon, help lower the risk of heat-related illnesses and deaths, improve stormwater control and water quality, reduce noise levels, create habitats, improve aesthetic qualities, and increase property values.
*   *Cool roofs* (Chapter 4) can lower cooling energy use, peak electricity demand, air pollution and GHG emissions, heat-related incidents, and solid waste generation due to less frequent re-roofing.
*   *Cool pavements* – pervious concrete, brick pavers designed to allow a high degree of infiltration, and plastic "geo-tech" fabrics that allow for gravel and grass surfaces – can indirectly help reduce energy consumption, air pollution, and GHG emissions. Depending on the technology used, cool pavements can improve stormwater management and water quality, increase surface durability, enhance nighttime illumination, and reduce noise.

While cool roofs and cool pavements may benefit a single owner, community-wide use of these installations can result in reduction of air temperatures. Lower temperatures mean overall reduction in energy use and carbon dioxide emissions for larger communities. This cumulative effect is the meaning behind the phrase "droplets of water can create a lake!"

Effectiveness of Roof Gardens and Urban Vegetation

The Commerzbank Tower in Frankfurt, Germany has a triangular atrium. At nine different levels the atrium houses a large sky garden that also allows natural light into the building. Each office has a view to the city or the sky garden. Owing to more effectively and sustainably cooling the building, it does not radiate as

Figure 3.3.1   Commerzbank, using plants to improve thermal performance.
(Source: https://commons.wikimedia.org.)

much heat and thus contributes to the reduction in heat island effect.

Green Roofs or Living Roofs

In Europe, living or vegetative roofs have been used functionally and architecturally to cool buildings and consequently reduce heating costs. Green roofs not only look attractive, they also absorb pollution, purify air, and reduce noise. Green roofs cool buildings through plant respiration and lower rooftop temperatures, causing reduced heat transfer into the building. The heat island effect is minimized at the urban scale if many of the buildings in a city have living roofs. Additional benefits are that these roofs filter water from precipitation, reduce the load on stormwater infrastructure, and prevent run-off that can pollute streams and lakes. Typically, green roofs about six inches thick can be made in a modular pattern using some kind of interlocking system set on a water-proofing membrane with a well-designed drainage system. Depending on the location, they can be as simple as a two-inch covering of hardy groundcover or as complex as a fully accessible park complete with trees. Green roofs have longer life than conventional roof systems and therefore decrease life cycle maintenance costs. Also, a living roof can reduce energy demand by lowering the surface temperature and thus the amount of solar energy that is conducted into a building. Living roofs can also reduce stormwater run-off and improve air quality. In a city with limited available space for street-level planting, living roofs provide a good opportunity for the re-introduction of vegetation into the urban environment. Green roofs can be installed on a wide range of buildings, from industrial facilities to private residences, to reduce energy use and GHG emissions.

According to EPA estimates, green roofs are becoming popular in the USA, with roughly 8.5 million square feet installed in 2008. Figure 3.3.2 shows a green roof on top of the Chicago City Hall in Chicago, Illinois. The roof garden was implemented in 2001 in an effort to test the impact of green roofs on the urban heat island effect. Many roofs remain viable candidates to become green roofs.

Another good example of a large-scale green roof is in the GAP building in California, designed by

Figure 3.3.2 Chicago City Hall.
(Source: http://en.wikipedia.org.)

Figure 3.3.3 Green roof on the GAP building, San Bruno, California; designed by William McDonough. A good example of a large-scale green roof: a layer of grass and plants set on six inches of soil.
(Source: this file is licensed under the Creative Commons Source Share Alike 3.0 Unported License.)

William McDonough (Figure 3.3.3). Topping the roof of this building is a layer of grass and plants set on six inches of soil. The whole composition acts as insulation to the roof and also absorbs rainwater and some air pollution. This building also features many other green building concepts with considerable elegance.

Lessons Learned from Studies in Japan

The mean temperature in six large cities in Japan, including Tokyo and Nagoya, has risen 2–3 °C in the twentieth century, while globally averaged temperature has risen 0.6 °C.

Japan's study confirms that causes of the urban heat island phenomenon are:

- extensive use of air-conditioners;
- increasing amount of heat absorbed by buildings;
- heat released from manufacturing facilities;
- heat transfer from urban surfaces;
- fewer green spaces.

European Studies on Urban Heat Island Effect

At the beginning of the last century 15 percent of the world population lived in urban areas. At present, about 50 percent of the world population lives in urban areas, in approximately 2.8 percent of the total land area of our planet [1]. This increase in urban inhabitants has led to urban sprawl, especially in developing countries [2]. Increased density has caused the rise of urban temperatures up to 2 °C, contributing to the urban heat island effect.

Several European studies have confirmed the correlation between an increase in green areas and a reduction in local temperature, suggesting augmentation of urban vegetation as a mitigation strategy for the urban heat island effect. One possible solution is to convert flat roofs into green ones. Roofs constitute about 20–25 percent of the urban surface. Conversion of urban roofs into green roofs can offer many benefits, including reduction in urban heat island effect and building energy use, improved air quality, stormwater management, biodiversity, and urban amenities. Of

course, retrofitting an existing roof may prove to be, at times, expensive.

Summary

The heat island effect in cities raises temperatures, which results in higher demand for cooling and increased cooling costs. Designers can lessen these effects by thoughtful use of vegetation and green roofs and careful attention to alternatives in urban surface materials through cool roofs and pavements. Basic passive energy concepts introduced in earlier sections of this book can also be applied on a larger scale for urban environments. One drop at a time, consideration of site issues such as building placement and orientation can add up to sustainable benefits for an entire community.

References

[1] Millennium Ecosystem Assessment, *Ecosystems and Human Well-being: Biodiversity Synthesis* (Washington, DC: World Resources Institute, 2005).

[2] University of Michigan, Urbanization and global change, 2002. www.globalchange.umich.edu/globalchange2/current/lectures/urban_gc.

Further Reading

Inter-Ministry Coordination Committee to Mitigate Urban Heat Island, *The Policy Framework to Reduce Urban Heat Island Effects* (Japan: Inter-Ministry Coordination Committee to Mitigate Urban Heat Island, 2004).

New York City Regional Heat Island Initiative, *Mitigating New York City's Heat Island with Urban Forestry, Living Roofs, and Light Surfaces* (New York: New York City Regional Heat Island Initiative, 2006).

T. Susca, S.R. Gaffin, and G.R. Dell'Osso, *Positive Effects of Vegetation: Urban Heat Island and Green Roofs* (Italy: Polytechnic University of Bari, 2011).

Yoshika Yamamoto, Measures to mitigate urban heat islands, *Science and Technology Trends Quarterly Review*, 18, 2006, 65–83.

Web Support

www.unh.edu/unhsc/thermal-impacts
www.env.go.jp/en/air/heat/heatisland.pdf
www.epa.gov/hiri/mitigation/index.htm
education.nationalgeographic.com/education/
encyclopedia/urban-heat-island
www.sciencedirect.com/science/article/pii

Exercises

1 Many cities such as New York and Tokyo have observed and recorded the urban heat island effect and they are taking steps to mitigate it. Describe in detail the efforts of a city in your area.
2 Comment on retrofitting a green roof on an existing built-up roof. Specifically discuss architectural and structural implications.
3 Research, record, and sketch four green roof cross-sections for a moderate-size commercial building and the impact on that building's energy use.
4 One drop at a time, consideration of site issues such as building placement and orientation can add up to sustainable benefits for an entire community. Research and estimate, for your city, available exposed roof areas, in square feet, which can be retrofitted with green roofs. Calculate the energy benefits.

3.4 Site: Placement of Buildings

Orientation

A well-planned and appropriately oriented building supports energy efficiency for the community as a whole through:

* passive solar heating and cooling when needed;
* natural ventilation;
* daylighting.

Placement of a building on a site must also take into account the importance of site slopes, soil considerations, stormwater management and natural ecosystems.

In sustainable design, the site itself suggests possibilities for placement of buildings and for their configuration. Elements of building configuration such as interior layout, shape, size, number of stories, solar orientation, and openness to airflow and daylight contribute to sustainability.

In *Design with Climate* [1] Olgyay and Olgyay identified that in order to benefit from natural heating and cooling, building orientation needs to relate directly to regional climatic conditions (see Figure 3.4.1).

For example, designing in extreme climates presents unique opportunities to create informed and elegant solutions that respond to local conditions. In the hot and arid climate of the southwestern USA, Will Bruder designed the Phoenix Central Library, employing a variety of techniques and materials for shading and glazing that combine with orientation to

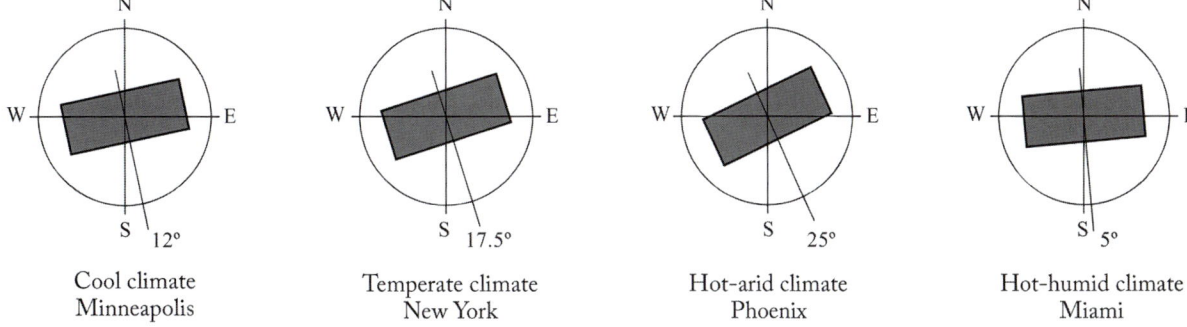

| Cool climate
Minneapolis | Temperate climate
New York | Hot-arid climate
Phoenix | Hot-humid climate
Miami |

Figure 3.4.1 Building orientation in response to US regional climates.
(Source: Professor Stephen D. Dent, University of New Mexico, School of Architecture and Planning.)

Figure 3.4.2 Phoenix Central Library by Will Bruder.
(Source: Photo by Cygnusloop99; this file is licensed under the Creative Commons Source Share Alike 3.0 Unported License.)

achieve maximum cooling and lighting effects while minimizing solar gain (Figure 3.4.2).

In hot and humid climates summer sun can be severe and windows and roofs need overhangs. For residential scale, the length of the overhang is the critical factor. For tall commercial buildings, there are several new solutions called "smart façades" which incorporate well-insulated windows with light shelves to minimize the effects of the sun. Also, in these climates buildings should be elongated and open in plan to maximize summer winds, in the manner of many classic buildings in India, Indonesia, and the Caribbean Islands. U-shaped and courtyard buildings also are good design solutions in hot, humid climates. If these principles cannot be employed due to the size of the site and other restraints on physical properties, then technical solutions include extra insulation in the walls and floors and the use of smart glass in windows, which has greater U-value and reflectivity.

Placement and configuration work together to optimize the sustainable functionality of a building,

and therefore it is difficult to discuss them separately. Locating and orienting a building on a site requires using the existing contours of the land to minimize site disturbance and to respect the living things that pre-exist on site. Adjacent buildings can block sun and wind and as a result can create their own microclimates. The general direction of wind and position of the sun, as well as the shape of building forms, determine the correct location of both interior and exterior spaces. Many examples of this in reference [2] can be found on p. 140. There are many different combinations for locating outdoor spaces in a building for different climates. Indeed, climate is central to the discussion of placement of sustainable buildings that will rely on passive lighting, heating, and cooling.

A note of caution: Except in new urban developments, existing street patterns, location of amenities, and other neighborhood details are fixed and therefore difficult to alter to suit any particular sustainability need, such as channeling wind direction for passive cooling or heating.

Building Configuration and Energy Use

The basic concept here is to make buildings "large" to the positive environmental forces and "small" to the negative environmental forces on the site.

1. Variation of Surface Area with Configuration

A building's configuration largely determines the amount of energy it uses. Configurations can minimize heat gains or losses, resulting in buildings that are more sustainable. For example, a low building with a square configuration will have less surface area than a rectangular plan of the same area, resulting in less thermal effect. How tall the building is, however, alters this relationship for the building as a whole. See Figure 3.4.3, where a tall building is least affected by solar gains on the roof. Typically, tall buildings are affected by wind loads and exfiltration and infiltration due to heat exchange, and also receive little protection from plants against wind and sun. Low buildings may have greater heat gain, resulting in the need for bigger

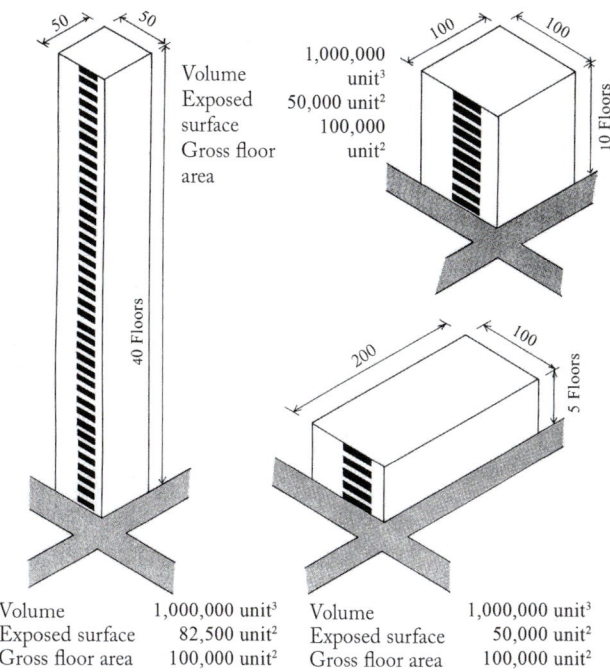

Figure 3.4.3 Variation of surface area with configuration. (Source: Craig B. Smith (ed.), *Efficient Electricity Use* (Elmsford, NY: Pergamon Press, 1978).)

Figure 3.4.4 Architecture of Hassan Fahey, New Gourna Village, Egypt. (Source: photo by Marc Ryckaert; this file is licensed under the Creative Commons Source 3.0 Unported License.)

mechanical cooling systems. However, this situation is fairly easy to control with light roofs and insulation. Glazed areas pose a more difficult problem.

For a designer, therefore, *form responses* become most interesting in dealing with building membrane and natural environmental forces. If a building is in the form of a sphere, it will have the least exposed surface area to the volume. Since it is not practical to have only spherical buildings, designers interested in sustainability tend to make their building approximate a sphere with straight line geometries. For instance, a convex surface spreads out the solar radiation, a technique that is used in several traditional buildings in hot and arid regions, including many buildings in parts of Africa and others designed by Hassan Fahey in the Middle East (Figure 3.4.4). In temperate climates it can be useful to make buildings smaller on the side exposed to high summer sun and larger on the parts exposed to low winter sun. Local climates may alter this general guideline.

2. Creative Shading

For very hot climates such as that of India, sun-shading devices are absolutely necessary, offering creative shading opportunities. For example, the shading devices by Le Corbusier for the Secretariat Building in Chandigarh, India (Figure 3.4.5).

3. Cross Ventilation

Cross ventilation is extremely useful in cooling a building in hot and humid climates. Ventilation helps building occupants feel a cooling sensation through evaporation, a process that lowers humidity. Typically, in hot climates a building should be oriented so that it is open to prevailing breezes on one side, with openings on the opposite side to create suction to help cooling. In climates where wind speeds drop at night, it might be useful to combine cross ventilation and stack ventilation to maintain the desired level of thermal comfort.

Figure 3.4.5   Secretariat Building in Chandigarh, India, by Le Corbusier.
(Source: http://en.wikipedia.org.)

A 22-story office building in Berlin, Germany, uses cross ventilation effectively (Figure 3.4.6). Outside air is admitted from the east façade to pass through the 35-foot-wide building to exit through the west façade. The west façade creates the stack effect. By using sound-baffled partitions, the entire office building allows decent airflow. During heating season the three-layer façade acts like a thermal buffer when the windows are closed. The warm air from the stack is returned to the central plant for heat recovery.

In his study of house forms Donald Watson [3] generated building form responses to the requirements of minimum wind resistance and maximum thermal retention, solar gain, and internal airflow. This study established different building forms and interpretation of construction in response to different climates, offering interesting design opportunities.

4. Daylighting and Building Forms

All green buildings place emphasis on using as much daylight as possible. It is well known that natural daylight sets the standard for high quality, reduces costs for operation of buildings, and also improves health of building occupants.

If energy can be saved by use of natural lighting, the building perimeter should be increased and its interior may have to be decreased. Creating more perimeter or exterior walls open to the outside may result in different forms such as multiple courtyards, light wells, tall or low buildings with skylights, or long, skinny, narrow buildings. There are many ways to get daylight deep into buildings in addition to windows and skylights. These include light monitors, clerestories, light shelves, atria, courtyards, glass, glass bricks, glass top-level partitions, top silvered Venetian

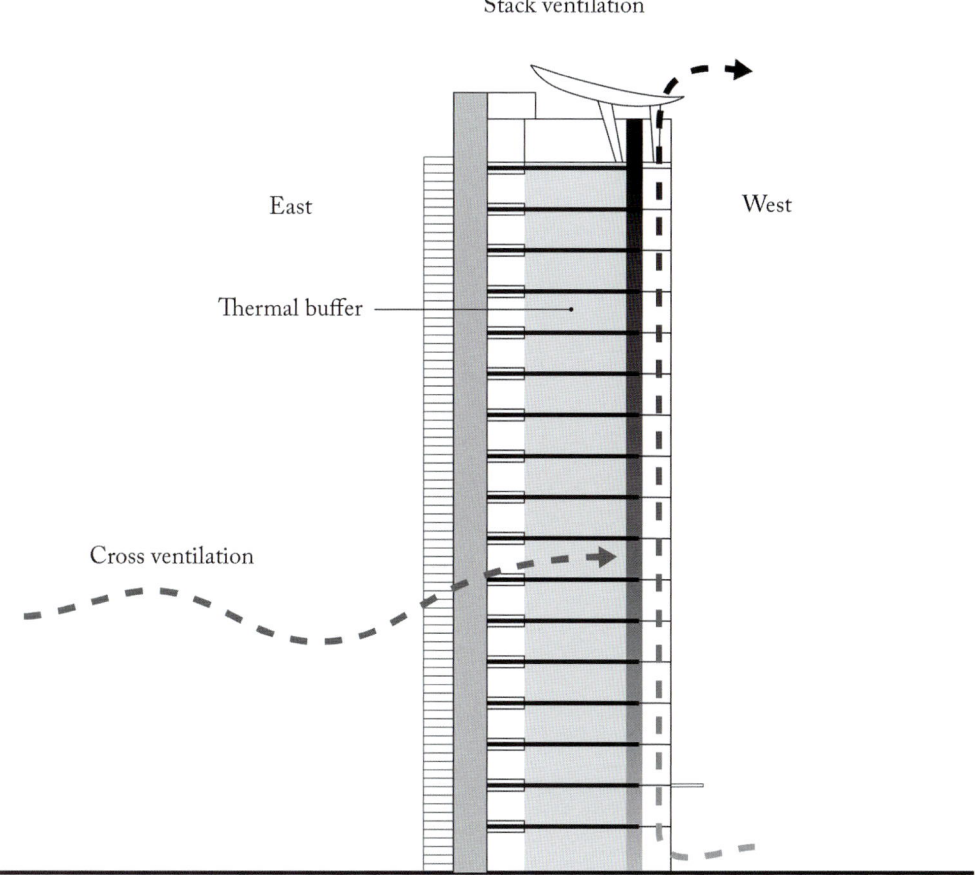

Figure 3.4.6 Building placement for cross ventilation, GSW building in Germany.
(Source: prepared by the Building Technologies Program, Environmental Energy Technologies Division at the Ernest Orlando Lawrence Berkeley National Laboratory, University of California, Berkeley.)

blinds, laser-cut prisms, and light-colored paint on walls and ceilings.

A light shelf (Figure 3.4.7) is an opaque horizontal surface placed on the interior of a window, dividing it into two unequal parts. Daylight enters the smaller top part of the window and bounces off the shelf. This allows both sun and daylight to reflect from the interior ceiling to provide uniform light in the building.

Careful attention should be paid for light distribution and quality of light to avoid problems with glare.

Buildings that depend on sun for light and heating can be put into two categories: long, thin, narrow buildings and deep, thick buildings. In thin buildings the amount of light that reaches the interior depends on the depth of the room and the height of the window opening. A rule of thumb: Light penetrates into a building at 1.5 times the height of the window opening. This condition helps determine the overall depth of the building. The Multiple "Fingers" Science and Technology Park, Gelsenkirchen in Germany, by Kiessel & Partners, is an example of a long, thin building.

Deep buildings pose a challenge to a designer when light and solar heat are desired. Some formal design ideas are illustrated by Brown and DeKay (see p. 156 in reference [2]). For solar effectiveness in deep, thick buildings, plans and sections must be well organized. Plans having two or three rooms can gain solar benefits by staggering rooms in plan or changing elevations in sections. The designer may select a site with appropriate topography to take advantage of the sun.

With a firm understanding of passive design and its relation to energy efficiency for individual

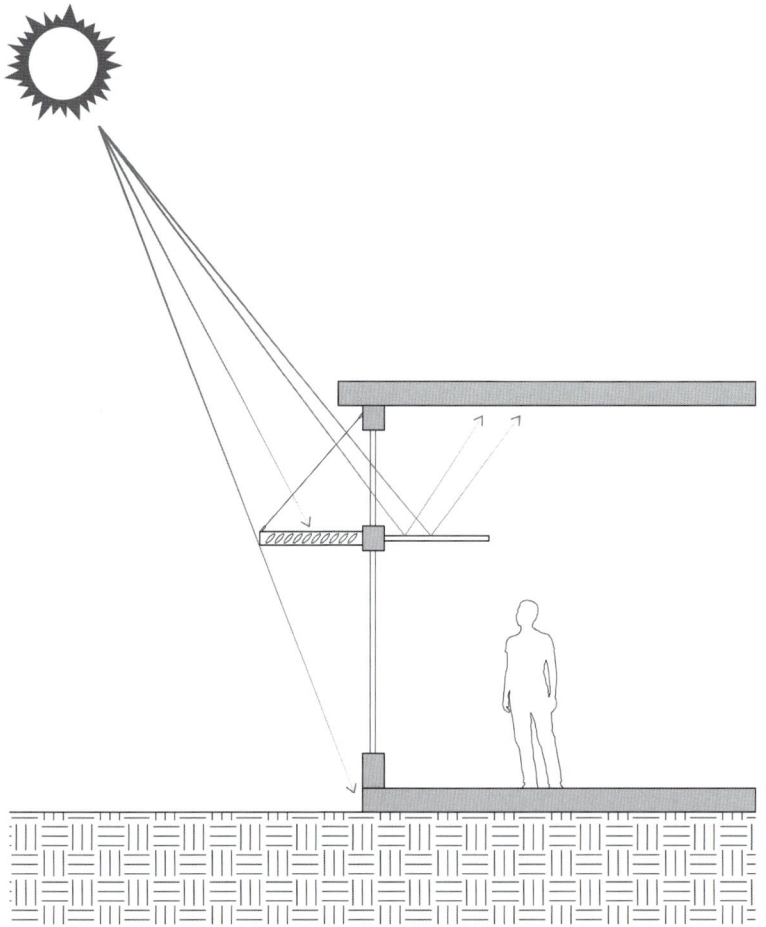

Figure 3.4.7 Light shelves for daylighting.
(Source: Kuppaswamy Iyengar.)

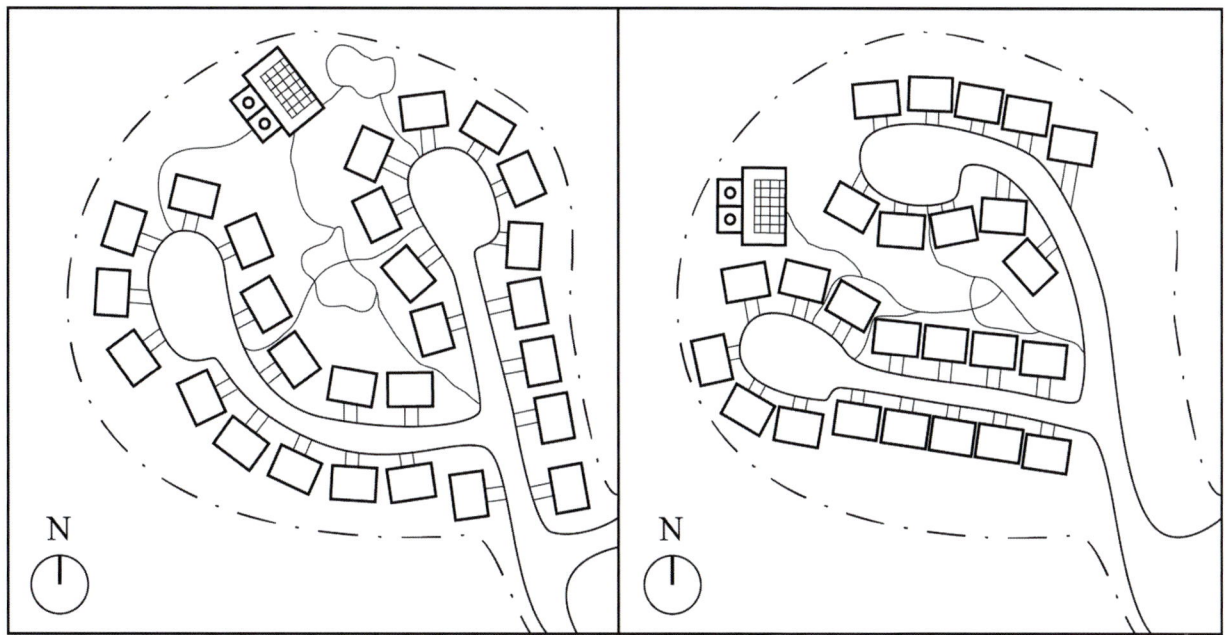

Original Plan - A   Alternative Plan - B

Figure 3.4.8 Site plan illustrating variations in housing layout. Layout B has very good solar orientation – north/south – for all buildings.
(Source: US Department of Energy.)

buildings, designers can turn their attention to site plans for larger buildings or urban areas (Figure 3.4.8). The housing layout in Figure 3.4.8b clearly takes advantage of southern exposure for all buildings, thus gaining energy benefits.

Summary

A sustainable building should be placed on a site so that it meets or exceeds the expectations of energy efficiency and carbon neutrality, as well as indoor air quality and comfort. Configuration of buildings refers to shapes and forms that take advantage of interior spaces. Buildings and enclosures can block sun or wind, thus creating their own microclimates, which enters into the following discussion of building clusters.

References

[1] Victor Olgyay and Aladar Olgyay, *Design with Climate* (Princeton, NJ: Princeton University Press, 1963).

[2] G. Brown and Mark DeKay, *Sun, Wind & Light* (New York: John Wiley & Sons, 2001).

[3] Donald Watson, *Designing and Building a Solar House* (Charlotte, VT: Garden Way Publisher, 1977).

Further Reading

BuildingGreen Inc., *Greening Federal Facilities* (Brattleboro, VT: NREL and DOE, 2001).

Stephen Dent (James C. Snyder and Anthony J. Catanese, eds.), *Introduction to Architecture* (New York: John Wiley & Sons, 1979).

Ralph Knowles, *Sun Rhythm and Form* (Oxford: Architectural Press, 2011).

Kevin Lynch, *Site Planning* (Cambridge, MA: The MIT Press, 1971).

Rocky Mountain Institute, *Green Development* (Golden, CO: RMI, 2001).

Craig B. Smith (ed.), *Efficient Electricity Use* (Elmsford, NY: Pergamon, 1978).

Derek Thomas, *Architecture and the Urban Environment* (Oxford: Architectural Press, 2002).

Michael Wigginton and Jude Harris, *Intelligent Skins* (Burlington, MA: Architectural Press, 2003).

Web Support

www1.hunterdouglascontract.com/NR/rdonlyres/1.
www1.eere.energy.gov/femp/pdfs.

Exercises

1   How can a designer have control over the interior climate of a cluster of residential buildings? Explain with sketches.
2   How can a designer utilize cross ventilation and stack ventilation to manipulate building comfort in tropical climates? Give examples of small, medium, and tall commercial buildings.
3   Which building forms would work for hot and humid climate zones recommended by Donald Watson in his book, *Designing and Building a Solar Home*?

3.5   Site: Building Clusters

At the scale of building clusters, the site resources of sun, wind, light, and natural topography, and how effectively they are used, will have major impacts on the resources a building will use over its lifetime. Even when a designer has control over just one building in a cluster, the form and relationship of that building with others has a long-term effect on the neighborhood by creating a distinct microclimate. Designers have frequently ignored this aspect of design, which has contributed to permanent environmental inefficiencies and undesirable microclimate conditions in many of our cities.

USC Professor Emeritus Ralph Knowles reminds us that the sun is fundamental to all life [1]. It is the source of our vision, our warmth, our energy, and the rhythm of our lives. Its movements inform our perceptions of time and space and our scale in the universe. Without access to the sun, our perceptions of the world and of ourselves are altered. The natural world appears to abound with examples of arrangements based in some measure on exposure to the sun.

Solar Orientation

Norbert Lechner [2] documents that ancient Greeks took pride in the solar design of their buildings, which took advantage of east–west orientation of the streets. Romans enacted the great Justinian Code (sixth century) that sunshine cannot be blocked from entering the sunroom. A community with row houses oriented east–west ensures proper solar access to all units except the end units, which will be exposed to low sun angles during morning and evening.

For both energy and quality of life, solar access is a legitimate area of public policy in which the aim is to regulate how and when neighbors may shadow one another.

It is desirable to orient a building to have access to winter sun and avoid summer sun, but thus far building orientation is largely determined by the street orientation in urban areas. While east–west streets assure decent solar access, it may not be possible to achieve this in all terrains. Figure 3.5.1 illustrates the importance of orientation to solar access. East–west aligned streets are too cold and dark in the winter. In contrast, streets that are oriented on a diagonal north–south orientation maximize annual insolation, resulting in streets that are bright and warm in the winter.

Architects might not have control over infrastructure and development and, yet, for sustainable design awareness, these issues remain important.

The Solar Envelope and Building Clusters

The amount of sun available at any site establishes the volume of a building. While this may not be a problem in a rural site, it can become complex in suburban and urban sites. In cold climates this requirement becomes essential for passive design solutions. For example, users of the famous Seagram building in New York City, designed by Mies van der Rohe, have shown that users overwhelmingly prefer the sunny side of the plaza, which has been a celebratory space for decades. In response to the difficulties with solar access in cities, Knowles and others defined the concept of the *solar*

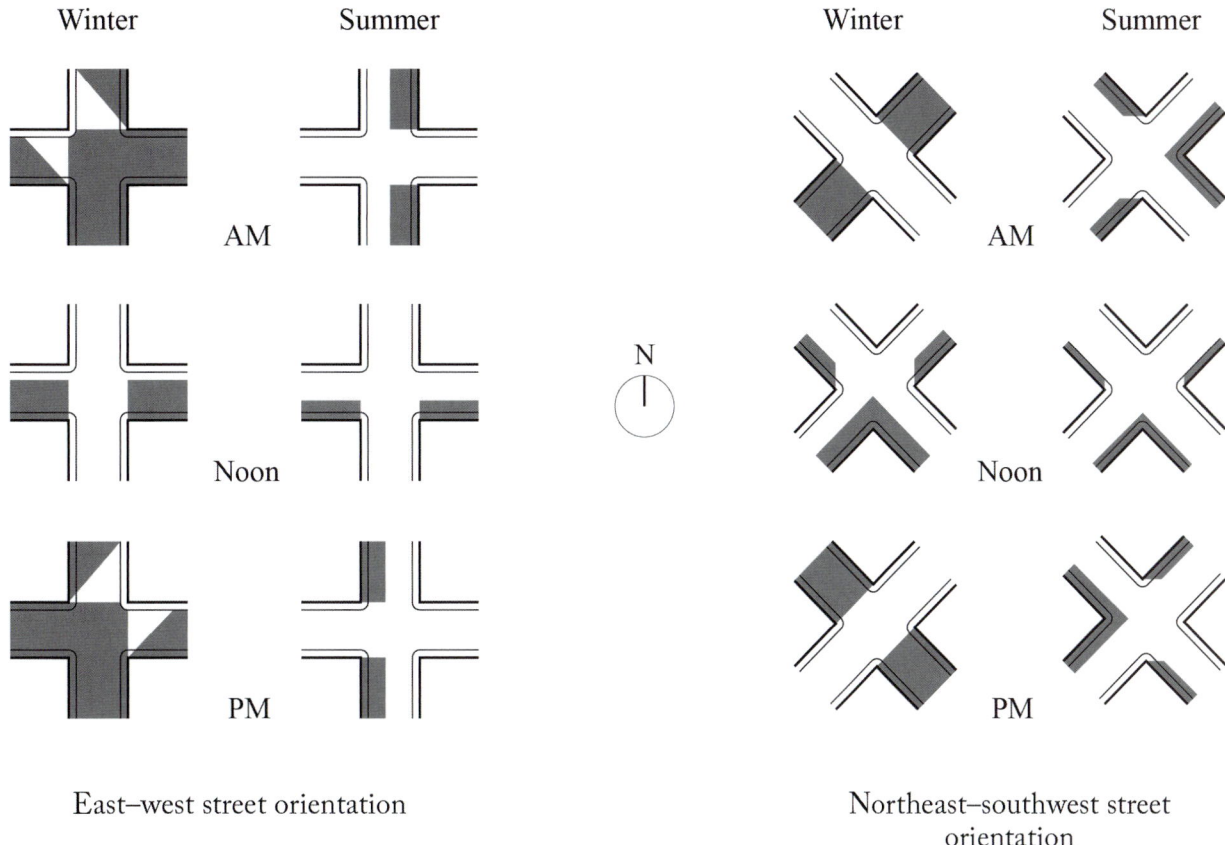

Winter   Summer

AM

Noon

N

PM

East–west street orientation

Winter   Summer

AM

Noon

PM

Northeast–southwest street
orientation

Figure 3.5.1 Streets that are oriented on a north–south diagonal offer maximum insolation throughout the year.
(Source: Ralph Knowles, *Energy and Form: An Ecological Approach to Urban Growth*, Figures: Solar Envelope, © 1975
Massachusetts Institute of Technology, by permission of The MIT Press.)

envelope as a zoning and design principle. The size and shape of the solar envelope of a building depends on site size, orientation, latitude, ground slope, and when sun energy is needed at the site.

By regulating urban development within imaginary boundaries derived from the sun's relative motion, buildings within this container will not overshadow their surroundings during critical periods of the day and year. If massing models are constructed for all sites for all types of buildings for a city block, a city can ensure solar access to all buildings. That takes strict zoning controls by a city government. Another consideration is how much any adjacent buildings shade the future building. By limiting the size and shape of a building (Figure 3.5.2), solar shading can

be avoided to gain solar access. With all this information it is possible to develop a massing model for a building.

Designers of future tall buildings should seriously consider sustainability of initial design concepts and incorporation of sustainable technologies. The biggest impact on a building's energy consumption depends on how fundamental early decisions are taken with respect to size, form, shape, skin, and the positioning of service cores. These, in turn, are controlled by sun, wind, and light. Tall buildings also provide opportunities for harnessing wind energy as well as access to view, light, air, and a sense of place. There are now universities offering accredited graduate degrees in the design of tall sustainable buildings.

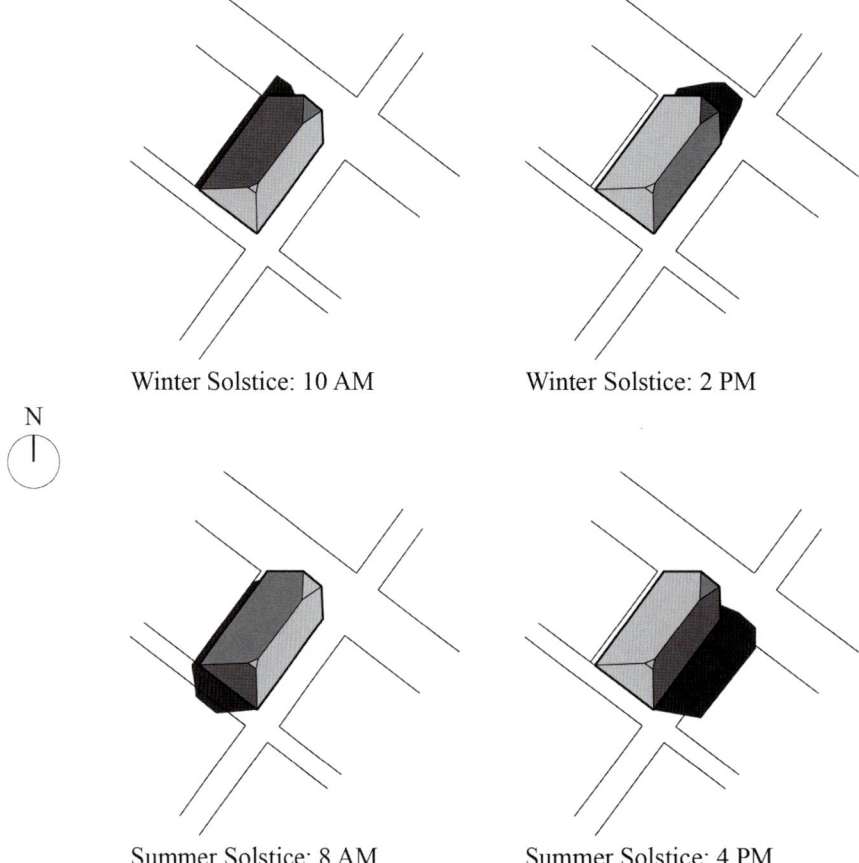

Winter Solstice: 10 AM

Winter Solstice: 2 PM

Summer Solstice: 8 AM

Summer Solstice: 4 PM

Figure 3.5.2 Illustrates the reduction of cast shadows throughout the year by altering the solar envelope of a building. (Source: Ralph L. Knowles, "The Solar Envelope," wwwbcf.usc.edu/~rknowles/sol_env/sol_env.html.)

Best Use of Sun and Light for Tall Buildings

The issues involved with the solar envelope are further complicated by a new call for density of urban settings. With rapid urban development worldwide, "dense and more concentrated cities are widely seen now as an essential part of a more sustainable way of life," explains Antony Wood, Executive Director of the Council on Tall Buildings and Urban Habitat (CTBUH), based in Chicago.

> These dense, smaller-footprint cities can cut energy consumption and climate-change emissions by reducing the suburban spread of cities and therefore the need for extensive transportation and infrastructure networks. In this regard, tall buildings play a key role in creating denser cities

by accommodating more people on smaller parcels of land and therefore reduce the overall impact of buildings upon the environment and upon the world's climate.

Wood explains that tall buildings, vertical clusters, need to better respond to environmental concerns and their specific urban locations. "They need to be creative beyond their standard functions – office, residential, and hotel space – to include more sustainable functions."

Some recent tall buildings have alternative design approaches, which include innovative building forms such as vertical farms to help alleviate the environmental problems of agricultural imports, and vertical aquifers to maximize rainwater capture, which will help address the growing global decline of water resources. Tall buildings also may accommodate more social-communal spaces within them, such as sky gardens and sky plazas.

Clustering of Buildings for Different Climates and Terrain

A designer should be knowledgeable about the micro-climate of a site where buildings may be clustered, which can be predicted based on certain physical properties of the land. First, since dense, cold air settles at lower levels, it will move upwards when heated by the sun. This creates wind movement up and down the slope of a terrain between day and night. Second, elevation above the mean sea level determines the temperature of that land. Higher elevations tend to have cooler temperatures, typically about 3.5°F for every 100 feet. Third, large bodies of water alter

Figure 3.5.3 Closely connected dwellings in Tunis, Tunisia offer shade and comfort.
(Source: https://commons.wikimedia.org.)

temperatures of a site. A designer should collect local data for these conditions.

By making the streets narrow and varying the heights of buildings, a city can provide significant shade for its residents (Figure 3.5.3). For example, in Jaipur, India, solar access poses a different kind of problem. In this city the summers are very severe, coupled with sandstorms. Ornamental screens, an elegant architec-tural solution, provide protection from the sand as well as the sun. While many residents in Jaipur do not have air-conditioning, they have managed to bring down the shade temperature to a manageable level. Many hot climates such as Alhambra, Spain, and Rajasthan, India, have used the concept of layering (from courtyard to verandah to transitional space to the interior of a building) to manage strong sunlight. Figure 3.5.4 illustrates use of ornamental concrete for similar solar protection in modern times. A Buddhist monastery in India (Figure 3.5.5) takes advantage of principles of wind movement and slope in the design of clustered buildings.

Clustering and Adaptive Reuse

Urban design and the resultant clustering of buildings can be a positive, sustainable response to issues of sprawl if the building clusters are designed with attention to site and microclimates. A designer should be concerned with relationships between buildings and between buildings and open spaces, with or without plants. For example, a new development away from the existing city center forces development of infrastructure such as highways, electrical distri-bution systems, water and wastewater management systems, stormwater disposal, and many other public works demanding expense and resources. It may impose new schools, hospitals, and other commercial establishments.

Adaptive reuse is one solution to the problem of sprawl and increased infrastructure. Designers and developers can investigate the possibility of using and redesigning existing structures in an urban center. In this way, an enormous number of resources can be preserved, especially if building planners know how to apply passive energy concepts to buildings in clusters.

Figure 3.5.4   Traditional Jali (ornamental concrete work) to control light and dust.
(Source: http://en.wikipedia.org.)

Figure 3.5.5   The Gompa, a Buddhist monastery in Ladakh, India, rises up in the sky. It is situated in the hilltop and adapts to the local climate and terrain.
(Source: photo by Michael Hardy at en.wikipedia; this file is licensed under the Creative Commons Source 2.0 Generic License.)

Figure 3.5.6 At Positano, Italy, development adapts to climate, terrain and culture. The microclimate and topography of a site affects building clusters, and building clusters themselves can cause their own microclimates.
(Source: this file is from the Wikimedia Commons and is in the public domain.)

Passive Systems Within Clusters

When buildings are clustered, a designer also is concerned with making sure that individual buildings receive daylight and sun energy for passive heating and cooling of the building. Urban design techniques include breezy streets, ventilation corridors, and urban patterns with adequate parks and plants dispersed among the buildings. Several strategies have evolved to manage the local environment of building clusters when severe sun is a factor. Among these design ideas are dense urban dwellings (Rajasthan, India; Cairo, Egypt), green belts with wind breaks, and overhead shade from tall buildings.

Sense of Place

The topography of a site not only creates microclimates impacting building clusters, but can also lend character to the development, whether it has flat or rolling or steep slopes. Today, most developments have bulldozed sloping land into flat land. Of course, there are advantages to flat sites, but land should not be leveled only for monetary and technical advantage. The relationship between man and the land is transactional and that contract cannot be violated. This is a way of saying that every place has a spirit and that spirit will have an impact on the users of the place.

Summary

Clustering of buildings can be preferable to sprawl. The microclimate and topography of a site affects building clusters, and building clusters themselves can cause their own microclimates, which must be addressed through design. It is possible to develop an urban pattern that supports sustainability through sensible street and block layout. In response to the difficulties with solar access in cities, the concept of the *solar envelope* as a zoning and design principle should be followed as defined by Knowles and others. Orientation of the street and building blocks should take advantage of sun, wind, and local terrain to focus on the priorities of the climate.

References

[1] Ralph Knowles, *The Solar Envelope* (Golden, CO: Solar Energy Information Data Bank, 1999).

[2] Norbert Lechner, *Heating, Cooling, Lighting*, 3rd edition (New York: John Wiley & Sons, Inc. 2009).

Further Reading

G. Brown and Mark DeKay, *Sun, Wind & Light* (New York: John Wiley & Sons, 2001).

Ralph Knowles, *Sun Rhythm and Form* (Oxford: Architectural Press, 2011).

Kevin Lynch, *Site Planning* (Cambridge, MA: The MIT Press, 1971).

Derek Thomas, *Architecture and the Urban Environment* (Oxford: Architectural Press, 2002).

Exercises

1 Research and find examples of how tall buildings and clusters can address the need for solar access to all buildings in urban settings.

2 How can a designer take advantage of sloping terrain and bodies of water for building design? Give specific examples, one in a mountainous region and the other near water.

CHAPTER FOUR

Building Envelope

4.1 Building Envelope: Thermal Loads

Need for "Zero-Net Energy" Buildings

The Energy Independence and Security Act of 2007 calls for all new commercial buildings to be zero-net energy by 2030. An integrated approach provides the best opportunity to achieve significant GHG reductions from the buildings sector, because many different building elements interact with one another to influence overall energy consumption.

Designing building forms is a complex process. For a building to be sustainable, all of the individual building components must be built to perform like a symphony. Form, function, and aesthetic requirements all contribute to the whole. External loads such as sun, wind, vegetation, and outside noise, as well as people loads from inside, all inform the relationship of the building internally and externally.

Therefore, the design of the building envelope/shell – the separation between interior and exterior environments of a building – becomes critical. Technical information in this section supports the sustainable goal: Actions must be taken to reduce carbon dioxide and other GHGs through energy efficiency.

Impact of Building Envelope on Sustainability

The term "building envelope" refers to a building's walls, windows, skylights, floors, roof, and foundation, which shield living spaces from the elements. An effective building envelope provides additional services, such as blocking outside noise, protecting a home's structure from weather, and improving indoor air quality. The typical family spends an average of $2,000 per year to heat and cool a home ($1,423 in California to $3,065 in New Jersey) in the USA, according to Energy Information Agency (EIA) data in 2009. Even in extreme climates this spending can be reduced by up to 50 percent through investment in building envelope improvements such as adding adequate insulation, upgrading window features, and sealing air leaks. Once the building is sufficiently sealed and passive thermal control is implemented, one can downsize existing heating or cooling systems or switch to low-energy alternatives to save even more energy. A holistic thinker and designer will be able to resize all envelope components proportionately and appropriately for new constructions as well as existing buildings, and will demonstrate to a client energy-saving possibilities and their benefits.

Sustainable efforts also require reduction of waste, which can add up quickly when expressed at the national level. According to the *American Council for an Energy Efficient Economy*, an average home in the USA loses over $150 per year in the form of heat or cold air, through the cracks in their homes, which is a national total of $130 billion.

The operation of both passive and active technologies is dependent on the principles of thermodynamics, and the potential for creating effective sustainable designs relies on the designer's grasp of these thermo-physical properties.

Thermo-physical Properties and Heat Transfer

Of all the building elements with sustainable design potential, those that offer the greatest array of choices are in the building envelope – its outer shell. To design ecologically efficient building envelopes, an understanding of heat transfer mechanisms is essential. Heat transfer refers to when thermal energy passes

between bodies with different temperatures. It is a general condition of nature to seek balance, in this case thermal equilibrium. Where differences in temperature occur, this process of transfer cannot be stopped, only slowed. Heat transfer in buildings takes place in four ways:

1   radiation
2   conduction
3   convection
4   evaporation or condensation.

Radiation is the process by which heat flows from a higher temperature body to a lower temperature body when the bodies are separated in space or when a vacuum exists between them (the sun and Earth). *Conduction* is the flow of heat through a material by transfer from warmer to colder molecules in contact with each other. *Convection* is a process in which the motion of molecules transfers heat from one region

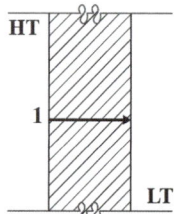
Solid material
Heat transfer by conduction.

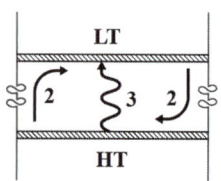
Air space in a roof
Heat transfer by convection and radiation.

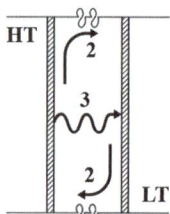
Air space in a wall
Heat transfer by convection and radiation.

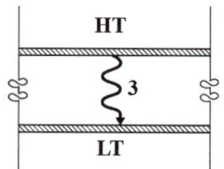
Air space in a floor
Heat transfer by radiation.

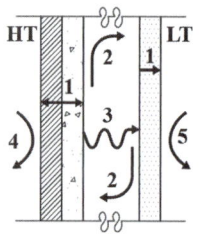
Air composite assembly of a wall
Conduction at varying rates in different materials. Convection currents and radiation carry the heat across the air space.

Legend:

1. Conduction
2. Convection
3. Radiation
4. Inside air motion
5. Outside air motion

Figure 4.1.1   Heat transfer mechanisms.
(Source: Craig B. Smith (ed.), *Efficient Electricity Use* (Elmsford, NY: Pergamon Press, 1978).)

to another. *Evaporation or Condensation* involves condition changes or changes in matter (liquid to gas or vice versa), which absorb or reject heat. Heat transfer mechanisms in a building are illustrated in Figure 4.1.1.

Material properties that cause heat transfer in and out of a building and consequently affect indoor thermal conditions and occupant comfort are thermal conductivity, resistance, surface characteristics with respect to radiation, surface convective coefficients, and heat capacity of the building material. These material properties vary in the degree and manner in which they transmit energy flow. This enters into calculations of heat transfer. Calculations of heat transfer are not only important to gauge thermal comfort, but also to predict and ensure the energy efficiency of a building.

Heat Loss and Heat Gain

Technical understanding of heat loss and heat gain is an essential requirement to properly design a building envelope. Heat naturally flows from warmer objects to cooler objects via the processes of radiation, convection, and conduction. *Radiation* of heat from objects takes the form of electromagnetic waves that travel through space. Most of us are familiar with radiant energy from the sun, and its effect on the building envelope (Figure 4.1.2).

A dark built-up roof on a hot sunny day will absorb 70–90 percent of the sun's energy and re-radiate this into the building. Without adequate attic ventilation or insulation this heat gain can add 40 percent to the cooling load on the air-conditioner. In cold weather, in a poorly insulated space or near a window, heat radiates from our bodies to the colder space, making

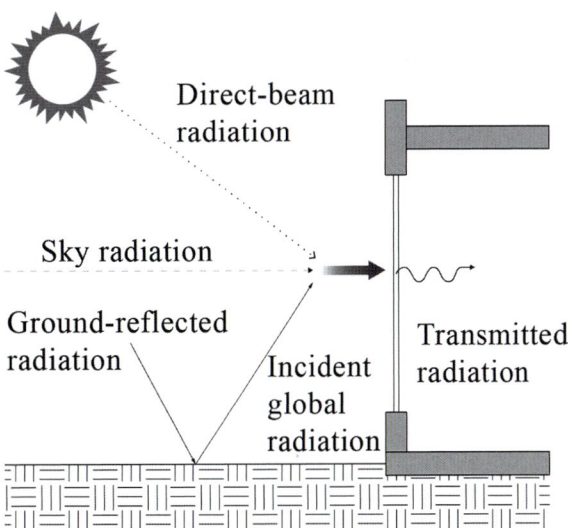

Incident global solar radiation includes direct-beam, sky, and ground-reflected radiation.

Figure 4.1.2 Incident global solar radiation.
(Source: adapted from Edward Mazria, *The Passive Solar Energy Book* (Emmaus, PA: Rodale Press, 1979).)

us feel chilly. The movement of this air is convection. *Convection* is the driving cause of air leakage through seams, cracks, and other openings in the building envelope. Typically, warmer air flows upward, due to stratification of air, through a building attic or chimney, pulling cooler air in from the basement and in through gaps around windows and doors. Sealing air leakages also helps prevent moisture infiltration, improves ventilation systems, and makes living spaces draft-free. A well-sealed building should also have a well-designed ventilation system to offset any problems associated with indoor air quality.

Conduction is the transfer of heat through a solid object, from its warmer side to its cooler side. Glass objects (such as windows) and metal are good conductors of heat and bad insulators, whereas foam and fiberglass make poor conductors and thus good insulators. *R-value* is a measure of a material's resistance to heat transfer by conduction – the higher the R-value, the better its insulating properties. The reciprocal or inverse of the sum of the R-values of all construction components in a wall or roof sections is the *U-value*.

In general, denser materials conduct heat better than less dense materials, with the critical property being the amount of trapped dead-air pockets which retard the continuous transfer of heat.

The terms that define heat flow through building materials are:

- *K, thermal conductivity*: rate of heat flow in British thermal units (BTU/hr) through 1 sq.ft of homogeneous material 1 inch thick per °F temperature change through the material. Also called unit conductance (BTU in.) / (hr sq.ft F) *or* (watts) / (m × K).
- *C, thermal conductance*: Rate of heat flow in BTU/hr × sq. ft. for 1 °F temperature difference across the material. BTU / (hr sq.ft F) *or* Watts / (sq.m × K).

  R, thermal resistance: The temperature difference in °F required causing heat to flow through 1 sq.ft of material at the rate of 1 BTU/hr. It is the reciprocal of thermal conductance. The total R-value of a wall or roof section is equal to the sum of the individual resistances for each separate material plus the resistance due to the surface conduction coefficients. R-values are the most commonly used

to denote effectiveness of insulation. (hr sq.ft F) / BTU *or* (sq.m × K) / watt.

- *U, overall thermal transmittance coefficient*: The number of BTUs/hour that pass through one sq.ft of wall, floor, or roof when the difference between the inside and outside air temperature is 1 °F under a steady state of heat flow. The U-value may be calculated by taking the reciprocal of the ΣRt value, i.e., (U = 1/ΣRt). The U-values may only be taken for the complete construction section, i.e., from outside air to inside air. Component heat transmissions are not additive, as the value of the overall coefficient is less than any of its parts.
- *H, surface conduction coefficient*: The rate of heat flow in BTUs per hour through 1 sq.ft of surface for a 1 °F temperature difference due to air motion across the surface. The surface conduction coefficient varies with the speed of the air across the surface. BTU / (hr sq.ft F) *or* watts / (sq.m × K).

It is the objective of a designer to keep indoor temperatures within a comfortable, stable range despite outdoor conditions by properly managing heat transfer. This generally means keeping heat transfer into a building at a minimum while also retaining indoor heat as needed for comfort. For detailed thermal properties of conventional building and insulating materials see the tables in Appendix E of Stein *et al.*'s *Mechanical and Electrical Equipment for Buildings* [1].

It is appropriate to discuss a few other aspects of building envelope design at this point. These are the effect of wind and of controlled air spaces in buildings. Glazing, infiltration, exfiltration, and their effects will be discussed in later chapters.

Effect of Wind and Air Films on Surfaces of Buildings

Heat loss from a building envelope is also dependent on the outside wind velocity and the nature of inside air in contact with the envelope. In calculating the rate of heat flow between indoor and outdoor air, the thermal resistance of air adjacent to the surfaces should be considered. In winter, the inside surfaces of walls are usually cooler than the room temperature. Because of convection, warm air collides with the cooler wall surface and increases its temperature. The outside air temperature is less than the temperature of the outside wall's surface. When the wind blows, the wall is cooled, thereby increasing the rate of heat loss. Thus, inside and outside air films have heat resistance coefficients. These coefficients affect heat flow from the surface to the ambient air. Still air inside a building has higher thermal insulation properties than outside air, which is affected by wind speed. There are several tables in Appendix E of MEEB [1] that will be useful when calculating heat loss from a building. When using the tables in MEEB to get your air film resistances, make sure you select the correct surface orientation and direction for heat flow. For example, let's say a wall is oriented vertically and the heat flow is horizontal to the outside. For finding the outside air film, use a 15 mph wind in winter and a 7.5 mph wind in summer [1]. (See *MEEB*, Table 4.3, p. 158.)

Air Space as Insulators

Dead air spaces in building construction may be effective insulators, depending on the boundary surfaces, position of the space, and direction of heat flow, not simply on the thickness of the air space. Reflective surfaces such as aluminum foil are highly effective in reducing radiant transmission between two opposing surfaces. It is only necessary to use the reflective surface on one face because it will absorb or emit only a small part of the radiation transmitted across the air space. The reflective surface must face an air space to be effective in retarding heat flow. If it is sandwiched between other building materials or faces an air space of less than 0.5 inches it will have no appreciable effect. (See *MEEB*, Table 4.4, pp. 160–162 for thermal resistance of air spaces.) When using the tables to find resistances of air spaces, use the highest value for emittance (E = 0.82) as most typical construction materials are not reflective. Use the table for the closest thickness of air space in your construction section. Also, use the table for all air spaces of 3.5 inches or greater.

Determining Composite R-value and U-value for Wall Assembly

Heat Transfer by Conduction

Conduction heat transfer is directly related to the type of materials used in construction. Each material conducts or resists the flow of heat differently than other materials. Resistance and conductance values for typical building materials have been tested and charted by ASHRAE.

The following example illustrates how to calculate R-value and U-value for a wood-framed wall with stucco finish on the exterior. First, R-value is determined by adding R-values of all wall components:

$$\text{U-value of wall} = 1/\text{SUMMATION OF R} = 1/R_1 + R_2 + R_3 \ldots$$

Wall components	Void	Solid
1. Outside air film	R = 0.17	R = 0.17
2. Stucco, 1"	R = 0.20	R = 0.20
3. Sheeting, insulating, 1/2"	R = 1.32	R = 1.32
4. 3.5" fiberglass batt insulation	R = 11.0	N/A
5. 2" × 4" studs, pine, 16" oc	N/A	R = 4.38
6. Gypsum board, 1/2"	R = 0.45	R = 0.45
7. Inside air film	R = 0.68	R = 0.68
Summation of R-values; hr. sq.ft. °F/Btu	Rt = 13.82	Rt = 7.05
U = 1/Rt; Btu/hr. sq.ft. °F	U = 0.07	U = 0.14

The combined U-value for the frame wall = (U void × percentage of wall that is void) + (U solid × percent solid).

The percentage of the construction section that is solid wood is called the "framing factor." The percentage solid + the percentage void should, of course, equal 1.0. Following are typical framing factors:

Framing Factors		
Spacing, o/c	Studs	Joists and rafters
12"	0.17	0.13
16"	0.15	0.10
24"	0.10	0.06

To calculate the combined U-value for the above wall section we use the framing factor for studs at 16" o/c (on center) and fill in the formula:

$$\text{Combined U-value} = (0.07 \times 0.85) + (0.14 \times 0.15)$$
$$= 0.08 \text{ Btu/ hr sq.ft } {}^\circ\text{F}$$

Controlled Air Spaces as Insulation

Air space can also play an important role in sustainability due to its insulating abilities. Properly introduced air spaces in building walls, roofs, and floors can significantly reduce heat transfer from the building. The resistance of an air space is not related to its thickness but to other factors such as its position, the direction of heat flow as shown, and the emittance of the material (see Figure 4.1.4).

For example, by lining the sky side of an attic space with a reflective foil and introducing ¾" to 4" air space between outer and inner surfaces, it is possible to achieve the equivalent insulating value of 3 inches of insulating material. Being able to use air space in this manner saves the cost and production costs of using insulation (see Figure 4.1.3).

Environmental Loads on Building Envelope

Loads from the building envelope, especially windows and skylights, are among the most significant loads that affect heating and cooling energy use. The principal components of heating loads are infiltration through the building and conduction losses through building envelope components, including walls, roofs, floors, slabs, windows, and doors. Cooling loads, however, are dominated by solar gains through the windows. Outside air for ventilation and lighting loads are also quite significant.

Since the building envelope has such potential (or liability) for sustainability, it has become a focus of building codes and standards. The design of the building envelope is generally the responsibility of an architect, although others such as contractors or engineers may also do the design. The designer is responsible for making sure the building envelope complies with local standards. Likewise, the building official/inspector is responsible for making sure the building envelope is designed and built in conformance with the standards.

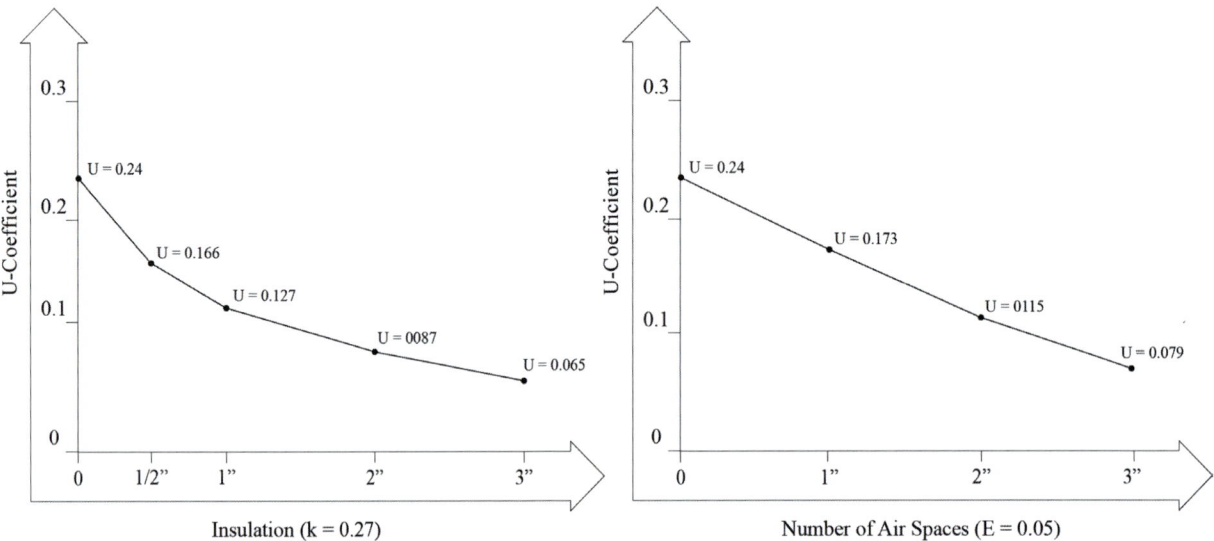

Figure 4.1.3 Effectiveness of air spaces as insulation. (Source: Kuppaswamy Iyengar.)

Building Heat Loss Calculations [2]

The effectiveness of a building's response to temperature will vary with both the external climatic variables and with properties of the building's construction. All building materials have varying abilities to resist the flow of heat and may be classed as insulation if they are used *especially* to reduce or delay heat flow. If the material reduces the total amount of heat flow, i.e., decreases the amplitude, it is referred to as "resistance" insulation. If it delays the passage of heat with respect to time, i.e., causes a shift in phase, it can be termed "capacity" insulation. This discussion is limited to resistance insulation, the generally preferred method of controlling heat transfer through composite construction.

A building gains and loses heat through a variety of paths. In order for the architect to determine how well a building performs in terms of energy conservation he or she must understand the nature and magnitude of those pathways for a particular design. A good rule is to "insulate, then isolate," or in other words, reduce your unwanted heat gains and losses and then add

solar gain as needed. Figure 4.1.4 shows the various paths of heat transfer in a typical house between inside and outside.

$$Qscemp +/- Qinfil = \text{net heat flow}$$

Qs = solar heat gain
Qc = conduction heat flow
Qe = electrical heat (lights, equipment)
Qm = miscellaneous heat gains (pilot lights, gas stoves, etc.)
Qr = people-generated heat
$Qinfil$ = ventilation and infiltration heat flow

The direction of heat flow for conduction and ventilation is dependent on the temperature differences between inside and outside. A positive sign indicates heat flow or gain *to* the building from the warmer exterior, while a negative sign indicates heat flow or loss *from* the building to the cooler ambient temperature outside. Consequently, note the sign changes in the formulas presented below:

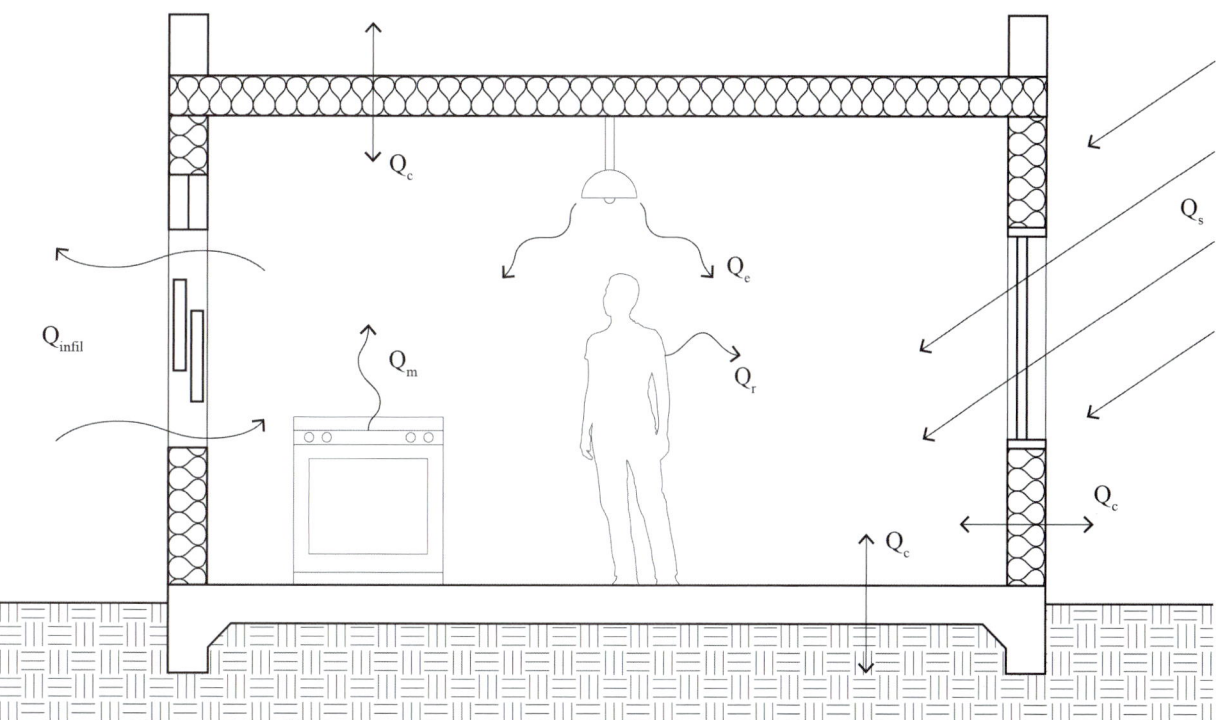

Figure 4.1.4 Paths of heat transfer.
(Source: Professor Stephen D. Dent, University of New Mexico, School of Architecture and Planning.)

Winter (typical case when outside is colder than inside):

$$Q\ total = +\ Qs - Qc + Qe + Qm + Qr - Qinfil$$

Summer (typical case when outside is warmer than inside):

$$Q\ total = +\ Qs + Qc + Qe + Qm + Qr + Qinfil$$

Importance of Understanding Heat Transfer in Buildings

Here, we follow the example of heat loss calculations for a small building. First, we will calculate heat loss for individual surfaces of a building, then use total heat loss figures to determine whether or not modifications are needed to the design. Once modified heat loss figures are recalculated, these numbers can be used to determine energy use over an entire heating season. Finally, use of online sources reveals the energy efficiency of the design or building as compared to energy-use profiles for typical commercial and residential buildings.

Example: Heat Loss Calculations for a Small Building [3]

Following are the necessary steps to determine heat loss from a building:

- Calculate heat loss for individual surfaces.
- Calculate total heat loss for the entire building from conduction and convection.
- Determine if modifications for the building surfaces are necessary.
- Find out modified heat loss after recalculation.
- Use this information to determine energy use over a heating season.
- Use online sources to reveal the energy efficiency of the design or building as compared to energy-use profiles for typical commercial and residential buildings.

Calculating heat loss for individual surfaces of a building provides the basis for calculating the overall heat loss, or heat load, for a building. The following example illustrates one of the methods used to calculate the heat load of a small building.

To calculate the overall heat loss (or heat load) of a building, sum the losses through all surfaces and cracks. The heat load of a building depends on its insulation and construction, and varies with the outside temperature and wind velocity.

As an illustration, consider a drafty, uninsulated, wood-frame building. Assume it is 50 feet long and 30 feet wide, as shown in the plan (Figure 4.1.5). It has uninsulated stud walls and a hardwood floor above a ventilated crawl space. The ceiling has acoustical tile but is otherwise uninsulated, and it sits below a low,

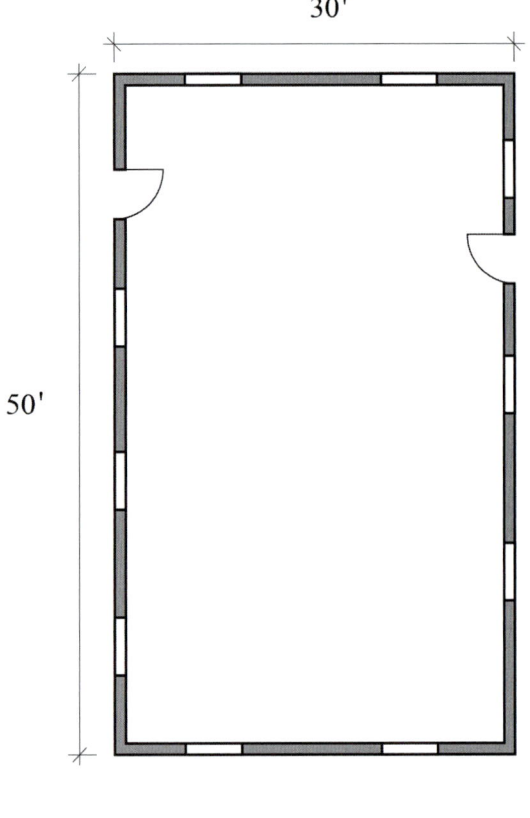

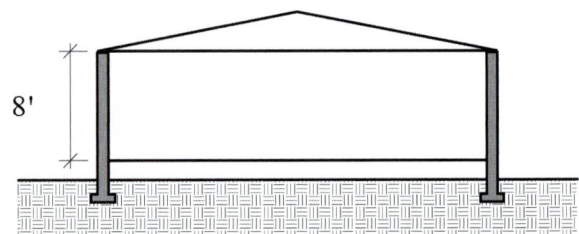

Figure 4.1.5 Plan and section of a small building. (Source: Kuppaswamy Iyengar.)

Building assembly	U-value		Ref in MEEB
1. Uninsulated stud wall	0.23	See earlier discussion to compute U-values including air films	Calculate from example
2. Single pane 1/8" glass windows	1.13	Including resistances of outside and inside air films	Table E.15
3. Oak doors 1" thick	0.59	R = 0.61 for the door plus inside and outside air films	Table E.10
4. Hardwood floor	0.34	R = 2.94 for finish, felt, wood subfloor and air films	
5. Hardwood floor + carpet	0.24	R = 4.16 all of the above plus carpet	
6. Ceiling and roof	0.24	R = 4.12 comprising eight layers: acoustical tile, gypsum board, attic space, plywood, building paper, asphalt shingles and air film	

Figure 4.1.6 Building construction details. (Source: Kuppaswamy Iyengar.)

pitched roof of plywood and asphalt shingles. The house has ten single-pane, double-hung, wood-sash windows (each 4 feet high by 2.5 feet wide) and two solid oak doors (each 7 feet by 3 feet). Building construction details, U-values of surfaces derived from references or calculations are listed in Figure 4.1.6.

First, we need the U-values of each surface. An uninsulated stud wall has a U-value of 0.23. Again, from Appendix E[1], U = 1.13 for single-pane windows, and R = 0.61 for a 1" oak door. Adding the resistance of the inside and outside air films, we get R_t = 1.69 or U = 1/1.69 = 0.59 for the doors.

The calculation of the U-values of the floor and ceiling is a bit more involved. For that, refer to the detailed "example calculation" (*see determining composite R-values, above*). The hardwood floor has three layers – interior hardwood finish, felt, and wood subfloor – and still air films above and below. The resistances of all five layers are added to give R_t = 2.94, or U = 1/2.94 = 0.34. However, about half the floor area is covered by carpets (R = 4.16, including the rubber pad), and this half has a U-value of 0.24. Finally, the total resistance of the ceiling and roof is the sum of the resistances of eight different layers, including the acoustical tile, gypsum board, attic space, plywood, building paper, asphalt shingles, and the inside and outside air films. These add to R_t = 4.12, and the U-value of the ceiling is U = 1/4.12 = 0.24.

For a 1 °F temperature difference between indoor and outdoor air, the conduction heat loss through each surface is the product of the (area of the surface) times the (U-value of the surface). If the design temperature is 35 °F, for example, multiply by 30 (= 65

– 35) to get the design heat loss through that surface. The conduction heat losses through all surfaces are summarized in Figure 4.1.7.

Infiltration heat losses are calculated using Q-values from Appendix E, "Estimated Overall Infiltration Rates for Small Buildings." Double-hung poorly fitted wood-sash windows have a Q-value of 111 in a 15 mph wind. Around poorly fitted doors, the infiltration rate is twice that: 220 ft³/hr, for each foot of poorly fitted opening. And there is still some infiltration through cracks around window and doorframes, with a Q-value of 11.

These Q-values are then multiplied by the heat capacity of a cubic foot of air (0.018 Btu/ft³/°F) and the total length of each type of crack to get the infiltration heat loss. *Note that only windows and doors on two sides of the building (that is five windows and one door) are used to get total crack lengths because the wind is blowing from one side of the building.* The infiltration heat losses through all cracks are also summarized in Figure 4.1.7.

In a 15 mph wind, the conduction heat loss of this building is 1,195 Btu/hr for a 1 °F temperature difference between indoor and outdoor air. Under the same conditions, the infiltration loss is 244 Btu/hr – or a total heat loss of (1,195 + 244) 1,441 Btu/hr/°F. Over an entire day, the building loses 24 (hours) times 1,441 (Btu per hour) for each 1 °F temperature difference, or 43,225 Btu per degree day. Under design conditions of 35 °F and a 15 mph wind, the heat load of this building is 43,225 Btu/hr (= 35,850 + 7,375). The furnace has to produce almost 43,225 Btu/hr to keep this building comfortable during such times (Figure 4.1.7)

Surface	Area (ft²)	U-value (Btu/hr/ft²/°F)	Conduction Heat Losses:*	
			1°F temp diff (Btu/hr/°F)	35 °F outside (Btu/hr)
Walls	1,138	0.23	262	7,860
Windows	100	1.13	113	3,390
Doors	42	0.59	25	750
Bare floor	750	0.34	255	7,650
Carpeted floors	750	0.24	180	5,400
Ceiling	1,500	0.24	360	10,800
Total Conduction Heat Losses			**1,195**	**35,850 (83 percent)**

Crack Around	Length (ft)	Q-value (ft³/hr/ft)	Infiltration Heat Losses:*	
			1°F temp diff (Btu/hr/°F)	35 °F outside (Btu/hr)
Window sash	65	111	130	3,900
Door	20	220	79	2,376
Window and door frames	85	11	17	499
Other	–	–	20	600
Total Infiltration Heat Losses			**246**	**7,375 (17 percent)**

*NOTE: All calculations assume 15 mph wind.

Figure 4.1.7 Summary of heat loss in the building.
(Source: Kuppaswamy Iyengar.)

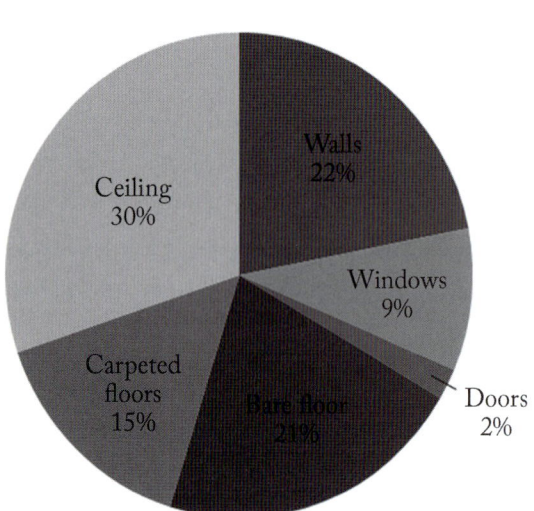

Figure 4.1.8 Conduction losses (83%).
(Source: Kuppaswamy Iyengar.)

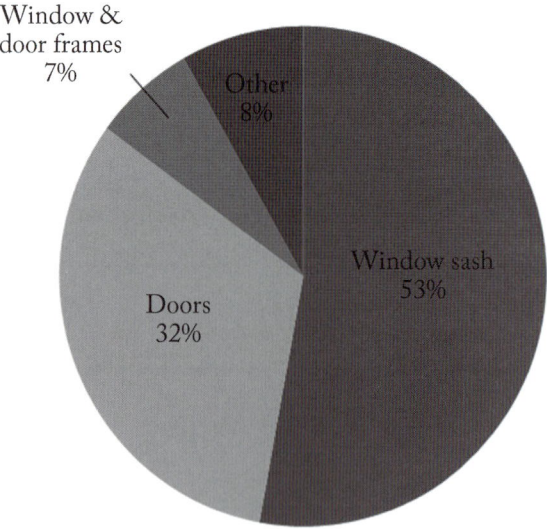

Figure 4.1.9 Infiltration losses (17%).
(Source: Kuppaswamy Iyengar.)

We see from this example that construction and insulation, as well as outside conditions, affect heat loss and as a result impact the energy efficiency of the building envelope. Again, note that conduction losses for this building are 83 percent (Figure 4.1.8), while infiltration losses account for 17 percent (Figure 4.1.9) of the total heat loss.

By making the following simple design or retrofit modifications the energy performance of this building can be significantly improved (see Figure 4.1.10).

| Surface | Area (ft²) | U-value (Btu/hr/ft²/°F) | Conduction Heat Losses* | |
			1°F temp diff (Btu/hr/°F)	35° outside (Btu/hr)
Walls	1,138	0.14	159	4,770
Windows	100	0.81	81	2,430
Doors	42	0.59	25	750
Bare floor	0	0.34	0	0
Carpeted floors	1,500	0.24	360	10,800
Ceiling	1,500	0.15	225	6,750
Total Conduction Heat Losses			850	25,500 (89 percent)

| Crack around | Length (ft) | Q-value (ft³/hr/ft) | Infiltration Heat Losses* | |
			1°F temp diff (Btu/hr/°F)	35°F outside (Btu/hr)
Window sash	0	111	0	0
Door	20	220	79	2,376
Window and door frames	0	11	0	0
Other	–	–	21	630
Total Infiltration Heat Losses			100	3,006 (11 percent)

*NOTE: All calculations assume 15 mph wind.

Figure 4.1.10 Modified heat loss calculations.
(Source: Kuppaswamy Iyengar.)

1 Add insulation to walls and ceiling.
2 Carpet the entire floor.
3 Double glazing for windows with select coating.
4 Seal (caulking) around window sash and doors.

Final modified heat loss of 25,500 + 3,006 = 28,506 Btu/hr is 66 percent of the original 43,225 Btu/hr, which is a *34 percent reduction in energy use*. In more detailed analysis direct heat gain from windows and internal loads (people, lights, plug loads, pilot lights, gas stoves, etc.) will tend to lower the total loss values. Computer simulation programs will account for these types of loads as well as exact building orientation and hour-by-hour climate changes.

Before we can assess our sample building design's energy efficiency, we must consider requirements for heating over a full day and for the heating season. The heat loss we have calculated is only for one hour. A designer should account for heating for 24 hours per day, as well as the entire heating season. To complete this calculation we need to address two more issues:

1 Net load coefficient (NLC): defined as the amount of heat that would be required to maintain the air temperature per day.

$$28,506 \times 24 \text{ hours} = 684,144 \text{ Btu/day}$$

2 To determine the heating load for the entire season requires calculating heating degree days. A heating degree day is defined as the difference between the base temperature of 65 °F and the daily average temperature of a location. These numbers are added per month for the entire season.

For example, the number of heating degree days for Albuquerque in January is 955, for February 700, and March 561. For the entire heating season the total is 3,597 heating degree days, which includes other heating months.

From this information a designer can calculate the total heat required for the entire season: (850 + 100) × 24 hours/day × 3,597 degree days = 82,011,600 Btu/year or 82,011,000/1500 (area of the building) = 54,674 Btu/sq.ft/year (EUI for this building).

The question remains, is this building energy efficient or not? To determine the answer we need to know about *Target Finder* and the *Energy Utilization Index (EUI)*. For any selected sustainable building this number should be less than the number from Target Finder.

Energy Utilization Index (EUI) and Target Finder

The US EIA has established statistical data on energy use for typical buildings, known as the 2003 Commercial Building Energy Consumption Survey (CBECS) (Figure 4.1.11) and the 2001 Residential Building Energy Consumption Survey (RECS).

To assess what should be the target energy use for any selected building there are two options:

1. *Target Finder program by Energy Star*. This is an online tool for target setting and rating during the design phase. Target Finder is a no-cost online tool that enables architects and building owners to set energy targets and receive an EPA energy performance score for projects during the design process, found at: *www.energystar.gov/index.cfm?c=new_bldg_design.bus_target_finder.*

   A designer can establish what the energy use for a proposed building should be in comparison

to a CBECS building and then make changes to the building envelope to lower the target. When the modified EUI is at 75 percent of the target, that building will be eligible for the Energy Star award. The EPA is constantly working to expand the number of building types for which the energy performance rating is offered.

2. *Portfolio Manager*. This is an online database for actual energy use from utility bills for rating and benchmarking over time. The rating system is currently available for K–12 schools, offices, courthouses, warehouses, supermarkets, residence halls/dormitories, retail, different healthcare facilities (acute care and children's hospitals, and medical offices) and many other building types.

   Even if a building does not fit into these categories, it can still be benchmarked and receive an EUI score to determine if it is at, below, or above a national, weather-normalized, EUI for that building type.

Lessons from a Model Energy Efficiency Standard (Title 24) from California

California's Title 24, initiated in 1998, reveals advanced thinking and deep awareness in its treatment of energy and environmental standards. Typically, this standard is revised frequently, but as it stands now the present standard of 2008 will be updated in 2013. Many local standards could be designed around the California model to better support sustainability in the USA and abroad. The US National Academy of Sciences has urged the entire country to follow California's lead on such efforts, saying that conservation and efficiency should be the chief element in energy and global warming policy. Their first efficiency recommendation is simple: Adopt nationwide energy-efficient building codes. Energy-efficiency improvements will not only increase comfort levels and save money, but will also play a vital role in creating and maintaining a healthy environment. Title 24 requirements not only serve as a progressive model and source for best practices nationwide, but they also inform many of the strategies for sustainable design proposed in this book.

The California Public Utility Commission's (CPUC) California Long Term Energy Efficiency

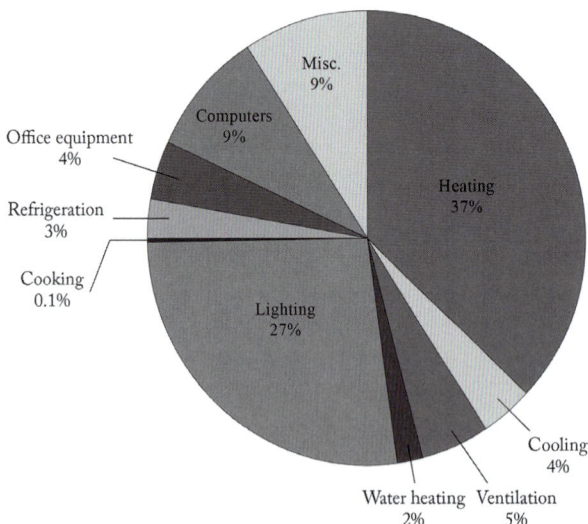

Figure 4.1.11   CBECS energy-use profile indicates typical energy use in commercial buildings. (Source: US EIA.)

Strategic Plan, dated July 2008, endorses the Energy Commission's *"zero net energy"* goals for all newly constructed homes by 2020 and for all newly constructed commercial buildings by 2030. The California Investor Owned Utilities are now implementing public goods-funded incentive programs that support the implementation of this strategic plan. Also, the California Energy Commission is progressively improving the Title 24 standards toward "Zero Net Energy" buildings.

The Title 24 Energy Standards have both mandatory measures and prescriptive requirements that affect the design of the building envelope. These requirements establish a minimum level of performance, which can be exceeded by advanced design options or construction practices. This standard does not compromise comfort, economy, or environmental benefit.

Summary

Designing building forms is a complex process involving form, function, and aesthetic requirements. Loads from the building envelope, especially windows and skylights, are among the most significant loads that affect heating and cooling energy use, and thus can greatly impact energy savings. Technical understanding of heat loss and heat gain is an essential requirement to properly design a building envelope and to assess its performance. *R-value* is a measure of a material's resistance to heat transfer by conduction – the higher the R-value, the better its insulating properties. The reciprocal of this R-value is conductance, termed as U-value. These calculations are helpful in planning and determining the effectiveness of the building envelope design. California's 2013 Title 24 is an example of a model standard that exceeds typical local standards that designers must meet for building envelope design. By determining the Energy Utilization Index, a designer can decide on changes to the building elements for sustainability.

References

[1] Benjamin Stein, John Reynolds, Walter Grondzik, Alison Kwok, *Mechanical and Electrical Equipment for Buildings*, 10th edition (New York: John Wiley and Sons, 2009).

[2] Stephen D. Dent, Class notes, School of Architecture & Planning, University of New Mexico, 2010.

[3] Bruce Anderson and Michael Riordan, *The Solar Home Book* (Harrisville, NH: Cheshire Books, 1976).

Further Reading

California Energy Commission, *Building Energy Efficiency Standards, Compliance Manual* (California: California Energy Commission, 2008).

Rob Bolin, *Sustainability of the Building Envelope* (New York: Whole Building Design Group, 2009).

Edward Mazria, *The Passive Solar Energy Book* (Emmaus, PA: Rodale Press, 1979).

Rocky Mountain Institute, *Green Developments* (Golden, CO: RMI, 2001).

Web Support

www.c2es.org/technology/factsheet/Building Envelope

www.wbdg.org/resources/env_sustainability.php

http://buildingsdatabook.eren.doe.gov/CBECS.aspx

www.greenbiz.com/

www.mckinsey.com/client_service/electric_power_and_natural_gas/latest_thinking/unlocking_energy_efficiency_in_the_us_economy

Exercises

1 Determine the R-value for a wall assembly consisting of 1" stucco, 5/8" plywood sheathing, 5.5" fiber-glass batt insulation, 2" × 6" studs of Douglas fir and 0.5" gypsum board.

2 Using the EPA's *Target Finder* tool, determine the annual target energy use for a 150,000 sq.ft commercial building in Dallas, TX.

4.2   The Role of Insulation

Proper insulation of any building envelope will stem the flow of heat or cold from outside. Determining whether insulation is adequate depends on a number of factors: where it is installed, how it is installed, and what and how much material is used. Just providing higher insulation for roofs alone can be enormously beneficial. A study from Bayer's (supplier of insulating materials) material science division – *Energy and Environmental Impact Reduction Opportunities for Existing Buildings with Low-Slope Roofs* – shows that higher insulation levels in commercial roofs can contribute to significant energy savings and carbon dioxide emission reductions. If 1.5 billion square feet of roofs are replaced for each of the next five years (for a total of 7.5 billion square feet of roofs):

- the energy savings would be 0.08 quads at the site (0.17 quads of source energy), and the 20-year cumulative energy savings would be 0.47 quads (1.03 quads of source energy). One quad is equal to 1 quadrillion BTU (about 1 percent of the total US energy consumption in 2005); and
- the reduction in carbon dioxide emissions, based on source energy, over the first five years would be 12.2 million metric tons (MMT), and 73.5 MMT over the cumulative 20-year time period (equal to the carbon dioxide emissions from an average coal-fired power plant over 16 years).

Insulation is the product that can provide the greatest return and offer the most carbon abatement, according to the McKinsey Report, "Pathway to a Low-Carbon Economy," which has received support from ten leading global companies. Designers with a working knowledge of basic forms of insulation can reduce energy use and carbon emissions and support sustainability.

Basic Forms of Thermal Insulation

Types of thermal insulation include flexible blankets or batts, rigid foam boards, loose-fill, sprayed foam, cellulose, and radiant barriers/reflective systems.

Blankets, in the form of *batts* or rolls (Figure 4.2.1), are flexible products made from mineral fibers.

Blankets are also made from mineral wool, plastic fibers, and natural fibers such as cotton and sheep's wool. They are available in widths suited to standard spacing of wall studs and attic or floor joists. Batts with a special flame-resistant facing are available in various widths for basement walls where insulation will be left exposed. They are available with or without vapor retarder facings, in various thicknesses. High-performance, medium- and high-density fiberglass blankets have R-values between 3.7 and 4.3 per inch of thickness.

Foam boards and *rigid* insulation are made from fibrous materials or plastic foams that are pressed or extruded into board-like forms and molded pipe coverings. These provide thermal and acoustical insulation, strength with low weight, and coverage with few heat loss paths. Such boards may be faced

Figure 4.2.1   Proper insulation will stem the flow of heat or cold from outside. (a) batt insulation; (b) foam board. (Source: http://en.wikipedia.org.)

with a reflective foil that reduces heat flow when next to an air space. Molded expanded polystyrene (MEPS) is a closed-cell material that can be molded into many everyday items, such as coffee cups and shipping materials, or large sheets of insulation. R-values range from 3.8 to 4.4 per inch of thickness. Since spaces between the foam beads can absorb moisture, a vapor barrier is necessary if water transmission through the insulation is a potential condition. MEPS is often used as the insulation for structural insulated panels (SIPS) and insulating concrete forms (ICFS).

Blown-in or loose-fill insulation includes loose fibers or fiber pellets that are blown into building cavities or attics using special pneumatic equipment. Another form includes fibers that are co-sprayed with an adhesive to make them resistant to settling. The

blown-in material can provide additional resistance to air infiltration if the insulation is sufficiently dense. Sprayed wall insulation can be effective to deal with the irregularities of wall and ceiling cavities, especially the spaces around pipes, electric cables, junction boxes, and other equipment that is embedded in cavities.

The most common types of materials used in loose-fill insulation include cellulose, fiberglass, and mineral (rock or slag) wool. All of this material is produced using recycled waste products. Cellulose is primarily made from recycled newsprint. Most fiberglasses contain 20–30 percent recycled glass. Mineral wool is usually produced from 75 percent post-industrial recycled content.

Sprayed foam or foamed-in-place (Figure 4.2.2) polyurethane foam insulation can be applied by a

Figure 4.2.2 Sprayed and blown-in insulation.
(Source: (a) US Department of Energy; (b) flickr user Jesus Rodriguez.)

professional applicator using special equipment to meter, mix, and spray into place. Polyurethane foam can also help to reduce air leaks. Also, it is important to select foaming agents that don't use chlorofluorocarbons (CFCS) or hydrochlorofluoro-carbons (HCFCs), which are harmful to the ozone layer. Liquid foam insulation materials are cementa-tious, phenolic, polyisocyanurate (also in boards) and polyurethane.

Liquid foam insulation – combined with a foaming agent – can be applied using small spray containers or in larger quantities as a pressure-sprayed product. Both types expand and harden as the mixture cures. They also conform to the shape of the cavity, filling and sealing it thoroughly. Liquid foam insulation costs more than traditional insulation. Since the foam insulation forms an air barrier it can eliminate some cost associated with weatherization.

Cellulose insulation (Figure 4.2.3) is made from recycled wood fiber, such as newspaper, or discarded cotton fiber from blue jeans. One hundred pounds of cellulose insulation contains 80–85 percent recycled newspaper and the remainder is borax or boric acid and non-toxic fire retardants. Fibers of cellulose insulation are finer than fiberglass, making it easy to fill around cracks and completely fill the voids. In new construction cellulose insulation can be installed using a spray technique. Also, since 2006, an Arizona-based cotton fiber insulation manufacturer (Bonded Logic) and an association of cotton manufacturers, growers, and retailers (Cotton Incorporated) have teamed up to reuse approximately 200 tons of unwanted denim

Figure 4.2.3 Denim insulation.
(Source: Image Courtesy by Bonded Logic Inc.)

from landfill to new homes in the USA, in the form of denim insulation.

Radiant barrier systems are fabricated from aluminum foils with a variety of backings such as kraft paper, plastic film, polyethylene bubbles, or cardboard. The resistance to heat flow depends on the heat flow direction, and this type of insulation is most effective in reducing downward heat flow. Reflective systems, a subset of radiant barrier, are typically located between roof rafters, floor joists, or wall studs. Often, reflective insulation materials have flanges that are to be stapled to the wall studs or to joists in attics or floors. If a single reflective surface is used alone and faces an open space, such as an attic, it is called a *radiant barrier*. Radiant barriers are installed in buildings to reduce summer heat gain and winter heat loss. They are more effective in hot climates than in cool climates. All radiant barriers must have a low emittance (0.1 or less) and high reflectance (0.9 or more). Since reflective insulation materials will conduct electricity, one must avoid making contact with any bare electrical wiring.

Radiant Barriers in Ceilings

In the performance approach, radiant barriers are modeled (in computer simulations) as separate adjust-ments to the heating U-factor and the cooling U-factor.

Radiant barrier construction practice (Figure 4.2.4) dictates that a radiant barrier must have an emittance of 0.05 or less and must be certified by the Department of Consumer Affairs. The most common way of meeting the radiant barrier requirement is to use roof sheathing that has a radiant barrier bonded to it in the factory. Oriented strand board (OSB) is the most common material available with a factory-applied radiant barrier. The sheathing is installed with the radiant barrier (shiny side) facing down toward the attic space. Alternatively, a radiant barrier material that meets the same ASTM test and moisture perfo-ration requirements that apply to factory-laminated foil can be field-laminated. Field lamination must use a secure mechanical means of holding the foil to the bottom of the roof decking, such as staples or nails that do not penetrate all the way through the roof deck material.

Other acceptable methods are to drape a foil-type radiant barrier over the top of the top chords before the sheathing is installed, stapling the radiant barrier between the top chords after the sheathing is installed, and stapling the radiant barrier to the underside of the truss/rafters (top chord).

Installation of radiant barriers is somewhat more challenging in the case of closed rafter spaces when sheathing is installed that does not include a laminated foil. Foil may be field-laminated after the sheathing has been installed by "laminating" the foil as described above to the roof sheathing between framing members.

Structural Insulated Panels

Structural insulated panels (SIPS) are an advanced method of constructing walls, roofs, and floors. SIPS consist of rigid insulation (usually expanded polystyrene) sandwiched between two sheets of OSB or plywood (Figure 4.2.5). Little or no structural framing penetrates the insulation layer. Panels are typically manufactured at a factory and shipped to the job site in assemblies that can be as large as 8 ft by 20 ft.

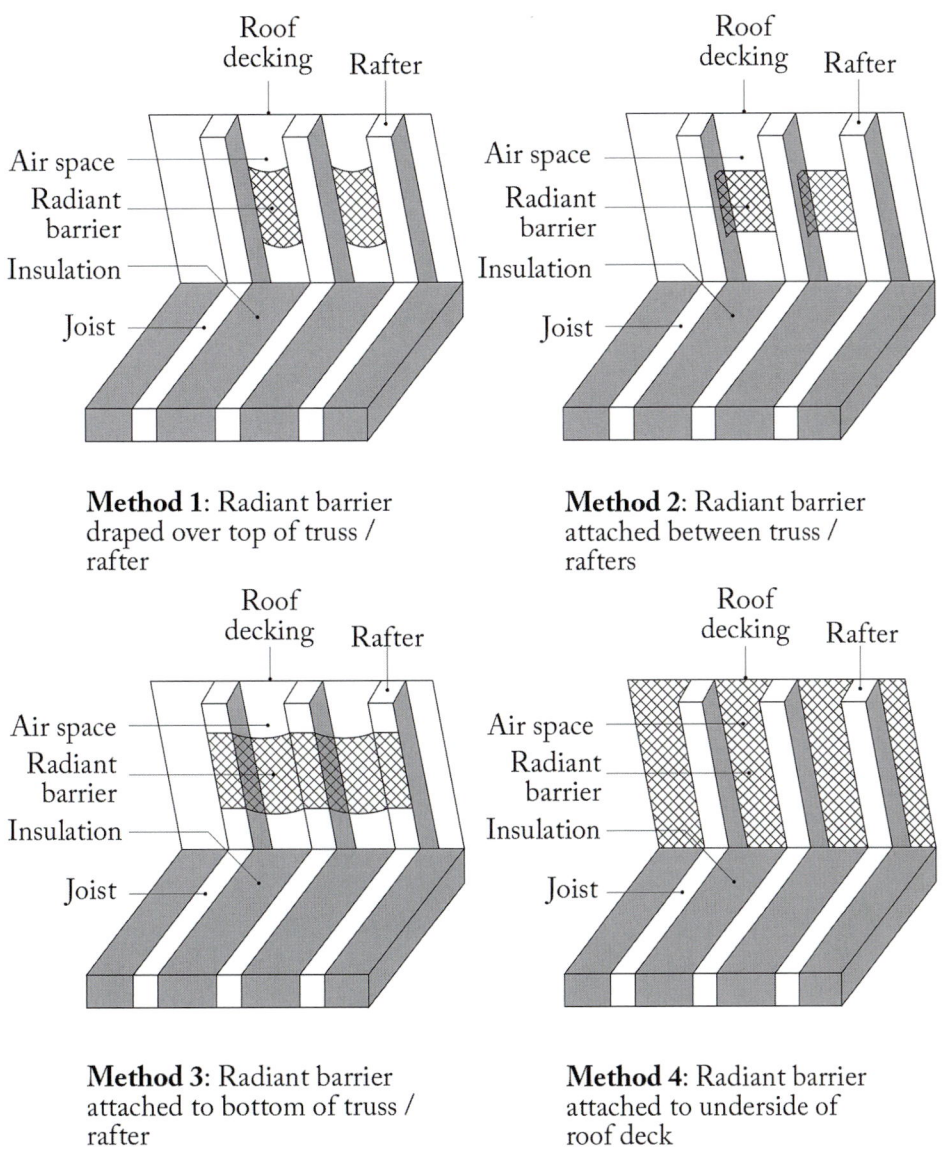

Method 1: Radiant barrier draped over top of truss / rafter

Method 2: Radiant barrier attached between truss / rafters

Method 3: Radiant barrier attached to bottom of truss / rafter

Method 4: Radiant barrier attached to underside of roof deck

Figure 4.2.4 Methods of installation for radiant barrier.
(Source: California Energy Commission, 2008-005-004 *Residential and Non-residential Standards Building Energy Efficiency Standards, Compliance Manual*, 2008.)

Figure 4.2.5 Composite sandwich structural panel used for testing by NASA.
(Source: https://commons.wikimedia.org.)

In the field the SIPS panels are joined in one of two ways and the choice affects thermal performance. The first way is to use wood spacers at the joints. These spacers allow thermal bridging but they are spaced no closer than 48 inches. The second way of joining SIPS panels is to use an OSB spline. With this technique, the insulation is notched or routed just in the back of the OSB panels on each side. An OSB strip is then inserted into the pocket on each side of the panel and the assembly is fastened together with wood screws. Because of its tight SIPS construction, Burnside Inn at Dexter, MI (Figure 4.2.6) is 63 percent more energy efficient than 2006 buildings and also has excellent indoor air quality.

Straw Bale Construction

Recently, the California Legislature and a few other states adopted building codes for houses with walls constructed of straw bales. These states provided guidelines for moisture content, bale density, seismic bracing, weather protection, and other structural requirements. The thermal mass benefit of straw bale construction can be credited only through the use of the computer performance compliance approach

Figure 4.2.6 A SIPS construction: Burnside's Inn (residence), Dexter, MI.
(Source: Fireside Home Construction.)

by modeling straw bale construction using the heat capacity characteristics of the straw bales given below. Straw bales that are 23 inches by 16 inches are assumed to have a thermal resistance of R-30, whether stacked so the walls are 23 inches wide or 16 inches wide.

Performance data on other sizes of bales are not available, but Oak National Laboratory plans to conduct additional tests. The minimum density of load-bearing walls is 7.0 pounds per cubic foot, and this value or the actual density may be used for modeling straw bale walls in the performance approach. Specific heat is set to 0.32 Btu/lb/°F. Volumetric heat capacity (used in some computer programs) is calculated as density times specific heat. At a density of 7 lb/ft³, for example, the volumetric heat capacity is 2.24 Btu/ft³/°F. The minimum dimension of the straw bales when placed in the walls must be 22 inches by 16 inches. There are no restrictions on how the bales are stacked. Due to the higher resistance to heat flow across the grain of the straw, a bale laid on edge with a nominal 16-inch horizontal thickness has the same R-value (R-30) as a bale laid flat.

How Much Insulation?

New construction and existing buildings will require different types of assessments. For new construction, determining how much insulation to use and how thick it should be depends on the method of assessment a designer has chosen to follow, either a performance method or prescriptive method. Local standards will most likely apply to the prescriptive method of assessment as well as recommendations from *2013 Title 24* of the California Standard, if a designer wants to be stringent. For the performance method, a designer or his/her consultant should be proficient in using the following types of energy modeling software to determine the required level of insulation and manipulate the options in wall surfaces, windows, and infiltration:

- DOE2/eQuest
- Energy Plus
- Autodesk: Ecotect™/Project Vasari
- EnergyPro
- Green Building Studio

- Blast/Energy 10
- Trane's Trace + Carrier's HAP
- RemRate & HEED (for Residential)

For existing structures, it can be difficult to see insulation in finished walls and other areas. Two simple ways to assess insulation are to remove a power outlet cover or to drill a hole in a closet or hidden area. By identifying the type of insulation and measuring the thickness of insulation, resistance to heat transfer, R-value, can be ascertained or calculated from Figure 4.2.7 (see also tables E10 and E15 in MEEB [1]), or by simply adding R-values for each additional inch of material. Alternatively, a local building professional with infrared technology can give an accurate reading of the insulation's effective value.

What Kind of Insulation to Use?

A designer has several tools to use in making the proper insulation determinations. From a designer's point of view, what trade-offs are considered in the final selection of insulation? Obviously, choosing a ceiling with high walls and greater ceiling surface area will require large quantities of insulation materials, which involves higher costs. Once the designer has identified the location of the areas in a building requiring insulation and has determined what R-value is needed, then it is time to decide what type of insulation to use. One should consider the several forms of insulation available, their R-values, and the thickness needed. Note that for a given type and weight of insulation, the thicker it is, the higher its R-value.

The EPA's recommended levels of insulation for different heating types in some wood-frame building envelope components are listed in Figure 4.2.8.

Construction Recommendations for Different Insulation Applications

A number of basic requirements apply to insulation in general:

- Insulating materials must be certified and labeled by the manufacturer.
- Urea-formaldehyde foam insulation may be

R-Value for Typical Building Materials	
Thermal Resistance	**R Value (ft² · °F · h/Btu)**
Concrete	0.10
Stone	0.05 - 0.10
Brick	0.10 - 0.35
Hardwood	0.9
Softwood/plywood	1.25
Particle board	0.85 - 1.85
Insulating board	2.30 - 2.60
Sidings	0.80 - 1.00
Asphalt shingles	0.44
Wood shingles	0.94
Built-up roofing	0.70 - 0.90
Rock wool	3.20 - 3.70
Mineral wool or fiber batt	2.90
Cellulose	3.20 - 3.70
Lightweight aggregate concrete	1.00 - 2.00
Cement board	1.50 - 2.30
Stucco / plaster	0.20
Gypsum / plaster board	0.90
Fiberglass	3.16
Fiberboard	3.45
Polystyrene - extruded	5.00 - 5.40
Polystyrene - expanded	3.85 - 5.40
Polyurethane foam	5.80 - 7.70
Building paper / felt	0.06
Cork	2.00
Ceramic tile	0.15
Vinyl / linoleum / rubber tile	0.64
Synthetic carpet (jewel loop)	3.50 - 5.90
Synthetic carpet (plush)	2.40 - 4.50
Wool carpet	4.50
Fiber / hair / jute cushion	3.88
Flat rubber cushion	2.72
Rippled rubber cushion	1.82
Prime urethane cushion	4.44
Bonded urethane cushion	3.96
Solid wood door	1.56
Single glass window	0.89
Insulating double glass	1.89
Energy plus double glass	4.50

Figure 4.2.7 Typical R-values for building materials.
(Source: US Department of Energy.)

(a)

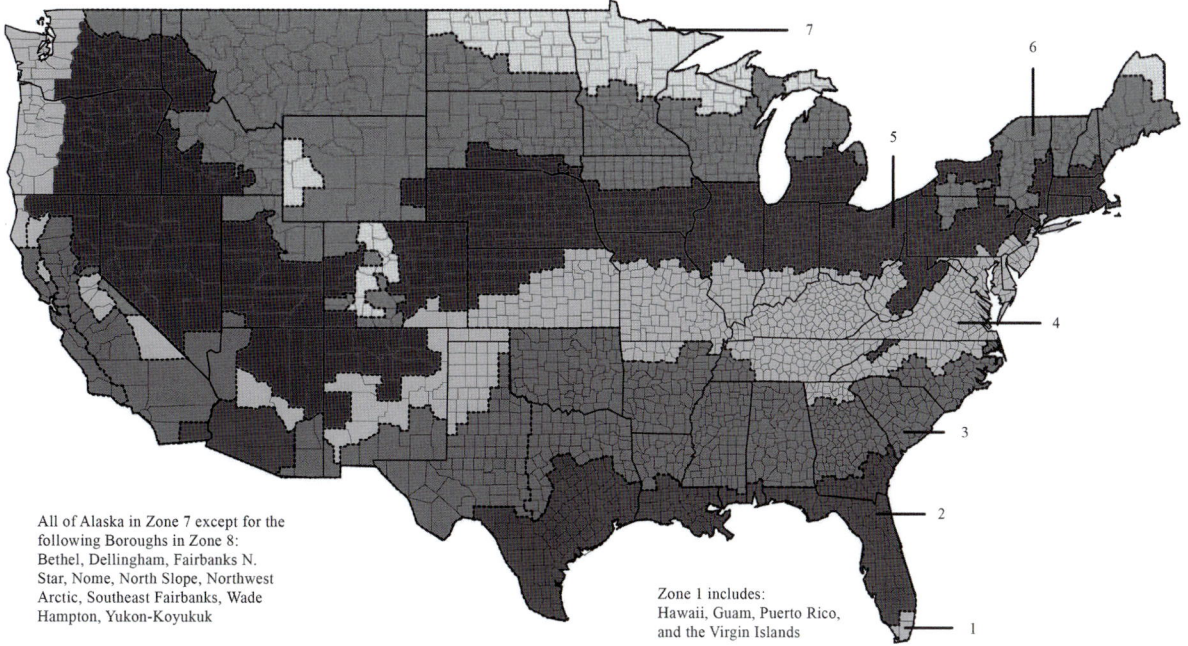

All of Alaska in Zone 7 except for the
following Boroughs in Zone 8:
Bethel, Dellingham, Fairbanks N.
Star, Nome, North Slope, Northwest
Arctic, Southeast Fairbanks, Wade
Hampton, Yukon-Koyukuk

Zone 1 includes:
Hawaii, Guam, Puerto Rico,
and the Virgin Islands

(b)

| Zone | Heating system | Attic | Cathedral ceiling | Wall | | Floor |
				Cavity	Insulation sheathing	
1	All	R30 to R49	R22 to R38	R13 to R15	None	R13
2	Gas, oil, heat pump	R30 to R60	R22 to R38	R13 to R15	None	R13
	Electric furnace					R19-R25
3	Gas, oil, heat pump	R30 to R60	R22 to R38	R13 to R15	None	R25
	Electric furnace				R2.5 to R5	
4	Gas, oil, heat pump	R38 to R60	R30 to R38	R13 to R15	R2.5 to R6	R25-R30
	Electric furnace				R5 to R6	
5	Gas, oil, heat pump	R38 to R60	R30 to R38	R13 to R15	R2.5 to R6	R25-R30
	Electric furnace		R30 to R60	R13 to R21	R5 to R6	
6	All	R49 to R60	R30 to R60	R13 to R21	R5 to R6	R25-R30
7	All	R49 to R60	R30 to R60	R13 to R21	R5 to R6	R25-R30
8	All	R49 to R60	R30 to R60	R13 to R21	R5 to R6	R25-R30

Figure 4.2.8   Recommended levels of insulation by EPA's Energy Star program.
(Source: prepared by Oak Ridge National Laboratory for the US Department of Energy, 2008.)

installed only in exterior walls with an interior vapor barrier.

- Insulating materials installed in exposed applications must have a flame spread of 25 or less and a smoke development rating of 450 or less.

Recommendations for different insulation applications (floors, walls, ceilings) follow.

Floor Insulation

The CEC recommends that raised wood-framed floors (Figure 4.2.9) have at least R-13 insulation installed between framing members, or the construction must have a U-factor of 0.064 or less. The equivalent U-factor is based on R-13 insulation in a wood-framed floor with no crawlspace or buffer zone beneath the floor. If there is a crawlspace under the floor, the equivalent U-factor should be 0.046. Other types of raised floors, except for concrete raised floors, must also meet these maximum U-factors.

Floor insulation should be installed in direct contact with the sub-floor so that there is no air space between the insulation and the floor. Support is needed to prevent the insulation from falling, sagging, or deteriorating. Options for support include netting stapled to the underside of floor joists, insulation hangers running perpendicular to the joists, or other suitable means. Floor insulation should not cover foundation vents. For more detailed information, refer to the California Energy Commission's Title 24 [2].

Wall Insulation

Depending on climate and location, local codes determine the R-values for a building.

Framed walls: In many parts of the USA, prescriptive requirements for framed walls call for R-19 and R-21 in many climates. R-13 insulation is required in the few zones where the climate is mild.

Mass walls: Prescriptive requirements have separate criteria for heavy mass walls. While the standards

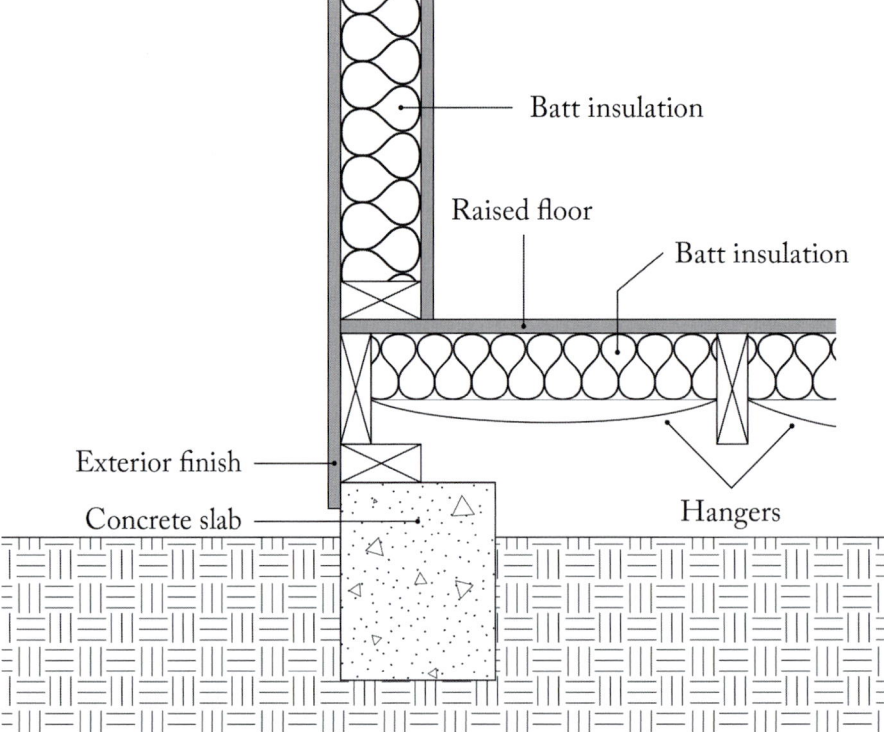

Figure 4.2.9 Raised floor insulation should be installed in direct contact with the sub-floor (no separation between the insulation and the floor).
(Source: California Energy Commission, 2008-005-004 *Residential and Non-residential Standards Building Energy Efficiency Standards, Compliance Manual, 2008.*)

recognize both heavy mass and light mass walls, separate criteria are presented only for heavy mass, those that weigh more than 40 lb/ft². For a light mass wall the assembly must comply with 0.102 U-factors for climate zones that require R-13 for wood-framed walls, or 0.074 for where R-19 is required, or 0.069 where R-21 is required. Those walls that have a heat capacity (HC) greater than or equal to 8.0, and a density greater than 40 lb/ft³, qualify as heavy mass walls.

These points help guide construction practice for wall insulation (Figure 4.2.10):

- Behind tub/shower enclosures these wall sections should be inspected during the framing inspection.
- If kraft or foil-faced insulation is used, it should be installed per manufacturer recommendations to minimize air leakage and avoid sagging of the insulation.
- Wall insulation should extend into the perimeter floor joist (rim joist) cavities along the same plane as the wall.

- If a vapor barrier is required, it must be installed on the conditioned space side of the framing.

Metal framed walls: A change from wood framing to metal framing can significantly affect compliance. Metal and wood framing are not interchangeable. Metal-framed wall construction generally requires a continuous layer of rigid insulation to meet the mandatory minimum wall insulation levels and/or the prescriptive requirements.

Curtain walls in high-rise buildings should perform thermally with respect to conduction, solar radiation, thermal break, and occupant comfort. The curtain wall's thermal performance depends on the glazing infill panel, the frame, construction behind opaque (spandrel and column cover) areas, and the perimeter details.

When highly conductive materials such as aluminum frame are employed, it is common practice to incorporate thermal breaks of low-conductivity materials, traditionally PVC, neoprene rubber, polyurethane, and more recently polyester-reinforced nylon, for improved thermal performance. Some

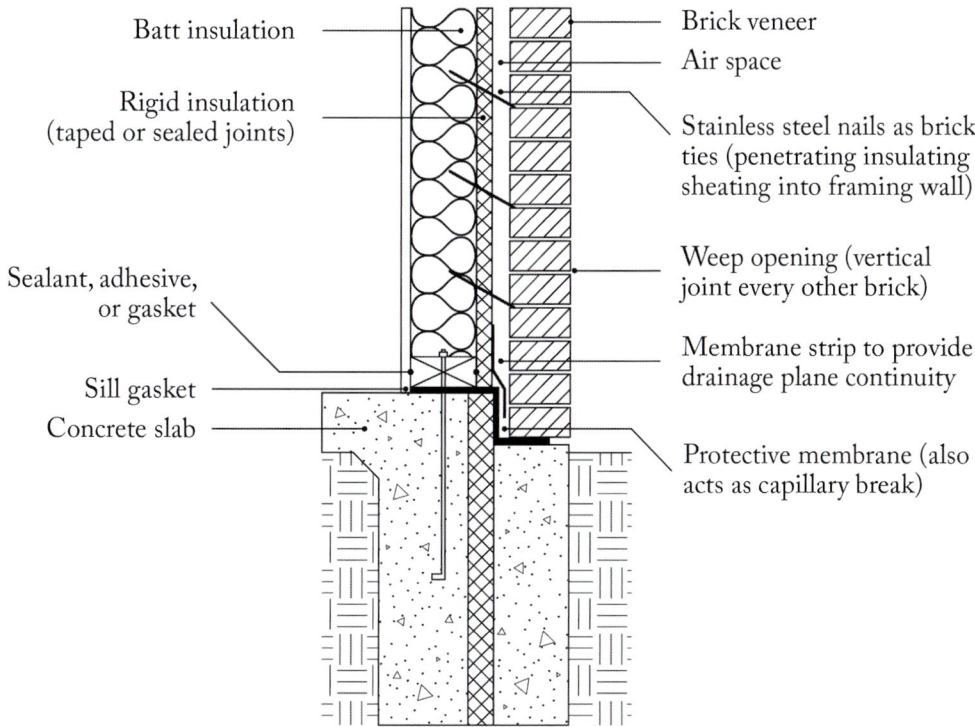

Figure 4.2.10 Wood-framed wall with brick veneer, R-13 to R-19 insulation.
(Source: California Energy Commission, 2008-005-004, *Residential and Non-residential Standards Building Energy Efficiency Standards, Compliance Manual, 2008.*)

thermal breaks shrink, since exterior aluminum frames move differently from interior aluminum. Specially designed mechanical systems are utilized to improve thermal performance and condensation resistance of the curtain wall system. More details of high-performance curtain wall systems will follow in Section 4.4.

Ceiling and Roof Insulation

Standards developed by the California Energy Commission through Title 24 provide guidance for improved energy-efficient performance for most ceiling and roof insulation as shown:

- In the attics of existing buildings, at least R-30 to R-38 should be installed depending on climate zones. Insulation in roof/ceiling constructions should be placed in direct contact with the infiltration barrier. As shown in Figure 4.2.11, the insulation must lie directly on top of the ceiling.
- Typically, wood-framed ceiling/roof construction assemblies must have at least R-19 insulation or a maximum U-factor of 0.051. These standards vary for different parts of the country.

- Designers should make every effort to achieve the weighted average U-factor for the overall ceiling/roof, 0.051 or less or as prescribed by local codes.
- Although standards vary depending on region, typically in new construction the minimum level of insulation applies when the performance method is adopted. Otherwise, the R-19 minimum prescriptive requirements are replaced by R-30 or R-38, depending on climate zone.
- It is recommended by the California Energy Commission that metal-framed and ceiling/roof constructions must have a U-factor of 0.051 or less to be energy efficient.

Wet insulation systems are roofing systems where the insulation is installed above the roof's waterproof membrane. Water can penetrate this insulation material and have an effect on the energy performance of the roofing assembly in wet and cool climates. The insulating R-value of continuous insulation materials installed above the roof's waterproof membrane must be multiplied by 0.8 before choosing the value from standard tables.

For roof structures where a metal deck is in direct

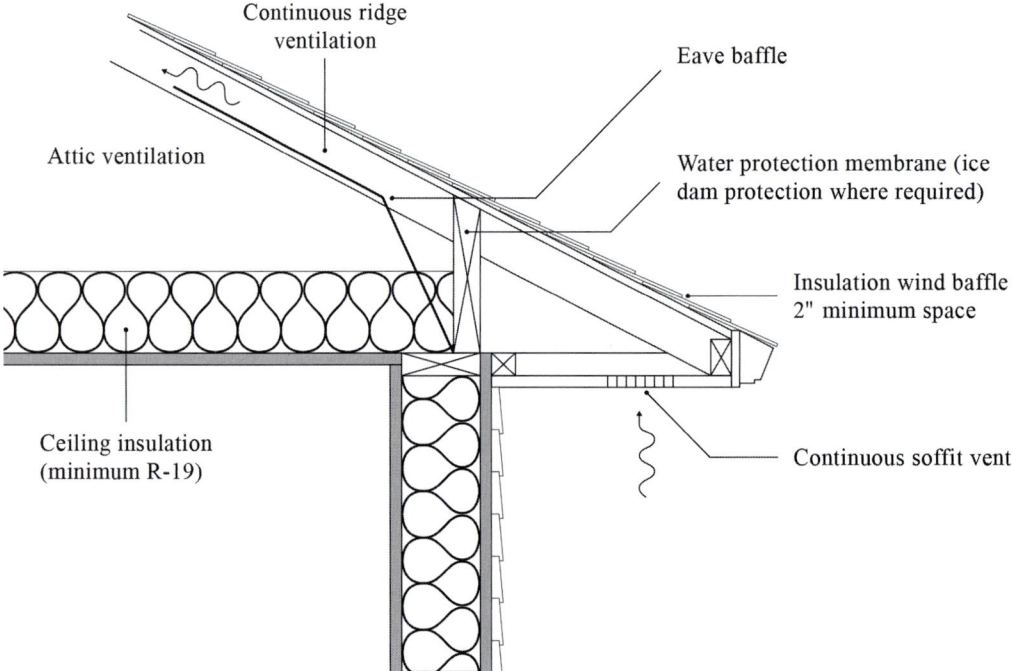

Figure 4.2.11 Ceiling insulation recommendation.
(Source: California Energy Commission, 2008-005-004, *Residential and Non-residential Standards Building Energy Efficiency Standards, Compliance Manual,* 2008.)

contact with metal supporting members, the standard R-value may be used only if the required insulation is continuous over the top of the metal deck or continuous and installed between the metal supports and the metal deck.

Insulation for retrofits: Loose-fill insulation can be installed in either enclosed cavities, such as walls, or unenclosed spaces, such as attics. Installation usually involves using special equipment that blows the insulation through and into the cavity or space. This includes the "two hole" method, which entails drilling two holes spaced vertically between the exterior walls' framing studs. The holes should be 2" in diameter. Working between each stud, drill one hole 16" from the top of the wall. Drill the other hole 24" from the bottom of the wall. Blow the insulation into the holes and then seal the insulation holes. In conventional ceilings, blow the insulation between roof rafters (Figure 4.2.12).

Summary

Insulation types, such as blankets, foam boards, blow-in or loose-fill, sprayed foam, and reflective, all have different methods of installation. R-value recommendations vary by location, and there are different considerations for the insulation of roofs, ceilings, walls, and floors. All insulation supports sustainable performance for building envelopes by stemming the flow of heat or cold into or out of buildings.

References

[1] Benjamin Stein, John Reynolds, Walter Grondzik, Alison Kwok, *Mechanical and Electrical Equipment for Buildings*, 10th edition (New York: John Wiley and Sons, 2009).

[2] California Energy Commission, 2008-005-004, *Residential and Non-residential Standards Building Energy Efficiency Standards, Compliance Manual* (California: CEC, 2008).

Further Reading

Oak Ridge National Laboratory, *Recommended Levels of Building Insulation by Energy Star* (Washington, DC: US Environmental Protection Agency, 2008).

Public Technology, Inc. and US Green Building Council, *Sustainable Building Technical Manual: Green Building Design, Construction and Operation* (Alexandria, VA: Public Technology, Inc., 1996).

Web Support

www.eere.energy.gov
www.buildings.com/article-details/articleid/8692/title/the-importance-of-existing-insulation-technology.aspx
www.nrdc.org/business/design/denim.asp

Exercises

1. Explain the benefits of using "radiant barriers" in building attics and also under basement floors. Your answers should discuss thermal flow in both cases.
2. Determine how much insulation you should use for a residence in your area. Research the applicable building codes and illustrate the insulation requirements for walls, windows, floors, and ceilings.

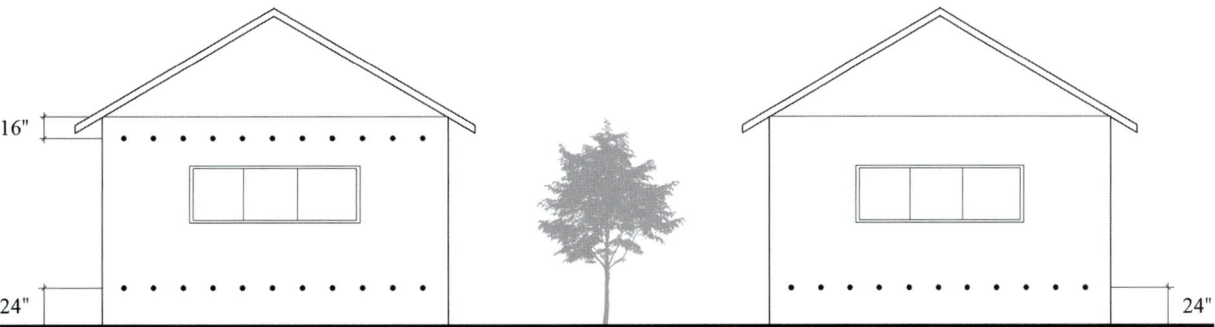

Figure 4.2.12 Insulation for retrofits.
(Source: US Department of Energy.)

4.3   Sustainable Materials and Minimizing Waste

The Beams of New College, Oxford, Gregory Bateson (That is the way to run a culture.)

In 2005 Dr. Robert Glossop, Ph.D, gave a Convocation Address to the graduating students of the College of Social and Applied Human Sciences in Ontario. In that address he narrated an extremely important story about New College, Oxford (see Figure 4.3.1) for the benefit of sustainable designers. He said,

> we simply cannot build a good life, a just economy, a sustainable world, on the basis of quarterly economic indicators, immediate gratification, disposable relationships, four or five year electoral cycles. To live a meaningful life not only takes time; it requires us to think about the small place that we occupy within TIME. There is an illuminating story that was told by Gregory Bateson about New College at Oxford University. It is a little sobering to those of us here in the colonies to realize that New College was built in the 1600s. The ceiling of its Great Hall was supported by 2' × 2' forty foot long oak beams. When Bateson was teaching there in the 1950s, a Committee had been struck to figure out what could be done to salvage the great hall now that its ceiling was about to give way to dry rot and old age. This was, for the principal of the college, an immediate crisis of no small proportion. Fortunately, however, the Committee discovered that there was a College Forester. When apprised of the situation, he said something like this: "It's about time someone would ask us." He continued and explained, "When this building was constructed 350 years ago, the architects had insisted that a grove of oak trees be planted and maintained in order to replace the ceiling beams whenever they might fail." As Bateson said, "That's the way to run a culture."

Figure 4.3.1   The beams in the roof of New College, Oxford. (Source: http://en.wikipedia.org.)

Designers from 350 years ago at New College, Oxford, demonstrated the foresight and whole-system thinking that remain an inspiration today.

The Bateson story teaches us to design buildings for generations of use through thoughtful foresight and planning. In this spirit, this section emphasizes how to build for the long haul through careful selection of materials. A second aspect of materials use is the reduction of waste and toxins generated by building construction, operations, and occupants. This is waste that otherwise would have to be hauled to landfills or incinerated. Specific techniques are purchasing sustainable products for construction and operation of buildings, including products that improve indoor air quality; recycling and reusing construction and demolition debris; and reduction of mercury and other toxins. Once a building is in operation, the waste stream must be assessed in order to target areas that need more sustainable practices. The main goal is to develop a waste reduction plan that serves sustainable aims for the entire life of the building. Procurement should include awareness of the impact of building materials on the environment and whole-system thinking. Prudent designers go through the four Rs – Reduce, Reuse, Recycle, and Rejuvenate – whenever they are in a position to make choices about construction materials.

Environmental Impact of Building Materials and Embodied Energy

Buildings create a large amount of waste through their operation and use. Construction of a typical house produces 2.5 tons of waste and demolition produces 20 tons of waste, all of which ends up in landfills. For sustainable buildings the goal should be to reduce this waste while improving the environment through responsible procurement practices. This goal can be partially met by carefully choosing the materials brought into the site, building with reductions in environmental impacts in mind, and keeping waste at a minimum through efficient design.

Materials selection plays a significant role in sustainable building operation because of the environmental and health consequences associated with the entire lifecycle of materials, including extraction, processing, fabrication, transportation, installation,

building use, and ultimate disposal. These activities pollute water and air, destroy habitat and deplete natural resources. On the positive side, materials containing recycled content create opportunities for new markets, slow the consumption of raw materials and reduce the amount of waste disposal to landfills. Use of local materials reduces transportation impacts and reduces the use of nonrenewable resources, thus supporting healthier societies. Building designers should avoid VOCs (volatile organic compounds) and formaldehyde glues to minimize polluting the atmosphere, thereby developing healthier indoor environments.

A useful measure of the impact of building materials is the lifecycle analysis (LCA) of the individual parts of a building over the life of that building. For example, a fluorescent lamp fixture has three parts: a reflector made up of some metal, a lamp, and a ballast. The reflector lasts over 20 years, while the lamp may be replaced four or five times and the ballast two or three times. The lifecycle cost of this lamp fixture includes the original cost plus replacement of lamps and ballast. This idea can be applied to the entire building and any of its components. Unfortunately at this time there is no commonly accepted standard LCA for materials. For now, the building sector is encouraging the use of LCA with help from the Athena Institute (www.athenasmi.org). The Athena Institute does work for the common good, as seen in the continued development of its LCA design tools, the Impact Estimator and the Eco Calculator.

Criteria for the selection of building materials and components must appreciate aesthetics, performance, availability, and cost. Environmentally conscious designers include an additional component in their specifications: the amount of *embodied energy* required for producing these materials.

Embodied energy is the total energy inputs used throughout a product's lifecycle. The initial embodied energy in buildings represents the nonrenewable energy consumed in the acquisition of raw materials, their processing, manufacturing, transportation to site, and construction. This initial embodied energy has two components: indirect energy used to acquire, process, and manufacture the building materials, including any transportation related to these activities: and direct energy used to transport building products to the site, and then to construct the building (Figure 4.3.2).

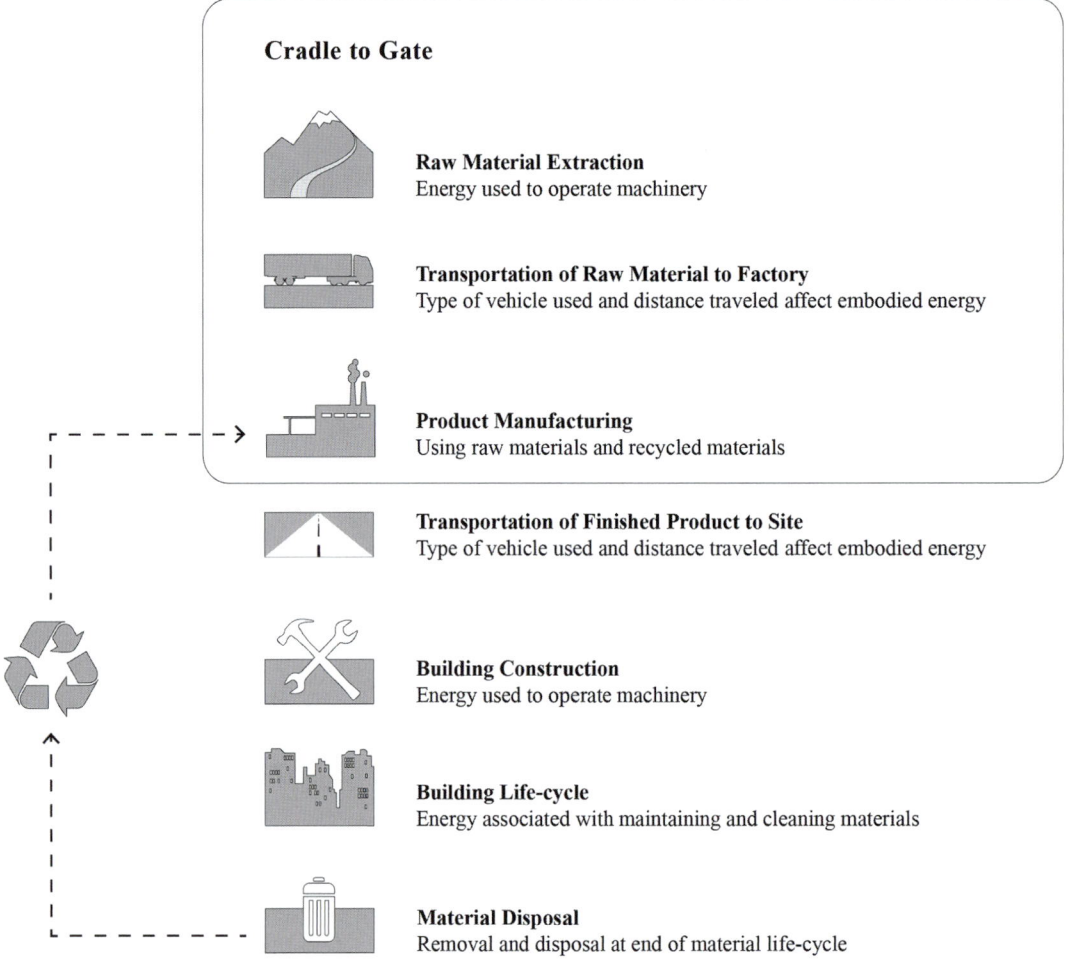

Cradle to Gate

Raw Material Extraction
Energy used to operate machinery

Transportation of Raw Material to Factory
Type of vehicle used and distance traveled affect embodied energy

Product Manufacturing
Using raw materials and recycled materials

Transportation of Finished Product to Site
Type of vehicle used and distance traveled affect embodied energy

Building Construction
Energy used to operate machinery

Building Life-cycle
Energy associated with maintaining and cleaning materials

Material Disposal
Removal and disposal at end of material life-cycle

Figure 4.3.2 Energy inputs throughout a building's life cycle.
(Source: CannonDesign.)

The recurring embodied energy in buildings represents the nonrenewable energy consumed to maintain, repair, restore, refurbish, or replace materials, components or systems during the life of the building.

Embodied energy is typically expressed in MJ/kg, where a megajoule (MJ) equals 0.948 kBtu or 0.278 kWh. Figure 4.3.3 illustrates the embodied energy of common building materials.

Overall use of sustainable building materials selection criteria should concentrate on resource efficiency and affordability, energy efficiency, waste reduction, and indoor air quality.

Resource efficiency includes the use of renewable natural products certified by independent agencies, identifiable recycled content, locally available materials,

and manufactured products that are resource efficient through wise use of energy in the manufacturing process and by keeping waste to a minimum. Efficiency should be encouraged in as many building components as possible. Typical resource-efficient products include wood certified by the Forest Stewardship Council, structural steel having nearly 75 percent of recycled scrap steel, and those products manufactured within a 500-mile radius of the construction site.

An excellent example is the selection of sustainable building materials by Environmental Dynamics, Inc. in Albuquerque, NM (Figure 4.3.4) which includes

- Use of recycled materials found on the property for interiors and site development.

Embodied energy by weight			Embodied energy by volume		
Material	MJ/kg	MJ/m³	Material	MJ/kg	MJ/m³
Aggregate	0.1	150	Straw bale	0.2	31
Straw bale	0.2	31	Cellulose insulation	0.2	112
Soil-cement	0.4	819	Mineral wool insulation	14.6	139
Stone (local)	0.8	2030	Aggregate	0.1	150
Concrete block	0.9	2350	Soil-cement	0.4	819
Concrete (30 Mpa)	1.3	3180	Fiberglass insulation	30.3	970
Concrete (precast)	2.0	2780	Lumber	2.5	1380
Lumber	2.5	1380	Stone (local)	0.8	2030
Brick	2.5	5170	Concrete block	0.9	2350
Cellulose insulation	3.3	112	Concrete (precast)	2.0	2780
Gypsum wallboard	6.1	5890	Concrete (30 Mpa)	1.3	3180
Particle board	8.0	4400	Polystyrene insulation	117.0	3770
Aluminum (recycled)	8.1	21870	Particle board	8.0	4400
Steel (recycled)	8.9	37210	Shingles (asphalt)	9.0	4930
Shingles (asphalt)	9.0	4930	Brick	2.5	5170
Plywood	10.4	5720	Plywood	10.4	5720
Mineral wool insulation	14.6	139	Gypsum wallboard	6.1	5890
Glass	15.9	37550	Aluminum (recycled)	8.1	21870
Fiberglass insulation	30.3	970	Steel (recycled)	8.9	37210
Steel	32.0	251200	Glass	15.9	37550
Zinc	51.0	371280	Carpet (synthetic)	148.0	84900
Brass	62.0	519560	PVC	70.0	93620
PVC	70.0	93620	Paint	93.3	117500
Copper	70.6	631164	Linoleum	116.0	150930
Paint	93.3	117500	Steel	32.0	251200
Linoleum	116.0	150930	Zinc	51.0	371280
Polystyrene insulation	117.0	3770	Aluminum	227.0	515700
Carpet (synthetic)	148.0	84900	Brass	62.0	519560
Aluminum	227.0	515700	Copper	70.6	631164

Figure 4.3.3 Embodied energy in common building materials.
(Source: Post Carbon Institute.)

- All the wood-based products are certified.
- Building materials were further evaluated on the basis of performance, low embodied energy values, and their potential to be diverted from landfills at the end of their usable life.
- Nearly 70 percent of construction and demolition waste was diverted from landfill to recycling or salvaging operations.

- Convenient bins throughout the building facilitate recycling of paper, plastics, and other materials by staff and guests.

Designers have received a LEED® Platinum award for their efforts.

Figure 4.3.4 Environmental Dynamics, Inc. an architectural firm, Albuquerque, NM. (Source: photo by Patrick Coulie.)

Purchase Sustainable Products for Operation and Lifecycle Maintenance

Organizations interested in sustainability should maintain a sustainable purchasing program covering at the bare minimum office paper, office equipment, furniture, and building materials for use in the building and on the site. Such a procurement specifications program contains at least:

1 Forest Stewardship Council (FSC) certified wood;
2 rapidly renewable materials;
3 materials harvested in close proximity to the project;
4 significant percentage of salvaged material from off-site and on-site;
5 post-consumer (at least 10 percent) or post-industrial (20 percent) material;
6 equipment reuse program.

The EPA's Environmentally Preferable Purchasing (EPP) Program urges the federal government to "buy green" and stimulates demand for green products and services; it also assists commercial and residential consumers to make sustainable environmental purchasing decisions along with traditional factors such as performance and price. The EPP Program has summarized information about environmental attributes to look for, procurement guidance, tools, case studies, and other useful resources.

Materials for Interior Air Quality

Since a building's envelope has both external and internal components, issues of indoor air quality (IAQ) also influence choices of materials for maximum sustainability. Designers and building managers should develop both policies and purchasing requirements for product groups: for building materials that are used inside the building for construction, improvements, upgrades, retrofits, renovations, or other construction modifications; for paint and coatings, adhesives, sealants, carpet, composite panels, and agrifiber products. According to LEED®, IAQ can be enhanced by utilizing materials that meet the following principles:

1 low or non-toxic materials that emit few or no carcinogens, reproductive toxicants, or irritants and minimal emissions of VOCs;
2 low-VOC assembly with minimal VOC-producing compounds;
3 moisture-resistant products and systems that inhibit the growth of biological contaminants in buildings;
4 systems or equipment products that promote healthy IAQ by identifying indoor air pollutants or enhancing the air quality, and also low-VOC methods of cleaning.

Energy efficiency can be improved by downsizing operating equipment during the life of the project following these principles:

- Passive design strategies, explained in earlier chapters, such as building shape and orientation, appropriate insulation, passive solar design, and the use of natural lighting for productivity and well-being.
- Use of computer simulations for optimizing building design and electrical and mechanical systems.
- High-efficiency lighting systems with advanced lighting controls.
- Properly sized and energy-efficient heat/cooling systems in conjunction with a thermally efficient building shell which includes high R-value floor, wall, and ceiling insulation, minimal glass on east and west exposures, low-E glass for other windows, light colors for roofing and wall finish; and appropriately sized electric equipment and appliances.
- Alternative renewable energy sources such as photovoltaics, wind energy, and fuel cells that are now available in new products and applications.

Waste Reduction During Building Operation

In addition to careful selection of sustainable building materials, buildings can be operated to minimize waste. To reduce the amount of toxic material reaching the ground and groundwater sources, every building should establish minimum source reduction and recycling program elements and quantify waste stream production volume. For example, overdesigning a building or its systems for redundancy because the designer is ambivalent about the design accuracy will lead to overuse of materials. Hence, a plan to minimize the use of materials at the outset is important to reduce the embodied energy.

- Once the building is occupied, conduct a systematic audit to determine the amounts for paper, glass, plastics, cardboard, and metals in the waste stream. It is a good practice to identify opportunities for source reduction purchasing strategies, collection station equipment, recycling, and occupant education.
- Establish a waste baseline, and then evaluate how each type of waste identified in the waste stream can be reduced through procurement/management policies, reuse, and recycling.

Facilitate the reduction of waste and toxins generated by building occupants and building operations that are hauled to and disposed of in landfills or incineration by the separation, collection, and storage of materials for recycling, including (at a minimum) paper, glass, plastics, cardboard/OCC, metals, batteries, and fluorescent light bulbs. With decent effort it is possible to divert/recycle nearly 50 percent of the total waste stream by weight or volume.

Establishing Recycling Areas

During new construction or renovation, builders, building owners, and managers, after estimating the area required for recycling, should arrange to provide a convenient, easily accessible area that serves the entire building and is dedicated to the separation, collection, and storage of materials for recycling. The recycling area needs to include space for wood, paper, glass, plastics, cardboard, and metals. Identify local waste handlers and buyers for glass, plastic, office paper, newspaper, cardboard, metals, organic wastes, and other waste. Instruct occupants on building recycling procedures. Commitment and dedication is needed to explore source reduction and waste management programs for an existing building if they have not been planned when the structure was initially designed

Minimization of Toxic Products

The products that we use to build, renovate, light, furnish, and clean our buildings must contain as few toxins as possible. A designer should be aware of the product's contents, the sources of its raw materials, emissions during manufacture, the toxins in the final product, and lifespan and recyclability. Minimizing negative environmental impacts requires thought and knowledge about how the products are used to build and maintain, and where they end up. (These are the seven stages of the lifecycle of a building product as shown earlier in Figure 4.3.2.) Decision-makers have the option to select materials that reduce the most significant environmental and health impacts throughout their lifecycles.

Taking Future Needs into Account

To claim sustainability in a building a complete Waste Management Policy should cover any future building retrofit, renovation, or modification on the site. As a first step, quantify by weight construction, demolition, and land-clearing debris that might reach landfill and disposal by incineration. Redirect recyclable recovered resources back to the manufacturing process. Redirect reusable materials to appropriate sites. Efforts should be to divert a significant amount of this waste from landfill and incineration disposal.

Specification writers and construction managers should identify licensed haulers and processors of recyclable materials, markets for salvaged materials, and the cost for recycling, salvaging, and reusing materials.

Summary

Sustainable designs focus on the reduction of waste and toxins generated by construction, operation, and building occupants. Building materials selected can be analyzed for resource efficiency from original extraction, processing, and manufacture, to transport and installation; for recurring costs of operation and maintenance; to eventual disposal and recycling of components at the end of the building's life. Recycling, reusing, and reduction or diversion of the waste stream from landfills all contribute to the efficiency of a building. LEED®, GBI, and others offer many suggestions for the minimization of toxic products such as mercury, VOCs, cleaning, and other building products that affect indoor air quality.

Further Reading

California Department of Resources Recycling and Recovery, *CalRecycle* (Sacramento, CA: California Department of Resources Recycling and Recovery, 2011).

Green Globes Certification, *Green Building Initiative (GBI) for Environmental and Sustainability Assessment* (Portland, OR: Green Globes Certification, 2004).

Owen J. Lewis, *A Green Vitruvius* (London: European Commission, 1999).

Public Technology, Inc. and US Green Building Council, *Sustainable Building Technical Manual: Green Building Design, Construction and Operation* (Alexandria, VA: Public Technology Inc., 1996).

US Green Building Council, "Materials and Resources," in *LEED® Certification for New Commercial Buildings*.

Web Support

www.ciwmb.ca.gov/greenbuilding/Materials
www.cbe.berkeley.edu/mixedmode/nrdc.html
http://media.cannondesign.com/uploads/files/MaterialLife-9-6.pdf
www.calrecycle.ca.gov/GreenBuilding/CaseStudies/#Commercial
www.thegbi.org/about-gbi/#sthash.UVKdVZVf.dpuf
www.epa.gov/osw

Exercises

1 Define embodied energy. Show how this concept might be applied to increase sustainability for a small-scale building in Texas.
2 Suggest a minimum of five new ideas for future generations to manage solid waste in building construction.
3 What is the value of "lifecycle cost" for sustainability? Research and discuss briefly how it is computed based on the Department of Energy's suggested method.

4.4 Walls and Superstructure

As we have seen in previous sections, materials and their inherent properties of heat transfer, conductance, and resistance are essential to choices made in architectural design. Materials most frequently used for walls and superstructure of buildings are timber, steel, cement, concrete, brick, adobe and rammed earth, and straw bales. What are the benefits and drawbacks to producing and selecting each of these materials?

Designers have an obligation to reduce the use and depletion of finite raw materials and long-cycle renewable materials by replacing them with rapidly renewable materials made from plants that are typically harvested within a ten-year or shorter cycle. Typical rapidly renewable materials are bamboo, wool, cotton insulation, agrifiber, linoleum, wheat board, strawboard, and cork. In addition, there are several products available that are sustainable, durable, and less toxic than their counterparts. For example, innovative building materials from recycled glass, tires, and plastic have been used to create construction material. While selecting a building material designers interested in environmental sustainability should also consider lifecycle costs.

An example of innovative material development and architectural design comes from *Rural Studio's* design-build program at Auburn University. The program, begun in 1993 by D.K. Ruth and Samuel Mockbee, has established an ethos of recycling, reusing, and remaking. It gives architecture students a more hands-on educational experience while also assisting an underserved population in West Alabama's Black Belt region. Rural Studio has expanded the scope and complexity of its projects, focusing largely on community-oriented work. This program is an illustration of what a new generation of design thinkers is exploring in terms of sustainability, materials, and design. Figure 4.4.1 offers an example of a thesis project of this university in 2005, exploring paper products for building.

A discussion of most commonly used construction materials for walls and superstructure follows, with special attention paid to sustainable issues. Use of building materials and products that are extracted and manufactured within the region, a radius of 500 miles, not only supports the use of indigenous resources but also reduces the environmental impacts resulting from transportation.

Sustainable Wood and Timber

Timber is a renewable material. Wood is a highly popular building material: light, strong, durable, easy to work, and beautiful. It has been a building material of choice for centuries.

Unfortunately, tropical forests are shrinking by 11 million hectares per year; 31 million hectares of forests in industrial countries are damaged by air pollution or acid rain. An estimated 26 billion tons of topsoil are lost, and this is in excess of any new soil formation annually. Some six million hectares of new desert are formed annually by land mismanagement. The World Wildlife Foundation (WWF) asserts that the timber trade is now the primary threat to the world's forests.

Forests vary enormously in type and quality, and measurement of forested areas is highly misleading, often equating diverse natural forests with monocultural plantings. The oldest forests are rich in strong and rare trees as well as varieties of wildlife. Old forests also contain mature trees, making them attractive to timber traders. Along with tropical forests, many temperate and boreal forests are also disappearing. Many indigenous people have faced displacement and extinction due to legal and illegal operations and forest cuttings [1]. It is also tempting for impoverished indigenous peoples to deforest their own land to earn money and meet demands of other countries.

From this we see that designers must select wood from suitably managed forests. Many labeling systems claim that they are "sustainable" but most are not

Figure 4.4.1 A Rural Studio thesis project, 2005, by Masons Bend Alabama. Use of innovative material for construction – paper-crete.
(Source: photo by Tim Hursley.)

truly tested and verified for their integrity. The Forest Stewardship Council (FSC), an international body that verifies certification systems, offers the following ten principles:

1 Compliance with international and national law.
2 Documented and legally established tenure and use.
3 Rights of indigenous peoples respected.
4 Community relations and workers' rights supported.
5 Efficient use of the many yields of the forest.
6 Conservation of the biological integrity of the forest.
7 Existence of a management plan with long-term aims clearly stated.
8 Monitoring and assessment carried out.
9 Natural forests conserved and not replaced with other land uses.
10 Plantations properly managed and used to reduce pressures on natural forests.

To encourage environmentally responsible forest management, designers can establish a project goal for FSC-certified wood products and identify suppliers that can achieve this goal. Wood products carrying the FSC logo should be treated as being from a properly managed forest and any claim of sustainability made by a non-FSC organization should be viewed with caution. Also, designers should avoid over-sizing structural members and be careful in detailing in order to optimize the use of wood products for maximum efficiency and minimal waste.

The US Green Building Council (USGBC) encourages designers and builders to reuse existing buildings up to 80 percent, with material reuse up to 75 percent and recycle content and materials up to 20 percent of the extracted building products to receive its LEED® certifications. USGBC also encourages rapidly renewable and FSC-certified materials.

Sustainable Engineered Lumber

There are six types of engineered wood and three standard manufactured products (trusses, I-beams, and girders) that are sustainable. These products use waste lumber, fast-growing trees, and make use of appropriate epoxies to reconstitute building materials for sustainable use. They are:

- plywood
- oriented strand board (OSB)
- glulam
- parallel strand lumber (PSL)
- laminated strand lumber (LSL)
- laminated veneer lumber (LVL).

These are used for walls, beams, columns, and other structural uses. They can be assembled to form structural timber beams and trusses, structural elements for quick and easy installations.

A sustainable timber wall section is shown in Figure 4.4.2. The details indicate how to retrofit an existing construction for energy efficiency and sustainable efforts. Modified details can be adopted for a new construction. A designer should be able to calculate the composite R-values of any of these wall assemblies to establish heat transfer from these walls and the whole building as discussed in Section 4.1.

Recycled Steel

Most metals are derived from mining some form of ore, which requires destroying land. This operation often alters the topography and produces toxic emissions. Mined land requires expensive rehabilitation after the mine is closed and in most cases these lands

are not useful for centuries. Metal extraction is an energy-intensive process. The use of energy starts the moment the mining process begins and then continues with the transportation of the ore to the processing plants. Manufacturing and again transporting metals to the fabrication and installation location requires additional energy input. James Womack and Daniel Jones, in their book *Lean Thinking* [2], trace the tedious manufacturing process of aluminum cans and the energy required to produce them (see Section 1.2 for the whole story, which is an illustration of how wasteful we are in the use of some materials). It is estimated that the embodied energy to produce steel is 63 MWh/m^3, while aluminum requires 195 MWh/m^3.

Two technologies that are used to produce steel require old steel to make new steel. Basic oxygen furnace (BOF) technology uses approximately 25 percent steel scrap to make new steel. Steel manufactured by the BOF is used in products to include automotive (requiring formability) outer body panels, exterior panels for refrigerators and stoves, residential door skins, architectural panels, and packaging such as soup cans.

Scrap-based electric arc furnace (EAF) technology uses nearly 100 percent steel scrap as the base material and is used to produce products that require strength. Steel from the EAF process is used to produce structural beams, steel plates, and reinforcement bars. Of the recycled steel used for both technologies, up to 50 percent is post-consumer generated material, and the balance is pre-consumer and home scrap. Both types of steel are fully recyclable, and one type should not be favored over the other.

Recycling offsets the energy requirement for mining operations and initial cleaning and therefore is preferred in sustainable constructions. Recycling of structural materials has increased from 68 percent in 1988 to almost 90 percent in 2010.

Steel gets oxidized and therefore requires paint or some other coating for longevity. This additional treatment can make steel non-sustainable if the paint used is toxic. See www.aiasdrg.org/sdrg.aspx for additional information.

Now there are many sustainable steel buildings using recycled steel content. One such example is Rush University's Medical Center in Chicago (Figure 4.4.3). In the Rush buildings more than 90

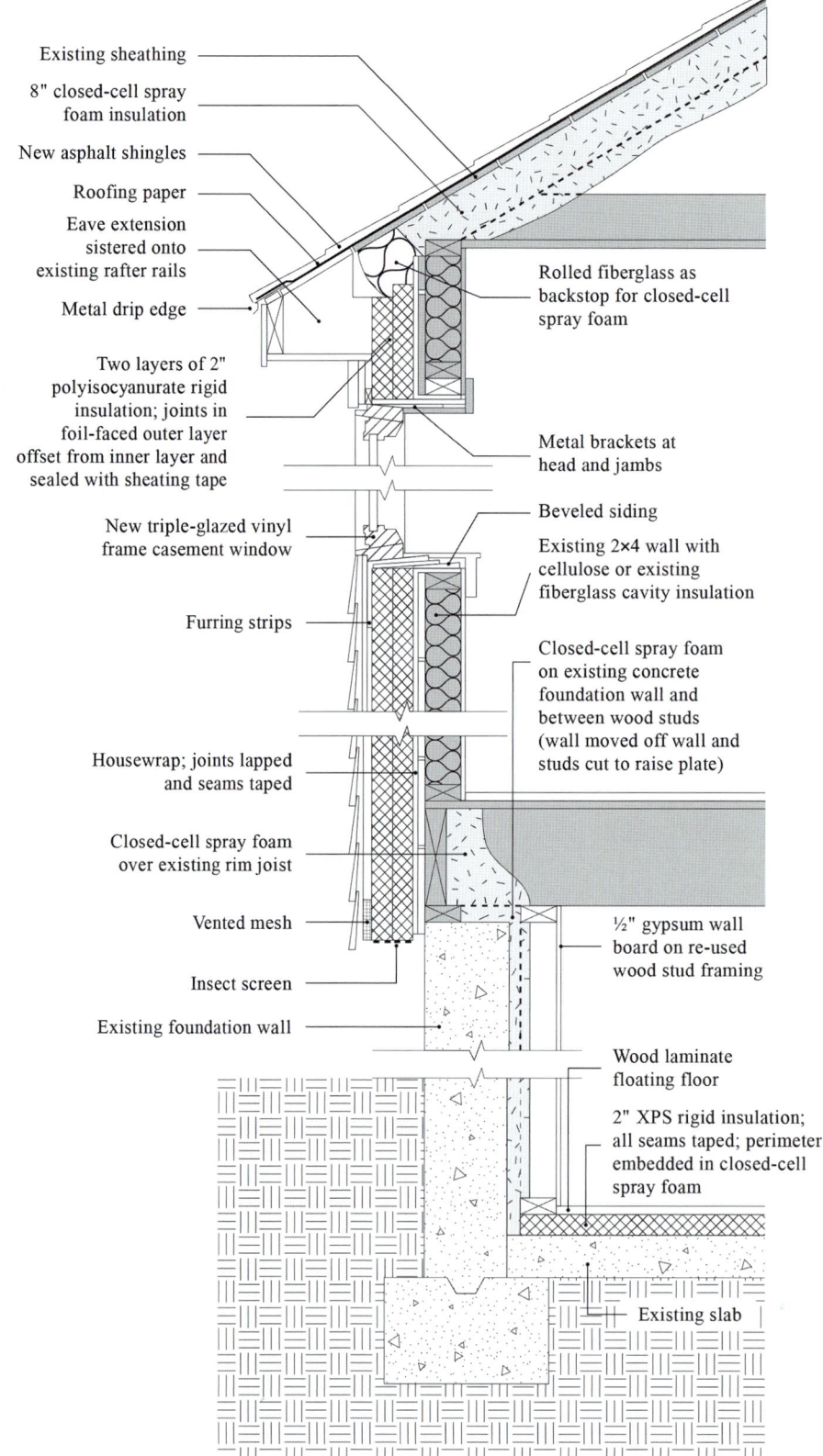

Existing sheathing

8" closed-cell spray foam insulation

New asphalt shingles

Roofing paper

Eave extension sistered onto existing rafter rails

Metal drip edge

Rolled fiberglass as backstop for closed-cell spray foam

Two layers of 2" polyisocyanurate rigid insulation; joints in foil-faced outer layer offset from inner layer and sealed with sheating tape

Metal brackets at head and jambs

New triple-glazed vinyl frame casement window

Beveled siding

Existing 2×4 wall with cellulose or existing fiberglass cavity insulation

Furring strips

Closed-cell spray foam on existing concrete foundation wall and between wood studs (wall moved off wall and studs cut to raise plate)

Housewrap; joints lapped and seams taped

Closed-cell spray foam over existing rim joist

Vented mesh

½" gypsum wall board on re-used wood stud framing

Insect screen

Existing foundation wall

Wood laminate floating floor

2" XPS rigid insulation; all seams taped; perimeter embedded in closed-cell spray foam

Existing slab

Figure 4.4.2 Typical timber wall details for new (to be modified to suit code) and retrofits. (Source: Building Science Corporation.)

Figure 4.4.3 Rush University Medical Center in Chicago.
(Source: photo by Nathan Hicks; this file is licensed under the Creative Commons Source 3.0 Unported License.)

percent of the steel structure is recycled – and other recycled building products include structural concrete, wallboard, and interior finishes. Designers claim that everything in the in-patient rooms is made from at least 20 percent post-consumer recycled content and some of the products, like sofas and recliners, are 95 percent recycled content. Over half of the wood is FSC-certified to promote the responsible management of the world's forests.

Cement

To make cement, calcium carbonate (usually in the form of limestone), silicates (from sand, clay or fly ash, a by-product of coal power plants) and some admixture (aluminum or iron and other minerals) are ground and mixed together and burnt at high temperatures of up to 1,500 °C. The exact mix depends on the required properties (quick setting, slow setting, seawater tolerant, etc.) of the cement. The burnt mixture of chemicals is now a combination of calcium, silica, and oxygen, which will be pulverized to form a fine powder capable of reacting as a binder when combined with water. Manufacture of cement is an energy-intensive process and releases carbon dioxide. It is estimated that 1 lb of cement produces 1.1 lbs of CO_2 (60 percent from fossil fuel and 40 percent from the calcining process). One bright spot in this manufacture is that waste products such as motor oil, old tires, and other such materials can be used as fuels for burning.

Since cement is alkaline, if it gets into human or fish food chains it can produce toxic effects and negative environmental impacts.

Reinforced Cement Concrete

Concrete can be a friend of the environment in all stages of its lifespan, from raw material production to demolition, making it a good choice for sustainable building construction.

Concrete is an admixture of cement (13 percent), sand (30 percent), aggregate (51 percent), and water (7 percent). By varying the amount of the ingredients, especially the amount of water and cement (water:cement ratio), quality and strength can be adjusted depending on the building requirements. Production of concrete is a non-renewable building process that uses considerable energy in manufacture of cement, crushing of stones, dredging of sand, and hauling of all of these. It cannot be recycled except when the demolished and reclaimed concrete is crushed again and the aggregate is reused in pavements and other such structures. However, even these recycling operations require energy in transportation. Most carbon dioxide emissions from concrete come from cement production and hauling. A designer should also be aware that improper disposal of concrete can lead to environmental pollution. When steel reinforcements are introduced into the concrete for building structural elements, such as beams and columns and other structural members, it becomes *reinforced cement concrete (RCC)*, creating abundant opportunities for extremely elegant sustainable architectural building solutions (Figure 4.4.4). In developing countries RCC is the preferred building construction material except for very tall structures, which typically demand structural steel. According to the Portland Cement Association and the Environmental Council of Concrete Organizations, the advantages of reinforced concrete are many.

Advantages of concrete:

- It is resource efficient because its raw material is limestone, the most abundant mineral on earth. It can also be made with fly ash and all waste by-products from power plants and steel mills.
- It has relatively high compressive strength, 3,000 psi to 8,000 psi.
- It has better resistance to fire than steel.
- It has long service life with low maintenance cost.

- It is the most economical structural material for large structures like dams.
- It can take any required shape.
- It yields rigid members with minimum apparent deflection.
- Buildings built with concrete walls, foundations, and floors can take advantage of concrete's inherent thermal mass for cooling and heating.

Disadvantages of reinforced concrete:

- It needs mixing, casting, and curing, all of which affect the final strength of concrete. The cost of the forms used to cast concrete is relatively high.
- It has low tensile strength as compared to steel (the ratio is about 1:10, depending on the material), which leads to large sections.

Concrete Masonry Unit Blocks

Concrete masonry unit (CMU) blocks are similar to concrete in environmental issues. By hollowing the solid concrete, the voids created in the CMU make the resultant blocks much lighter while taking advantage of their dimensional stability. Though the air voids in the blocks offer some insulation, it is not enough to compete directly with insulating materials. To be sustainable, insulation must be incorporated into the wall assembly. Composite insulating blocks are made by infusing an insulating layer of one to two inches between the cement concrete blocks. A designer has several options to combine CMU with insulation depending on the design requirement. Figure 4.4.5 shows a couple of ways to incorporate insulation into CMU construction. Manufacturers should avoid insulating materials that contain CFCs or HCFCs since they deplete the atmosphere's ozone layer.

Burnt Bricks

Brick masonry has existed for centuries and there are exemplary brick buildings all over the world. They have decent compressive strength but require reinforcements to support lateral forces like earthquakes and severe wind. Like ceramics, bricks are made by baking clay at high temperature. Although clay is available in

Figure 4.4.4 Examples of elegant reinforced concrete structures (a) Concert Hall, Tenerife, Canary Islands, Spain, design by Santiago Calatrava; (b) Boston City Hall, Massachusetts, design by G. Kallmann and M. McKinnell.
(Source: this file is licensed under the Creative Commons Source 3.0 Unported License.)

(a)

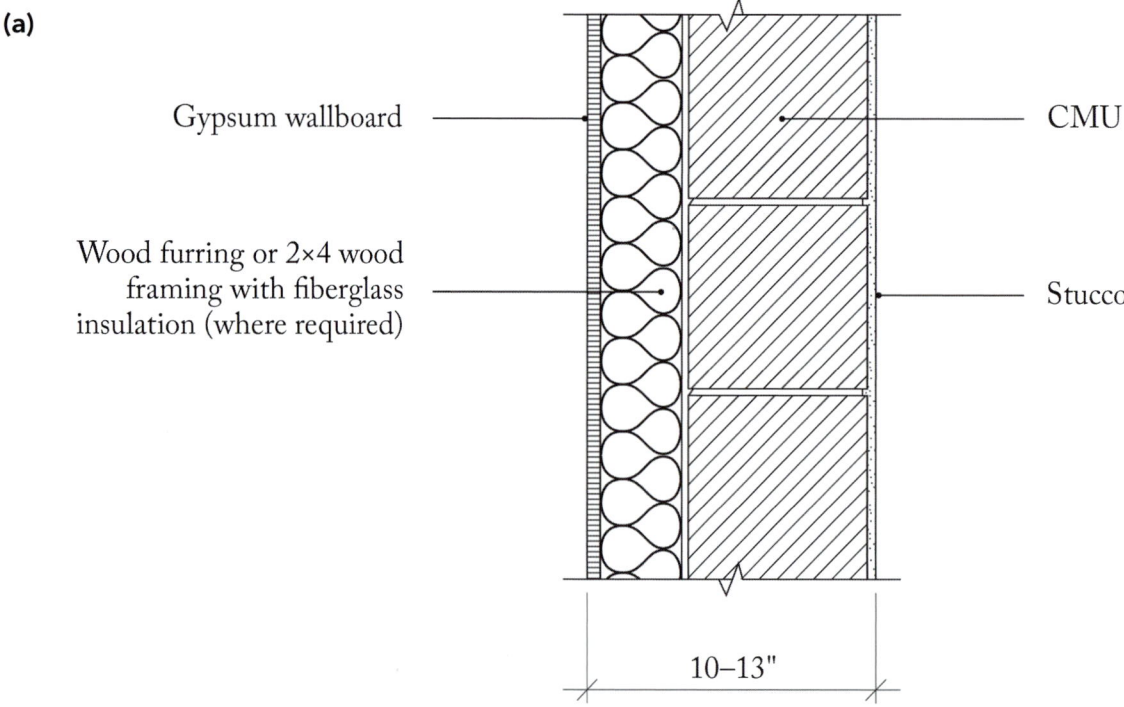

Gypsum wallboard

Wood furring or 2×4 wood framing with fiberglass insulation (where required)

CMU

Stucco

10–13"

(b)

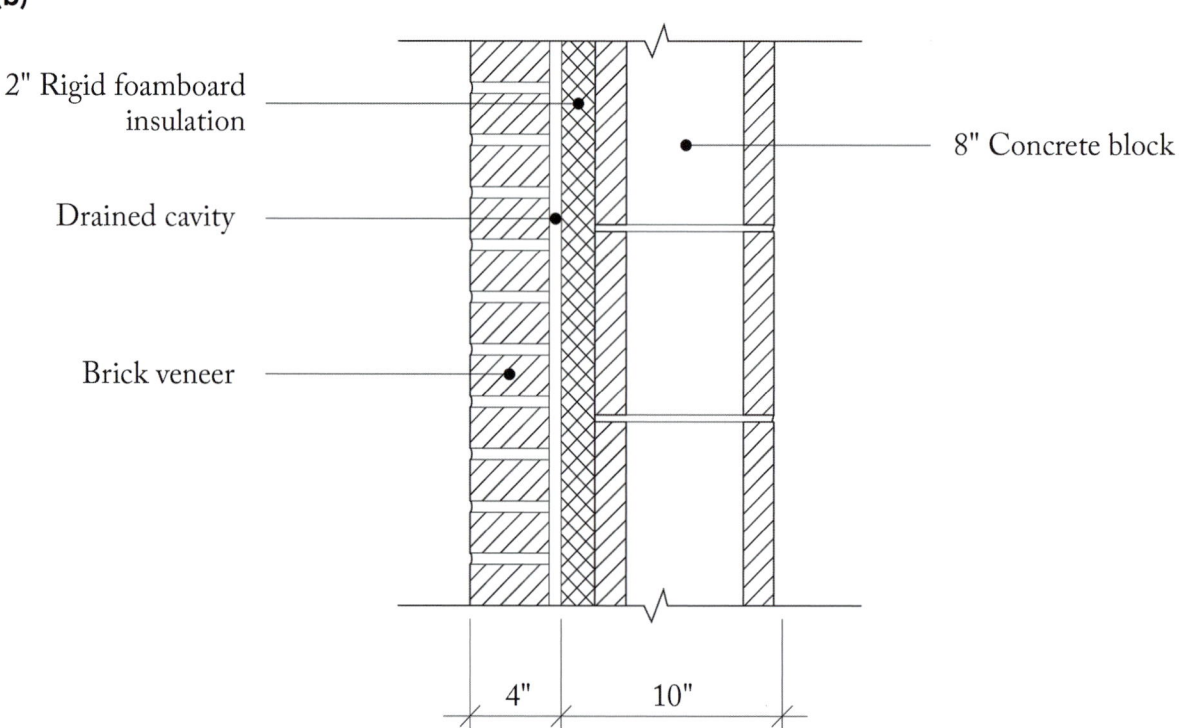

2" Rigid foamboard insulation

Drained cavity

Brick veneer

8" Concrete block

4"   10"

Figure 4.4.5 Different types of composite CMU construction with insulation (a) external insulation; (b) CMU with insulation and masonry veneer.
(Source: Kuppaswamy Iyengar.)

abundant quantities, its quarrying can have a negative impact on the local community due to marring of the landscape. Hauling of the material from the quarry to the manufacture site also incurs fuel costs. The brick firing process involves the use of fuel oil, natural gas, electricity, and, in some countries, timber. Producing bricks results in significant CO_2 emissions of 0.33 kg/kWH. Bricks alone contribute 0.25 kg/kWH of CO_2. Consider, for example, that cement manufacture produces four times the CO_2 when compared with brick. However, concrete contains only 13 percent cement, or one-half of brick's CO_2 emissions. If one compares the environmental impact of concrete and brick, it can be concluded that bricks produce twice the amount of CO_2. Therefore, contrary to the popular perception that bricks are natural material and come from the earth, brick is an energy-intensive building material. Brick's insulating properties are not very good, but they have good thermal mass, which can be used to retain heat or cold if superstructures are designed properly.

Brick masonry is easy to handle and light compared to CMU and yields a warm quality to interior and exterior spaces, as seen in Figures 4.4.6 and 4.4.7.

Figure 4.4.6 Indian Institute of Management in Ahmadabad, India, by Louis Kahn.
(Source: photo by students of IIMA; this file is licensed under the Creative Commons Source 3.0 Unported License.)

Figure 4.4.7 Indian Institute of Management in Ahmadabad, India, by Louis Kahn. Exterior and interior spaces.
(Source: © Indian Institute of Management, Ahmadabad.)

Adobe and Rammed Earth

Some claim adobe construction was popular before 10,000 BC in the Middle East. Nadir Khalili, an Iranian architect practicing in Hisparia, California, has extensively documented earth constructions such as adobe in Iran and other ancient countries, as well as in the USA.

Earth consists of various grades of small stones, sand, clay, and water. Clay binds all the ingredients. Any organic matter present in earth makes the earth construction unsuitable for shelter, since it weakens the structure upon its decay. In adobe construction, earth with a proper mix of sand, clay, and other inorganic matter is simply removed from the ground and "puddled" with water, mixed thoroughly, placed in forms to dry, and piled as a wall. Local practices include mixing with straw and other fibrous materials, depending on availability at the location.

Many states and cities in the USA have developed local standards in terms of maximum height and thicknesses of buildings built using adobe (see Figure 4.4.8 for a section of typical construction details). When greater strength is required, the same adobe mixture is compacted with the addition of cement and other stabilizing materials such as lime and asphalt, which is referred to as "rammed earth." Rammed earth buildings require form work and can even be made to resemble concrete buildings. Several residential buildings using rammed earth can be seen in the US southwest, particularly in New Mexico and Arizona.

Earth can also be packed into forms in situ and compressed by simple hand-pressing machines. In India a hand-packed earth brick called a CEB (compressed earth block) is popular in some areas. For low-height buildings, earth is a suitable building material and is usually available close to the construction site, requiring minimal hauling and extraction cost. When it has reached the end of its useful life it can be easily disposed of without harming the environment.

Heating or baking earth also can be a consideration in the strength of adobe construction. *Nadir Khalili* has documented very strong earth buildings in Iran that have survived severe earthquakes. One such building had been exposed to intense fire and it baked in that fire as though in a kiln, which made it as strong as a ceramic building. In another tradition called "geltaftan," a specially designed earth building is packed with fuel and later used as a kiln for pottery. This type of building becomes very durable, having been baked at high temperatures.

Most US standards require earth walls to have the same strength as brick for design purposes, and therefore thickness of structural adobe is similar to that of brick buildings.

The New Mexico Building Code stipulates that adobe shall not be used in any building more than two stories in height. The maximum height of every wall of adobe block without lateral support is specified in the New Mexico Administrative Code (NMAC), Table 1. The height of the wall is defined as the distance from the top of the slab or top of the stem wall to the underside of the bond beam. The maximum height of exterior walls, which are laterally supported with those supports located no more than 24 feet apart, are as defined in 14.7.4.8 NMAC, Table 1. The bottom story of a two-story structure is allowed a minimum thickness of 14 inches, with the upper story allowed a thickness of ten inches, providing the structure meets other provisions of the NMAC.

Adobe walls are not good insulators but have a thermal storage property that makes them suitable as "thermal walls." Traditional adobe construction found in Taos Pueblo ruins, and in other areas of New Mexico, appears to have provided comfortable dwelling conditions for native occupants. Today, adobe constructions remain popular for their thermal storage properties and beauty.

Straw Bale Construction

Straw comes from wheat, barley, oats, rye, and rice plants left over after grains are harvested. Straw is renewable and readily available in the USA and also in many other parts of the world; it has been used as a binder in earth bricks and structures for centuries. Since the invention of the baler, straw bales have been used as building blocks for highly insulating walls. In most codes, however, bales serve as filling materials between structural supports as in post-and-beam construction. Current methods of development ensure that well-designed buildings with tightly packed bales do not suffer from moisture, pests, or susceptibility to fire (Figure 4.4.9). Typical construction involves inserting steel or bamboo stakes through the bales

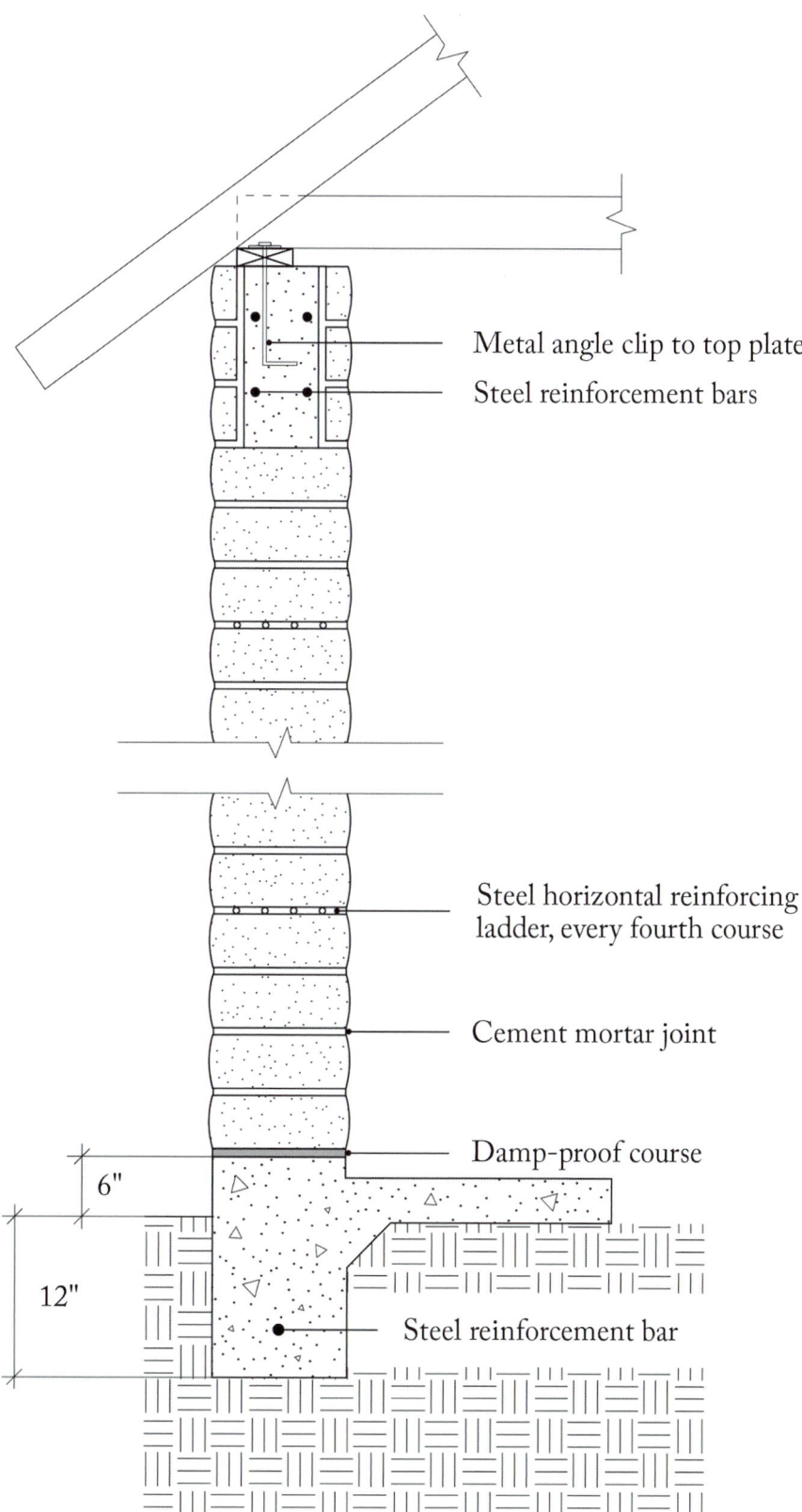

Metal angle clip to top plate

Steel reinforcement bars

Steel horizontal reinforcing
ladder, every fourth course

Cement mortar joint

Damp-proof course

6"

12"

Steel reinforcement bar

Figure 4.4.8 Typical construction details of adobe buildings.
(Source: Kuppaswamy Iyengar.)

and anchoring them into the foundations and walls. The straw walls are plastered inside and outside. Construction-grade straw bales offer an R-value of 1.45/inch thickness based on studies conducted by the Oakridge National Laboratories. The environmental impact of straw bales and other plant-based construction material is low. The only ecological impact through CO_2 comes from burning bales when there is over supply and hauling those from place to place, incurring transportation fuel use. The US Department of Energy has measured and endorsed the energy and cost savings of this type of construction.

In New Mexico and other parts of this country the governing code is the Uniform Building Code (UBC, Chapter 23) for dealing with vertical and lateral loads. Straw bale walls are only infill in most applications and cannot be structural. Straw bale walls cannot be below grade and must have a vapor barrier between the foundation and the wall. Actual details of the loading can be reviewed in Bruce King's *Buildings of Earth and Straw* [3].

Selection of Walls and Superstructure

The quantity of materials necessary for walls and superstructure of buildings has a corresponding impact on possible waste through non-sustainable practices. A designer who is concerned with the environmental impact of a building must consider the source of the material, how it is extracted, processed, transported, built, used, and disposed of at the end. In other words, the environmental impact of a building is proportional to the quantity of materials used in its construction from beginning to end.

That said, one cannot ignore that even small quantities of paint, adhesive, and other surface materials used in a building can have significant impact on the environment.

Figure 4.4.9 A public library built using straw bales, located in Mattawa, Washington. When straw bales are from a local area, the environmental impact can be low.
(Source: https://commons.wikimedia.org.)

Summary

During its life, a building can produce great quantities of CO_2 through the first procurement of materials, to electricity and other energy uses during its operation, to final disposal or recycling at the end of the building's usefulness. Reducing this use of energy through careful design of walls and superstructure and through selection of materials with minimal environmental impact can have a direct effect on reducing pollution and resource depletion. A designer interested in sustainability uses knowledge of strength, durability, toxicity, and heat transfer to explore properties of materials to capture the benefits of natural systems like sun, wind, and light.

References

[1] WWF, *Living Planet Report* (2006): assets.panda. org/downloads/living_planet_report.pdf.

[2] James Womack and Daniel Jones, *Lean Thinking* (New York: Simon & Schuster, Inc, 1996).

[3] Bruce King, *Buildings of Earth and Straw* (Sausalito, CA: Ecological Design Press, 1996).

Further Reading

US Green Building Council, *LEED for New Construction* (Washington, DC: USGBC, 2009).

Owen J. Lewis, *A Green Vitruvius* (London: European Commission, 1999).

James G. MacGregor, *Reinforced Concrete Mechanics and Design*, 4th edition (Englewood Cliffs, NJ: Prentice Hall, 2005).

American Institute of Steel Construction, *Manual of Steel Construction*, 9th edition, (Chicago, IL: American Institute of Steel Construction, 2006).

Earthen Building Materials Code – NM Adobe Code [New Mexico] (Santa Fe, 2003)

Non-Load Bearing Baled Straw Construction Building Standards [New Mexico] (Santa Fe, 2009).

Forest Stewardship Council Certification, *FSC US Forest Management Standard (v1.0)* (Bonn: FSC, 2004).

Web Support

www.certifiedwood.org

Exercises

1 What principles does the Forest Stewardship Council adopt to ensure sustainability in timber use? Locate an FSC-certified wood supplier in your area.

2 Show two examples of recycled steel buildings in your city. Calculate the amount of recycled steel content in these buildings.

4.5 Windows and High-performance Glazing

Windows and other glazing components are critical for the sustainable performance of the building envelope. This section looks at appropriate choices for more sustainable windows, skylights, and their glazing components, and examines options for window frames and materials for frames, including aluminum, wood, vinyl, hybrid options, and more. These choices, when made with sustainability in mind, can have a large positive impact on energy use and the environment. Information regarding daylighting is discussed in Chapter 5.

Window Requirements

Some estimates claim that the energy losses through windows in the USA alone equal twice the energy that is flowing through the Alaskan pipeline. Until recently, windows used to have single panes with low resistance to energy transfer. Now there are many more options. To begin, for sustainable architectural design decisions consider three crucial questions for windows:

1 What kind to satisfy architectural requirements?
2 How many?
3 Where on the envelope?

Every building should also balance the need for heat and daylight through windows by minimizing infiltration loss. This requires an understanding of the area of windows in the building envelope, along with the *shading coefficient* and *solar heat gain (U-factor)* of the selected glass. These terms are mathematically related and both describe the solar energy blocked from passing through a glass material.

- The *shading coefficient* is the ratio of solar energy that passes through a piece of glass relative to a piece of 1/8" clear glass with a shading coefficient of 1.0.
- *Solar heat gain coefficient (SHGC)* represents the solar gain through the glass relative to the incident solar radiation; it is equal to 86 percent of the shading coefficient. In either case, a lower number indicates improved solar control over the 1/8" clear glass baseline.

What is better, a high or low shading coefficient? In colder, heating-dominated climates such as Canada or the northern USA, windows with higher shading coefficients generally are preferred and conserve energy. This is so because in the longer heating season, more solar radiation, which becomes "free" heat, is allowed to pass into a home. In the south, with a long air-conditioning season, it is most important to reduce solar gain and therefore reduce air conditioning loads. A lower shading coefficient is preferable in warm climates.

In addition, it is essential to locate windows with access to views and ventilation. While specifying the windows, a designer should indicate the spectral characteristics such as heat gain (U-factor), emissivity (SHGC), and visual transmittance (VT) for different solar conditions. There should be different glazing packages for different faces of a building. It is quite likely that south-facing windows should be different from west-facing windows. If that is not possible, use windows with a low shading coefficient to prevent overheating of the south- and west-facing building envelope.

To minimize the use of nonrenewable fuels, significant strides have been made in the development of windows by adding additional layers of glasses and air spaces in the window frames to improve the resistance to heat transfer through them. Eliminating wind drafts and the "chill factor" of cold glazing are important considerations for good window design.

The introduction of so-called "super windows" is a dramatic development in window design. These windows have two or three layers of glazing. The space between the layers is filled with an inert gas such as argon or krypton, and contains a low-emissivity invisible film or coating. The low-E film(s) can be on the inner face of one of the glazing layers, which will allow short-wave radiation to enter the building while preventing long-wave radiation from entering or leaving the building. The R-values (resistance to heat transfer) typically range from 3 to 8 in comparison to 1 for a single-pane glass window. In most cases these super windows can save 15–50 percent in energy use. They come in a variety of colors and meet the aesthetic and climatic needs of any given locality. For example, a super window can let in all the light one wants without letting in much heat in a hot climate such as Phoenix or Albuquerque, while it can allow enough heat to warm a building in colder climates such as Buffalo, New York, or Toronto. As an additional bonus, these super windows prevent noise and will help maintain colors of furniture and furnishings by preventing ultraviolet light damage. Also, in some cases, note that certain buildings may not warrant low-E windows on south-facing passive solar collection areas.

Here is an interesting example of a window design for ING Bank in Amsterdam (refer to Figure 3.2.4), which was designed by a team of stakeholders interested in creating a sustainable green building. The windows have three parts. The middle part has fixed glass for viewing, the top part has louvers for daylight, and the bottom part has operable shutters. Some people object to operable windows, which can cause problems for mechanical designers, yet this workable solution for the bank satisfied many requirements. Most people prefer that there should be at least one operable window in every room to let in outside fresh air along with, hopefully, the fresh scent of a fragrant plant or birdsong. Studies have shown that people are willing to bear a few degrees of higher temperature if they can have an operable window in their office or home.

Ventilation, light and solar gain can be accommodated with separated or combined openings. Separate ventilation openings can be designed for that purpose in hot climates.

Operable windows are not always desirable. In

heavily populated cities such as Mumbai and New York, dirt, dust, pollution, and other urban problems can prevent recommending operable windows. In such cases sealed windows with mechanical ventilation and air-conditioning will become the only solution.

Sustainable Window Components

Gas-filled Multiple Glazing and Low-E Coatings

Figure 4.5.1 illustrates the characteristics of a typical double-glazed window with a high-transmission, low-E glass and argon/krypton gas fill. These low-E glass products are often referred to as pyrolitic or hard coat low-E glass due to the glass coating process. The properties presented here are typical of a low-E glass product designed to reduce heat loss but admit solar gain. High solar gain low-E glass products are best suited for buildings located in heating-dominated climates. This low-E glass type is preferred for passive solar design projects due to its performance qualities relative to other low-E glass products that reduce solar gain.

In heating-dominated climates with a modest amount of cooling, or climates where both heating and cooling are required, low-E coatings with high, moderate, or low solar gains may result in similar annual energy costs depending on the building design and operation. While the high solar gain glazing performs better in winter, the low solar gain performs better in summer. Low solar gain low-E glazing is ideal for buildings located in cooling-dominated climates.

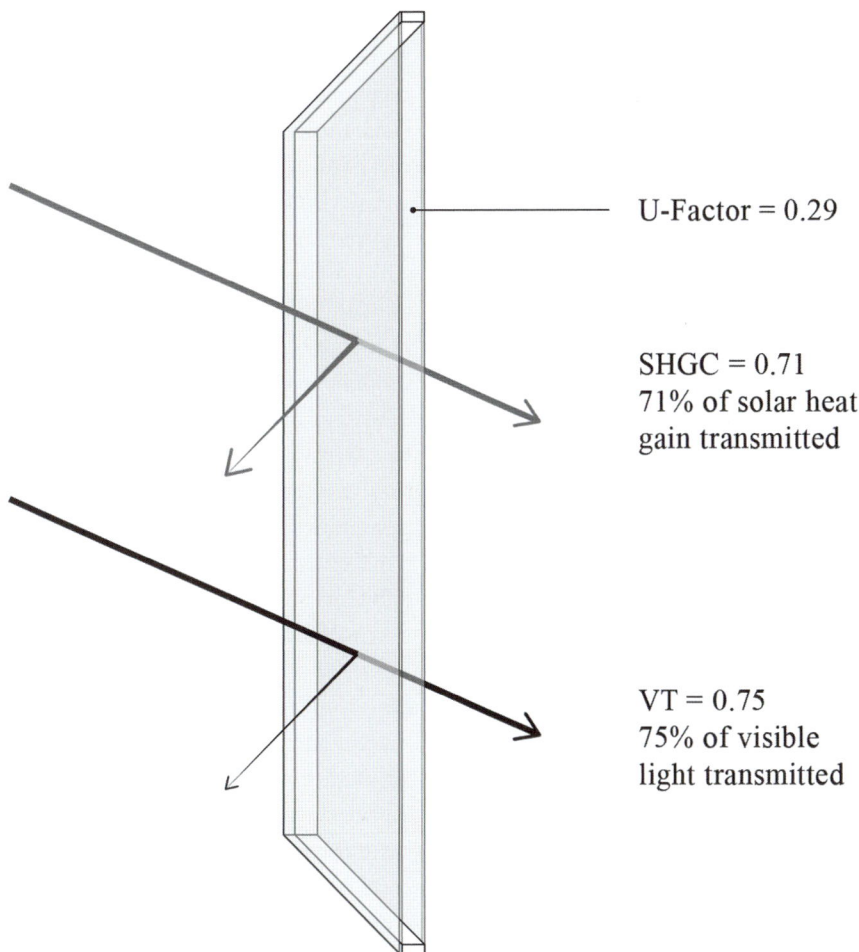

U-Factor = 0.29

SHGC = 0.71
71% of solar heat gain transmitted

VT = 0.75
75% of visible light transmitted

Figure 4.5.1 Properties of multiple glazing windows. (Source: www.efficientwindows.org/index.cfm.)

The values shown in Figure 4.5.1 are for the center of the glass only. They should only be used to compare the effect of different glazing types, not to compare total window products. Frame choice can drastically affect performance.

Prescriptive Requirements for Windows

Windows, doors, and skylights can gain and lose heat through:

- direct conduction through the glass or glazing, frame, and/or door;
- the radiation of heat into a building (typically from the sun) and out of a building from room objects, such as furniture, interior walls, and people.

These energy performance characteristics are measured and rated by:

- *Window area*, the amount of window surface in each face of the building envelope.
- U-factor, expressed in units of Btu/hr/sq.ft/°F, the rate at which a window, door, or skylight conducts non-solar heat flow. For windows, skylights, and glass doors, NFRC U-factor ratings represent the entire window performance, including frame and spacer material. The lower the U-factor, the more energy efficient the window, door, or skylight.
- *Solar heat gain coefficient (SHGC)*, the fraction of solar radiation admitted through a window, door, or skylight – transmitted directly and/or absorbed, and subsequently released as heat inside a building. The lower the SHGC, the less solar heat it transmits and the greater its shading ability. A product with a high SHGC rating is more effective at collecting solar heat during the winter. A product with a low SHGC rating is more effective at reducing cooling loads during the summer by blocking heat gain from the sun. A building's climate, orientation, and external shading will determine the optimal SHGC for a particular window, door, or skylight.
- *Visible transmittance (VT)*, a fraction of the visible spectrum of sunlight (380 to 720 nanometers) that is transmitted through the glazing of a window,

door, or skylight. VT is expressed as a number between 0 and 1. A glass product with a higher VT transmits more visible light. The required VT for a window, door, or skylight should be determined by the designer, depending on daylighting requirements regarding glare in a space.

ASHRAE 90.1-2010 compared its standards with the 2011 International Energy Conservation Code (IECC), which closely resembles the State of California's 2008 Title 24 Energy Standards developed by the California Energy Commission (CEC). ASHRAE Standards and Title 24 can be modified and adopted as a model for local building codes in many parts of the USA to encourage sustainable practices, since designers are obligated to follow the local building codes.

The National Fenestration Rating Council (NFRC) is a voluntary program that tests, certifies, and labels windows, doors, and skylights based on their energy performance ratings. Energy Star, a nationally accepted certification, bases its qualification only on U-factor and solar heat gain coefficient ratings. All of the EPA's ENERGY STAR® qualified window, door, and skylight products will have the NFRC label.

Windows that have the Energy Star designation will be labeled showing the climatic zones in which they are qualified. Since energy-efficient performance of windows, doors, and skylights varies by climate, product recommendations are given for four US climate zones. The Efficient Windows Collaborative has developed properties required for windows in these four climatic zones (also see Section 2.1) for the designer's guidance. For details of Energy Star rated window products with the NFRC label, refer to www.efficientwindows.org/energystar.php.

The following brief summary outline of the 2008 Title 24 standard has useful information for the design of windows and skylights, which includes mandated prescriptive window requirements. There are three aspects of the envelope component approach for windows:

1 maximum area;
2 maximum U-factor;
3 maximum relative solar heat gain.

Window Area

Under the envelope component approach, the total window area may not exceed 40 percent of the gross wall area (encompassing conditioned space) for the building. Likewise, the west-facing window area may not exceed 40 percent of the west gross wall area (encompassing conditioned space for the building). This maximum area requirement will affect those buildings with very large glass areas, such as high-rise offices, automobile showrooms, or airport terminals. Under these circumstances a designer can use simulation tools to satisfy the code requirements and arrive at the appropriate energy performance. As a practical matter, window area is generally calculated from the rough opening dimensions. Calculation of the percentage can be made by dividing the window area by the gross exterior wall area, which does not include demising walls.

Window U-factor

Each window must meet the required U-factor criteria (see Table 3-2 of Title 24). In California for non-residential buildings, the U-factor criterion is $0.47\,\mathrm{Btu/h/°F/ft^2}$ for the valley, desert, and cold climates. The criterion is $0.77\,\mathrm{Btu/h/°F/ft^2}$ for the middle coast and south coast climates. For residential buildings, the criterion is 0.47 for all climates. In general, an NFRC-rated double-glazed, low-E window with a thermal break frame will comply with the 0.47 criterion, and an NFRC-rated double-glazed, low-E window with a standard frame will comply with the 0.77 criterion; however, other window constructions may also comply. Window manufacturers will be able to provide the required data.

Window Relative Solar Heat Gain (RSHG)

Each window or skylight must meet the required relative solar heat gain (RSHG) (see Table 143-A of Title 24). The required value for relative solar heat gain is less stringent (higher) for north-facing windows. Either an RSHG of 0.56 or the "north" value, whichever is greater, may also be used for windows in the first-floor display perimeter that are prevented from having an overhang because of building code restrictions (such as minimum separation from another building or a property line). The relative solar heat gain criteria also depend on the window–wall ratio, becoming more stringent with larger window areas.

Prescriptive Requirements for Skylights

As with windows, there are three aspects of the envelope component approach for skylights:

1 maximum area
2 maximum U-factor
3 maximum solar heat gain coefficient.

Skylight Area

The area limit for skylights is 5 percent of the gross exterior roof area. This effectively prevents large skylights under the envelope component approach. The limit increases to 10 percent for buildings with an atrium over 55 feet high. The 55-foot height is also the height limitation at which the Uniform Building Code requires a mechanical smoke-control system for such atriums. This means that the 10 percent skylight allowance is not allowed for atriums unless they also meet this smoke-control requirement.

Skylight U-factor

All skylights must meet the maximum U-factor criteria. For skylights the U-factor represents the heat loss per unit of rough-framed opening (the denominator). However, the heat loss (the numerator) includes losses through the glazing, the frame, and the part of the curb that is integral with the skylight and included in the skylight test. Large skylights are treated differently. In such cases the skylight area is the surface area of the glazing and frame/curb (not the area of the rough framed opening), regardless of the geometry of the skylight (i.e., could be flat pyramid, bubble, barrel vault, or other three-dimensional shape).

For skylights, the U-factor and solar heat gain coefficient (SHGC) criteria are different depending on whether the skylight glazing material is plastic or glass. For glass skylights, the U-factor criteria depend on whether or not the skylight is intended to be mounted on a curb. It is assumed that all plastic skylights are mounted on a curb.

Skylight SHGC

Skylights are regulated only for SHGC, not RSHG, because skylights cannot have overhangs. The SHGC criteria vary with the skylight-to-roof ratio (SRR). Two ranges are represented in the standards: up to and including 2 percent of the exterior roof and greater than 2 percent but less than or equal to 5 percent.

Skylights in Large Enclosed Spaces

Appropriately sized skylight systems when combined with daylighting controls can dramatically reduce the energy consumption of a building. With too little skylight area, insufficient light is available to turn off electric lighting; with too much skylight area, solar gains and heat losses through skylights negate the lighting savings with heating and cooling loads.

Types of Window and Skylight Frames

Several common window types and frames are discussed briefly in terms of their contributions to the sustainability of building envelope design. Windows and skylights are manufactured with different frames to satisfy varying design needs. These frames are made from aluminum, aluminum with thermal breaks, wood, wood clad, vinyl, insulated vinyl, composite materials, and fiberglass and hybrid/double hybrid. These different frames cause the window to have different solar gain properties. Manufacturers will be able to provide detailed specifications for their windows and skylights (properties of selected examples are in Figures 4.5.2 and 4.5.3). In all these cases attention should be on three important properties: U-factor, SHGC and VT, and on local codes.

Aluminum

Aluminum window frames are light, strong, durable, and easily extruded into the complex shapes required

Frame	Aluminum	Aluminum with thermal break	Wood	Wood clad	Vinyl	Hybrid / composite	Insulated vinyl	Fiberglass
U-Factor	.61	.50	.37	.37	.37	.37	.29	.29
SHGC	.64	.58	.53	.53	.53	.53	.56	.56
VT	.62	.58	.54	.54	.54	.54	.58	.58

Figure 4.5.2 Properties of multiple glazing windows.
(Source: data provided from the Efficient Windows Collaborative (www.efficientwindows.org).)

Glazing	Single-glazed clear	Double-glazed clear	Double-glazed with low-solar-gain low-E, argon / krypton gas
U-Factor	2.48	.94	.75
SHGC	.78	.68	.40
VT	.70	.70	.55

Figure 4.5.3 Skylight properties for aluminum frames
(Source: data provided from the Efficient Windows Collaborative (www.efficientwindows.org).)

for window parts. Aluminum frames are available in anodized and factory-baked enamel finishes that are extremely durable and low-maintenance. These can be recycled, which preserves nearly 90 percent of their embodied energy.

The biggest disadvantage of aluminum as a window frame material is its high thermal conductance. Therefore, the overall U-factor of a window unit also can increase. In cold climates, a simple aluminum frame can easily become cold enough to condense moisture or frost on the inside surfaces of window frames. Even more than the problem of heat loss, the condensation problem has spurred development of better insulating aluminum frames (see *Aluminum with Thermal Break*, below). In hot climates, since solar gain is more important than heat conduction, improving the insulating value of the frame can be much less important than using a higher-performance glazing system.

Aluminum with Thermal Break

A common solution to the heat conduction problem of aluminum frames is to provide a "thermal break" by splitting the frame components into interior and exterior pieces by using a less conductive material at their connections. Current technology with standard thermal breaks has decreased aluminum frame U-factors (heat loss rate) by about 50 percent. Again, in hot climates, where solar gain is often more important than conductive heat transfer, improving the insulating value of the frame can be much less important. It may be best to use a high-performance glazing system, in any case.

Wood

The traditional window frame material is wood, because of its availability and ease of milling into the complex shapes required to make windows. Wood is favored in many residential applications because of its appearance and traditional place in house design. From a thermal point of view, wood-framed windows perform well. Wood is not intrinsically the most durable window frame material because of its susceptibility to rot, but well-built and well-maintained wood windows can have a long life. Scheduled painting protects the exterior surface and allows an easy change in color schemes.

Wood clad

To create a permanent weather-resistant surface, the wood-framed window is clad with either vinyl or aluminum on the exterior face of the frame. Clad frames thus have lower maintenance requirements, while retaining the attractive wood finish on the interior. While vinyl and enameled metal claddings offer much longer protection to wood frames, they are generally only available in a limited number of colors.

Vinyl

Vinyl, also known as polyvinyl chloride (PVC), is a plastic with good insulating value. Vinyl window frames do not require painting, have good moisture resistance and, as there is no finish coat that can be damaged or deteriorate over time, the surface is therefore maintenance-free. Some vinyl window manufacturers are now offering surface treatments like wood laminates and other maintenance-free coatings. These products increase color selection and surface appearance options. Recent advances have improved dimensional stability and resistance to degradation from sunlight and temperature extremes.

Vinyl frames are comparable with wood in terms of their thermal performance. Small hollow chambers within the frame reduce convection energy exchange, as does adding an insulating material.

Insulated Vinyl

Insulated double vinyl frames are identical in most of their characteristics to standard vinyl frames. The major difference between insulated vinyl and standard vinyl frames is improved thermal performance. In insulated vinyl frames, the hollow cavities of the frame are filled with insulation, making them thermally superior to standard vinyl and wood frames. Usually, these high-performance frames are used with high-performance glazing.

Composite

For a long time, the timber industry has used such materials as particle board and laminated strand lumber, in which wood particles and resins are compressed to form a strong composite material. Now the industry has taken this process a step further by creating a new generation of wood/polymer composites that are extruded into a series of lineal shapes for window frame and sash members. These windows are very stable, and have the same or better structural and thermal properties as conventional wood, with more moisture and decay resistance. They can be textured and stained or painted much like wood. They were initially used in critical elements, such as window sills and thresholds in sliding patio doors, but are now being used for entire window units. This sustainable approach has the added environmental advantage of reusing a volume of sawdust and wood scrap that would otherwise be discarded.

Fiberglass

Glass-fiber-reinforced polyester or fiberglass or extruded engineered thermoplastics (as used in automobiles and appliances) are all being used to produce insulated double window frames, which are extruded into lineal forms and then assembled into windows. These frames are dimensionally stable and have air cavities that are filled with insulation. Their thermal performance can be superior to wood or vinyl because the material is stronger than vinyl and can have smaller cross-sectional shapes and thus less exposed area. Usually these high-performance frames are used with high-performance glazing.

Hybrid/Double Hybrid

U-values for windows should be specified as being for the whole unit rather than "center-of-glass" values, which apply only to the glass. There are several hybrid windows available in the market now with a good combination of solar control and visible light transmittance. For effective window selection, instead of identifying individual values, a good measure of quality is a light-to-solar-gain (LSG) ratio. For example, PPG Glass Company has introduced *Solarban 70 XL*, which has combined clarity, solar control (SHGC 0.27) and visible light transmittance (VLT 63 percent). This results in a VLT of 2.33, which is an excellent window from a sustainability point of view.

Today, manufacturers are making hybrid frame designs that use two or more frame materials to produce a complete window system. The wood industry has long built vinyl- and aluminum-clad windows to reduce exterior maintenance needs. Vinyl manufacturers and others offer interior wood veneers to produce the finish and appearance that many homeowners desire. Split-sash designs may have an interior wood element bonded to an exterior fiberglass element. The Green Builders Association is encouraging an ever-increasing selection of such hybrid designs as manufacturers continue to try to provide better-performing products at lower cost. It is important for a builder or a homeowner to learn about these windows from the perspective of energy efficiency, maintenance requirements, and options for interior finishes. However, it becomes increasingly difficult to estimate the thermal properties of such a frame from simple inspection. The best source of information is a National Fenestration Research Council (NFRC) label and/or manufacturers' data that provide the thermal properties of the overall window.

High-Performance Glazing

There are many high-performance commercial buildings in the world now. High-performance, energy-efficient window and glazing systems can dramatically cut energy consumption and as a result reduce pollution. These glazing systems have lower heat loss (conduction effect), less air leakage (convection effect), and warmer window surfaces that improve comfort and minimize condensation (creating a clear view). High-performance windows feature double- or triple-glazing, specialized transparent coatings (low-E), insulating gas (argon or krypton) between panes, and improved frames.

For high performance windows:

- *U-values* are around 0.2 for a multi-paned, high-performance window with low-emissivity coatings and insulated frames.

- *SHGC* is 0–1.00. Windows with low values are desirable in buildings with high air-conditioning loads (hot climates) while windows with high SHGC values are desirable in buildings where passive solar heating (cold climates) is needed.

Note that for the *Heat Mirror 77 Superglass* in Figure 4.5.4 the U-value is 0.10, effectively bringing the R-value to 10, which is ten times better than 1/8" single-pane glass. It is also interesting to note that this type of glazing is better than a typical wood wall.

For high-performance buildings it is recommended that a designer use simulation tools such as DOE.2.1e, an hourly simulation software, or PowerDOE, similar to DOE2.1e. For manual calculations use the *Glazing*

Design Handbook for Energy Efficiency by the American Institute of Architects (AIA) [1].

Intelligent Building Façades

An intelligent building façade operates as a sustainable window. These façades have the ability to know their optimum shape, anticipate the environmental impact on the building, and respond appropriately to keep the occupants comfortable. They can also optimize the use of energy in most cases. The intelligent building incorporates the idea that the building fabric or the skin is not a static but a dynamic situation. It can change its behavior to respond to the environmental conditions by altering its color, adding shade

Glass type	Glass thickness (inches)	Visible transmittance (% daylight)	U-factor (Winter)	Solar heat gain coefficient (SHGC)
Single Pane Glass (standard clear)	0.25	89	1.09	0.81
Single White Laminated w/Heat Rejecting Coating (*Southwall California Series®*)	0.25	73	1.06	0.46
Double Pane Insulated Glass (standard clear)	0.25	79	0.48	0.7
Double Bronze Reflective Glass (*LOF Eclipse®*)	0.25	21	0.48	0.35
Triple Pane Insulated Glass (standard clear)	0.125	74	0.36	0.67
Pyrolitic Low-e Double Glass (*LOF Clear Low-e®*)	0.125	75	0.33	0.71
Soft-coat Low-e Double Glass w/Argon gas fill (*PPG Sungate® 100 Clear*)	0.25	73	0.26	0.57
High-efficiency Low-e (*Solarscreen 2000 VEI-2M™*)	0.25	70	0.29	0.37
Suspended Coated Film (*Heat Mirror™ 66 Clear*)	0.125	55	0.25	0.35
Suspended Coated Film w/ Argon gas fill (*Azurlite ® Heat Mirror SC75*)	0.125	53	0.19	0.27
Double Suspended Coated Films w/ Krypton (*Heat Mirror™ 77 Superglass*)	0.125	55	0.1	0.34

Figure 4.5.4 Representative glass specifications.
(Source: performance calculations by Lawrence Berkeley National Laboratory WINDOW 5.2 (www.wbdg.org/resources.windows.php).)

as required, or orienting itself to minimize the energy impact. Typically, intelligent façade designs are found in modern commercial buildings. Of course, the concepts derived from this idea can be incorporated into any building, provided there is economic justification. Intelligent building façades should manipulate several building functions (adopted from *Intelligent Skins*, p. 36 [2]):

- enhance daylight (light shelves/reflectors);
- maximize daylight and passive heat (full-height windows);
- protection from the sun and heat avoidance (louvers/blinds/overhangs);
- insulation from heat loss (nighttime shutters);
- ventilation for indoor air quality (automatic dampers);
- collection of heat for hot water (solar collectors);
- control of sound (acoustic dampers);
- generation of electricity (photovoltaics).

Intelligent features of a façade should be able to manipulate several functions as layers or as an independent item as needed. Most important of all is the building management system (BMS), which will evaluate the conditions (temperature, humidity, and light levels) at the façade inside and out. Based on the conditions at any given time the BMS system will react and respond to all environmental data, natural and artificial lighting, occupants' need, ventilation requirements, heating and cooling needs, and will use the double skin, typical of intelligent skins, to meet the desired design conditions.

For example, the 22-story GSW Headquarters in Berlin, completed in 1999 (Figure 4.5.5), has two intelligent systems to provide comfort and energy efficiency. The first system is a thermal flue, one meter wide, extending from the inner glazing for the entire height of the building. Air enters at the base of the building and exits at the top. The quantity is controlled by a BMS and offers occupant control at each floor. The second system, by using red and green lights, recommends whether or not to use the mechanical system to control lighting, depending on the ambient light levels. Signals to solar cells control the lights. Occupants can always override the signals.

The second example is the Commerzbank in Frankfurt (Figure 4.5.6). The clients wanted their ecological values expressed in an environmentally friendly and functionally futuristic building design. The intelligent skin of the external windows and the atrium are equipped with motorized sashes controlled by a BMS depending on the environment (weather, etc.), while the lighting is controlled by an automatic system based on occupancy and daylight penetration. Night cooling is achieved by motorized opening and closing of windows.

Behind the façade of the alkiTECHNIK headquarters building (Figure 4.5.7) in Germany lies an innovative and trend-setting energy concept that uses 50 percent less energy. Whole-system design thinking is employed here.

Summary

Significant quantities of valuable energy can be lost through poorly designed window systems. In this regard windows and skylights in the building envelope play a significant role. By using appropriately sized and well-designed double- or triple-glazed low-E windows, energy use in a building is minimized and its sustainability improved. California's Title 24 provides prescriptive standards for windows and skylights based on area, U-factor, and solar heat gain. Manufacturers are developing more options for glazing and frames, including hybrid designs. For passively designed buildings, energy-efficient windows also aid in heating and cooling (by suitable ventilation) the buildings. Intelligent façades can actually adapt to changing conditions, thus optimizing the use of energy and responding to other environmental factors.

References

[1] The American Institute of Architects (AIA), *Glazing Design Handbook for Energy Efficiency* (Washington, DC: AIA, 1997).
[2] Michael Wigginton and Jude Harris, *Intelligent Skins* (Burlington, MA: Architectural Press, 2002).

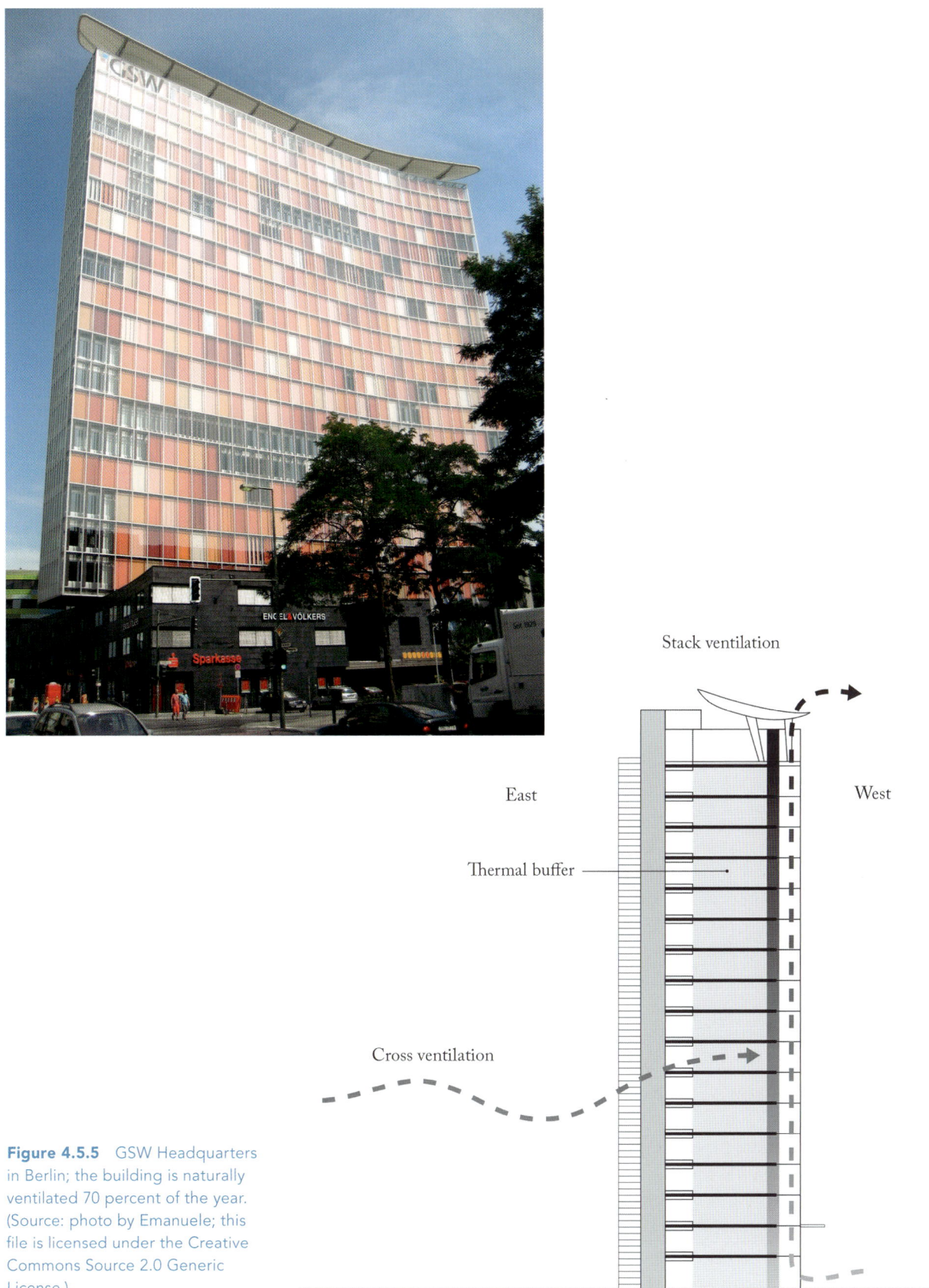

Stack ventilation

East

West

Thermal buffer

Cross ventilation

Figure 4.5.5 GSW Headquarters in Berlin; the building is naturally ventilated 70 percent of the year. (Source: photo by Emanuele; this file is licensed under the Creative Commons Source 2.0 Generic License.)

Figure 4.5.6 Commerzbank, Frankfurt.
(Source: Photo by Roland Meinecke; this file is licensed under the GNU Free Documentation License.)

Figure 4.5.7 The new headquarters of alkiTECHNIK in Ingolstadt, Germany.
(Source: this file is licensed under the Creative Commons Source 3.0 Unported License.)

Further Reading

Owen J. Lewis, *A Green Vitruvius* (London: European Commission, 1999).

California Energy Commission, *Residential and Non-residential Standards: Building Energy Efficiency Standards, Compliance Manual* (California: CEC, 2008).

E.J. Makela, J.L. Williamson, and E.B. Makela, "Comparison of Standard 90.1-2010 and the 2012 IECC with Respect to Commercial Buildings," US Department of Energy, 2011.

Web Support

www.efficientwindows.org/index.cfm
www.ppgideascapes.com

http://energy.gov/energysaver/articles/energy-performance-ratings-windows-doors-and-skylights
www.energydesignresources.com/resource/20

Exercises

1 Explain the three components of "Prescriptive Requirements for Windows" and apply the concept for a 12,000 sq.ft commercial building in Denver, Colorado. Assume the building to be properly oriented to take advantage of southern exposure.
2 Explain high-performance glazing and how it compares with low-E glazing.
3 How do intelligent building façades support sustainability? Research and explain the concept with a building you admire.

4.6   Floors and Roofs

Typically, floors carry self-weight and live loads, while roofs support environmental forces such as heat, wind, hail, rain, and others, in addition to resisting their own weight and live loads. In this section several types of floors and roofs, standards and codes for each, and sustainable options are discussed. At present, materials such as timber, concrete, and steel are commonly used for roof and floor structures. Although heat transfer is an issue for all building envelope components, in terms of floors and roofs, the discussion also centers on time factors, the rate of heat loss or gain. This is because roofs are exposed to the sun for a prolonged period and the floor slabs are in contact with constant ground temperature. While roofs can be altered if the thermal properties are not optimum, it is extremely difficult and expensive to add insulation and/or alter thermal properties to a floor that is in contact with the ground if it is not designed appropriately at the outset.

Benefits of Thermal Time Lag

Two points have to be made. One, when heat flows through a material a certain amount of heat is absorbed by the material. Two, heat flow is not instantaneous, but depends on the U-value and thickness of the material. Therefore, for any material of a given thickness, there is a certain amount of time lag before the heat is transmitted. Since some of the heat is absorbed, not all of it is transmitted. This leads us to two other significant properties of materials – *the time lag* and *the decrement factor*. The time it takes the peak temperature on the outside of a wall or a roof to make its way to a peak temperature on the inside face is called *time lag* or *decrement delay*. The time lag is the time difference between the maximum outdoor and maximum indoor temperatures and the decrement factor is the ratio between the two. Therefore, specific heat and transmittance are values intrinsic to a material. Depending on its thickness we can know the amount of heat absorbed and transmitted and the time taken for this transmission. This information can help architects design energy-efficient walls, floors, and roofs.

When it comes to heat exchanges, concern is with both the specific heat of the material and the amount (or mass) of the material. The product of mass and specific heat is known as the thermal mass. While the specific heat is a property of the material, the thermal mass depends on the amount of the material as well. The thermal mass (or capacity) is an indicator of the heat-storing ability of a material. Heat flow through materials is determined by the conductance and the resistance of the material. It is essential to know both the heat flow from or to a space and also the air-to-air resistance of materials. We need to take into account not just the resistance of the material itself, but also that of the air film at the surface of the material (Figure 4.6.1). A detailed discussion of heat transfer in building materials, the U-value and its reciprocal effect which is the resistance to heat flow, R-value, was given in Section 4.1.

Architects and building designers know that different building materials allow the passage of heat at different rates. The effects of decrement delay becomes of concern when the outside temperature fluctuates significantly higher or lower than the desired inside temperature (see Figure 4.6.2). Decrement delay is an important issue in the design of lightweight buildings, typically steel- or timber-frame in warm climates. By controlling decrement delay it is often possible to control and prevent the overheating of a building.

Typically, a timber-frame wall with brick veneer can have a decrement delay of 7.5 hours, while a masonry wall with a cavity can have a delay of 10.5 hours. A heavy mass timber construction can hold heat and slowly transfer it to the interior, delaying turning on the energy systems.

Floor as Thermal Mass

Mass surface absorbance for interior thermal storage should be high to absorb radiation, while non-massive surfaces should be reflective to redirect radiation to mass. When solar radiation strikes a surface, a portion of the sun's energy is absorbed and the rest is reflected. The amount of energy stored in the flooring material depends on color, finish, and type of material. Massive floors should be dark-colored for direct gain in a given space. General rules for collecting energy from solar radiation are:

- when the ratio of mass surface to solar glazing area is 3:1 or less, materials used to absorb and

Material	Specific Heat (Btu/lb.-°F)	Density (lb./cu.ft.)	Volumetric Heat Capacity (Btu/cu.ft.-°F)	Thermal Conductivity (Btu/hr.-ft.°F)
Sand	0.19	94.6	18	0.09 - 0.14
White Pine	0.67	27	18	0.07
Gypsum	0.26	78	20	0.28
Adobe	0.24	106	25	0.30
White Oak	0.57	47	27	0.09
Concrete	0.2	140	28	1.0
Brick	0.21	140	28	0.40
Rock	0.21	180	38	1.2 - 4.0
Water	1.0	62.4	62.4	0.33
Air 75°F	0.24	0.075	0.018	0.014
Hollow Concrete Block (~30% air)			20	
Rock Bed (void fraction ~ 1/3)			25	
Copper				232
Steel				25
Cotton Wool Insulation				0.017
Fiberglass Insulation				0.023

Figure 4.6.1 Specific heat and thermal properties of some building materials.
(Source: Harlan H. Bengtson, "Concrete Blocks as Thermal Mass for a Hot Air Heat Storage System," www.brighthub.com/environment/renewable-energy/articles/89823.aspx.)

store solar radiation should be at least 50 percent absorptive [1]; and

• the surfaces of lightweight, non-massive materials should be light in color, at least 50 percent reflective, so that they can redirect the energy to other massive surfaces.

In Figure 4.6.3, solar energy is stored in ten concrete floors (see also Figure 2.2.5 for direct gain and *trombe* wall details) of an office.

The work of African architect Mick Pearce demonstrates properties of thermal storage for a large commercial facility, as seen in his signature design for the Eastgate Building in Harare, Zimbabwe (Figure 4.6.3). This building employs common-sense passive systems for climate control based on thermal gradient, and was inspired by the work of a tiny insect, the termite. The termite, one of nature's more accomplished builders, erects the tallest earth structures on our planet when compared proportionately, and

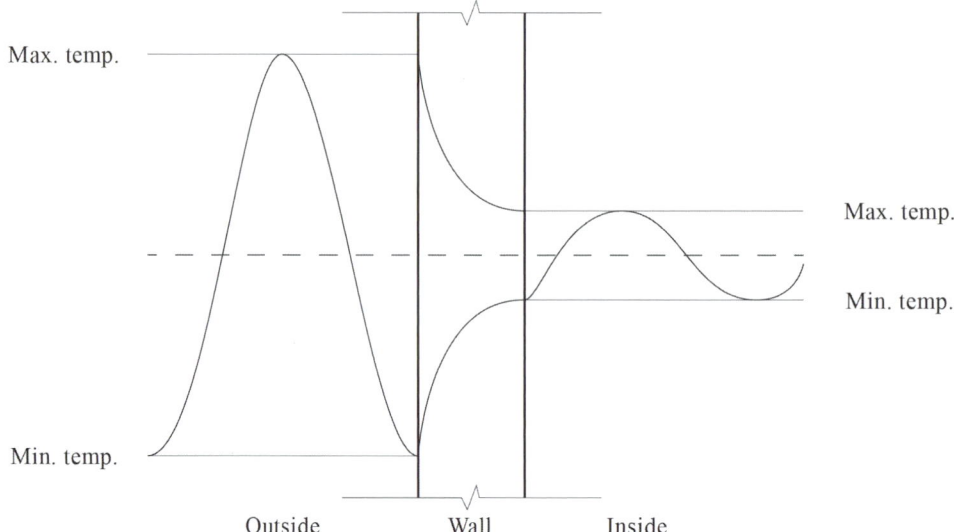

Max. temp.

Min. temp.

Max. temp.

Min. temp.

Outside   Wall   Inside

Figure 4.6.2   Decrement delay.
(Source: Kuppaswamy Iyengar.)

Figure 4.6.3   Atrium flanked by offices (Eastgate Building in Harare, Zimbabwe).
(Source: photo by Gary Bembridge; this file is licensed under the Creative Commons Source 2.0 Generic License.)

yet termite mounds maintain a constant temperature inside despite a daily fluctuation from 40 °C to less than 0 °C.

The Eastgate building is actually two buildings: an interior atrium and adjacent offices on both sides of the atrium. Heat gain is reduced by passive systems such as limited glazing, deep overhangs, and building mass, and the architect took advantage of night cooling, thermal storage and convective air currents to moderate temperatures. During the day the heavy building mass and rock storage in the basement absorb the heat of the environment and human activity. At night, cool air is allowed into the base of the building and initiates the convective flow that vents the hot daytime air through roof vents. This cool air is also stored in hollow floors and baseboard vents, and distributed the next day into offices.

If the energy is directed to a thermal storage wall or floor, these mass walls or floors should have a high absorbance color such as black, or a selective coating with low emittance. Figure 4.6.6 shows absorbance/reflectance of finishes.

In hot climates, dark surfaces absorb heat and increase the air temperature around them. Increasing the reflectance of this surface can reduce the solar load into the building. It is estimated that cooling energy requirements can be lowered by 7–12 percent in new construction built to current standards. This value can vary in older structures, depending on their location and construction.

A floor can be subjected to temperature fluctuations between its top and bottom surfaces, and also may be in contact with the ground, which can be quite cool. Under these circumstances adequate rigid insulation with proper moisture protection should be installed. The required R-value for insulation should follow local code (also see Section 4.2).

Typical Floor and Roof Construction

There are numerous types of floor and roof constructions. Figures 4.6.4 and 4.6.5 identify the most frequently used construction types: timber and steel. Adequate insulation should be installed to reduce the use of energy and support sustainability (see more in Section 4.2). Also, note that floors and roofs are usually connected to a wall and therefore their connections are critical for sustainable performance.

Sustainable Floors

As seen in earlier parts of this book, careful selection of construction materials is essential to sustainable design. Some useful flooring options are offered below.

Engineered *hardwood* floors are sustainably harvested and made with non-toxic adhesives and finishes. Floors made from FSC maple, oak, walnut, cherry, and pecan are typical sustainable floors.

Bamboo is a truly sustainable harvested grass that regenerates at least eight times faster than hardwood. Not only does bamboo mature rapidly, but harvesting does not kill the plant. It is a renewable resource that can be harvested every four years. Most bamboo flooring is made with zero VOC finishes without any added urea formaldehyde. It is quite hard and lasts a very long time.

In addition to bamboo, strand bamboo, eucalyptus, tamarindo and FSC-certified woods can be effectively used as flooring material.

Cork is a renewable bark from a tree which can be harvested every 8–10 years. It has excellent thermal and acoustical qualities. It's beautiful, lightweight, warm to the touch, hypoallergenic, fire- and insect-resistant, and stable.

Marmoleum is made from natural linoleum and is bio-based, highly durable, non-toxic, anti-microbial, and easy to maintain. It is made in sheets and tiles.

Reclaimed wood: Typically, reclaimed pine and oak come from the eastern countryside and old barns, factories, and miles of pasture fencing which shaped the USA. After decades of exposure to the elements in an ever-evolving country, the now abandoned structures have become sources for very sustainable wood structures. Many flooring companies have reclaimed these condemned structures and brought them back to life as flooring materials in interior spaces for future generations. This aged wood has unmatched durability and beauty.

Sustainable Roof Concepts

Choices for sustainable roofing move beyond conventional roofs through cool roof and green roof design.

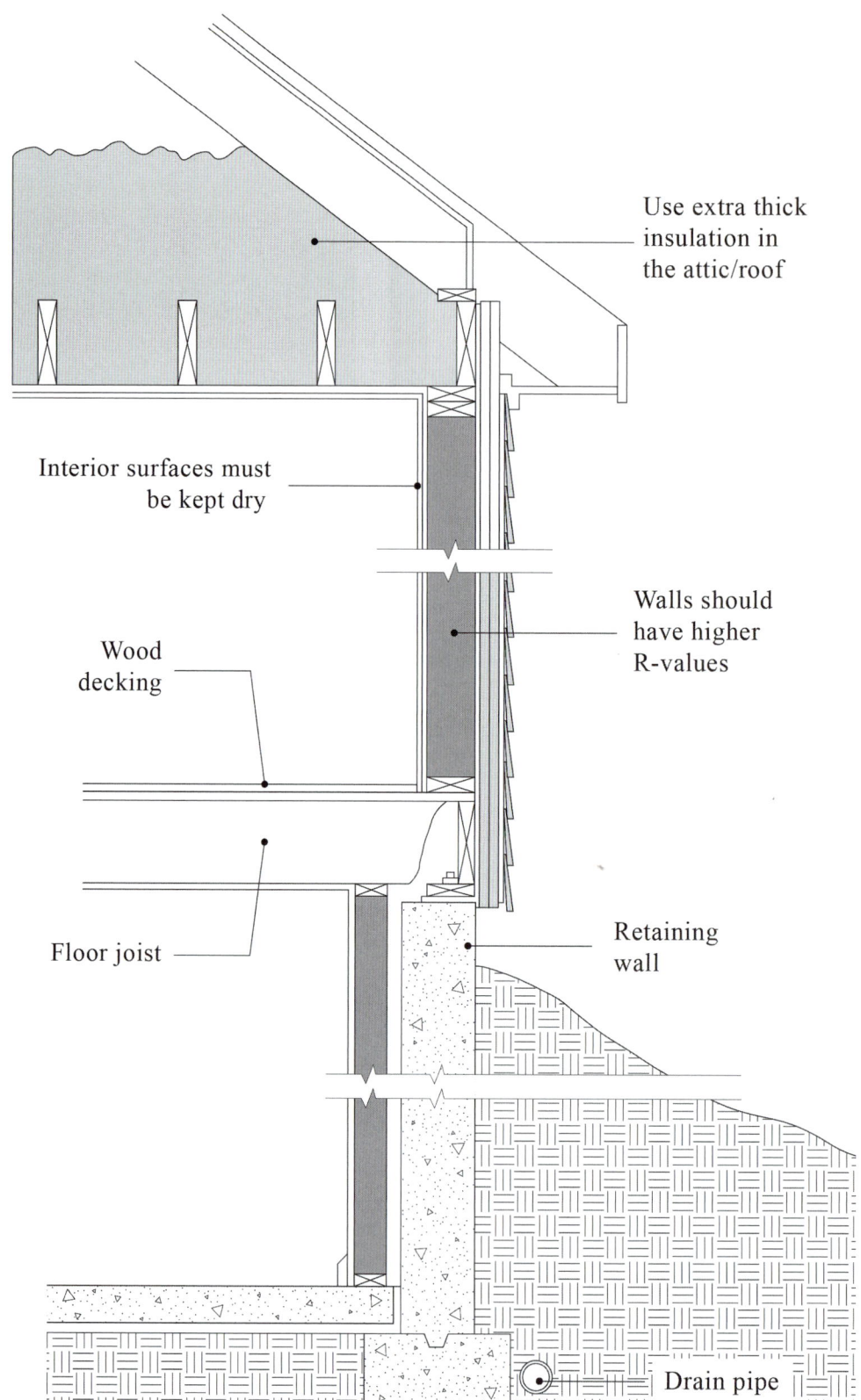

Use extra thick insulation in the attic/roof

Interior surfaces must be kept dry

Walls should have higher R-values

Wood decking

Floor joist

Retaining wall

Drain pipe

Figure 4.6.4 A typical timber floor and roof construction.
(Source: Kuppaswamy Iyengar.)

Figure 4.6.5 Typical steel floor and roof construction.
(Source: photo by Christopher Murphy.)

Cool Roofs

A cool roof is one that has been designed to reflect more sunlight and absorb less heat than a standard roof. The term "cool roof" refers to an outer layer or exterior surface of a roof that has high solar reflectance and high emittance and reduces heat gain into a building. As the term implies, the temperature of a cool roof is lower on hot sunny days than for a conventional roof, reducing cooling loads and the energy required to provide air-conditioning. Standard roofs can reach temperatures of 150 °F or more in the summer, while a cool roof under the same conditions could stay around 100 °F. The benefit of high reflectance is obvious: While dark surfaces absorb the sun's energy (visible light, invisible infrared, and

ultraviolet radiation) and become hot, light-colored surfaces reflect solar energy and stay cooler. It is also desirable to have high-emittance roof surfaces. Surfaces with low emittance (usually shiny, metallic surfaces) contribute to the transmission of heat into the roof components under the roof surface, while surfaces with high emittance allow heat to escape through radiation to the sky.

A cool roof has the following benefits:

- reduces energy bills by decreasing air-conditioning loads;
- improves indoor comfort in non-air-conditioned spaces;
- extends roof service life by decreasing roof temperature.

Cool roof coatings are white or have special reflective pigments that reflect sunlight. There are several ways to achieve the high emittance required to qualify as a cool roof. For low sloped roofs one of the best methods is to use a single-ply roofing membrane with high emittance properties as an integral part of the material.

Shingle roofs consist of overlapping panels made from a variety of materials such as fiberglass asphalt, wood, polymers, or metals. Another approach is to apply a coating to the surface of a conventional roof membrane such as modified bitumen or a mineral cap sheet. There are a number of qualifying liquid products, including elastomeric coatings and white acrylic coatings.

Metal roofs can qualify as cool roofs by using an industrial grade coating that has high reflectance and high emittance.

Several types of roof coatings are available, as discussed below.

Aluminum-Pigmented Asphalt Roof Coatings

Aluminum-pigmented coatings are silver-colored coatings, a shiny and reflective surface, that are commonly applied to modified bitumen and other roofing products. Because of the shiny surface and the physical properties of aluminum, these coatings have a minimum emittance rating of 0.75 according to CEC Title 24 [2].

Cement-Based Roof Coatings

These coatings, typically used in the central valley of California, among other regions, may be applied to almost any type of roofing product. Cement-based coatings must be manufactured to contain no less than 20 percent Portland cement. Coat thicknesses vary depending on the existing surfaces, such as metal, mineral cap, or rock/gravel.

Other Field-Applied Liquid Coatings

Other field-applied liquid coatings include elastomeric and acrylic-based coatings and should meet a number of performance and durability requirements. These coatings must be applied with a minimum thickness of 20 dry mils (0.5 mm) across the entire surface.

The Role of Color in Cool Roofs

The surface temperature of a material is a function of its ability to reject solar radiation and its ability to emit back to the environment infrared radiation. Many architects have used this property of building materials to their advantage in making their buildings more comfortable. One can observe in some older cities, in Greece and India, buildings have been painted white every year in order to keep them habitable.

Figure 4.6.6 illustrates the Solar Reflective Index (SRI) of materials, which is a measure of a color's ability to reject solar heat. Standard white has an SRI of 100, while the perfect black has an SRI of 0. It is recommended that designers should use an SRI of higher values to keep the building cooler.

Green Roofs

Using plant materials on the roof is an ancient tradition that is regaining popularity as "green roof" design. In the older traditions, sod was simply compacted on a roof and planted. However, modern green roofs are complex structures with several layers designed to deal with different functions.

Roof structures, typically, require strengthening to support the additional load due to earth for plants. This load can be nearly 120 pounds per cubic foot for wet soil plus plants. A green roof can be flat or inclined if the slope is less than 30°. Flat green roofs can become usable spaces as outdoor cafes, entertainment areas, and reading spaces. They also help cut down on noise, solar radiation and thermal transfer. Construction of green roofs requires care and attention to details, such as not leaving any protruding nails or other potential sources of water leaks into the building, and maintenance of green roofs can be a source of difficulty.

Figure 4.6.7 details the construction of a successful green roof system. The major components of a green roof include:

- *appropriate structural deck* (concrete or steel with 2 percent slope);

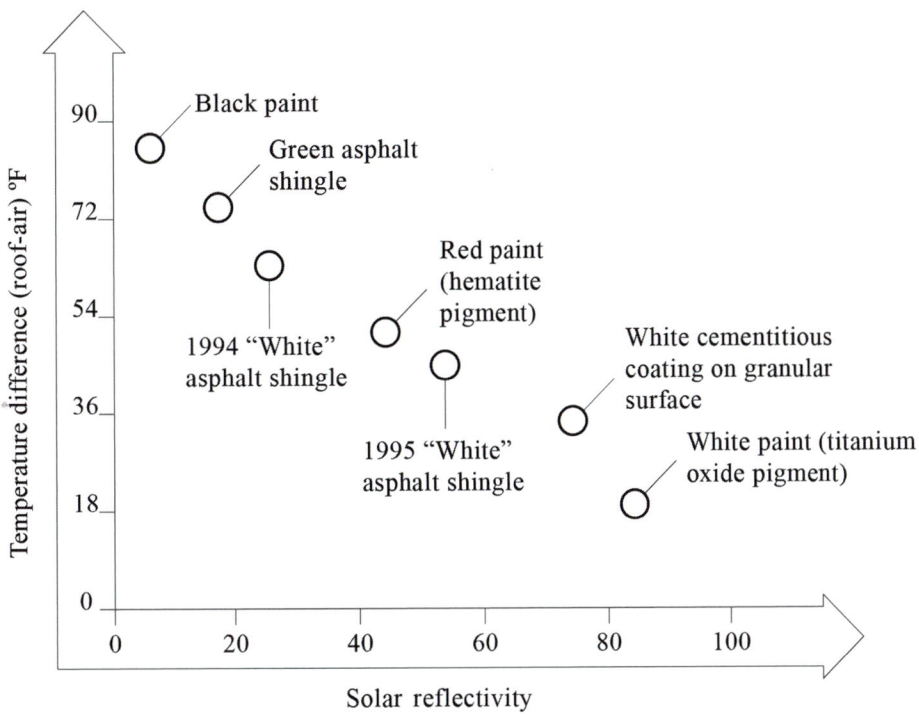

Figure 4.6.6 Solar Reflectivity Index.
(Source: www.heatisland.lbl.gov.)

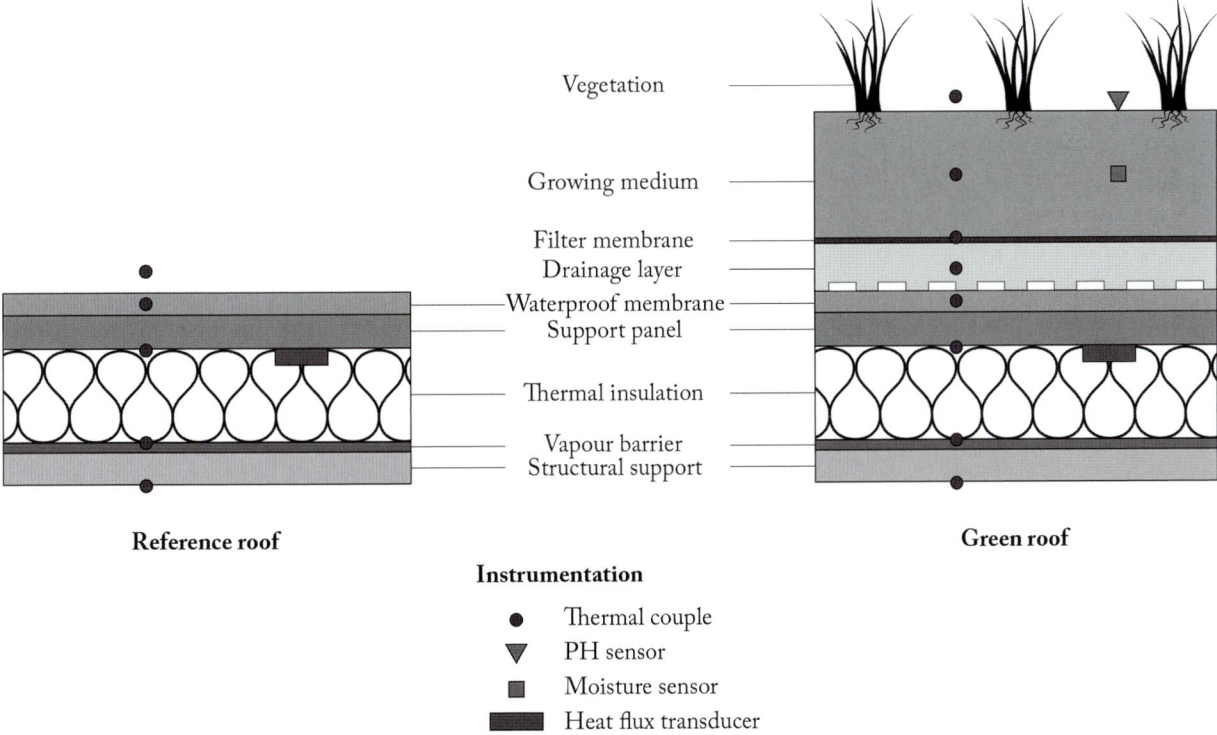

Figure 4.6.7   Cross-section of a typical green roof.
(Source: adapted from K. Liu and B. Baskaran, "Thermal Performance of Green Roofs through Field Evaluation," Greening Rooftops for Sustainable Communities Conference (www.greenroofs.org), Chicago 2003.)

- *membrane design* (field-formed membranes or factory-fabricated sheets and loose-laid or fully adhered membranes);
- *membrane properties* (low water absorption and vapor transmission, high tensile strength, high punching shear capacity and splicing resistance).

Until recently green roofs were mainly aesthetic, and it is not well documented how energy efficient they are. However, now there is increased interest in exploring the possibilities of using green roofing in many parts of the world. The Gap Building in northern California, designed by William McDonough; Eastgate in Zimbabwe by Mick Pearce; and CommerzBank in Germany, by Sir Norman Foster, are some of the modern buildings exploring the use of plant materials for controlling the building environment.

Codes and Standards for Roof and Ceiling Assemblies

The prescriptive requirements for roofs and ceilings in CEC's 2008 Title 24 [2] can be used as a model elsewhere in the USA. Exterior roofs and ceilings meet the energy-efficiency requirements in one of two ways: (1) by having the required R-value of insulation (applicable only if the roof does not have metal framing or a metal deck); or (2) by having an assembly U-factor that meets the maximum U-factor criterion (Title 24 Table 143A) for:

- most non-residential buildings, a U-factor of 0.065 is required (in areas like the south coast of California), and a U-factor of 0.059 is required in other temperate climates;
- high-rise residential buildings, the U-factor is 0.051 or R-value of R-19 (for non-metal framing or deck);
- hotel/motel guest rooms, the U-factor is 0.036 or R-30 for non-metal deck;
- relocatable public school buildings (portables), a U-factor of 0.051 or R-19 for non-metal is required in all climate zones.

Similar R-values are recommended for the walls that support these roofs and floors (see Section 4.4). It is recommended that the current 2008 CEC Title 24 standard be referenced for more information on these and other requirements.

Summary

For thermal considerations, roof and floor design is based upon the amount of heat transfer that takes place between the interior and exterior of a building. The color, thermal mass, and insulating properties of the roof materials determine the heat exchange between inside and outside and the time lag for thermal transfer. Typically, wood, concrete, and steel are the preferred floor and roof materials, though many others can be used. For sustainability, engineered lumber and recycled steel and concrete are used for roofs and floors. Different classes of coatings can also improve reflectivity and emittance of roofs, and green roofs use plants to help control building temperatures. Well-designed standards such as Title 24 can encourage the design of sustainable floors and roofs.

References

[1] J. Douglas Balcolm, *Passive Solar Heating Analysis: A Design Manual* (Atlanta, GA: ASHRAE, 1984).

[2] California Energy Commission, *Residential and Non-residential Standards: Building Energy Efficiency Standards, Compliance Manual* (California: CEC, 2008).

Further Reading

Owen J. Lewis, *A Green Vitruvius* (London: European Commission, 1999).

Public Technology, Inc. and US Green Building Council, Tom McKeag, "How Termites Inspired Mick Pearce's Green Buildings," *Zygote Quarterly*, September 2009.

Sustainable Building Technical Manual: Green Building Design, Construction and Operation (Alexandria, VA: Public Technology, Inc., 1996).

Web Support

www.engineeringtoolbox.com/heat-loss-buildings-d_113.html

http://energy.gov/energysaver/articles/cool-roofs

www.greenspec.co.uk/

Exercises

1 Describe "time decrement delay" and how you might use this concept in the passive heating or cooling of a building. Give two examples in different climatic regions.

2 Architect Mick Pearce employs biomimicry in his Eastgate Centre in Zimbabwe, as described in this chapter. Research biomimetic architecture and write a short presentation on a project that you admire. Explain sustainable aspects of the design and include images.

3 Sketch a proposal for a "cool roof" in a small commercial building. Make sure you explain the benefits of the cool roof components.

CHAPTER FIVE

Active Environmental Systems

5.1 Lighting Design

Sustainable Lighting Design

Designing sustainable, energy-saving lighting systems requires knowledge of daylight strategies, electrical lighting systems and equipment, typical lighting design load calculations, and the fundamentals of lighting power, including controls. This section also reviews computer programs that simulate lighting design, ideas for lighting retrofits, and specifications and model lighting standards [1]. *Daylight* is the least expensive and most efficient light energy source available. Of course, when the daylight is inadequate due to cloud cover or at dawn or dusk, it is essential to rely on electric lighting.

Design Considerations

A high-quality sustainable lighting environment is managed by two design paths:

1 Taking advantage of energy from natural daylight.
2 Using sustainable and efficient electric lighting.

To appreciate the human light sensory experience and other visual design experiences refer to *Perception and Lighting as Formgivers for Architecture,* by William M.C. Lam [2]. Lam was instrumental in using light to create more livable spaces and fully integrating natural

and artificial lighting to be an inseparable part of the architecture.

Careful use of daylighting can reduce heating and cooling loads, thus resulting in smaller HVAC equipment size and lowered fossil fuel use. Incorporating smart windows, skylights, atria, and light tubes can reduce the need for electric energy in both new construction and renovations. By providing dark louvers, light can be controlled on a bright day.

Objectives of sustainable daylighting are: (1) to let enough sunlight into a building without overheating the space in summer and still taking advantage of the sun for passive heating in winter; and (2) to reduce the use of electricity for lighting purposes. In order to achieve these objectives, a designer can follow many strategies at one time, from window opening options to the use of shades and layering, to understanding calculations involving the amount of sunlight that can penetrate a building.

Window Opening Options

Daylight penetration is about 2–2.5 times the height of the window opening. Whenever possible, windows should be placed near the ceiling to take advantage of greater daylight penetration. When views are important, windows at lower levels are essential. Also, horizontal windows evenly spaced will deliver more uniform daylight. Architect Le Corbusier designed ribbon windows near the ceiling in many of his buildings. It is advisable to avoid *unilateral* placement (windows on one wall) and adopt *bilateral* (on two walls – opposite or adjacent walls) placement. Placement of windows in *splayed edges* (an oblique angle or bevel given to the sides of an opening in a wall so that the opening is wider on one side of the wall than on the other) will help in the transition from very bright outside sunlight to more comfortable interior light. Use of trees, trellises, or any other form of screen can *filter* strong daylight. *Shades and Venetian blinds* are also important design elements to avoid excessive summer sun. Light can be diffused by reflecting it off of *light shelves*, as seen in two elegant examples of daylighting (Figures 5.1.1 and 5.1.2). Architects of these buildings have adopted many daylighting strategies to make their buildings energy efficient and comfortable to the users.

Notice how the architects of the Ventura Coastal Corporation Administration Office in Figure 5.1.1 utilized the light shelf and sloping ceiling to deliver diffused and uniform light levels from the south side of the building while installing vertical windows near the ceiling, and a clerestory skylight and sloping ceiling to capture daylight for the offices.

In the Emerald People's Utility District (EPUD), near Eugene, Oregon (Figure 5.1.2), daylighting strategies maximize the amount of daylight in the building and minimize the electric energy consumed,

following the 2.5*h* rule-of-thumb design criteria [3, p. 593]. The design intent is to achieve a target daylight factor of 4 percent for sufficient light during the daylight hours. The rule-of-thumb suggests that daylight will penetrate into a space that is 2.5 times the height from the floor or sill to the top of the window. In this building the T-shaped windows allow for a greater amount of light to enter at the top of the window, bounce off the light shelves and ceiling, and thus be distributed further into the interior spaces. A courtyard (not visible in the section drawing) between two buildings offers opportunities to take advantage of southern light, providing adequate daylight into two-story spaces. Virginia Cartwright, EPUD's daylight consultant, designed the light shelves. A post-occupancy study by the University of Oregon confirmed that the 2.5*h* rule holds true in this building.

Layering

In climates where the sunlight is very intense, the concept of layering has been the design solution for systematically stepping it down to manageable light intensity. In many parts of the ancient world, this practice has allowed sunlight to transition to a comfortable level for the user of the building without sacrificing architectural elegance. For example, in

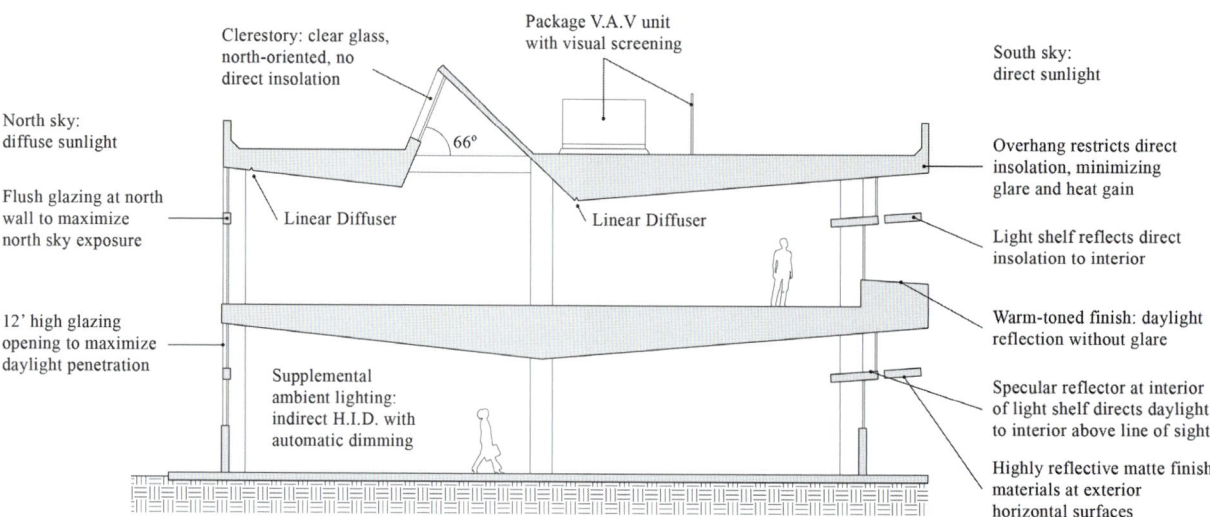

Figure 5.1.1 Daylighting section: Ventura Coastal Corporation Administration Office. (Source: design by Rasmussen and Associates, 1982, and sketch by Mike Urbanek.)

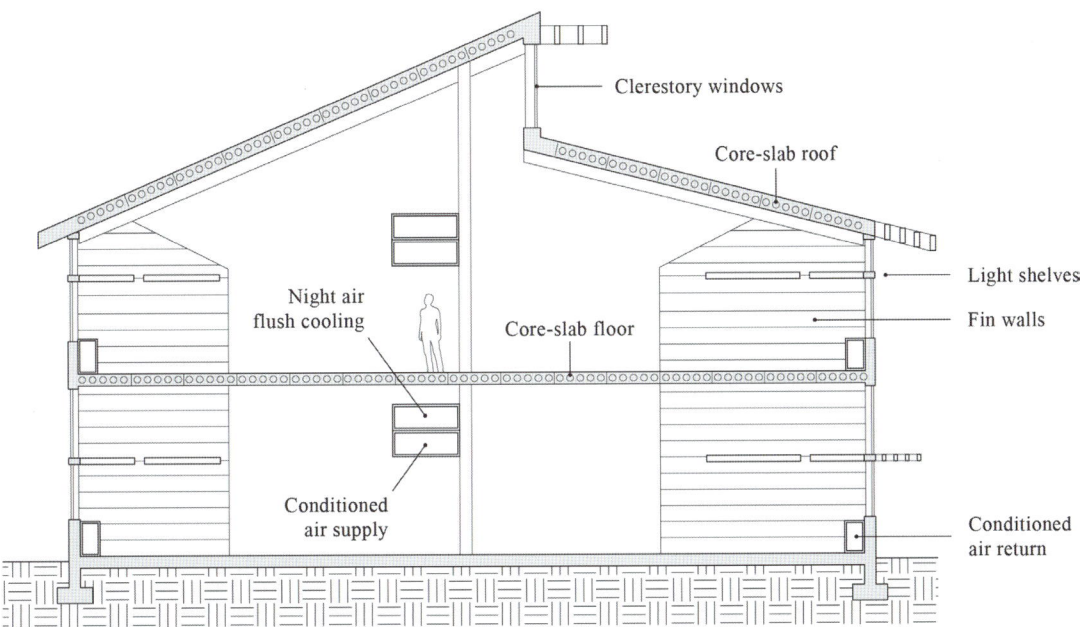

Clerestory windows

Core-slab roof

Light shelves

Fin walls

Night air
flush cooling

Core-slab floor

Conditioned
air supply

Conditioned
air return

Figure 5.1.2 Diagrammatic daylighting section, Emerald People's Utility District (EPUD), near Eugene, Oregon. Architects: WEGROUP pc and Equinox Design Inc.
(Source: Oregon Department of Energy.)

Figure 5.1.3 Courtyard in Alhambra, Spain.
(Source: photo by comakut; this file is licensed under the Creative Commons Source 2.0 Generic License.)

Alhambra, Spain (Figure 5.1.3), a courtyard reveals three layers of construction. The first layer is an exquisitely designed colonnade, followed by a second set of columns, and then a third layer of walls with windows.

Daylight Factor Recommendations

A range of sources exist to aid designers in calculating daylight penetration and determining the lighting needs for different tasks and in different locations. The daylight factor (DF) assists a designer in determining how much sunlight can be brought into a building for lighting purposes. DF is defined as the ratio of interior illuminance (Ei) to available outdoor unobstructed horizontal illuminance (Eh).

Therefore,

$$DF = \frac{Ei}{Eh \times 100}$$

Illuminance is measured in foot candles or lux.

Total daylight components comprise the sky component, the externally reflected component (from adjacent buildings, etc.), and the internally reflected component from floors, pavements and other surfaces [3, p. 590]. Recommended daylight factors are shown in Figure 5.1.4. According to the British Standards Institution, a space with a mean daylight factor between 2 percent and 5 percent is considered well lit and requires little or no additional lighting during daytime. A space with a daylight factor of less than 2 percent appears dimly lit. DF can be converted into a measurable quantity by the use of a foot candle meter which measures fc (foot candle) or lux (illuminance). Use smaller DF in southern latitudes where plentiful winter daylight is available.

Space Type	Target
Office/retail	2 percent
Classroom/conference room	3 percent
Circulation area	1 percent

Figure 5.1.4 Recommended daylight factors.
(Source: Tiffany Otis and Christoph Reinhart, "Daylighting Rules of Thumb," Harvard University Graduate School of Design.)

Determining Window and Skylight Size

Figure 5.1.5 shows how DF calculations can be used to estimate the size of windows, skylights, and other glazing options. The DFs so derived from the figure can assist a designer to come up with window or skylight sizes, to ensure that the daylighting design is correct for the building in consideration. Whatever DF is derived from this calculation should be compared with the code recommendation (Figure 5.1.4) for final design. By altering the window and skylight (atrium) areas, a designer can come close to the required DF [3, pp. 594–595].

Daylighting Design Example [4]

Consider an architectural space for a library and a graphic workshop of 120 feet (east–west) and 60 feet (north–south). It has 350 square feet of glazing on the north side, and 450 square feet of glazing on the south side.

From Figure 5.1.4, the building will require a DF of 2.5 percent, as it will require daylight for both office (2 percent) and conference spaces (3 percent).

To estimate the actual average DF for this building, use the diagram Figure 5.1.5:

DFav = 0.25 (window [or skylight area] area/ floor area)

= 0.25 ([450 + 350]) / 120 × 60)

= 0.027, or 2.7 percent

which is the exact DF required. In other real project examples if the answer is close to the calculated value (within 5–10 percent of DFav) it is acceptable.

Value of Room Reflectance

The light reflectance value is an indication of what proportion of an individual color will reflect the incident light. Reflectance is the ratio of light that a surface reflects as compared to the amount of light that falls on that surface. Dark and/or textured surfaces absorb a lot of light and thus have low light

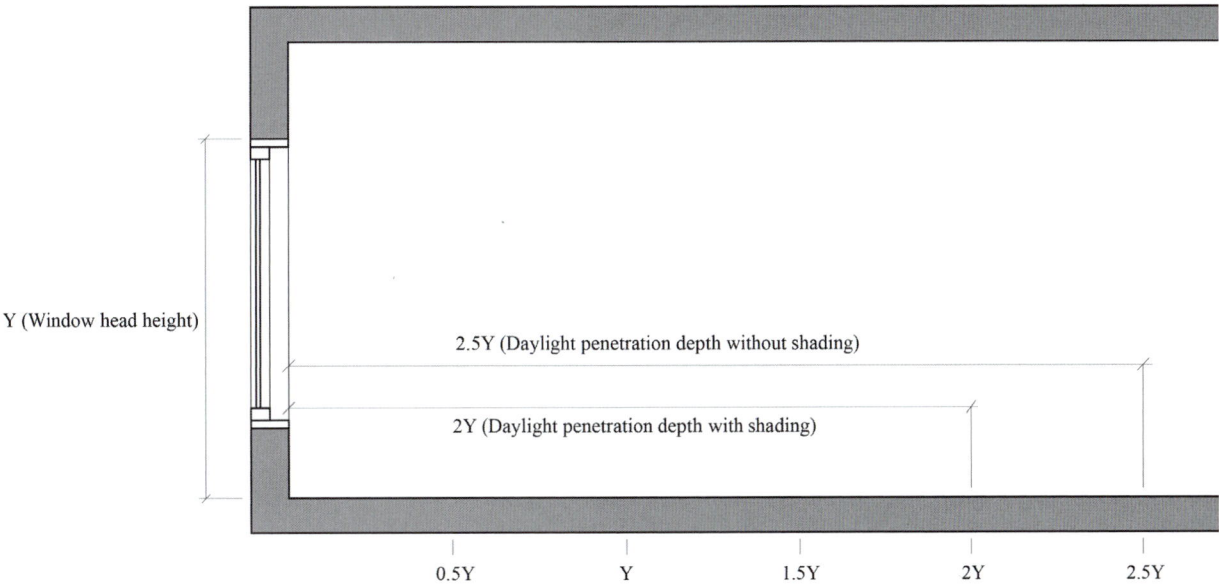

Figure 5.1.5 Depth of daylight area.
(Source: Tiffany Otis and Christoph Reinhart, "Daylighting Rules of Thumb," Harvard University Graduate School of Design.)

reflectance values. Light-colored and/or white smooth surfaces reflect most of the light that falls on them, resulting in high light reflectance values.

Black has a light reflectance value of zero and absorbs all light and heat. Dark surfaces with low light reflectance value can get very hot because they absorb all the heat. On the other hand, white has a light reflectance value of nearly 100, reflecting most of the incident light and thereby keeping a building light and cool. All colors fit between these two extremes. A color with a light reflectance value of 70 will reflect more light than a color with a light reflectance value of 35.

A designer interested in daylighting design has to pay close attention to the surface reflectance of the spaces. For additional guidance and case study examples refer to MEEB [3, pp. 579–617].

Controls and Software

A successful daylighting design should optimize architectural features with the electric lighting system. With advanced lighting controls, it is now possible to manipulate back and forth between daylight and electric lights, depending on sufficiency of daylight. There are several commercially available lighting controls to turn lights on and off, and stepped light levels and dimming conditions which can be integrated with the building management system (BMS).

Computer software tools can be used by a designer to assess different daylighting options. Tools include *Superlite 2.0* (1993), which analyzes daylight and electric lighting for various room geometries; *DOE-2*, a comprehensive hour-by-hour simulation for daylighting and glare calculations; and *Radiance*, a ray-tracing program that accurately predicts light levels and produces photo-realistic images of architectural space in all sky conditions (developed by Lawrence Berkeley National Laboratory).

Sustainable Electric Lighting Design

Daylighting options are often supplemented with efficient lighting systems that use the least amount of fossil fuel energy and are becoming increasingly important for economic and environmental reasons (Figure 5.1.6). Better design can cut lighting energy use by as much as 50 percent without causing any diminution of lifestyle and quality of life.

From the design point of view, task lighting with varying degrees of light levels can reduce the need for electric energy while enhancing the quality of the space and improving visibility. Lighting work surfaces more intensely than surrounding areas such as walkways, corridors, etc., will create the contrast necessary for performing tasks such as reviewing intricate work without eyestrain, while at the same time reducing usage for areas that need less light. Prior to the development of current lighting standards it was not uncommon to provide lighting levels up to and beyond three watts per square foot of building space. Now it is quite common to use less than one watt per square foot in many commercial buildings.

An appropriate lighting design must balance several factors, including light intensity, age of the user, intricacy of tasks, reflectance of surfaces, contrast, and tolerance for glare. For example, older people may require more light to see and certain tasks such as surgery might require higher light intensity. For specific detailed lighting design information, refer to the Illuminating Engineering Society's *Lighting Handbook*, 10th edition [4].

A lighting designer can determine the lighting needs based on different tasks of building users and with the assistance of new lighting standards such as ASHRAE 90.1-2010, California Energy Commission's 2008 Title 24 [1], the International Energy Conservation Code (IECC), and local codes for existing and new commercial buildings. Designers should meet with facility managers to ascertain the maintenance standards of the facility. A dirty light fixture, for example, might produce only 50 percent of the intended design illumination. Equipped with data about the correct level of illumination for new and existing buildings, the designer is able to plan an effective lighting system. Making viable suggestions involves familiarity with lighting systems and their components.

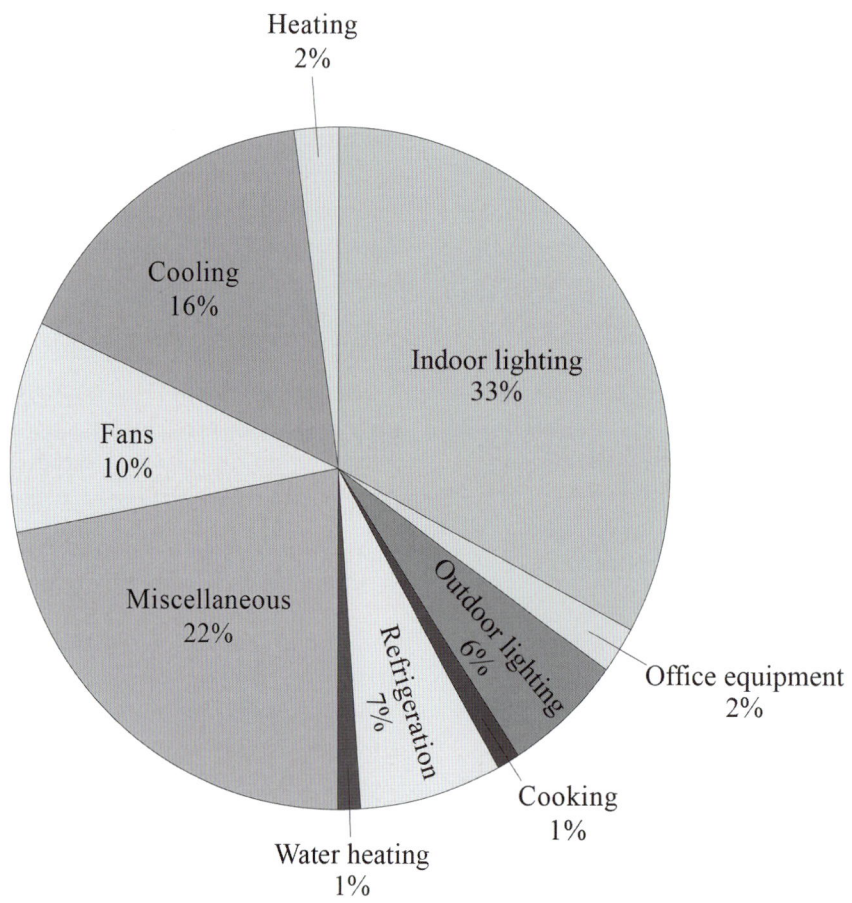

Figure 5.1.6 Energy use in commercial facilities in California (note nearly 40 percent goes to lighting). (Source: California Energy Commission.)

Fundamentals of Lighting Power (Single-Phase AC Circuits)

In order to meet sustainable goals and make appropriate lighting choices, designers need to understand the basics of lighting power and various equipment options. Most lighting systems are supplied by single-phase AC circuits. If a room is lit with incandescent lamps it is easy to compute the power needed for those lamps by simply adding the wattage of each lamp. When the supply voltage and measured current are known, the power can be computed as:

$$Q = vi \text{ watts}$$

where,

v = voltage in volts
i = current in amperes.

Lighting Systems and Equipment

Lighting systems consist of five main components to be discussed in this section:

1 lamp
2 ballast
3 reflector
4 lens
5 controls.

Lamps

The principle lamp types that are useful for a designer are fluorescent, compact fluorescent, metal halide, sodium vapor, tungsten, and LED.

Incandescent lamps consist of a resistive tungsten filament contained within an evacuated glass bulb containing a small amount of inert gas. They are connected directly to the lighting circuit and they were once prevalent and are now becoming obsolete due to lack of energy efficiency.

Fluorescent and other discharge-type lamps require a ballast, which is an inductor, to provide a high-voltage pulse to initiate the discharge through a vapor. Typically phosphor or other additives are incorporated in the lamp to modify the spectrum of emitted light to enhance colors and to improve the visible spectrum.

The current flow in the tube is controlled by the ballast. In these types of lamps, about 22 percent of the energy input is converted into light, 42 percent is dissipated as heat, and the remainder as infrared.

Energy-efficient T8 lamps, a recent development in lamp technology, not only save energy, they also offer substantial cost reductions. T8 lamps last 10–50 times longer than incandescent lamps and offer significant benefits over older T12 lamps. A 4-foot T8 can last 10,000–30,000 hours. A T6 and its cousins are under development and those are expected to perform 15–20 percent better than the T8s. T5s are especially common in Europe and are being specified more often in the USA.

Compact fluorescent lamps (CFLs), developed in the 1970s and introduced to US consumers in the 1980s and 1990s, have proven to be very efficient in all sectors. The first costs are higher for CFLs than incandescent products, but CFLs offer meaningful energy savings and longer lamp life, particularly in places where they are in use 24 hours a day, such as hospitals, manufacturing facilities with three shifts, research facilities, and so on.

Mercury vapor lamps typically have two main electrodes and a starter electrode. Upon application of a voltage to the starter electrode, argon gas is ionized and an arc is formed. Color rendition is very poor. A disappearing technology!

Figure 5.1.7 A compact fluorescent light bulb.
(Source: photo by Armin Kübelbeck; this file is licensed under the Creative Commons Source 2.0 Generic License.)

Metal halide lamps are similar to mercury vapor except that they contain various metal halides. When the lamp reaches operating temperature, the metal halide disassociates into metal and halogen. This type of lamp offers 50–100 percent efficiency over mercury vapor lamps, has a long life of 10,000–25,000 hours, and permits "white light" with improved color rendition. These types of light sources are good for department stores, schools, manufacturing units, and outdoor activities.

Sodium lamps operate on the principle of an electric current flowing through sodium vapor. In a high-pressure sodium lamp, energy is radiated over a band of wavelengths. In a low-pressure lamp, the light is almost a single color (wavelengths of 589 and 589.5 nanometers). Sodium lamps require special ballasts capable of providing high voltage.

Tungsten-halogen lamps offer superb color and brilliance and last longer than traditional incandescent alternatives. These lamps are used where high levels of light intensity are needed in small spaces like homes, theater stages, and some selected outdoor activities and as automobile headlights.

Light emitting diodes (LEDs), unlike incandescent and compact fluorescent lighting, are solid state semiconductor lighting (SSL) devices that produce visible light when an electrical current is passed through them (Figure 5.1.10). LEDs are organic light-emitting diodes (OLEDs) and light-emitting polymers (LEPs). LEDs produce light very efficiently and the heat produced is absorbed into an aluminum heat sink. LEDs can produce amber, red, green, and blue colors, which can be combined with phosphor to derive white color for general lighting purposes.

The EPA's Energy Star-rated LEDs use 75 percent less energy than traditional incandescent bulbs and last 25 times longer. LEDs even outdo CFL bulbs in efficiency, primarily because they have twice the lifespan of CFLs and they emit light in a targeted direction instead of scattering it in all directions. Equivalencies between the three lamp types are shown in Figure 5.1.9, which makes it obvious that LEDs produce more light by using significantly less electric energy.

The US Department of Energy's (DOE) report, *Adoption of Light-Emitting Diodes in Common Lighting Applications*, reveals that LEDs compete with traditional lighting sources (e.g., incandescent and fluorescent) extremely well. In 2012 about 49 million LED lamps and luminaires were installed in the nine locations, which saved approximately 71 trillion British thermal units (tBtu). The report estimates that if these markets switched to LEDs overnight, current and potential future savings could approach 3,873 tBtu,

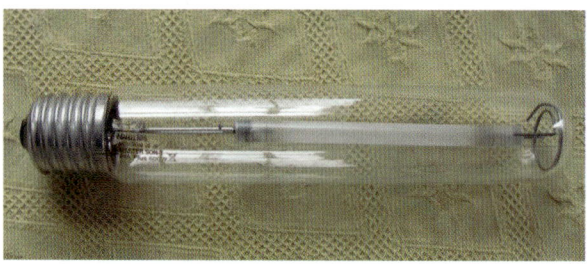

Figure 5.1.8   High-pressure sodium lamp.
(Source: photo by Bidgee; this file is licensed under the Creative Commons Source 3.0 Unported License.)

LED		**Fluorescent**		**Incandescent**
1 Watt	=	3 Watt	=	15 Watt
3 Watt	=	7 Watt	=	35 Watt
5 Watt	=	11 Watt	=	50 Watt
7 Watt	=	15 Watt	=	70 Watt
9 Watt	=	19 Watt	=	90 Watt
12 Watt	=	25 Watt	=	120 Watt
15 Watt	=	31 Watt	=	150 Watt
18 Watt	=	36 Watt	=	180 Watt

Figure 5.1.9   Equivalencies between three lamp types.
(Source: US EPA.)

Figure 5.1.10 Different types of LEDs.
(Source: photo by Geoffrey.landis at en.wikipedia; this file is licensed under the Creative Commons Source 3.0 Unported License.)

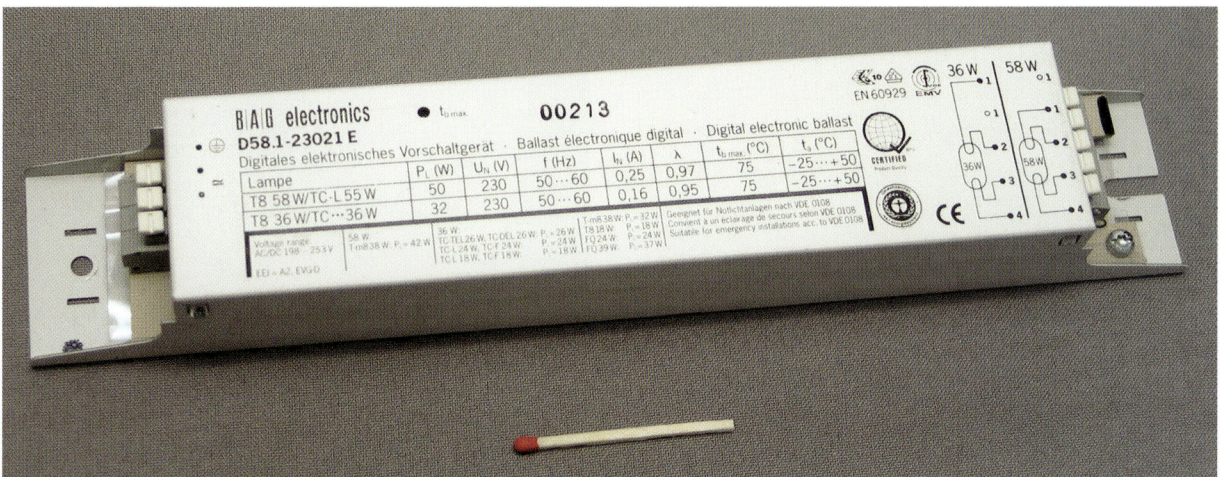

Figure 5.1.11 Electronic ballast with high capacity.
(Source: photo by Christian Taube Chiaube; this file is licensed under the Creative Commons Source Share Alike 2.0 Germany License.)

or about 3.9 quadrillion Btu (quads), saving nearly $37 billion in annual energy costs. This amount represents approximately half of the total national lighting energy consumption in 2012.

Other components of lighting systems include *ballasts*, *reflectors*, *lenses*, and *controls*.

Ballast

A ballast basically is an inductor to provide an initial high-voltage pulse to initiate the discharge through a conducting vapor or gas. Current electronic ballasts have replaced core coil ballasts in the marketplace. These electronic ballasts have a long life (Figure 5.1.11).

Reflector

Usually a reflector is made of a metal trough to redirect the light where it is needed. Several types and manufacturers are available for reflector design. The design philosophy here is to redirect the maximum amount of light to where it is most needed.

Lens

Typically, lenses cover lamps to better distribute or redirect light. Lenses come in various shapes and styles, from simple to ornamental. Interior design and the preferences of the designer dictate the final lens design. Many light manufacturers offer a variety of lenses for the user.

Controls

The simplest way to improve lighting efficiency is to turn off the lights when they are not in use. All lighting systems must have switching or control capabilities to allow lights to be turned off when they are not needed.

There are two major types of lighting controls. The first group includes manual controls, which control each light fixture or a group of lights. If daylighting is used in a building, usually a separate set of controls are employed to turn on the lights during dark or late day times or to dim the lights during bright hours to maximize lighting efficiency. Also, in an open office, groups of lights are controlled by a single switch to maximize the efficiency of electricity use. The second type includes automatic controls such as occupancy sensors. Occupancy sensors are divided into two types, passive infrared (PIR) and ultrasonic. PIR sensors cue into the human body's heat signature and can incorporate various lenses to limit the lighting's functional range. Ultrasonic models use high-frequency sound waves to detect occupancy based on movement. New passive dual-technology (PDT) sensors combine the benefits of both heat sensing and sound waves. Some of the control mechanisms recommended by the CEC are noted below. For detailed information refer to California Energy Commission's 2008 Title 24 [1].

Automatic Time Switches

Automatic time switches (Figure 5.1.12), sometimes called time clocks, are programmable switches that are used to automatically shut off the lights according to pre-established schedules, depending on the building's hours of operation. The device should have the capability to store two separate daily programs (for weekdays and weekends). To prevent losing the time of day and the programmed schedules, the time switch must contain back-up power for at least ten hours during a power interruption. Most building automation systems can meet these requirements.

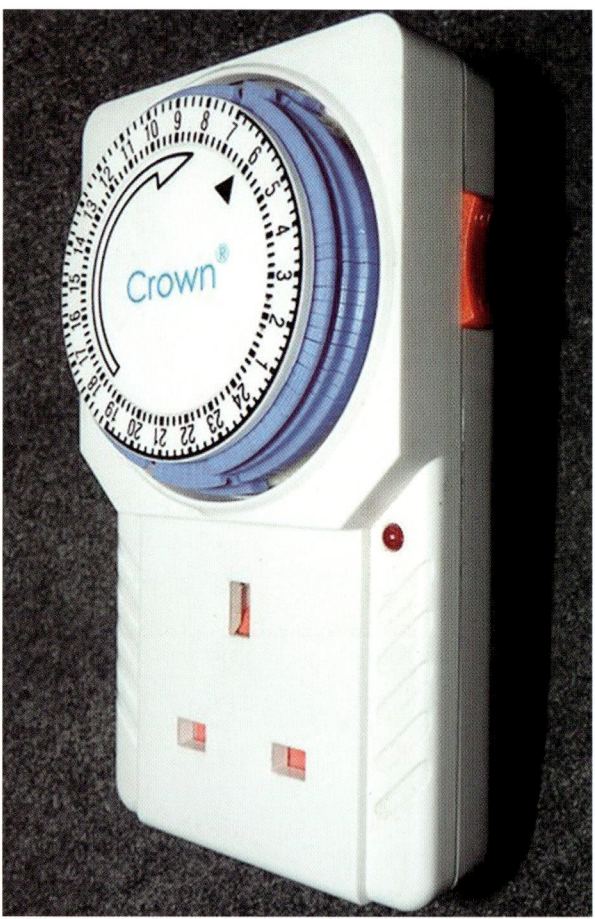

Figure 5.1.12   Automatic time switch.
(Source: photo by cmglee; this file is licensed under the Creative Commons Source 3.0 Unported License.)

Occupant Sensors

Occupant-sensing devices should be capable of automatically turning off all of the lights in an area no more than 30 minutes after the area has been vacated. Additionally, the ultrasonic type must meet certain minimum health requirements, and have the built-in ability for sensitivity calibration. Microwave devices, which are rarely used for occupancy sensors, must have emission controls, permanently affixed installation requirements, and built-in sensitivity adjustment.

Automatic Daylighting Controls

Daylighting controls (Figure 5.1.13) consist of photo sensors that compare actual illumination levels with a reference illumination level and reduce the electric lighting until the reference level has been reached. The photo sensor provides light-level information to the controller so it can decide when to increase or decrease the electric light level. These controls should have the ability to reduce the general lighting power of the controlled area by at least 50 percent uniformly.

Examples of Typical Lighting Design Load Calculations

Designers can use lighting design load calculations, Table 146-C of Title 24 [1], to plan for maximum lighting effectiveness and sustainability. All primary function areas (PFAs) are listed in Table 146-C. The "dominant" PFA refers to the function area with the largest floor area among all function areas contained within a space.

Use of common lighting system recommendations will ensure compliance and a lighting power density less than 1 W/sq.ft for almost any building space. Although this method will only work for some

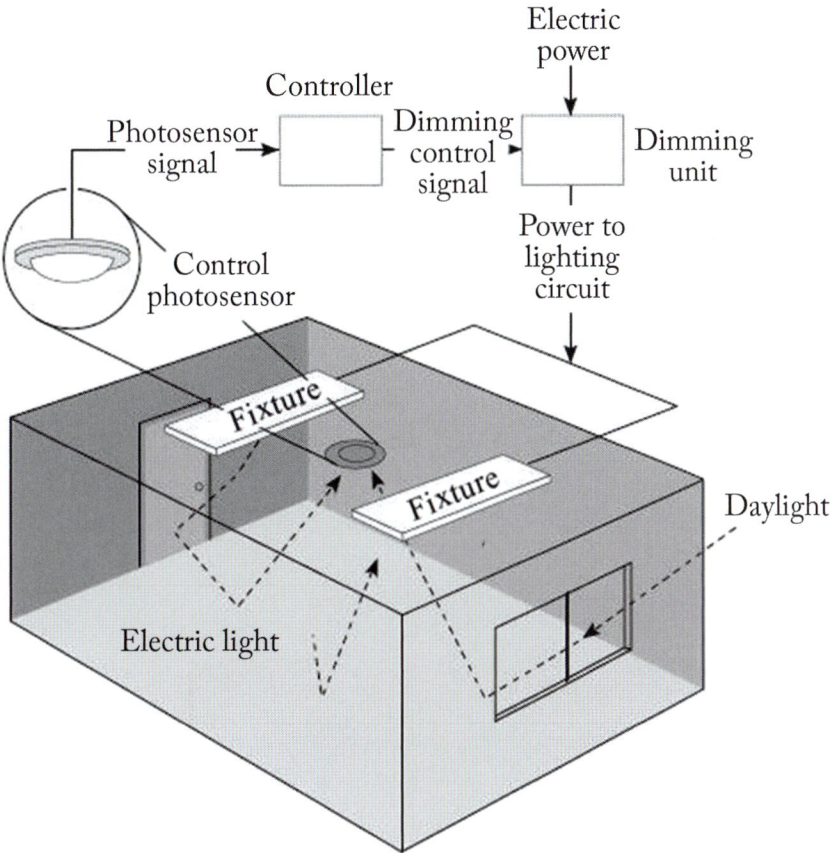

Figure 5.1.13 Typical daylight harvesting control system.
(Source: image courtesy of the Lawrence Berkeley National Laboratory.)

Standards Table 146-C Area Category Method (CEC 2008) - Lighting Power Density Values	
PRIMARY FUNCTION ALLOWED LIGHTING POWER	**Watts/sq.ft**
Auditorium	**1.5**
Classrooms, lecture, training, vocational room	1.2
Civic meeting place	1.3
Commercial and industrial storage	0.6
Convention, conference, multipurpose, and meeting centers	1.4
Corridors, restrooms, stairs, and support areas	0.6
Dining	1.1
Electrical, mechanical rooms	0.7
Exercise center, gymnasium	1
Exhibit, museum	2
Financial transactions	1.2
Multi-family	1
Dormitory, senior housing	1.5
Hotel function area	1.5
Kitchen, food preparation	1.6
Laundry	0.9
Library	
Reading areas	1.2
Stacks	1.5
Lobbies	
Hotel lobby	1.1
Main entry lobby	1.5
Locker/dressing room	0.8
Lounge/recreation	1.1
Malls and atria	1.2
Medical and clinical care	1.2
Office	1.2
Parking garage	0.4
Religious worship	1.5
Retail merchandise sales, wholesale showrooms	1.7
Tenant lease space	1
Transportation function	1.2
Theaters	
Motion picture	0.9
Performance	1.4
Waiting area	1.1
All other	0.6

Figure 5.1.14 Suggested power densities for different spaces.
(Source: extracted from CEC table 146-C.)

building types, these types make up a large portion of buildings in the USA.

Also, lighting design loads/compliance can also be achieved using the tailored method or the performance method, which requires computer modeling. The lighting power portion of the building energy performance allowed budgets is determined by following applicable local codes and standards for sustainability.

The following examples illustrate how to calculate the lighting power requirements for a sample building to easily comply with 2005 Title 24 lighting power requirements. For the latest revised design guidelines refer to 2008 Title 24 documents.

Function	Area	W/sq.ft	Watts
Bank (financial transactions)	4,700	1.2	5,640
Grocery store	4,500	1.7	7,650
Mechanical room	200	0.7	140
Common restrooms	300	0.6	180
Common corridors	1,500	0.6	900
Retail function	6,000	1.7	10,200
Retail restrooms	200	0.6	120
Retail corridor	600	0.6	360
Subtotal	18,216 SF		
Total building lighting power		25190 W	
The allowed lighting power is 25 kW			

Example 1 for new construction (the area category method)

Using Figures 5.1.14 and 5.1.15, determine the allowed lighting power by *the area category method* and refer to the sketch for approximate floor areas.

Example 2 for renovation by complete building method or area category method

Using the example above as an existing building with the retail store portion being renovated, the allowed lighting power for the retail would be:

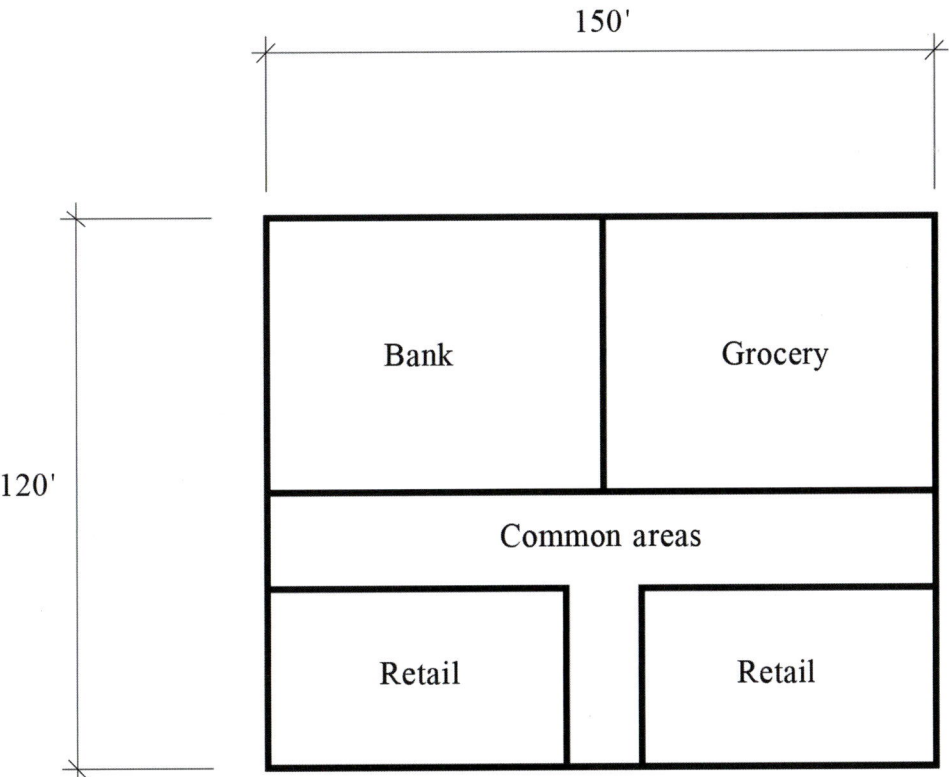

Figure 5.1.15 Sketch of floor plan for lighting design exercise (not to scale). (Source: Kuppaswamy Iyengar.)

Complete building method:
Allowed lighting power is 5,500 × 1.5 = 8,250 W or 8.25 kW

Area category method

Function	Area	W/sq.ft	Watts
(a) Retail	4,700	1.7	7,990
(b) Restrooms	200	0.6	120
(c) Retail corridor	600	0.6	360
Total allowed lighting power			8,470 W or 8.47 kW

One can see the final results are reasonably close for both methods.

Computer Programs for Electric Lighting Design

Computer programs such as *Radiance* or *AGI32*, *Superlite 2.0* and *DOE 2.0* are now available to simulate the required lighting design. *Radiance* can show the completed lighting quality in three dimensions to allow the designer to visualize the final product.

Specifications and Lighting Standards (from [1])

For detailed lighting design specifications refer to *The Lighting Handbook* [4] for both residential and commercial buildings. Typically, fixture catalog numbers listed on the designer's drawings and specifications should indicate manufacturer, design, appearance, and performance required. All integrally and remotely controlled lights and ballasts should be identified for proper lamp performance and should meet Underwriters Laboratories (UL) and Certified Ballast Manufacturers Association Standards. It is important to be aware that all fixtures must be tested in accordance with applicable sections of the National Electrical Manufacturers Association (NEMA) Standards. It is strongly recommended that a designer coordinate mechanical construction to avoid conflicts and ensure architectural integrity between light fixtures, supports, fittings, and mechanical equipment and systems.

Lighting Retrofits

Lighting upgrades for existing buildings can be evaluated using some of the current guidelines suggested above for new construction. When retrofitting an existing building, the first step is to conduct a lighting survey. If it is determined that lighting fails to meet the standards, there are several methods available for retrofitting lighting in buildings. The cost-effectiveness of retrofit approaches depends on the energy costs, lighting utilization, and the cost of these retrofits.

Residential Lighting

Residences can also make a significant contribution in reducing pollution and assisting the planet to recover from environmental damage by reducing the use of electric lighting. For new construction, follow the standards suggested in this chapter to design the appropriate lighting installation and follow a prudent use pattern. For an existing building, conduct an energy audit to see what corrections are needed. For a typical single-family residence the connected electrical load for all electricity using equipment should be around 3–3.5 kW. This load can be partially supported by photovoltaic (PV) systems, which help in reducing environmental pollution. In some ideal situations the excess power generated by a PV system can augment toward the initial cost of the PV system. For additional information on residential energy management refer to Energy Star guidelines by the Environmental Protection Agency (EPA) and local utilities.

Summary

Energy efficiency reduces energy costs for owners, increases reliability and availability of electricity for the state, improves building occupant comfort, and reduces environmental impact. Understanding of daylighting and electric lighting systems and their components (lamps, ballasts, reflectors, lenses, and controls) allows designers to make appropriate choices for sustainable design. Calculating energy requirements of lighting and awareness of California's 2008

Title 24 and 2010 ASHRAE 90.1 standards also allow planning for energy efficiency, whether for new construction or retrofitting existing structures.

References

[1] California Energy Commission, *Building Energy Efficiency Standards for Residential and Commercial Buildings, Compliance Manual* (California: CEC, 2010).

[2] William M.C. Lam, *Perception and Lighting as Formgivers for Architecture* (New York: McGraw-Hill, 1977).

[3] B. Stein, J. Reynolds, W. Grondzik, and A. Kwok, *Mechanical and Electrical Equipment for Buildings* (New York: John Wiley & Sons, Inc., 2006).

[4] David DiLaura *et al.*, *The Lighting Handbook* (New York: IES, 2011).

Further Reading

G. Brown and Mark DeKay, *Sun, Wind & Light* (New York: John Wiley & Sons, Inc., 2001).

California Institute for Energy Efficiency (CIEE), *Building Technologies Program, Tips for Daylighting with Windows – The Integrated Approach* (California: Lawrence Berkeley National Laboratory, 1997).

Kuppaswamy Iyengar, *Lighting the End of the Efficiency Tunnel* (Des Plaines, IL: Cahners Publishing Co., 1999).

Norbert Lechner, *Heating, Cooling and Lighting*, (New York: John Wiley & Sons, Inc., 2009).

Office of Energy Efficiency and Renewable Energy, *Building Energy Use* (US Department of Energy, 2007)

Craig B. Smith, *Energy Management Principles* (Oxford: Pergamon Press, 1981).

John M. Swift, Jr. and Tom Lawrence, *ASHRAE Green Guide* (Atlanta, GA: ASHRAE Publications, 2010).

Web Support

www.arch.ced.berkeley.edu/vitalsigns/bld/Casestudies/epud.pdf

http://wbdg.org/resources/daylighting.php

www.energystar.gov/index.cfm?c=lighting.pr_what_are

Exercises

1 What are the design considerations for a high-quality sustainable lighting design? Describe an efficient and aesthetically elegant cross-section of an office building. List all daylighting ideas.

2 What is the importance of the daylight factor in lighting design? Determine the required percentage of daylight factor for an office building in Los Angeles in March or September. You may use MEEB as a reference.

3 Use computer programs Radiance and DOE2.0 to simulate lighting design for a small retail facility of 1,500 square foot.

4 Using the "complete building method" explained in CEC's Title 24, determine the total building lighting power for a department store of 45,000 sq.ft.

5.2 HVAC Design

The main functions of a heating, ventilation, and air-conditioning (HVAC) system are to maintain thermal comfort (heating and cooling) and to provide adequate filtered ventilation for good indoor air quality. This section discusses typical HVAC system configurations in light of energy efficiency and sustainability. It begins with the reminder that all passive sustainable systems design opportunities such as those outlined in Chapter 2 should be utilized before turning to active HVAC design. Smart controls, retrofit, and sustainable initial design contribute to energy efficiency of HVAC systems.

From Figure 5.2.1 it can be seen that residential and commercial buildings share 39 percent of energy use in the USA.

HVAC systems require considerable energy. Depending on the climatic zone, a US commercial office building on average uses 12–32 percent of energy for space heating, 5–8 percent for ventilation, and 8–14 percent for space cooling. The average energy use for HVAC components in commercial buildings can be 8–18 percent. The amount of energy used for HVAC is increasing. In fact, roughly 90 percent of all new commercial facilities are air-conditioned.

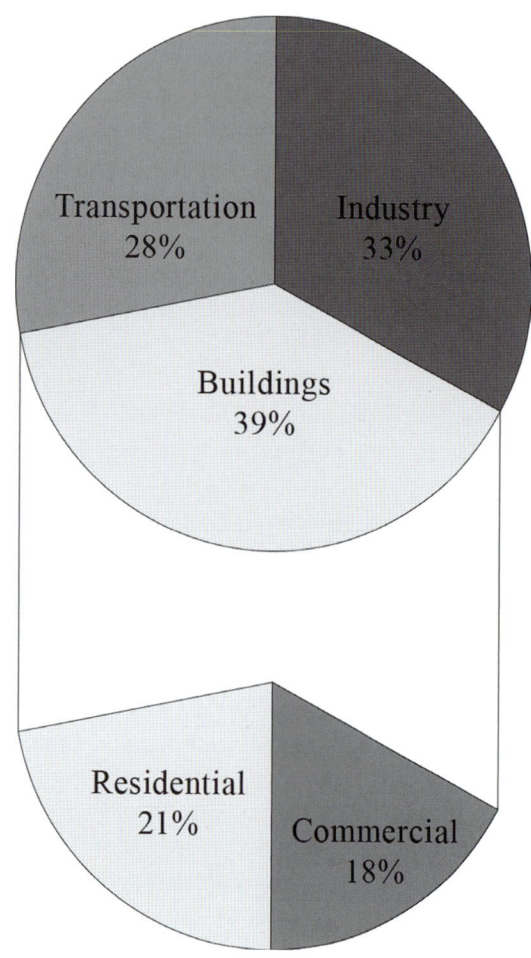

Figure 5.2.1 Buildings' share of US primary energy consumption.
(Source: US Department of Energy.)

Objectives of an HVAC System

The main objectives of an HVAC system in a building are:

- air movement is gently and evenly distributed throughout the room;
- cool air must be directed toward the walls and objects in the room;
- circulated air must be clean and healthy;
- normally air is not "thrown" more than 20 feet from a register;
- the system needs to be quiet;
- losses from ductwork must be reduced or eliminated;
- the system must be easy to install and maintain for decades.

HVAC Design Basics

A building designer and his consultant must be aware of several factors when designing an HVAC system:

- the specific functions and uses for each of the spaces in the building;
- an occupant count for each space;
- the location, climate, and orientation of the building;
- the building materials and construction methods for the foundation, walls, windows, and roofs, and their U-values, shading coefficients, and solar heat gain factors.

With this information, by using manual calculations or simulation programs (see Section 4.1) a designer can determine the heat gain/loss due to conduction, convection, and latent heat generated by people to establish the type of HVAC system appropriate for the building.

The Functions of HVAC

HVAC systems (Figure 5.2.2) address temperature and humidity control, ventilation, air motion and air filtration. In new construction, and in some retrofit situations, well-insulated and appropriately oriented buildings combined with passive design features using sun, night cooling, atriums, skylights, and daylighting to reduce heat from lighting can greatly reduce heating and cooling energy needs. Understanding interactions between all these systems offers a designer the opportunity to be creative in optimizing resource utilization and energy efficiency. In the US southwest, for example, evaporative cooling will use less energy than central HVAC systems. This option should be weighed against the cost of water use needed for evaporative coolers.

Except in certain commercial and institutional buildings, the purpose of an HVAC system is to heat or cool people, not buildings. This simple shift in viewpoint can offer changes in operational patterns, which make large energy savings possible. Instead of overheating rarely used hallways, designers can aim for optimum energy use based on the human needs for the space. Functions within a building, unrelated to

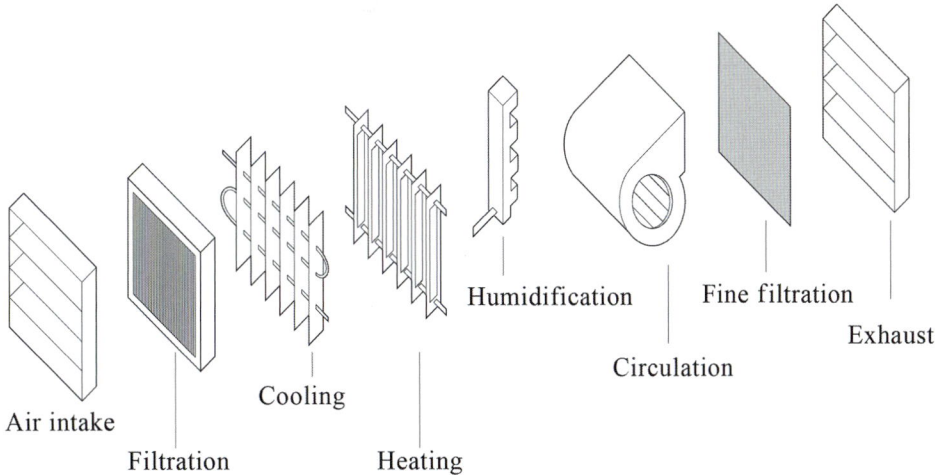

Humidification   Fine filtration

Circulation   Exhaust

Cooling

Air intake

Filtration   Heating

Figure 5.2.2 The functions of HVAC.
(Source: image courtesy of Tim Padfield, conservationphysics.org.)

HVAC, may restrict the extent to which energy can be successfully minimized, as in chemistry laboratories and clean-rooms, which might require 100 percent outside air. However, a focus on human requirements means that energy use is carefully directed, and may thus require smaller active systems.

Typical HVAC System Configuration

HVAC systems are configured to provide heating, air-conditioning, and suitable ventilation (Figure 5.2.3). They can be separate or combined systems. The following system descriptions are organized into three main categories: heating, cooling, and ventilation/air distribution, although there is considerable overlap of these three parts.

Heating Systems

Conceptually, heating is simple. A fuel is burned and the heat produced is distributed to different parts of a building. For heating a space, use of hot air, hot water, or steam can be employed. For both heating and cooling, an air distribution system requires a significant part of the building space for ducts. Water and electrical heating systems require less space than ducts to heat the same space. Also, sources of fuel for heating such as gas, oil, and solar require additional storage space in a building. These considerations will

have great effect on the resulting building architecture. For larger commercial buildings, mostly hot water or steam is used. In these systems, hot water or steam is piped to a finned heat exchanger located in the ducts. The air that passes over this exchanger picks up the required heat energy which then will be forced into the occupied space. Broadly, heating systems classify into:

- residential combined heating and cooling
- others
    - furnaces (air) and radiators (hot water/steam)
    - radiant floors
    - heat pumps (heating and cooling)
    - geothermal systems
    - active solar space heating.

Residential Combined Heating and Cooling Systems

For a small residence hot air can be moved by convection or forced draft using a small blower or fan. This equipment includes a furnace, air-conditioners, air filtration systems, humidifiers, and dehumidifiers designed to be energy efficient and help keep indoor air quality comfortable, healthy and clean.

Other residential split heating systems include both cooling and heating as illustrated in Figure 5.2.4. Cooling or condensing units to expel the hot air from

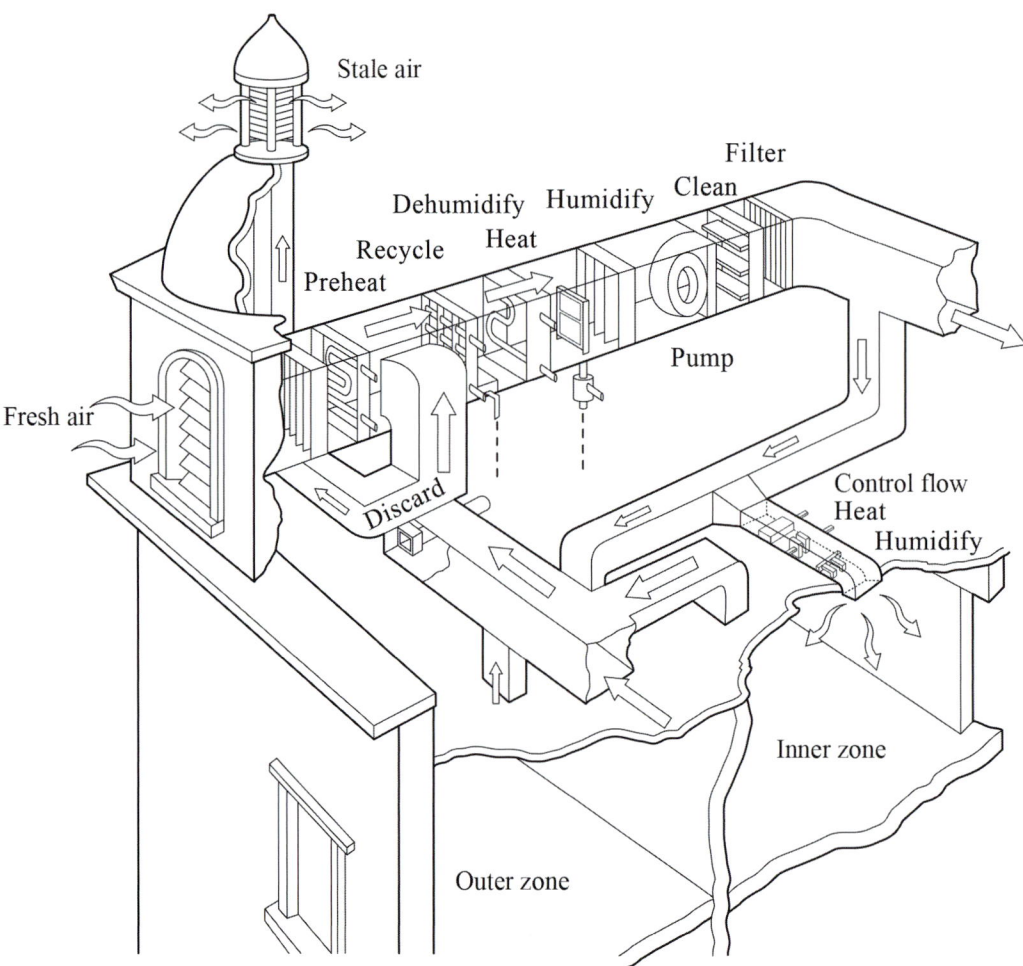

Figure 5.2.3 HVAC system configuration (functions and components).
(Source: image courtesy of Tim Padfield, conservationphysics.org.)

the house are placed outside the building, while the furnace is located in the house in an attic or some other convenient location.

Furnaces (Air Systems) and Boilers (Hot Water or Steam Systems)

Furnaces and boilers are the most common types of heating systems (Figure 5.2.5). Energy is saved by improving the efficiency of these systems through better maintenance and minor modifications. The federal minimum efficiency standards for furnaces took effect in 1992, requiring that new furnaces have an AFUE (annual fuel utilization efficiency – the percentage of fuel that is converted to heat, factoring

in combustion, seasonal use, and on/off cycling) of 78 percent. The most energy-efficient new furnaces rated by the US Environmental Protection Agency (EPA) under the voluntary Energy Star® label have an AFUE of 90 percent or higher. Energy Star-rated boilers have an AFUE of 85 percent or higher.

Radiant Floor Systems

A current popular radiant heating system (Figure 5.2.6) works by circulating hot water through a network of cross-linked polyethylene (PEX) pipes placed in the floor. The surface area of the floor gently radiates heat evenly and consistently throughout the room. The system works with a variety of heat sources and

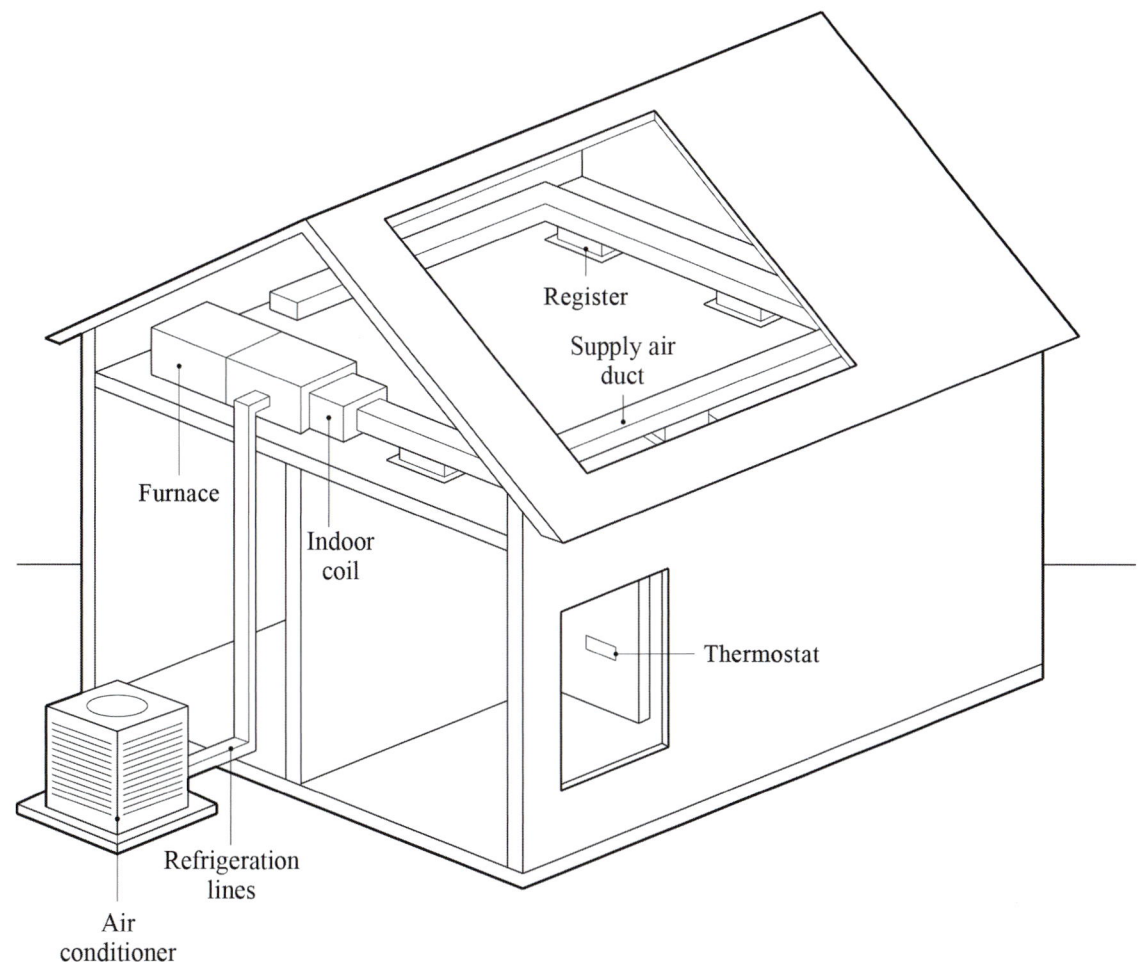

Figure 5.2.4 Residential split heating and cooling system.
(Source: Kuppaswamy Iyengar.)

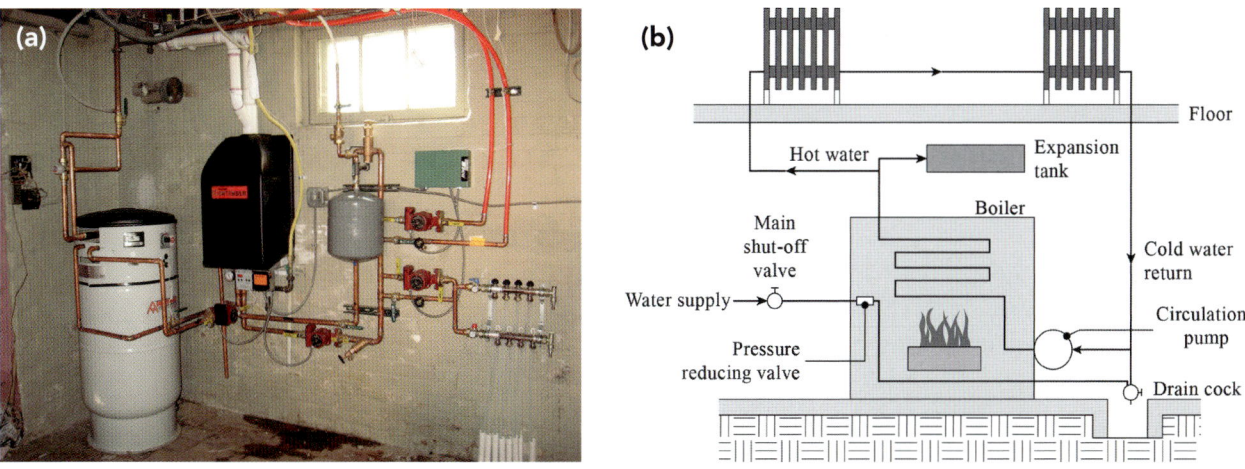

Figure 5.2.5 (a) High-efficiency furnace; (b) Schematic of a radiator boiler.
(Source: US Department of Energy.)

floor coverings. Room temperatures can be individually controlled, if used properly, by using multiple thermostats, allowing for lower thermostat settings to maintain the same comfort level. Additionally, it should be noted that because of the slow response of radiant systems, they should not be adjusted frequently nor used with night and occupancy setback scheduling thermostats.

A heat pump called a "reverse cycle chiller" generates hot and cold water rather than air, which can be used with radiant floor heating systems in a heating cycle. Unit heaters can also provide heating comfort for smaller buildings.

It is unlikely that all parts of a building will require the same amount of thermal energy and therefore the spaces are thermally zoned for different requirements in HVAC design. Separate thermostats are installed for different zones.

Heat Pumps (Heating and Cooling)

A heat pump can be used for both heating and cooling. The mechanical operation of a heat pump is identical to that of a chiller, except that the heat pump can also transfer heat from outside for use inside the building. In the summer it acts as an air-conditioner, removing heat from air inside the building and carrying it outside. In the winter it operates in reverse. There are two main types of residential heat pumps: air-source and geothermal, which are also known as ground source and geo exchange heat pumps.

Air-source heat pumps: Air-source heat pumps use

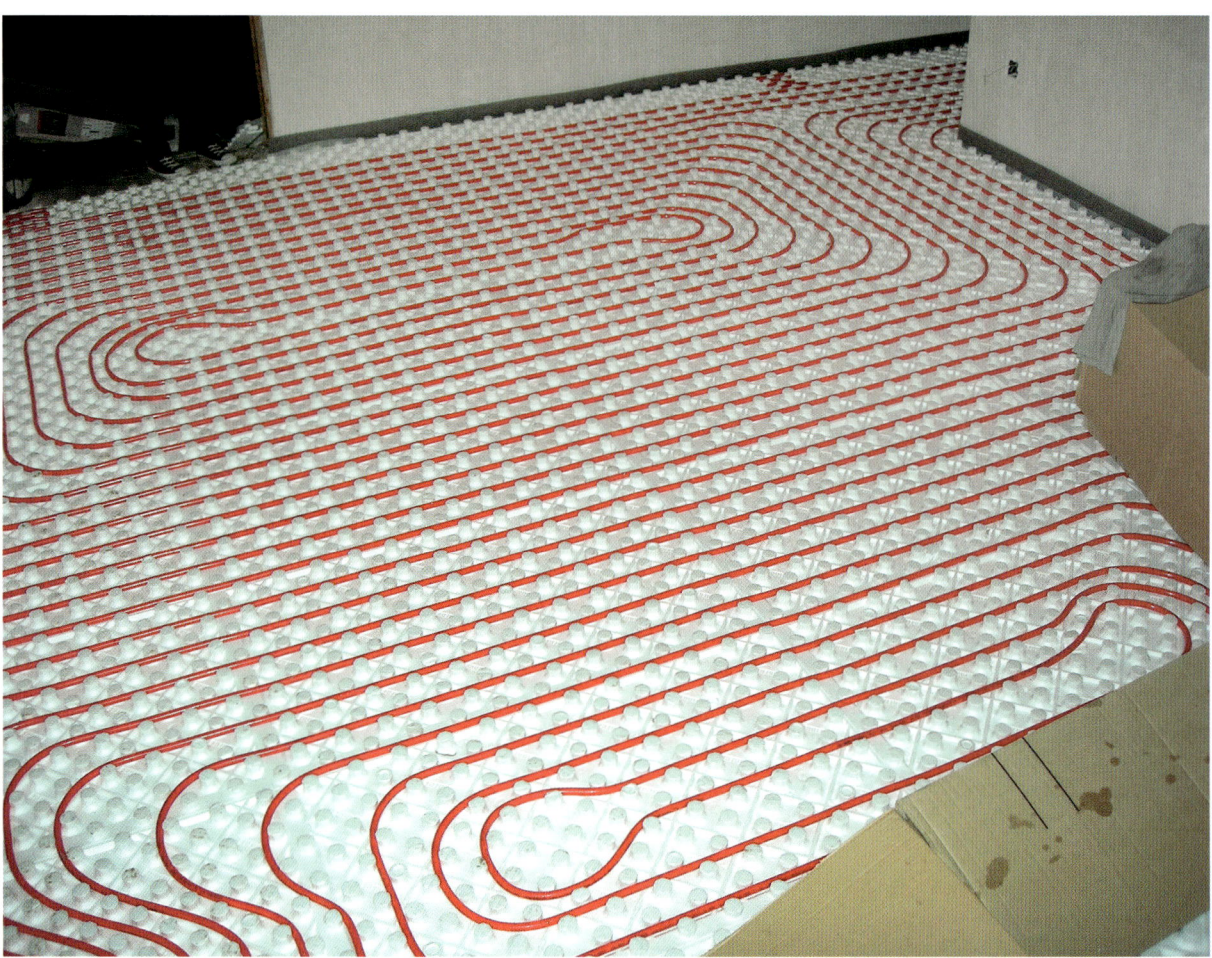

Figure 5.2.6 Radiant floor heating system.
(Source: photo by H. Raab; this file is licensed under the Creative Commons Source 3.0 Unported License.)

outside ambient air to cool a home. They are similar to conventional central air-conditioning systems except they also have the ability to heat the home. Some models can even provide air circulation, air filtration, humidification, dehumidification, and water heating services. While it appears to be an amazing system, it is important to note that air-source heat pumps might not heat a home any better than an electric heating system in extreme winter climates. A backup system is often necessary to help the air-source heat pump achieve comfortable temperatures in extreme winter climates. The efficiency of an air-source heat pump is measured in terms of its heating season performance factor (HSPF) and seasonal energy efficiency ratio (SEER). Currently, national standards require air source heat pumps to achieve a minimum HSPF of 6.8 and a minimum SEER of 10. However, many models are more efficient. Heat pumps with SEER of at least 13 and a HSPF around 9.0 are recommended. Energy Star labels ensure that one is purchasing a highly energy efficient product.

Geothermal Heat Pumps

Geothermal heat pumps use the ground, surface water, or underground water as a heat source and heat sink. They use underground pipes, typically buried 3 to 6 feet below the surface in horizontal loops, to take advantage of the ground's relatively constant year-round temperature. Some pumps use pipes buried in deep vertical loops (see Figure 5.2.7). Geothermal heat pumps are more efficient than air source heat pumps by about 22–44 percent, according to the EPA. They can save a typical homeowner 30–70 percent in heating bills and 20–50 percent in cooling costs. The efficiency of this system is measured by its coefficient of performance (COP) for heating and energy efficiency ratio (EER) for cooling. Present models with Energy Star labels will have COPs greater than 5.0 and EERs greater than 17.0. Also refer to Section 2.5 for geothermal energy sources.

As with all heating and cooling systems, appropriately sizing heat pumps is extremely important. Under- or over-sizing will result in inadequate performance, higher energy bills, and an uncomfortable

home. The best way to ensure correct sizing of both types of heat pump systems is to use the design methods developed by the American Society of Heating, Refrigerating, and Air-Conditioning Engineers (ASHRAE). Proper maintenance is essential to maintain the functionality of a heat pump.

Active Solar Space Heating Systems

In contrast to passive solar systems, active solar systems use supplemental electrical equipment, such as pumps or fans, to move heat around the home. In an active solar system, collectors harvest the sun's energy to heat either liquid or air that is then pumped or blown through pipes or ducts to the living space. Liquid systems are similar to boilers in that they can provide space heating and hot water, and some models combine these systems. Hot air systems operate much like furnaces. Active systems can be expensive to install and require electricity to operate. An active system will not provide all your heating needs, especially in cold, cloudy, northern climates where a backup heating system is required. In fact, solar heating systems are often designed to work in combination with other heating systems, which offers a lot of flexibility (Figure 5.2.8). Active solar heating systems are good choices in climates that have long heating seasons with high proportions of sunny days and above-average utility and fuel prices. Active solar systems can be expensive, but the operational savings can be exceptional, since typical efficiencies range up to 50 percent as compared to photovoltaics at 15–19 percent.

Cooling Methods

Basic methods of operation and pros and cons relative to building cooling are discussed here:

- vapor compression cycle
- absorption cycle
- heat pumps (reverse refrigeration)
- chillers
- chillers and cooling towers.

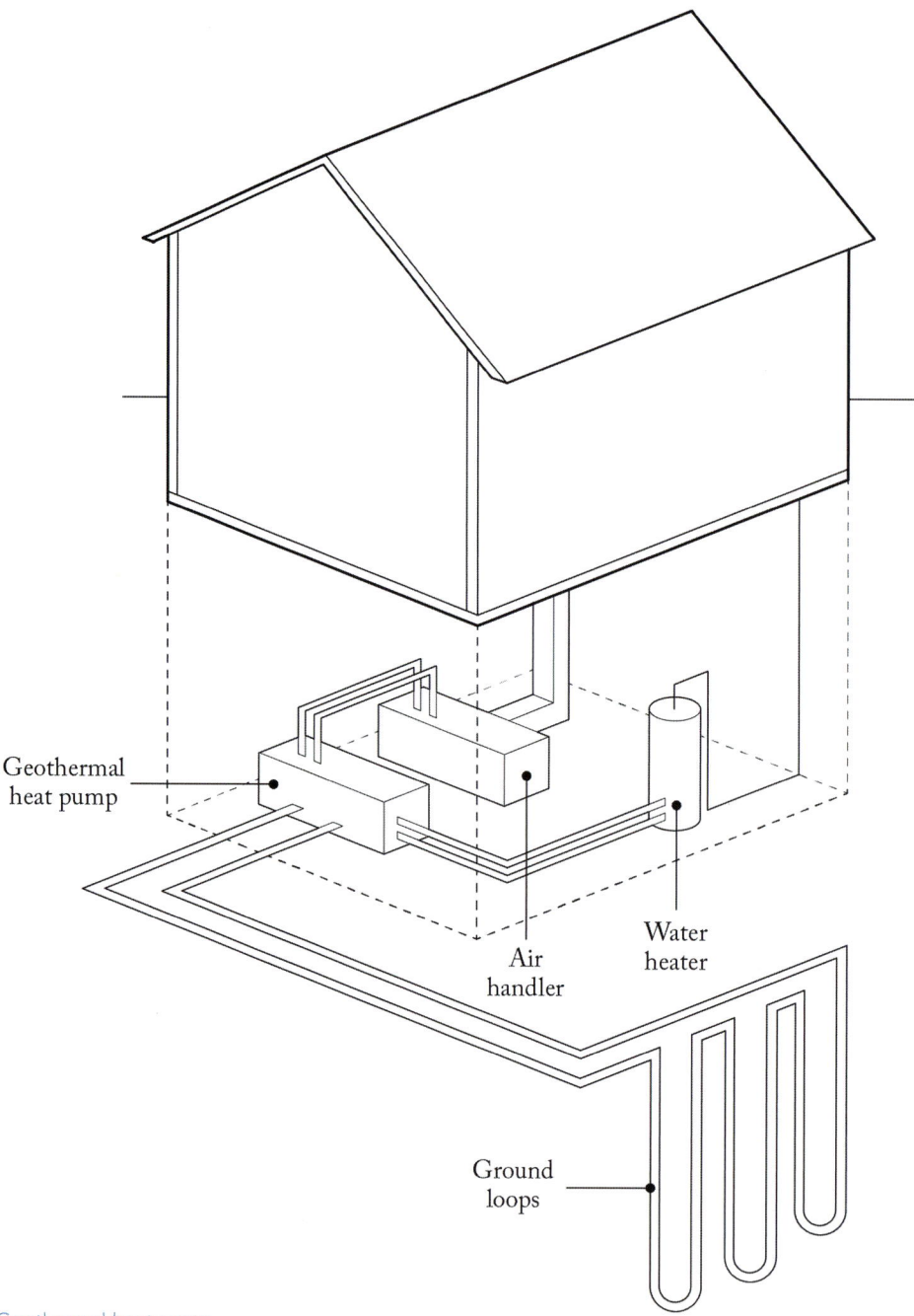

Figure 5.2.7   Geothermal heat pump.
(Source: Kuppaswamy Iyengar.)

Refrigeration Methods

There are three refrigeration methods: vapor compression, absorption cycle, and thermoelectric (Figure 5.2.9). *The vapor compression cycle*, which uses an electric compressor, is the most common type adopted in building cooling. *The absorption cycle* can be

effective when there is a low-cost heat source (waste heat from factories and heat from solar collectors), which substitutes a generator and absorber, called a thermal compressor, for an electric compressor. Because of its low efficiency, it can only compete with the vapor compression cycle when the electricity supply is unreliable.

Solar system components

Radiant system components

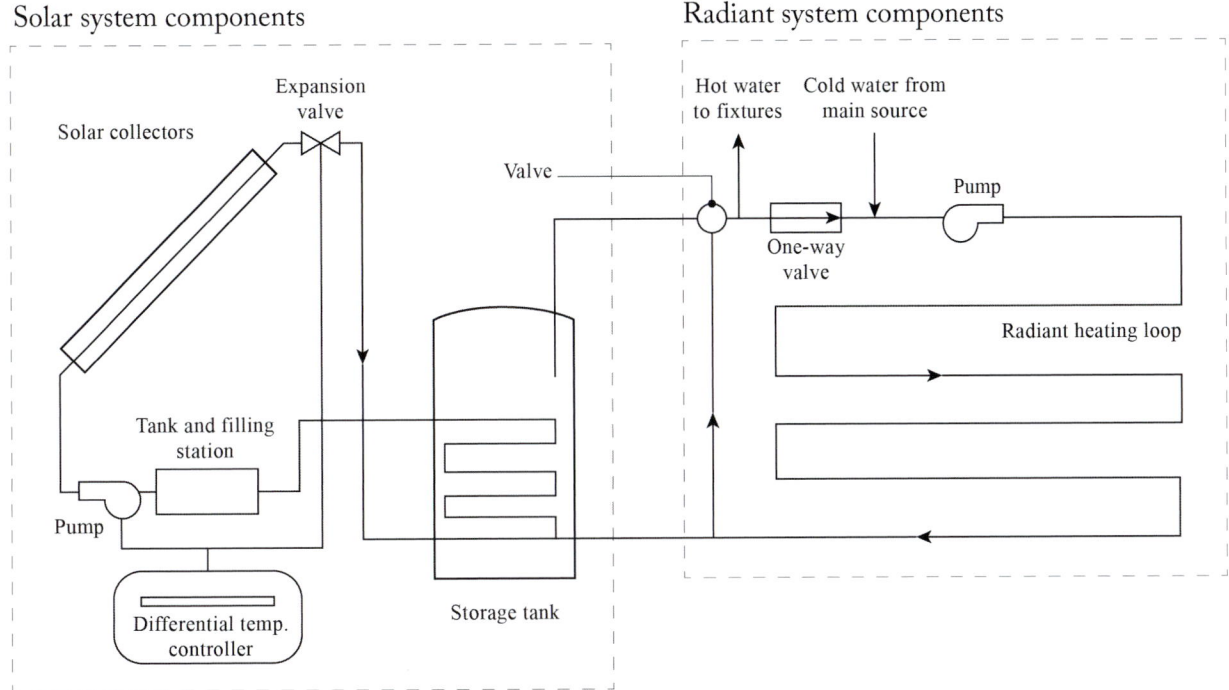

Figure 5.2.8   Solar space heating combined with in-floor radiant heating.
(Source: Kuppaswamy Iyengar.)

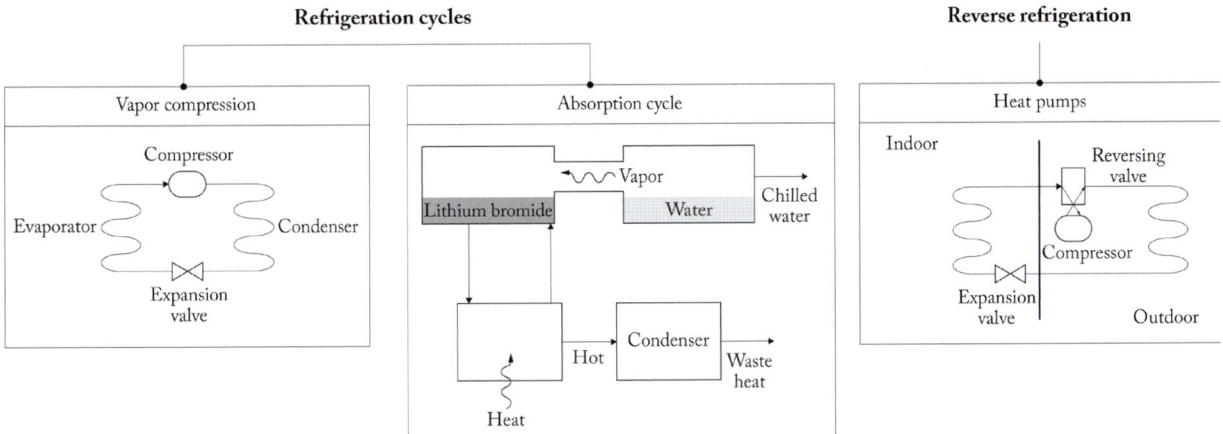

Figure 5.2.9   Basic refrigeration methods.
(Source: Kuppaswamy Iyengar.)

In *the thermoelectric cycle* electricity is directly used to heat and cool the building; it is not used as a part of an HVAC system.

Vapor compression: The basic vapor compression cycle is shown in Figure 5.2.10.

Step 1: In the *evaporator*, vaporization of the refrigerant, usually a hydrofluorocarbon, commences when

an expansion valve is partially opened at point C in Figure 5.2.10. The refrigerant gains heat from the outside air of the *evaporator* coil around 35 °F (cold low pressure).

Step 2: By using a *compression* pump, pressure and temperature of the refrigerant/vapor are raised (hot high pressure) and it will give up heat of vaporization at point A (170 °F). As it loses heat it will *condense* (become liquid) and collect at point B (120 °F).

Step 3: When the entire vapor has condensed at B (warm high pressure), the pressure is reduced by an *expansion* valve into the evaporator, and the refrigerant is back to its original condition. The process repeats again.

Step 4: The *expansion* starts the cycle again.

Vapor compression cooling systems have two types: *refrigeration* systems and *evaporative* systems. Refrigeration systems use electric-driven reciprocating, screw-type or centrifugal compressors to compress a refrigerant. The refrigerant is allowed to expand through a heat exchanger, causing cooling. In chilled water systems, water is pumped through the heat exchanger and then piped through cooling coils in the air-conditioning system.

Absorption cycle: Absorption chillers boil water, the refrigerant, at low pressure through absorption into a high concentration lithium bromide solution/water or ammonia/water. Both lithium bromide solution and ammonia absorb water vapor. Absorption chillers use low heat or waste heat from some other source, instead

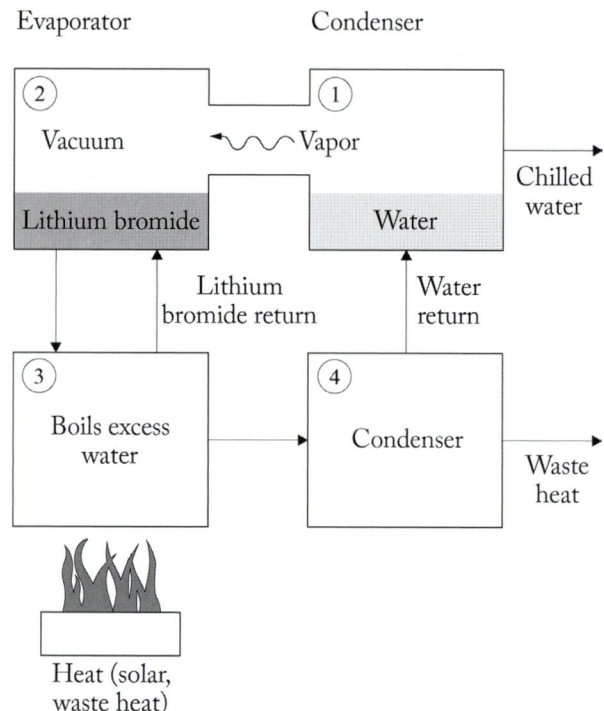

Figure 5.2.11   Absorption cycle.
(Source: Kuppaswamy Iyengar.)

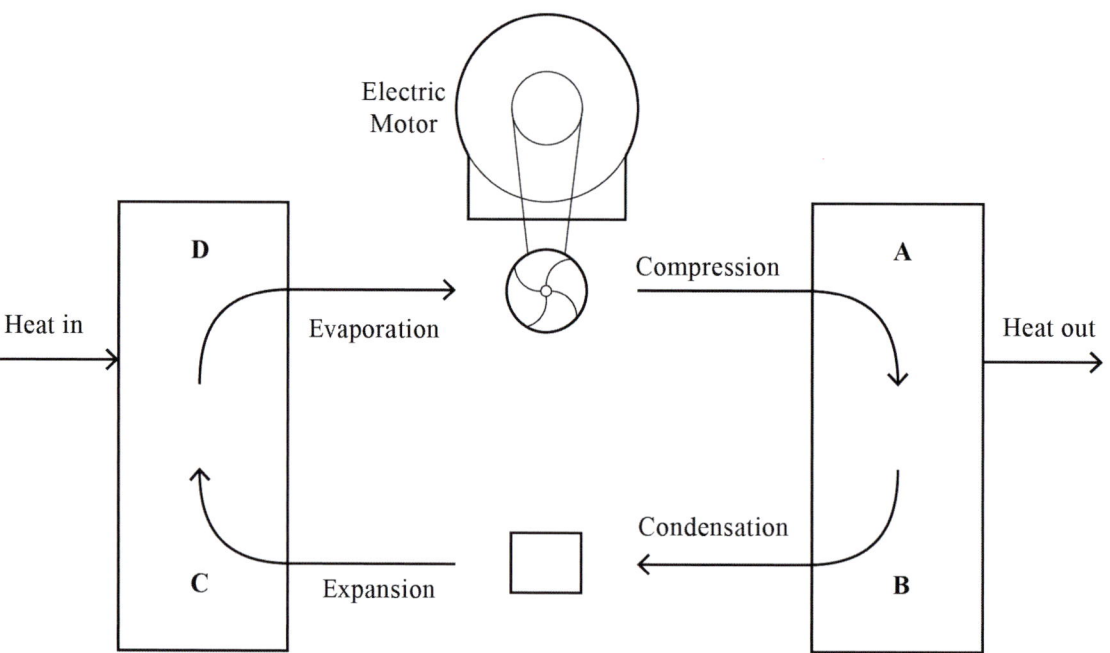

Figure 5.2.10   The vapor compression refrigeration cycle.
(Source: Kuppaswamy Iyengar.)

of mechanical energy (without the use of pumps or any other moving parts), to provide cooling. Otherwise, the principles used in vapor compression remain the same for absorption chillers, except in this case a mechanical vapor compressor is replaced by a thermal compressor that uses heat instead of mechanical energy. Compared to mechanical chillers, absorption chillers have a low coefficient of performance (COP = chiller load/heat input). They can substantially reduce operating costs if they use low-grade waste heat.

Heat pumps (also discussed earlier): During winter, the outdoors is cool and heat is required indoors. Every compressive refrigeration system pumps heat from evaporator to condenser following the vapor compression cycle (Figure 5.2.10). In heating mode, the refrigerant flowing from the evaporator (outdoor coil) carries the thermal energy from outside air (or soil) indoors (condenser). In cooling mode the cycle is similar, but the outdoor coil is now the condenser and the indoor coil is the evaporator. Instead of rotating a simple through-window air-conditioner, the flow of refrigerant is reversed by a *reverse valve*. By flipping a switch a heat pump can be converted from a heating unit to an air-conditioner. This type works well where winters are mild.

Chiller: For HVAC, whatever the system, a process for condensing and cooling the refrigerant is needed. In smaller systems this is done by *air-cooled* condensers

and in larger systems this is done by *water-cooled* condensers. A chiller (Figure 5.2.12) is a machine that removes heat from a liquid via a vapor-compression or absorption refrigeration cycle. This liquid can then be circulated through a heat exchanger to cool air. As a necessary by-product, refrigeration creates waste heat that must be exhausted to ambient air for greater efficiency, recovered for heating purposes.

Chillers, as part of the vapor compression process, are often the largest single energy user in the HVAC system. There are two types of chillers: mechanical and absorption chillers. Mechanical chillers cool through evaporation of a refrigerant at low pressure after it has been compressed, cooled, and passed through an expansion valve. Most mechanical chillers operate using different types of compressors. Reciprocating and screw-type (positive displacement units) and centrifugal chillers use a rapidly rotating impeller to pressurize the refrigerant. All of these chillers need a heat sink to capture the reject heat from the building. This is accomplished by exhaust fan and venting systems outside the building, or through use of cooling towers.

Cooling Tower: Some chillers use air-cooled condensers. Often in large systems a cooling tower is employed to cool the water, especially in large cities lacking adequate site area (see Figure 5.2.13). By making chiller operation more efficient through

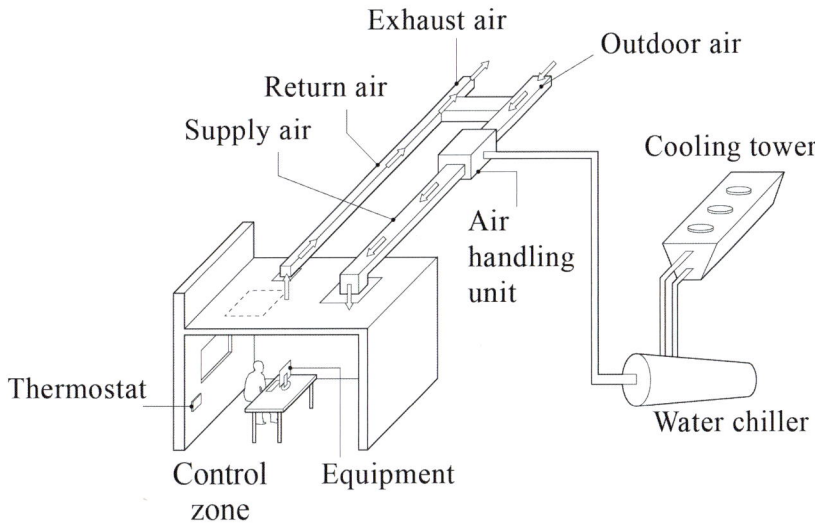

Figure 5.2.12 Central air-conditioning components with a chiller. (Source: Kuppaswamy Iyengar.)

sustainable cool tower use, whole HVAC system energy use is reduced.

In all HVAC systems there are pumps to pump the water and fans to move the conditioned or heated air. Generally, separate fans are provided to supply and exhaust air.

Categories of Cooling Systems

Cooling systems range from window units, small package units to large central plants.

The function of a cooling system is to transfer heat from the space to the refrigeration machine and then to dump the excess heat to a heat sink, usually to the atmosphere or a body of water. Typical systems vary widely with building size, type, and climate. Often cooling systems are classified by the fluids used to transfer the heat from building spaces to the refrigeration machine. They are shown in Figure 5.2.14.

Broadly, cooling systems classify into:

- small space *cooling systems* (Figures 5.2.4, 5.2.9, 5.2.15 and 5.2.16);
- others:
  - central air-conditioning for large spaces (Figure 5.2.13)
  - heat pumps – heating and cooling (Figure 5.2.7)
  - evaporative cooling (Figures 5.2.21 and 5.2.22)
  - solar and waste heat absorption chiller (Figure 5.2.23).

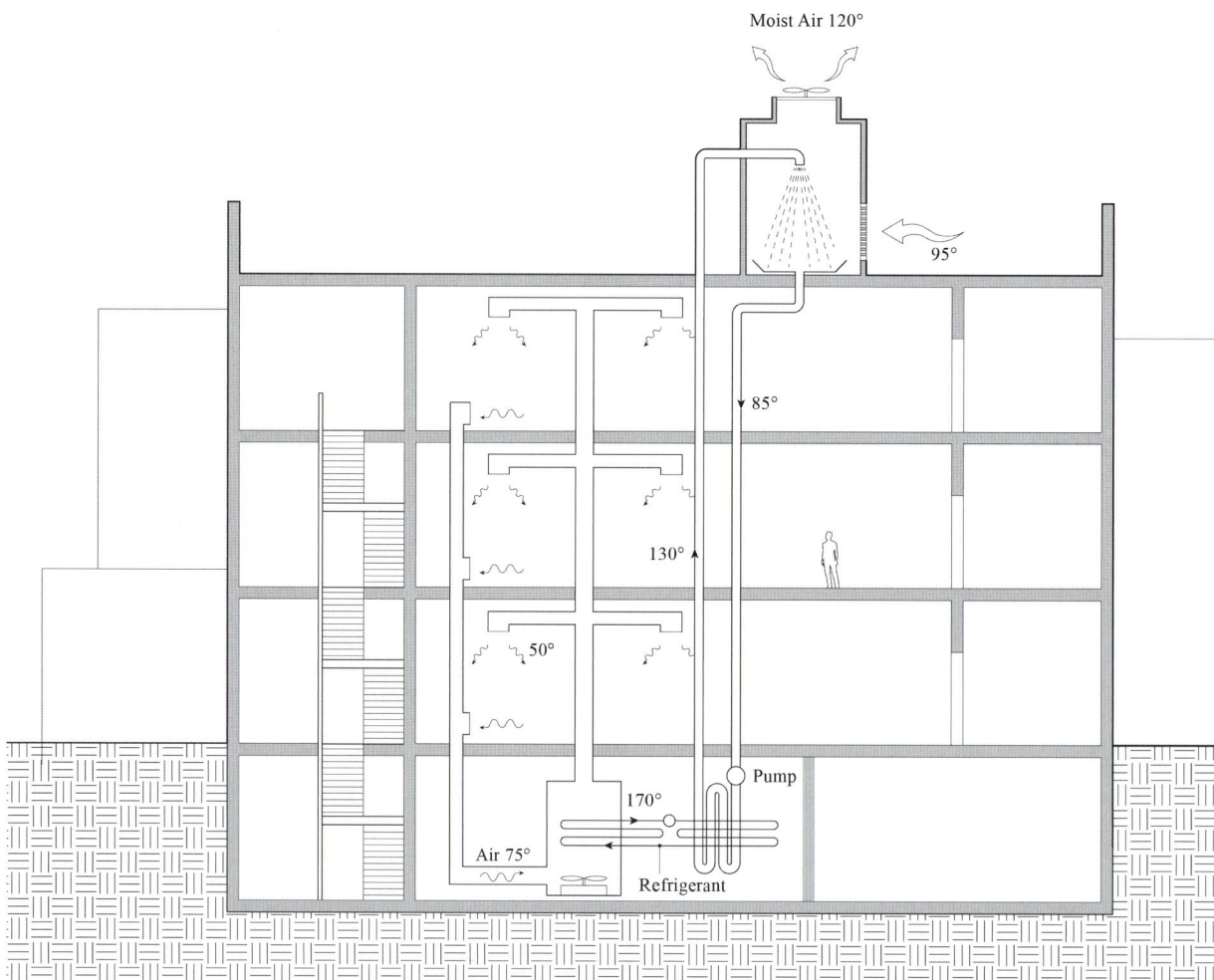

Figure 5.2.13 Cooling tower on rooftop.
(Source: Kuppaswamy Iyengar.)

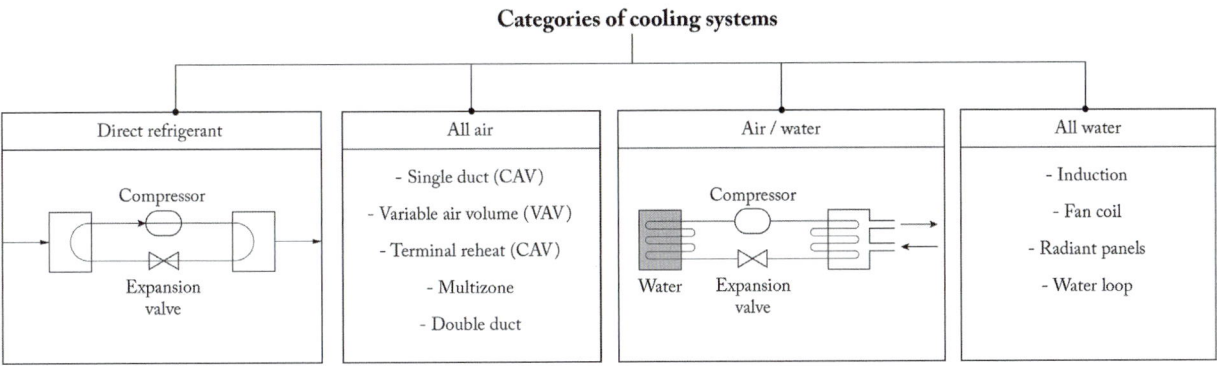

Figure 5.2.14 Categories of cooling systems.
(Source: Kuppaswamy Iyengar.)

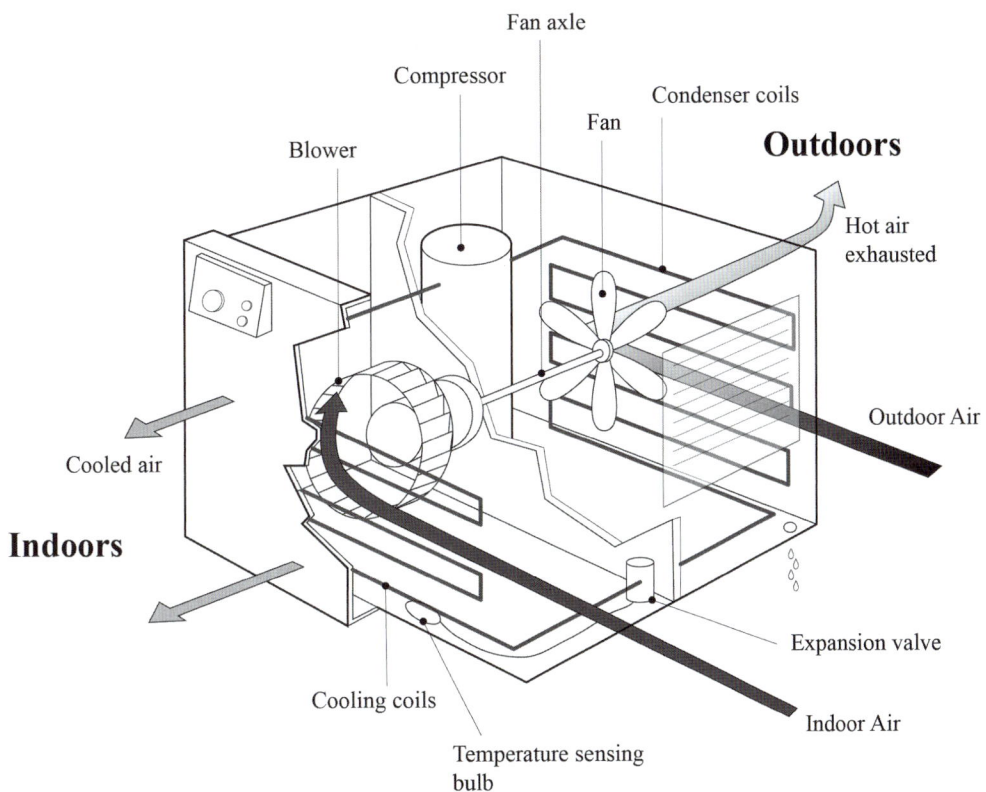

Figure 5.2.15 Typical direct expansion cooling hardware (DX system).

Following are brief descriptions of different *air-conditioning systems* for cooling (also used sometimes for heating) and how the *air distribution* is implemented.

Direct Refrigerant System

Conventional air-conditioners have two main types: central air-conditioners and room air-conditioners (Figures 5.2.14 and 5.2.16). Central air-conditioners

are ducted systems that can cool an entire building. They are the most common type of cooling system in the USA and the Western world. Room air-conditioners are generally smaller, individual units that have the ability to cool only a single room. Room air-conditioners are typically mounted on a wall or in a window, although there are portable units that can be moved all over the house. They typically use 2,200 kWh of electric energy per year. When purchasing a new air-conditioner, choose a central air conditioner with a SEER rating of 13 or higher or a room air-conditioner with an EER rating of 11 or higher. Make sure they are Energy Star compliant.

For small spaces, through-the-wall and rooftop cooling systems known as *direct expansion (DX)* systems (Figure 5.2.15) are used, where the cooling (evaporator) coils are placed in the path of indoor air. The refrigerant expands in the coils as described in the previous section, and as it moves through the coils it cools the air. In this design two fans are used, one on the compressor side and the other on the evaporator side. Condensation water is collected and drained away in this design.

Rooftop, package, or window units (single-zone system, Figure 5.2.16). These range from 0.3 kW to 30 kW and are self-contained. Cooling is performed by DX cooling coils. These systems consist of a simple refrigeration machine along with two fans and, usually, gas-fired furnaces. The indoor air is blown over the evaporative coil and the outdoor air is passed over the condenser coil. The cooled air is directly blown into the room.

All-Air Systems

Air systems have two types: (1) *constant air volume (CAV)*, in which the temperature of a space is controlled by changing the temperature of supply air and maintaining a constant volume of supply air; and (2) *variable air volume (VAV)*, in which the temperature and humidity of a space is achieved by varying the amount of supply air while maintaining a constant temperature. The VAV system is the preferred method since it is more versatile.

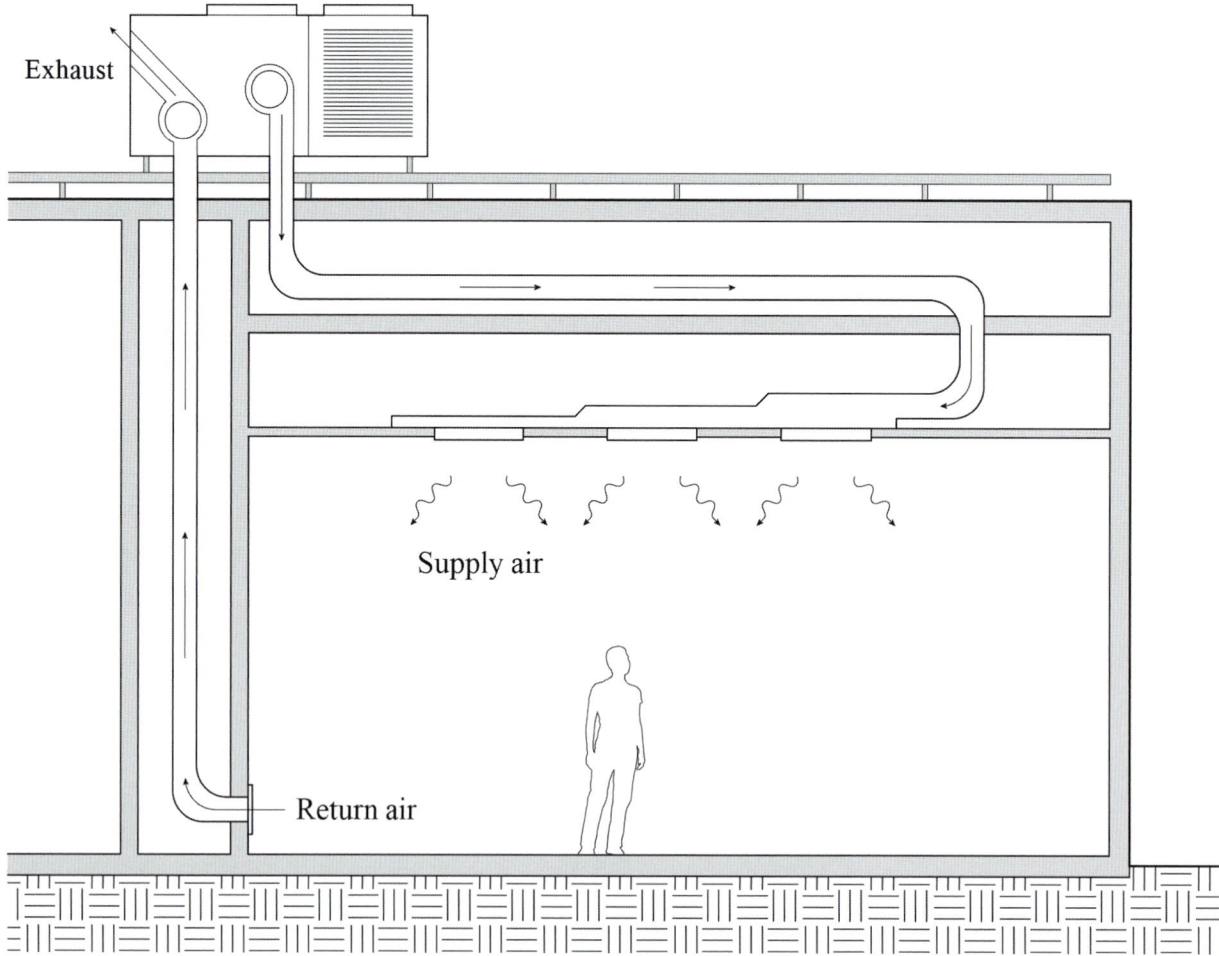

Figure 5.2.16 DX roof top units (RTU).
(Source: Kuppaswamy Iyengar.)

1 *Single duct and single zone (CAV):* This is usually for a one-zone system and therefore good for small- to medium-size buildings. It will have single supply duct, return plenum and an air-handling unit.

2 *Variable air volume (VAV) systems (Figure 5.2.17):* Simultaneous heating and cooling is avoided, and airflow is reduced to the need. VAV systems can handle changing load requirements by varying the amount of heated or cooled air circulated to the conditioned space in response to varying heating or cooling loads. This reduces fan power requirements, which saves energy and costs. A variable speed drive (VSD) is installed to control supply-fan speed. The VSD is controlled by supply duct pressure. VAV systems work either by opening or closing dampers or by modulating the airflow through mixing boxes powered by VAV fans as loads in various zones of the building.

In this system a control box is located wherever a duct enters a separate zone. A thermostat in each zone controls the airflow by operating a damper in the VAV control box. The quantity of air is controlled by the dampers. These systems are typically used for cooling. When heating is required, a separate heating coil downstream of the VAV box is used. The initial low cost and reduced energy use make this a popular system.

3 *Terminal reheat systems (Figure 5.2.18):* Chilled air is provided at each zone. Air is then reheated to temperature requirements. Though this system appears similar to a VAV system, it is actually very different. In place of VAV boxes, this system has terminal reheat boxes in which electric-strip heaters or hot water coils reheat previously cooled air. Typically, the building air is cooled to a desired cooling temperature and then the heat is added, if required, in different zones. Unfortunately, this is an energy wasteful system.

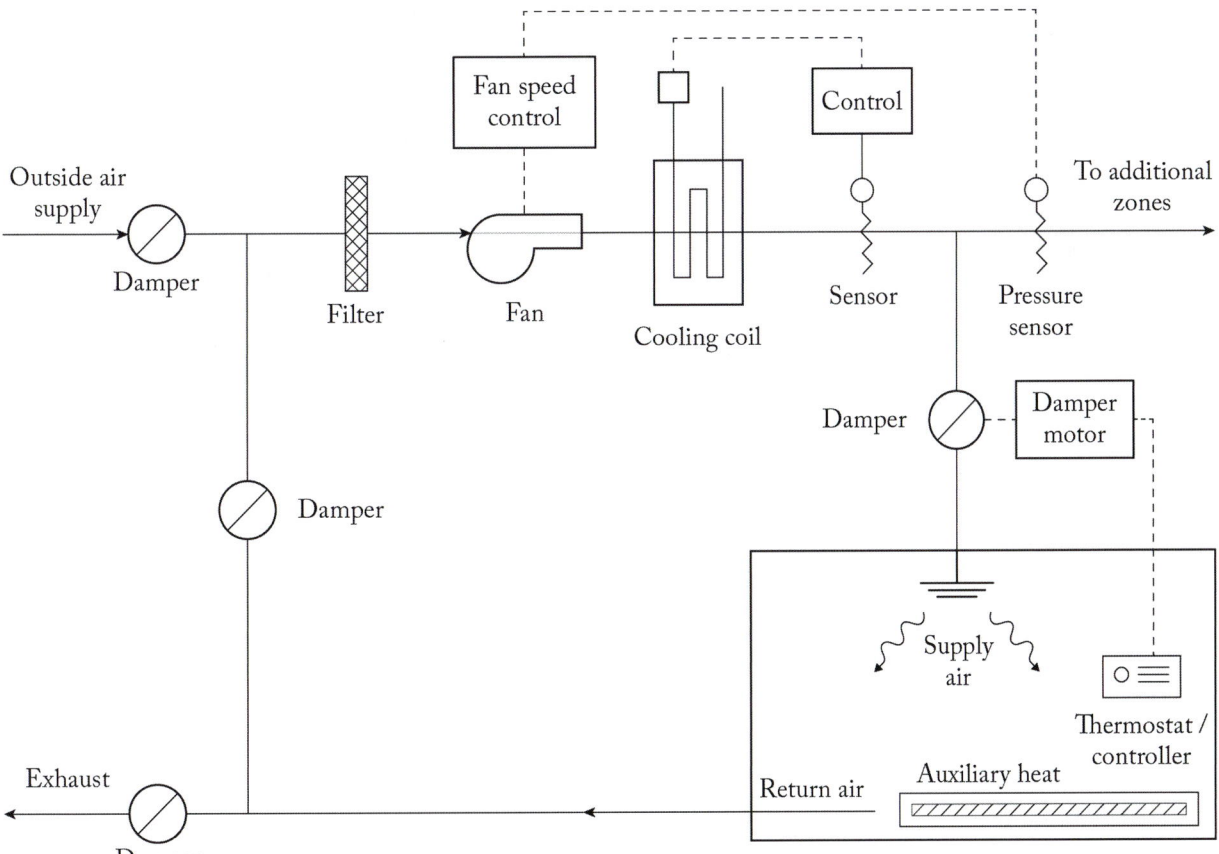

Figure 5.2.17 Variable air volume system.
(Source: Kuppaswamy Iyengar.)

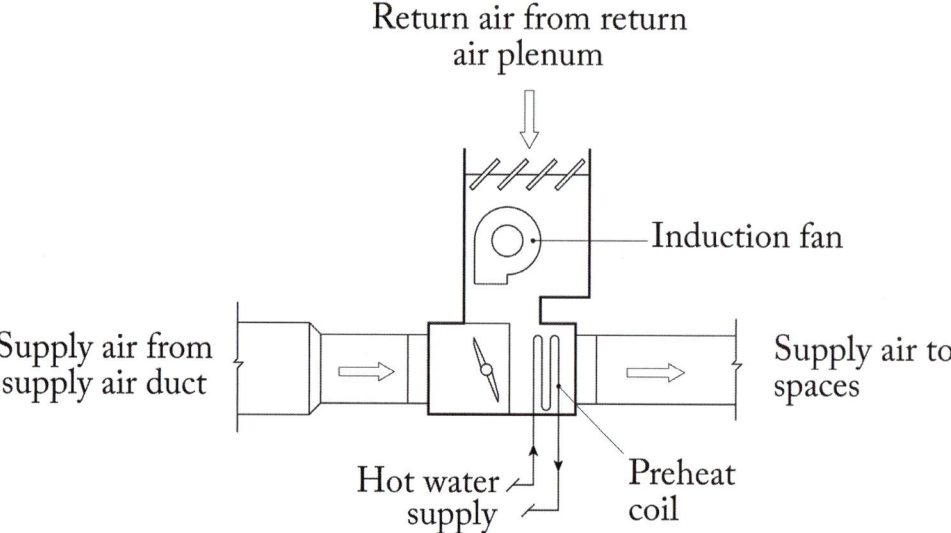

Figure 5.2.18 Terminal reheat system.
(Source: Kuppaswamy Iyengar.)

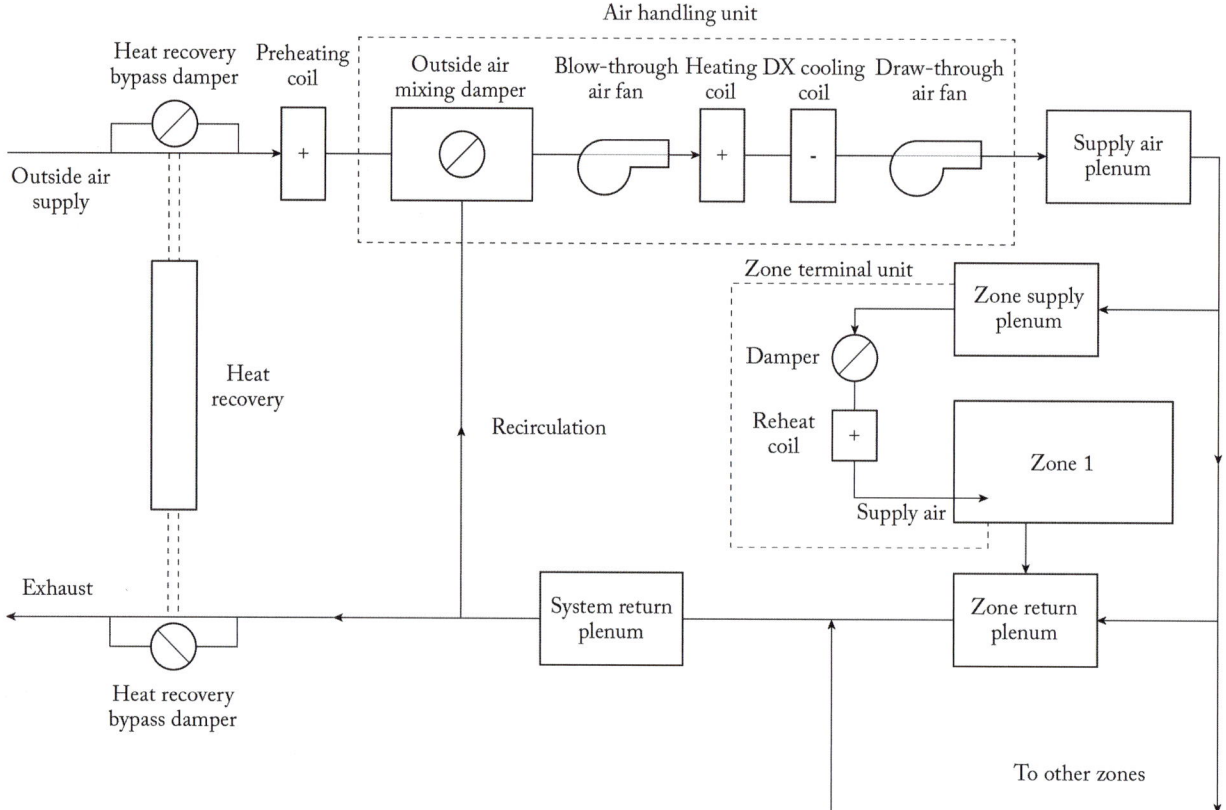

Figure 5.2.19 Multizone HVAC system.
(Source: Kuppaswamy Iyengar.)

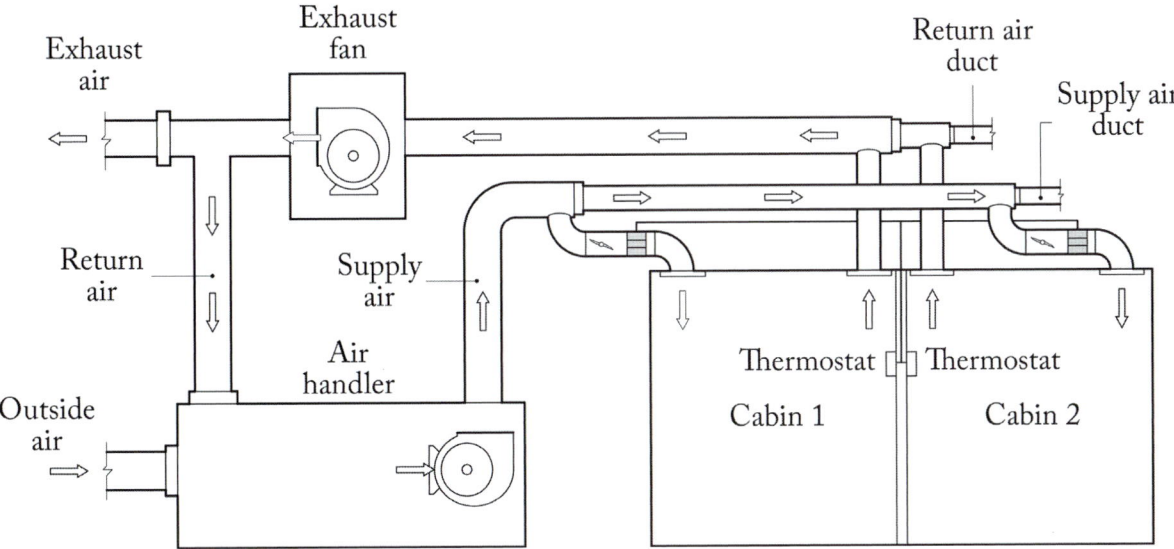

Figure 5.2.20 Dual duct systems.
(Source: Kuppaswamy Iyengar.)

4 *Multizone systems (Figure 5.2.19)* are similar to dual duct except that the mixing boxes are located at the fan and use a single fan to produce hot and cold air. Motorized dampers at the air-handling unit customize the required temperature for different zones controlled by a thermostat. Depending on the required temperatures the ratio of hot and cold air varies but the total amount is constant. Actuators are used to move mixing dampers in the discharge of the unit to meet the desired temperature. Multizone systems use hot water, cold water, and a small amount of fresh air. A single unit is made up of two or more zones serving different spaces. Each zone duct is controlled by a manual balancing damper that must be installed for proper airflow in each zone duct. These systems tend to be quieter because mixing dampers are not directly above the conditioned space. The disadvantages of multizone systems are the wasted energy to supply simultaneous heating and cooling and the high capital cost for the dampening unit. In addition, the placement of the mixing dampers directly downstream of the main supply fan demands high air velocity, thus creating significant pressure loss. The supply fan must compensate for this pressure loss to ensure adequate airflow to each zone. Dampers on the hot and cold supply streams

may leak, requiring additional energy to achieve the desired temperature in the space.

5 *Dual duct systems (Figure 5.2.20)* supply both hot and cold air in separate ducts, which means two sets of large supply ducts are necessary. In this system hot and cold air are blended together at mixing boxes placed at respective rooms in the building. No limitation is placed on the number of zones a building can have. Most of the advantages and disadvantages of the multizone system are applicable to the dual duct system also. This system is expensive since it requires more building space for separate ducts and mechanical equipment and is also inefficient in terms of energy use, but it provides the best level of comfort.

Air–Water Systems

Because of the huge heat-carrying capacity of water, system sizes can be quite small when air-water systems are used. Typically, water is used to transfer heat or cool energy while air is used for ventilation. There are three methods of air–water systems:

- *Induction system*: These units are situated at the perimeter of the building under windows. High-velocity air shoots into the room, which mixes with about 90 percent of the room air, and passes over heating or cooling coils using a water system. Due to high pressure requiring heavier-gauge ducts, the system becomes expensive and is rarely used.

- *Fan-coil with supplementary air*: For a building with interior and exterior zones, two separate systems are used. An air system is utilized for the interior zone and a water system (housed in cabinet-like fan-coil units next to windows) for the exterior zone. A fan blows air into the room after passing over coils containing circulated hot or cold water. Thermostatically controlled valves regulate the flow of water and thus the temperature.

- *Radiant panels with supplementary air*: A cool surface can create thermal comfort by lowering mean radiant temperature (MRT). Similar to the floor radiant heating described earlier, ceiling panels can be used for cooling purposes, provided their area is large. Cool water is circulated in plastic tubes in concrete. Floor slabs, metal tubes embedded in aluminum ceiling panels, and capillary tubes incorporated in ceiling plaster, gypsum, or any other ceiling materials can achieve the cooling needs. In this system condensation should be prevented by controlling humidity and temperature.

All-Water Systems

1 *Hydronic systems*: As the name implies there is no supply air in this system. Hydronic systems include four-pipe, three-pipe, and two-pipe systems. A four-pipe system has supply and return pipes for hot water and, similarly, supply and return pipes for cold water, enabling heating or cooling any time of the year. A condensation drain pan must be part of this system. For detailed design and descriptions of hydronic systems (water is the heat/cool transfer medium), including duct designs, refer to standard design details in the ASHRAE Handbook.

2 *Evaporative cooling systems*: Evaporative coolers (Figures 5.2.21 and 5.2.22) typically use less than one-quarter as much energy as conventional air-conditioners and can save hundreds of dollars a year on home cooling costs. They are used in residential and smaller spaces and limited to dry and hot climates. Water is evaporated into air, thereby cooling it. When water evaporates, it picks up a large amount of sensible heat from its surroundings, producing water vapor and converting this heat into latent heat. This conversion drops the temperature. If the water evaporates into the building, cools the air, and also produces humidification, this is called *direct evaporative cooling*. If the building is cooled without humidification, the process is called *indirect evaporative cooling*. These types of cooling systems use 3–11 gallons of water per day. A fan then circulates the moist, cool air into the home and pushes warmer air out through open windows or a relief vent for this purpose. (Note: windows or outside vents need to be open in order for an evaporative cooler to function properly.) There are three main types of evaporative coolers: portable swamp coolers, fixed room units, and whole-house systems. A portable swamp cooler is typically a small unit that can provide adequate cooling for a small room or a part of a room. Fixed room units are mounted in the wall or in a window and can provide enough cooling for the entire room. Whole-house systems include direct, indirect, or combined direct/indirect systems that are typically ducted. They provide cooling for the main living area of the home and/or each individual room. The cheap and high maintenance swamp coolers of yesterday are a thing of the past. Today they are a high-performance alternative to conventional air-conditioning systems. However, these systems are not effective in humid climates and use a fair amount of water. They need clean water and a drawdown system for periodic cleaning of dirt and unwanted build-up.

3 *Cool towers and thermal chimneys:* Cool towers use the evaporation of water to remove heat and cool the building. A thermal chimney, when heated by the sun, creates a natural upward draft, pulling air from the inside of a building due to pressure differences, and expelling hot air to the outside. The removed air is replaced with cooler air from outside (see full description in Section 2.4).

4 *Solar heat absorption chiller*: Figure 5.2.23 illustrates a simple schematic of solar air-conditioning for cooling (also refer to Figure 5.2.11 for a diagram of the absorption cooling process). In this system solar heat will be used to produce steam/hot water

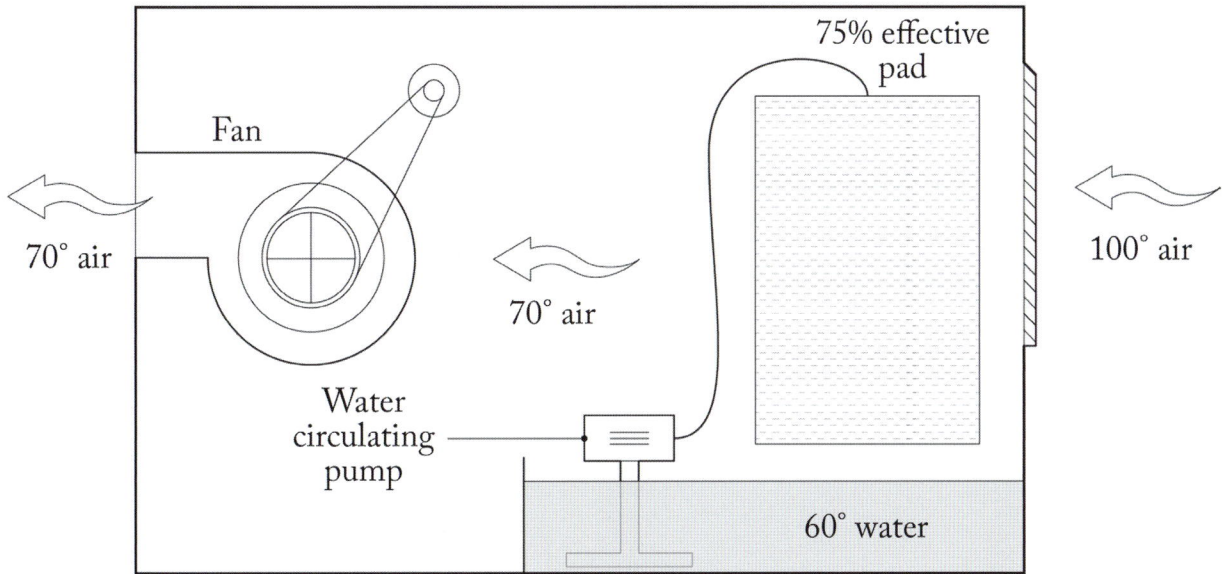

Figure 5.2.21 Evaporative cooling system diagram.
(Source: Kuppaswamy Iyengar.)

Figure 5.2.22 Evaporative cooling equipment.
(Source: https://commons.wikimedia.org.)

as a first step (chamber 3 in the diagram). This is a closed water loop and no external electrical or other heat is used.

Ventilation and Air Distribution

Ventilation is intentionally directing outside air inside a building and vice versa. According to ASHRAE standards it is ventilation that provides acceptable indoor air quality. Natural ventilation takes place when supply and exhaust of air through an indoor space is achieved without using mechanical systems. This action happens when the flow of external air to an indoor space occurs due to pressure or temperature differences. The ventilation rate is expressed by the volumetric flow rate of outside air being introduced to the building in cubic feet per minute (cfm) or liters per second (L/s). The ventilation rate can also be expressed on a person or per unit floor area basis, such as cfm/p or cfm/ft^2, or as *air changes per hour (ACH)*. Compliance with air quality requirements is important. For healthy air quality in a building, the ASHRAE standard recommends flushing the entire quantity of air from a building certain times in an hour based on the building type. Different ACH values vary with heating and cooling seasons and systems.

As an example, for residential buildings, the common ventilation rate is the number of times the whole interior volume of air is replaced per hour. During the winter, ACH may range from 0.50 to 0.41

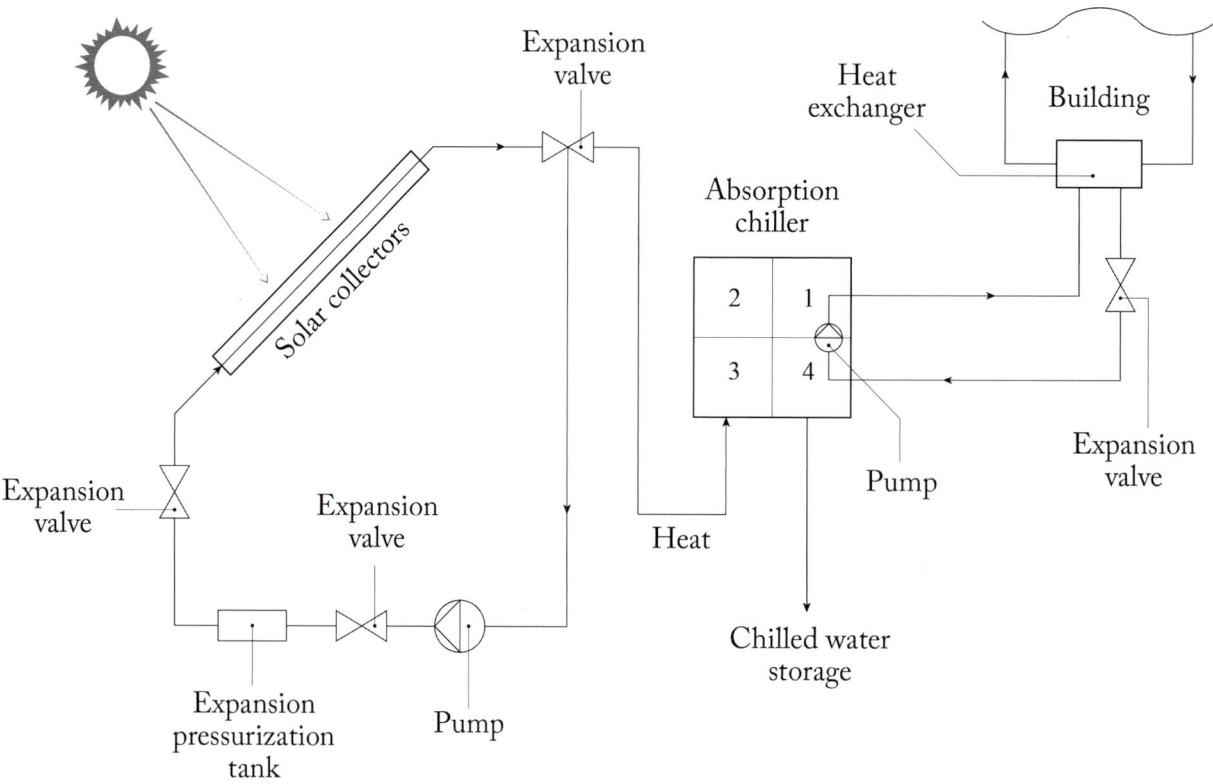

Solar Thermal System Flow Diagram

IWESS - Carnegie Mellon University
www.cmu.edu

Figure 5.2.23 Cooling by solar heat absorption chiller.
(Source: Ming Qu, Center for Building Performance & Diagnostics at Carnegie Mellon University.)

in a well-insulated house, to 1.11 to 1.47 in a loosely insulated house.

Fans in HVAC systems are required to move the air from a building at a certain rate, velocity (V). Building codes and standards require a certain air volume for keeping the environment in a building healthy:

$$V = \frac{\text{ACH} \times (\text{building volume in cubic feet})}{60 \text{ minutes/hour}}$$

$$= \text{fpm (feet per minute)}$$

For detailed ventilation rates refer to Table E.25, Appendix E, in MEEB [1].

For mechanical ventilation, whole-building fans can be used to ventilate a building, if the building is not very tightly constructed, to bring in fresh air and expel some unwanted indoor pollutants. A whole-house fan

can be a cost-effective way to cool a home in moderate climates. Portable fans and ceiling fans move the air in the building, making the environment comfortable. For large buildings, separate air-handling units with powerful fans assist in moving large volumes of air. For detailed ventilation rates refer to Appendix E, Table E.25 in MEEB [1]

Guide to Approximate HVAC System Sizing

Sizing of HVAC equipment relates to use of passive technologies, calculations of heating and cooling loads, as well as attention to indoor air quality requirements.

*   Implement passive design elements (Section 2.1) and calculate net heating requirements (Section

4.1). Manual calculations will give approximate results, while computer simulations will be more accurate. Based on the heat load requirements, select the equipment size, which should match equipment rating in Btu/hour (example: a 25,000 Btu/hr furnace). Follow EPA or ASHRAE guidelines for correct equipment size, manufacture and other details.

Similarly, cooling load can be calculated from heat gain calculations (for the cooling season). Cooling equipment ratings will be in tons (1 ton-hr = 12,000 Btu, 1 kWh = 3,412 kWh, and 1 ton = 3,516 kW). For example, a residence may require a three-ton unit. Approximate equipment sizes can be calculated from Figure 5.2.24 based on building occupancy. Be aware that equipment selected based on the MEEB tables could result in higher-capacity units since these tables may not take into account the effect of the designer's sustainable efforts. Therefore, incorporating sustainable design ideas and using simulation programs such as eQuest may result in significantly lower equipment sizes than the recommendation from Figure 5.2.24.

Take another example: a 10,000 sq.ft office may require a 20-ton A/C unit according to Figure 5.2.24. If sustainable design efforts add up to a 50 percent reduction in cooling loads (from simulation results or manual calculation) the final mechanical equipment size could be reduced by half to 10 tons.

Generic Design Strategies for Environmental Systems

For new and existing construction in support of sustainability, the most common improvements to HVAC systems involve use of all possible passive systems (Chapter 2), installing more efficient HVAC equipment or modifying existing units, increasing control capabilities, and resetting automatic controls. Architectural building design is site-specific and therefore systems design will respond to the specific site, too.

Type of Building	BTU per ft²	Ft² per Ton
Apartments, individual	26	450
Corridors	22	550
Auditoriums and theaters	40	300/18*
Banks	50	240
Bars and taverns	133	90
Churches	36	330/20*
Computer rooms	141	85
Dental offices	52	230
Dept. stores, basement	34	350
Main floor	40	300
Upper floor	30	400
Dormitory, rooms	40	300
Corridors	30	400
Factories	40	300
High-rise office, ext. rooms	46	263
Interior rooms	37	325
Hospitals, core	43	280
Perimeter	46	260
Hotel, guest rooms	44	275
Corridors	30	400
Public spaces	55	520
Industrial plants, offices	38	220
Plant areas	40	300
Libraries	50	240
Low-rise office, ext.	38	320
Interior	33	360
Medical centers	28	425
Motels	28	425
Office (small suite)	43	280
Residences	20	600
Restaurants	60	200
Retail stores	48	250
Schools & colleges	46	260
Supermarkets	34	350

*Persons per ton
12,000 Btu = 1 ton of air conditioning

Figure 5.2.24 Approximate HVAC sizing guide. (Source: RSMeans Mechanical Cost *Data*, p. 537.)

Guide to Energy Efficiency Improvements for HVAC Retrofit

Equipment modifications for energy efficiency of HVAC systems for a retrofit situation involve *four* items:

1 controls
2 retrofit
3 reduction of airflow rates
4 sustainable design of new elements.

Controls (fans and pumps): Understanding simple controls and maintaining their calibrations can save electrical energy. Examples include turning off large fan systems when relatively few people are in the building or turning off the ventilation systems half an hour prior to when the building closes. These types of sophisticated controls are already available in newer HVAC systems.

Retrofits (energy improvements to existing buildings): These include modifications to ventilation systems, chillers, and general principles for energy efficiency in HVAC systems.

Reduction of airflow rates: Ventilation systems are usually designed for maximum cooling or heating load. New codes permit lower lighting levels, reduced outside air input into the building, and wider acceptable comfort ranges. As a result, now it is feasible to decrease airflow in many commercial buildings. This operation is governed by fan laws. In brief, the volume rate of airflow through a fan, Q, varies directly with the speed of the impeller's rotation.

$$H_2 = [N_2/N_1]^3 \, H_1$$

where
H_1, H_2 are the energy need,
N_1, N_2 are fan speeds

The result of this equation is that if the airflow is doubled, the energy needed is the cube of 2, which is eight times. On the other hand, if the airflow is reduced by half, the power needed is cube power of one-half, which is one-eighth. This law holds for both fans and pumps to a great extent. By reducing the flow rates of air and water in HVAC systems, always

ensuring that they are within the allowable code limits, significant energy reductions can be achieved in both fan and pump systems. For example, even a small reduction of airflow (10 percent) can result in significant energy savings (27 percent).

• For improved energy efficiency the building codes permit the use of return air mixed with varying quantities of outside air by the use of a concept called "economizer cycle." Depending on the type of facility, a certain percentage of already used air can be recirculated by mixing it with fresh air.
• To finetune final environmental systems for building design, the assistance of an expert mechanical engineer is needed.

Sustainable design of new elements can follow current sustainable standards. Good sustainable practice applies to retrofits and to all HVAC design. These guiding principles address energy efficiency of HVAC systems:

1 *Optimize controls.* Use of controls to provide heating and cooling only when needed.
2 *Optimize capacity.* Review the system capacity for sustainability and avoid proving excess capacity. Note that use of passive systems, reducing heat from lighting, etc., should be considered.
3 *Reduce the load.* Minimize the heating and cooling loads by reducing infiltration, solar heat loads by proper orientation, etc.
4 *Heat and cool people, not the building.* Provide heating and cooling where people work rather than unused spaces. There are exceptions such as some computer equipment, some surgical areas, and freeze protection.
5 *Use efficient processes.* Select the most efficient heating and cooling process for the people, the climate and the building. Customize for special uses such as a one pass system in surgical wards, contaminant chemicals, etc. For an office, a recirculation system may be appropriate.
6 *Use efficient equipment.* Select the most efficient equipment such as EER and Energy Star rated.
7 *Operate equipment efficiently.* Ensure the equipment is operating efficiently and correct any deficiencies by regular maintenance.

8 *Use passive concepts.* Take advantage of building properties and the climate to do as much heating and cooling work as possible. *Trombe* walls, greenhouses, and rooftop night cooling systems are some examples.

9 *Employ heat and cool recovery.* Heat and cool can be recovered from the building, building exhausts, and other sources.

10 *Consider energy storage capability.* Energy stored can permit off-peak use of equipment (cool storage from off-peak hours), load leveling, and more efficient utilization of equipment.

Summary

Space heating and cooling accounts for 45 percent of total home energy costs. Furnaces and boilers are the most common types of heat systems. Pumps, active solar heating, and thermal mass systems also aid in heating spaces. The philosophy of cooling spaces is first to minimize the amount of heat that enters the building, as well as the amount that is generated. In addition to passive designs, many options exist for cooling spaces, including fans, evaporative coolers and pumps. Proper maintenance can contribute greatly to energy-efficient performance of HVAC systems. HVAC systems can be modified for energy efficiency through use of controls, retrofit, and sustainable initial design.

References

[1] B. Stein, J. Reynolds, W. Grondzik, and A. Kwok, *Mechanical and Electrical Equipment for Buildings* (New York: John Wiley & Sons, Inc. 2006).

Further Reading

Norbert Lechner, *Heating, Cooling and Lighting* (New York: John Wiley & Sons, Inc. 2009).

Craig B. Smith, *Energy Management Principles* (Elmsford, NY: Pergamon Press, 1981).

John M. Swift, Jr. and Tom Lawrence, *ASHRAE Green Guide* (Atlanta, GA: ASHRAE Publications, 2010).

Web Support

www1.eere.energy.gov/manufacturing/tech_assistance/pdfs/steam14_chillers.pdf)

Exercises

1 Briefly explain basic functions of an HVAC system using a typical system configuration diagram for a home.
2 Why would you recommend a radiant floor system for your residential client? Explain pros and cons of this system.
3 Provide a quick sketch for each of the principles listed under the sustainable design guide for cooling.

5.3 Indoor Air Quality

Any approach towards more sustainable lifestyles, buildings, or products must address human health and potential effects of exposure to pollutants and chemicals. The average person in a developed country spends approximately 90 percent of their time indoors, thus it is easy to see why indoor air quality (IAQ) is of importance.

In the USA IAQ design follows minimum standards established by the American Society of Heating, Refrigeration, Air-conditioning Engineers (ASHRAE 62.1-2004). It is important for building designers to appreciate the sources and severe effects of indoor air pollution in their building designs. This section deals with the IAQ requirements, impact of indoor environmental quality and risks, how to design HVAC systems for good air quality, and how to minimize pollutants at the source. It concludes with some guidelines from the USGBC LEED® programs.

Causes of Poor Indoor Air Quality

Excess carbon dioxide, water vapor, odors, and pollutants from building materials and building use must be exhausted from the building's interior. The amount of air that is polluted must be replaced with the same amount of fresh air. Pollution sources that release gases or particles into the air in homes and buildings cause IAQ problems. Poor ventilation can increase indoor pollutant levels. Proper ventilation to dilute emissions from indoor sources and to expel air pollutants out of the building is essential. High temperature and humidity levels can increase concentrations of some pollutants in a building. Figure 5.3.1 shows percentages and sources of indoor air pollution.

The effort to understand IAQ and its consequences is relatively recent. The building industry is aware of health effects of poor building design and has developed some methods to remedy the situation, but a good deal of research analysis and understanding of potential hazards is needed in this complex field. Over the past few years, several federal and professional organizations have invested in the research and development of science in this area, such as the US Environmental Protection Agency (EPA), the Occupational Safety and Health Administration (OSHA), and professional societies such as ASHRAE. Results of these activities have led to improved IAQ practices, standards, and performance targets.

Sources of Indoor Air Pollution

Indoor pollution sources are combustive materials such as oil, gas, kerosene, coal, wood, and tobacco products; building construction materials and furnishings containing asbestos insulation, wet or damp carpet, and furniture made of certain pressed wood products and fabrics; materials in central heating and cooling systems and humidification devices; and other outdoor sources such as radon, pesticides, and outside air pollution (Figure 5.3.2).

The importance of any single pollution source depends on the extent of pollutant it emits and how hazardous those emissions are. For example, an improperly adjusted gas stove can emit significantly more carbon monoxide than one that is properly adjusted. Similarly, smoking inside the house emits severe pollutants, affecting the health of occupants. Following are five major sources of indoor pollution:

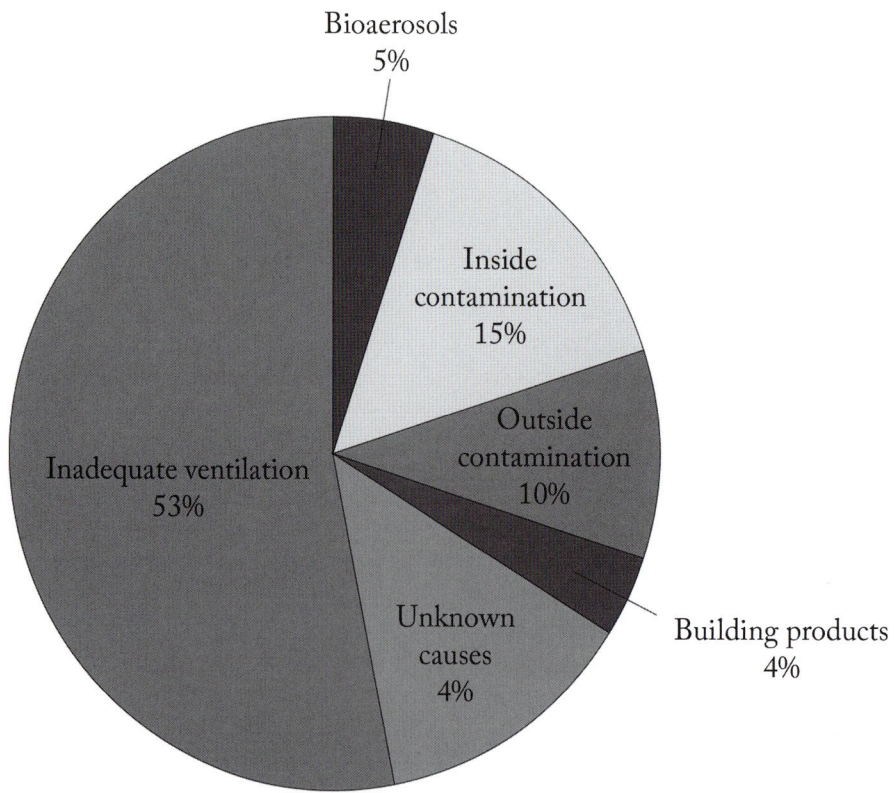

Figure 5.3.1   Reasons for indoor air quality problems.
(Source: National Institute of Occupational Safety and Health.)

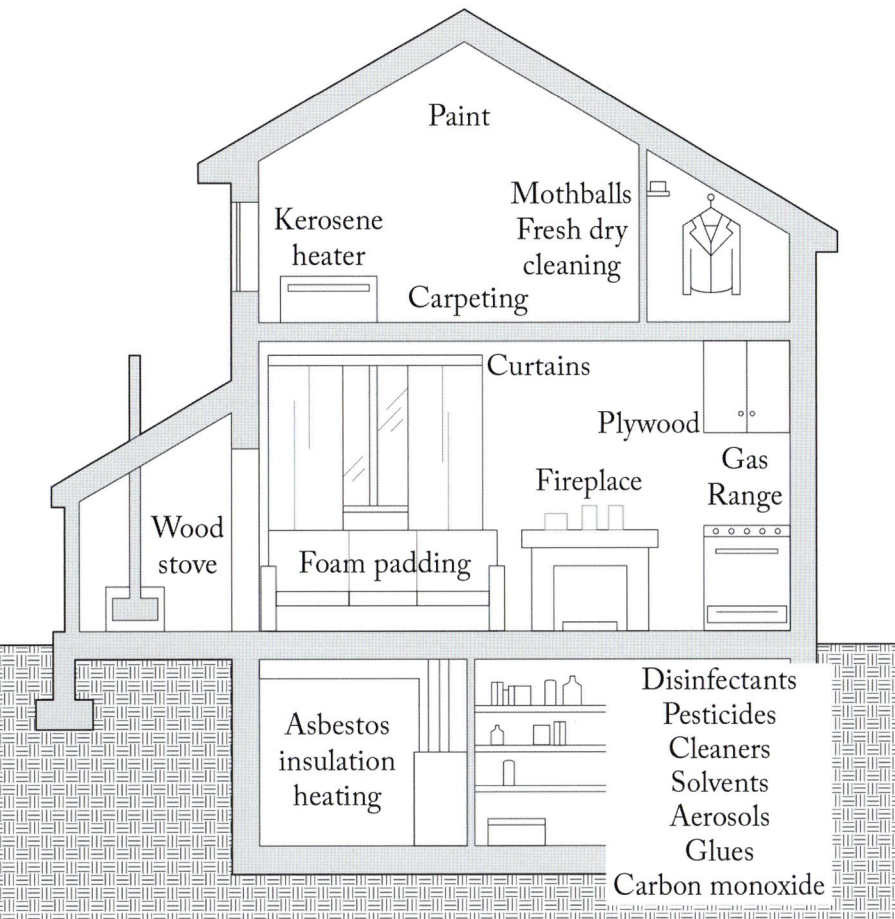

Figure 5.3.2 Sources of indoor air pollution.
(Source: Courtesy of Charles Welch, The Ozone Hole Inc.)

1 *Construction materials, furnishings, and equipment.* These items can emit odors, particles, and volatile organic compounds (VOCs). It is possible that VOCs from a specific material may combine with VOCs from other materials to form new hazardous chemicals. The building industry has established that VOCs and particulates can cause health problems for occupants upon inhalation or exposure. In certain situations levels of heat and moisture in a building can provide ideal conditions and nutrients that support the growth of molds and bacteria, which produce microbial volatile organic compounds (MVOCs). These organisms can affect occupants adversely if fungal spores containing mycotoxins and allergens or the MVOCs are inhaled. Research continues to fully identify the human response to molds and fungi.

2 *Building envelope.* The envelope controls the infiltration of outside air and moisture, and may include operable or inoperable windows to control the impact of air quality. Energy performance of a building is also determined by infiltration. Buildings that are designed and constructed to minimize the amount of outdoor air into and out of the building for energy efficiency may have higher pollutant levels than other buildings. Therefore, it is important to ensure that a sustainable building meets all ventilation standards stipulated by ASHRAE.

3 *Ventilation systems.* Acoustical materials in heating, ventilating, and air-conditioning (HVAC) systems may contribute to indoor air pollution in the same way as construction materials, mentioned above. Ventilation systems also control the distribution, quantity, temperature, and humidity of air.

4 *Maintenance*. Lack of maintenance allows dirt, dust, mold, odors, and particles to increase. The use of high-VOC cleaning agents pollutes air. Household products like air fresheners or solvents in cleaning and hobby activities and pesticides in housekeeping release pollutants more or less continuously. Poor maintenance of cooling towers has caused severe health effects, such as outbreaks of Legionnaire's disease.

5 *Occupants*. The number of occupants in a building and the amount of equipment contribute to indoor air pollution. People and pets are major sources of microorganisms and airborne allergens in indoor environments. Occupant activities can also pollute the air. Too many people in an area can lead to unacceptable air quality.

Infiltration, natural ventilation, and mechanical ventilation are the three methods by which air moves in and out of a building. The rate at which outdoor air replaces indoor air is described as the air exchange rate (see Section 5.2). Estimated air change per hour (ACH) is a measure typically used to indicate the air movement in a building. When there is little infiltration, natural ventilation, or mechanical ventilation, the air exchange rate is low and pollutant levels can increase. ACH is indicative of the *turnover* of air within a building or space. A tight building might permit an infiltration rate of 0.25 ACH while a leaky one might have an ACH of 1.0. ASHRAE standards list the allowable ACH for different buildings. Ventilation systems are designed to assist in appropriate air movement in a building.

Risk Assessment of Indoor Air Pollution

To analyze IAQ and its effects, ground samples (for radon), air samples, and samples from building surfaces should be collected to analyze for mold, bacteria, chemicals, or other pollutants.

Radon is the invisible, radioactive atomic gas that is found in foundations, rock building materials such as stone, and tile products themselves. Once radon is removed it will become benign since it has a half-life of 3.8 days. There are relatively simple and inexpensive tests for radon gas available in the market.

Molds and other allergens are biological agents that can arise from two common classes: (a) moisture-induced growth of mold colonies due to water penetrating compromised areas of the building skin, such as the roof, plumbing fixtures, condensation due to improper ventilation, or ground moisture penetrating a building slab; and (b) natural substances released into the air such as animal dander and plant pollen. Cellulosic materials (paper and wood, including drywall) can encourage mold colonies to propagate and release allergenic spores into the air, if the materials fail to dry within 48 hours. Low humidity levels (below 50 percent) and preventing leaks or moisture condensation and accumulation can inhibit visible mold growth.

Some of the Health Effects of Air Pollution

Indoor air pollution can cause immediate and/or long-term health effects for building occupants.

It is believed that *immediate effects* are short-term and treatable, whether they involve a single exposure or repeated exposures. Symptoms of asthma, hypersensitivity pneumonitis, humidifier fever, and other diseases can appear soon after exposure to some indoor air pollutants. Headaches, dizziness, fatigue, and irritation of the eyes, nose, and throat can be other symptoms. Age and pre-existing medical conditions can determine the extent of reactions due to exposure to pollutants.

Some experts claim that *long-term effects*, which may include some respiratory diseases, heart disease, and cancer, are due to exposure to pollutants. While pollutants commonly found in indoor air are responsible for many harmful effects, experts are still debating what concentrations, frequency, or periods of exposure are necessary to produce specific health problems. The following can cause poor IAQ.

Carbon monoxide (CO) is the most acutely toxic indoor air contaminant. This colorless, odorless gas is a by-product of incomplete combustion of fossil fuels in space heaters, defective central heating furnaces, automobile exhaust, and tobacco smoke. Carbon monoxide can produce flu-like systems, nausea, unconsciousness, and death. Proper ventilation and repairs to equipment will correct this problem.

Legionellosis or Legionnaire's disease is caused by a waterborne bacterium that grows best in slow-moving or still warm water from poorly maintained evaporative cooling towers, which release the bacteria to ventilation systems. Outbreaks can occur in medical facilities and nursing homes, where weak patients are likely to contract the disease. This bacterium is resistant to chemical and antimicrobial treatments. Very hot water flushes (160 °F), and sterilization of standing water in evaporative cooling basins will remedy the problem.

Asbestos fibers: Many common building materials like floor tiles, ceiling tiles, taping muds, pipe wrap, mastics, and other insulation materials used before 1975 contain asbestos. Inhalation of asbestos fiber, which may cause cancer, can occur from disturbed buildings due to cutting, sanding, drilling, or remodeling. There now exist particularly stringent regulations applicable to most commercial and industrial buildings for asbestos remediation. Use of asbestos has been banned in this country.

Carbon dioxide (CO$_2$) is emitted by humans and correlates with human metabolic activity. High levels of carbon dioxide indoors may cause occupants to function at lower activity levels. Indoor levels are an indicator of the adequacy of outdoor air ventilation relative to indoor occupant density and metabolic activity. ASHRAE recommends that carbon dioxide levels not exceed 700 ppm above outdoor ambient levels. Most building codes require alarmed monitors indoors.

Issues of IAQ in HVAC Design

Sustainable building designers of commercial and residential HVAC systems are paying more attention to the issue of IAQ throughout the design, construction, and maintenance stages of a building. The "Green Design" movement also joins in this effort.

Using *ventilation* to dilute contaminants, filtration, and source control are the primary methods for improving IAQ in most buildings. A basic way of maintaining the health of indoor air is by the frequency of effective turnover of interior air by replacement with outside air. In the USA, and according to ASHRAE standards, ventilation in classrooms is based on the amount of outdoor air per occupant,

not ACH. Since carbon dioxide indoors comes from occupants and outdoor air, the adequacy of ventilation per occupant is indicated by the concentration indoors minus the concentration outdoors. The value of 650 ppm above the outdoor concentration indicates approximately 15 cubic feet per minute of outdoor air per adult occupant doing sedentary office work. In classrooms, the requirements in the ASHRAE 62.1 standard, "Ventilation for Acceptable Indoor Air Quality," would typically result in about 3–4 air changes per hour, depending on the occupant density.

Dust on the wet coils and ducts in an air-conditioning system can reduce the efficiency of the coils and can serve as food to grow molds. Air filters are used to reduce the dust that reaches the wet coils and to trap air pollutants.

Moisture management and humidity control require operating HVAC systems as designed. This may conflict with efforts to try to optimize efficient use of energy. However, for most of the USA and many parts of Europe and Japan, during the majority of hours of the year, outdoor air temperatures are cool enough that the air does not need further cooling to provide thermal comfort indoors. High humidity outdoors creates the need for careful attention to humidity levels indoors. High indoor humidity can give rise to mold growth, and moisture indoors is associated with a higher prevalence of occupant respiratory problems.

Commercial buildings, and sometimes residential homes, are often kept under *slightly positive air pressure* relative to the outdoors to reduce infiltration. Limiting infiltration by keeping slightly positive air pressure inside a building helps with moisture management and humidity control.

Dilution of indoor pollutants with outdoor air is effective to the extent that outdoor air is free of harmful pollutants. Ozone in outdoor air occurs indoors at reduced concentrations because ozone is highly reactive with many chemicals found indoors. These reactions may produce organic compounds that are odorous, irritating, or toxic. These products of ozone chemistry include formaldehyde, higher molecular weight aldehydes, acidic aerosols, and fine and ultrafine particles, among others. The higher the outdoor ventilation rate, the higher the indoor ozone concentration and the more likely the reactions will occur, but even at low levels reactions will take place.

This suggests that ozone should be filtered from ventilation air, especially in areas where outdoor ozone levels are frequently high. Recent research has shown that mortality and morbidity increase in the general population during periods of higher outdoor ozone and that the threshold for this effect is around 20 parts per billion (ppb).

Steps to Improve IAQ

Most people spend 60–90 percent of their time indoors, either at home or at work. Therefore, poor indoor air quality can have a significant impact on people's lives, especially those who are most vulnerable: infants and children, pregnant women, the elderly, and those who have chronic illnesses. To address the special needs of children, for example, the US EPA has developed an "IAQ Tools for Schools" program (www.epa.gov/iaq/schools) to help improve the indoor environmental conditions in educational institutions.

Some of the following steps can be taken to help improve IAQ at home, the workplace, and in other indoor environments.

Avoid or use with caution citrus- and pine-based solvents since they react with ozone and form formaldehyde, higher molecular weight aldehydes, acidic aerosols, and fine and ultrafine particles. Ozone can be removed from outdoor air by filtration requiring large amounts of carbon. It is preferable to avoid these solvents since both the US EPA and the California Air Resources Board discourage their use.

Prevent carbon monoxide exposure by keeping gas appliances and the central heating system inspected, cleaned, and serviced at frequent intervals as well as prohibiting smoking in residences. Install carbon monoxide alarms.

Radon can seep into the house from contaminated earth and rock under the home, or from well water and/or building materials. Testing for radon is not expensive but to remedy a radon problem can be expensive. It is advisable to inspect the site for radon prior to building.

Inspect and tune air-conditioning systems regularly for poor IAQ, ensure good ventilation while tuning the HVAC, change filters on central cooling and heating systems, and avoid biological contaminants. Use natural household cleaning products and natural pest control techniques to reduce exposure to potentially toxic airborne substances and fill plumbing traps with water to avoid backflow of sewer gases.

Introducing plants to reduce the levels of indoor air pollution, while popular, is only minimally effective. Even minimal ventilation with outdoor air removes pollutants more quickly. The so-called "toxin-consuming plants" such as philodendron, spider plants, golden pothos, peace lilies, bamboo palms, mums, and English ivy remove dangerous toxins (e.g., formaldehyde, carbon monoxide, benzene, and others) from the air, but at extremely low rates.

Following are some of the USGBC LEED® recommendations for IAQ for commercial buildings:

- Prior to occupying a new building ensure that indoor chemical concentrations comply with permitted maximum concentrations.

Chemical contaminate	Maximum concentration
Formaldehyde	0.05 parts per million
Particulates (PM10)	20 micrograms per cubic meter above outside air conditions
Total volatile organic compounds (TVOC)	500 micrograms per cubic meter
4-phenylcyclohexene (4-PCH)	3 micrograms per cubic meter
Carbon monoxide (CO)	9 parts per million

- Install and maintain filters, inspect dampers, and prohibit smoking; operate permanent CO_2 monitoring systems for feedback on ventilation system performance.
- Review, record, and update asbestos and PCB work done in an existing building and site, including how the remaining asbestos/PCB is being addressed on an ongoing basis.
- Aim to use adequate daylight in the majority of occupied spaces and use a daylight factor of 2 percent.

Source Control of Indoor Pollutants

Products and materials used in buildings can release VOCs, which are harmful. For example, many paints release high amounts of VOCs as they are applied and dry, which calls for use of low- or no-VOC paints. Products such as furniture, flooring, or ceiling systems can release chemicals to the indoor environment over long periods of time. Building professionals must select products and materials that have minimal impact on IAQ while also paying attention to all other requirements.

Source control is the most effective method to achieve and maintain healthful indoor environments. Since the late 1980s, the EPA has promoted source control as a means of controlling indoor air pollution. Key products identified as sources of indoor pollution include furniture, flooring, paints and coatings, adhesives and sealants, cleaning agents, wall coverings, office equipment, wood products, and insulation. Sustainable building programs such as the USGBC LEED® Program and the Collaborative for High Performance Schools (CHPS) have adopted source control as a means to create high-quality indoor environments throughout the design, building, and maintenance processes.

Currently, several manufacturers have tested, improved, and certified their building products to meet IAQ criteria mandated by several governmental and professional agencies.

At present, good IAQ can be achieved without compromising functionality or individual design preferences and at no additional cost or effort.

Summary

Inadequate ventilation or poorly functioning systems can increase indoor air pollution. Indoor pollutant sources are numerous, including construction materials, furnishings, lack of maintenance, occupants and their activities, outdoor pollution, and more. Exposure to pollution can cause immediate and long-term health effects; thus, risk assessment for IAQ and pollutants such as radon, molds, carbon monoxide, asbestos, and the like is advisable. The US EPA and LEED® have issued guidelines for addressing issues of IAQ. Source control and careful selection of building materials are effective methods of achieving and maintaining healthful indoor environments.

Further Reading

Public Technology, Inc. and US Green Building Council, *Sustainable Building Technical Manual: Green Building Design, Construction and Operation* (Alexandria, VA: Public Technology, Inc., 1996).

T. Salthammer (ed.), *Organic Indoor Air Pollutants: Occurrence, Measurement, Evaluation* (Germany: Wiley-VCH, 1999).

J. D. Spengler, J. M. Samet, and J. F. McCarthy, *Indoor Air Quality Handbook* (New York: McGraw–Hill, 2001).

Web Support

www.epa.gov/iaq/ia-intro.html
www.epa.gov/ebtpages/airindoorairpollution.html
www.asumag.com/mag/university contaminant control
www.buildingecology.com

Exercises

1 Make a table showing sources of indoor pollution and the potential health effects for building users.
2 What steps should be taken to improve indoor air quality (IAQ) as recommended by the US EPA?

5.4   Water and Waste Management

For sustainable architectural design we should minimize waste and reuse much of the waste generated by human activities, and this goal includes paying careful attention to our use and recycling of liquid as well as solid waste.

The guiding philosophy in efficient water use is reduction in the generation of wastewater and potable water demand, while at the same time making every effort to increase the local aquifer recharge. Ideas for best design practices abound. Designers can plan and facility managers can implement decentralized on-site wastewater treatment and reuse systems as part of efforts to recycle water. It is possible to decrease the use of potable water for sewage conveyance by utilizing gray and/or black water systems. Non-potable reuse opportunities include toilet flushing, landscape irrigation, etc. Many municipalities are considering providing advanced wastewater treatment by employing innovative, ecological, on-site technologies including constructed wetlands, mechanical re-circulating sand filters or aerobic treatment systems. Institutions such as the University of California and Oberlin College have already implemented these wastewater treatment systems to meet the requirement of state and local regulatory authorities for effluent disposal. Disposal of treated effluent by applying it to the land, either by surface application or subsurface dispersal, should become integral to the wastewater treatment approach.

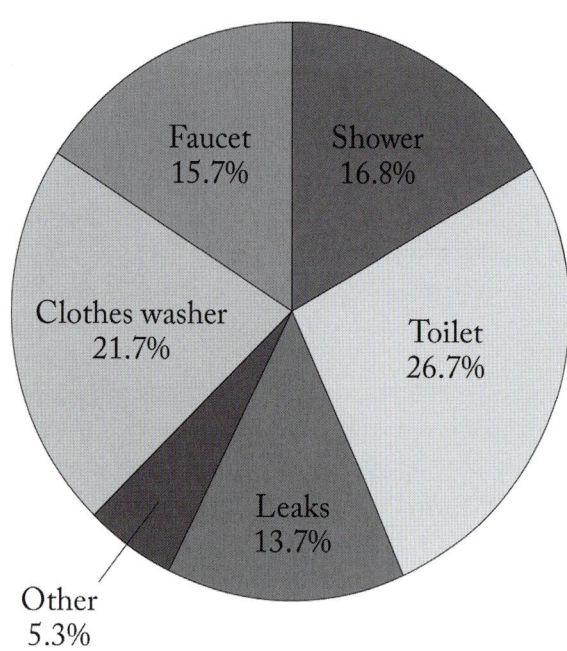

Figure 5.4.1 Residential end uses of water.
(Source: American Water Works Research Foundation, 1999.)

Efficient Use of Water

Efficient use of water supports sustainability by reduced use of fossil fuel energy and thus improves the environment. Designers can plan to:

- minimize water waste by best practices;
- reuse gray water;
- use solar hot water (reduction of fossil fuel use);
- lower stress on wastewater management systems (water harvesting, pervious surfaces, bioswales, living machines).

Minimize Water Waste

Daily indoor per capita water use, according to the American Water Works Association (waterfacts.net/html/water_use.html), is 72.6 gallons for the typical single family home in the USA. Figure 5.4.1 shows how it breaks down.

By installing more efficient water fixtures and regularly checking for leaks, households can reduce daily per capita water use by about 35 percent to about 45.2 gallons per day. Figure 5.4.2 shows water use for a household using conservation measures.

Fixtures that are efficient in terms of water use – some of them using no water at all – can be installed in commercial settings such as offices, airports, manufacturing units, etc., to minimize the use of potable water. Where practicable, gray water (non-industrial wastewater from domestic processes such as dishwashing), can be used for toilets and landscaping.

Use	Gallons per Capita	Percentage of Total Daily Use
Showers	8.8	19.5
Clothes washers	10.0	22.1
Toilets	8.2	18.0
Dishwashers	0.7	1.5
Baths	1.2	2.7
Leaks	4.0	8.8
Faucets	10.8	23.9
Other domestic uses	1.6	3.4
Total	**45.2**	**35%**

Figure 5.4.2 Efficient water use in residences.
(Source: American Water Works Association.)

Maximize fixture water efficiency within buildings to reduce the burden on potable water supply and wastewater systems. This USGBC LEED® requirement suggests that builders install, where possible, water-conserving plumbing fixtures that meet or exceed the Energy Policy Act of 1992 fixture requirements in combination with ultra-high efficiency or dry fixture and control technologies (waterless urinals, for example).

Figure 5.4.3 Efficient faucets and sinks.
(Source: this file is licensed under the Creative Commons Source 3.0 Unported License.)

Reuse Gray Water

Any water that has been used in the home or office, except water from toilets, is called gray water. Dish, shower, sink, and laundry water comprise 50–80 percent of residential "waste" water. This may be reused for other purposes, especially landscape irrigation.

It is a waste to irrigate with great quantities of drinking water when plants thrive on used water containing small bits of compost. Gray water reuse is a part of the fundamental solution to many ecological problems. The benefits of gray water recycling include:

- lower freshwater use;
- less strain on failing septic tanks or treatment plants;
- highly effective treatment for topsoil;
- the ability to build in areas unsuitable for conventional treatment;
- less energy and chemical use;
- groundwater recharge;
- plant growth;
- reclamation of otherwise wasted nutrients.

It is safe and legal to reuse gray water. In addition to conserving water and in many cases reducing water and sewer bills, using gray water can also "drought-proof" a family's yard. With landscaping valued at between 5 and 10 percent of the value of a home, this back-up supply of water may be an important economic insurance policy for a family. In climates where water is in limited supply, gray water use should be seriously considered. A sample exercise for calculating gray water use for a typical family home is found at the end of this section.

Use Solar Hot Water (Reduction of Fossil Fuel Use)

A solar hot water system (Figure 5.4.4) has a collector attached to a roof facing the sun, which heats some working fluid that is either pumped (active system) or driven by natural convection (passive system) through it. The collector is dark-colored and made of a simple glass-topped insulated box with a flat solar absorber made of sheet metal, attached to copper heat exchanger pipes. In this water-heating system the collector concentrates the sun's rays to heat water, which makes a closed loop through the heating tank. The hot water passes through an already installed in-the-home tank that contains a heat exchanger in the tank; the water is pumped back up to the solar collector (determined by a controller unit). Cold water that passes through the tank heats up and makes its way to building faucets. Since solar energy pre-heats the water in the water tank, it uses a reduced amount of electricity, thus minimizing use of fossil fuel.

Lower Stress on Wastewater Management Systems

Several techniques for easing wastewater issues include rainwater harvesting, installing pervious surfaces, creating bioswales, and using living machines to treat water on site.

Water harvesting involves collecting run-off from the soil's surfaces, paved surfaces, and other sources, and storing it for future use such as irrigation. Harvested water can include stormwater and irrigation run-off; water from cooling towers and heating, ventilating, and air-conditioning (HVAC) systems; and water

from swales and other drainage structures directed into collection areas. After collection in a storage tank or pond, harvested runoff must be pressurized in order to be used in an irrigation system. Water harvesting has been practiced in countries like India, Sri Lanka, and many other parts of the world successfully for centuries. Most of the ancient methods utilize gravity flow to collect run-off into harvesting areas such as storage tanks, open ponds, or detention basins. Also, rainfall from roofs and water from cooling towers can be directed into run-off harvesting areas.

Rainwater harvesting, practiced for centuries in arid parts of the ancient world, involves collecting and using precipitation from a roof or other catchment areas. This is an excellent way to take advantage of natural site resources, to reduce site run-off, and the need for run-off-control devices, and to minimize the need for utility-provided water. In the developing world where populations are dispersed, rainwater collection offers a low-cost alternative to a centralized piped water supply. In moist climate zones, rainwater collection is an excellent supplemental source of water.

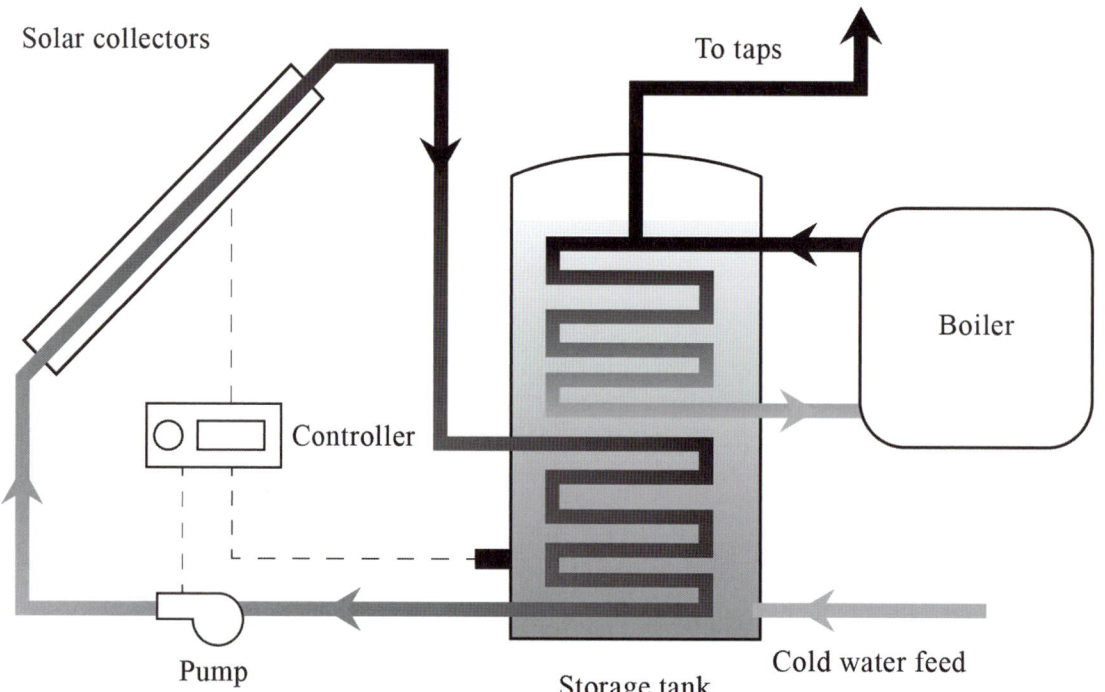

Figure 5.4.4 Solar hot water system.
(Source: Kuppaswamy Iyengar.)

Rainwater harvesting is simply collecting, storing, and purifying the naturally soft and pure rainfall that falls upon your roof. Rainwater may be utilized for both potable and non-potable requirements such as:

- drinking, cooking, bathing;
- swimming pool replenishment;
- toilet flushing;
- laundry (reduces detergent and bleach);
- landscape irrigation;
- livestock and animals.

Rainwater harvesting is the sustainable supply option. Rainwater can be utilized alone or together with other supply sources in residential, commercial, and industrial projects where pure water is desired.

Each *rainwater harvesting system* consists of at least the following components: a catchment area or roof surface to collect rainwater; delivery systems (gutters) to transport the water from the roof or collection surface to the storage *reservoir*; storage reservoirs or tanks to store the water until it is used; an extraction device (depending on the location of the tank, this may be a tap, rope and bucket, a pump, or an infiltration device if the collected water is used for well or groundwater recharge). Additionally, there are a wide variety of systems available for treating water before, during, and/or after storage.

Approximate Estimation of Rainwater Collection

The amount of rainwater that can be collected = catchment area in square feet × rainfall in inches × 0.62 gallons/sq.ft (conversion from inch units to gallons) × collection efficiency.

As an example, where the roof area is 2,500 sq.ft and rainfall is 1.97 inches, the amount of rainwater that can be collected is: 2,500 sq.ft × 1.97 inches rainfall × 0.62 gallons/in rain/sq.ft × 0.85 collection efficiency = 2,595 gallons.

In some developing countries (in Bangalore, India, for example) after filtering prior to sending it to the water tank, the rainwater is used for washing clothes, bathing and toilet flushing (Figure 5.4.5).

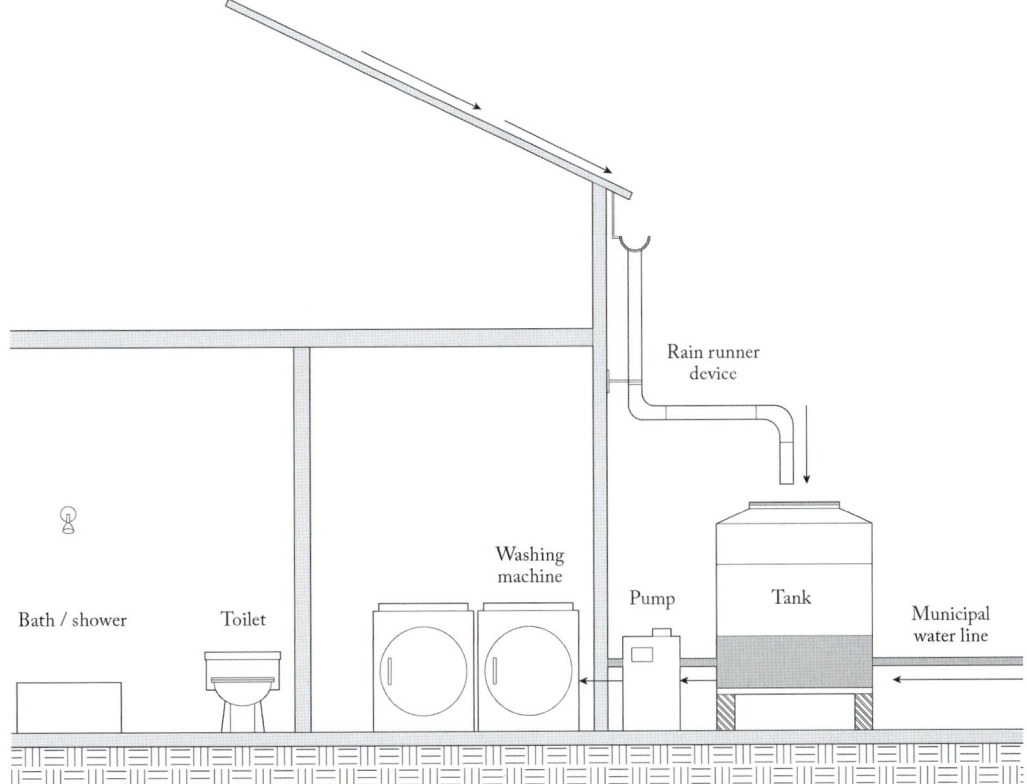

Figure 5.4.5 Rainwater harvesting in South India.
(Source: image courtesy of Padmini Décor.)

In urban settings it is important to consider the quality of rainwater. Areas with extremely poor air quality may yield rainfall of poor quality. Rainfall in some areas is highly acidic, and therefore undesirable for reuse without treatment. If the collection area has many overhanging trees, the collected rainwater can contain more debris and may appear brownish in color (caused by tannic acids drawn from plant debris). In areas with hard water, clean rainwater is preferable for its softness, cleaning abilities, and ability to extend the life of appliances such as water heaters and coffeemakers. There are few federal regulations for rainfall harvesting, and guidelines pertaining to the collection and use of rainwater are not clear. Pervious surfaces and bioswales help address issues of urban rainwater quality.

Pervious surfaces: These are ground covers that permit water to seep through to subsurface levels. One of the major advantages of this type of surface is that it will prevent storm run-off by absorption and thereby reduces the flow of pollutants to streams and rivers. These surfaces can be used for simple street walkways or entire parking lots. Portland and several other cities are experimenting with such surfaces.

A variety of commercial paving solutions are now widely available. They include:

- pervious concrete and asphalt that can be used for low-volume streets, parking lots, and sidewalks;
- brick pavers designed to allow a high degree of infiltration (compared to traditional cobbles, which are relatively impervious);
- plastic "geo-tech" fabrics that allow gravel and grass surfaces to have structural qualities;
- structured geo-grids below the paving surface.

These products should always be considered when making improvements to existing streets or building new roads. They are easy to install and maintain, and are an essential part of the solution for restoring stream and water quality, given that 20–30 percent of urban land is covered by streets and parking surfaces. All of these options reduce stormwater run off and increase on-site retention of water, though they vary in cost and aesthetics. When planning for pervious surfaces, consideration should be given to landscaping, site coordination, soil grade, and accessibility.

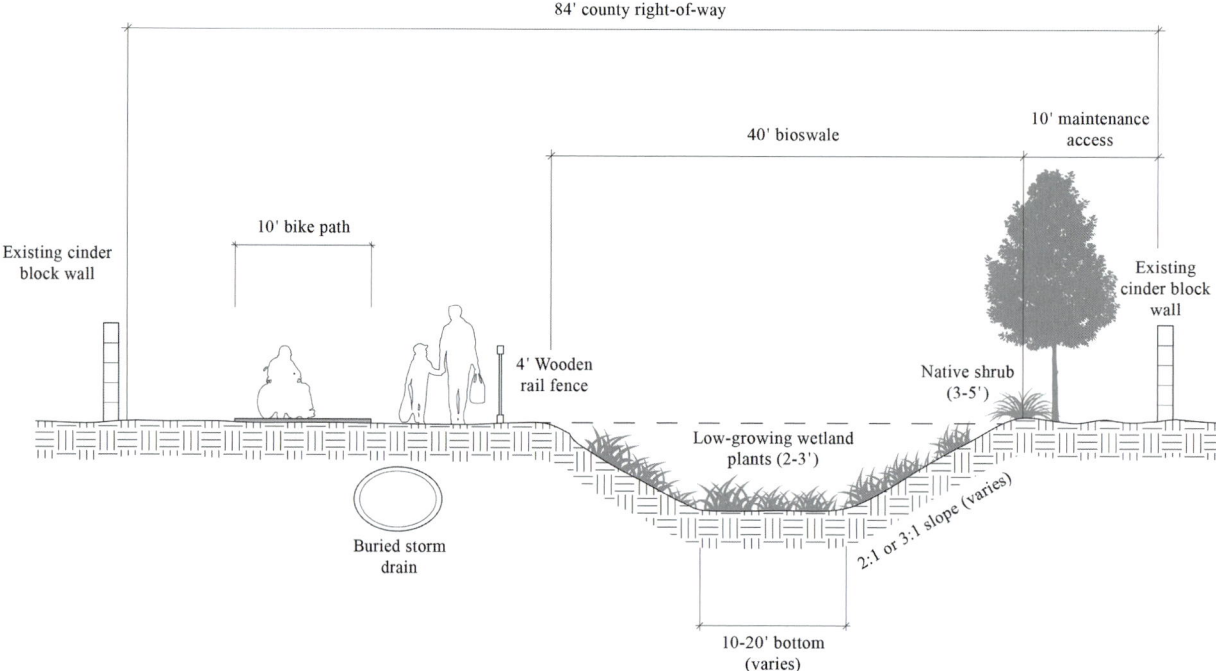

Figure 5.4.6 Typical cross-section of a bioswale.
(Source: image from the Tijuana Graduate Studio 2008, Sam Fox School of Design & Visual Arts at Washington University; instructors: Rene Peralta and John Hoal.)

Bioswales (Figure 5.4.6): These are land elements designed to stop silt and pollutants from joining the surface run-off. The slopes (less than 6 percent) of these elements are such that the water will flow smoothly and be filtered by vegetation and riprap stone. These types of swales are designed to slow down the water flow, elongating the filtering effect.

Bioswales are commonly used around parking lots to filter automobile pollution. A number of design options should be considered, such as the depth, wet or dry, grassed, rocky, and several other concepts. Also, a designer must take into account the direction of flow, slope, quantity of run-off, placement of swales relative to drainage surfaces, and integration of additional bio-remediation features.

Living machines are on-site wastewater treatment facilities. Based on the principles of wetland ecology, the patented tidal process treats wastewater to meet high-quality reuse standards, making living machine technology the most energy-efficient of wastewater treatment options. The treatment is accomplished through a sequence of activities in which anaerobic and aerobic containers hold key bacteria that consume pathogens, carbon, and other nutrients in the wastewater, rendering it clean and safe for reuse and recycling for landscape use. The most common type of living machines have two types of anaerobic tanks, a closed aerobic tank, and three open aerobic tanks – a clarifier, artificial wetland, and an ultraviolet filter. Living machines are very useful since they work off the grid (Figure 5.4.7).

Living machines require large land area and frequent maintenance. They require permits from city or local government (see *The Green Studio Handbook* [1]). Even though a typical living machine recycles thousands of gallons of gray water daily below the wetland surface, what an observer sees at the surface is lush greenery.

An example of gray water use for a typical family home

To verify whether a gray water system is right for a family, after checking with local codes, one has to learn approximately how much gray water the family will produce and how much landscape it can irrigate.

Estimating the Amount of Gray Water a Single Family Will Produce

The number of plumbing fixtures connected to the gray water system will determine how much gray water is available for irrigation use. The Greywater Standards use the following procedure to estimate a family's daily gray water flow.

Assuming four occupants in the family, they all use:

- Showers, bathtubs and sinks (total) 25 gal./day/occupant
- Clothes washer 15 gal./day/occupant
- = 40 gal./day/occupant × 4 occupants
- = 160 gallons each day.

Estimating the Amount of Landscape the Family Can Irrigate

Gray water is distributed subsurface and will efficiently maintain lawns, fruit trees, flowers, shrubs, and groundcovers. It can be used to irrigate all plants at the home except vegetable gardens. The following formula shows how to estimate the square footage of the landscape to be irrigated (from www.rainmaster.com/historicET.asp):

$$LA = \frac{GW}{ET} \times PF \times 0.62$$

where:
LA = landscaped area (square feet)
GW = estimated gray water produced (gallons per week)
ET = evapotranspiration – the amount of evaporation loss (inches per week) found from Figure 5.4.8
PF = plant factor (varies from 1.0 to 0.5 for lawn); 0.8 selected for this case.
0.62 = conversion factor (from inches of ET to gallons per week)

For the above family, which produces 160 gallons of gray water per day, how much lawn can be irrigated with that gray water?

$$LA = \frac{GW}{ET} \times PF \times 0.62 = \frac{1120}{2} \times 0.8 \times 0.62$$

$$= 1{,}129 \text{ square feet}$$

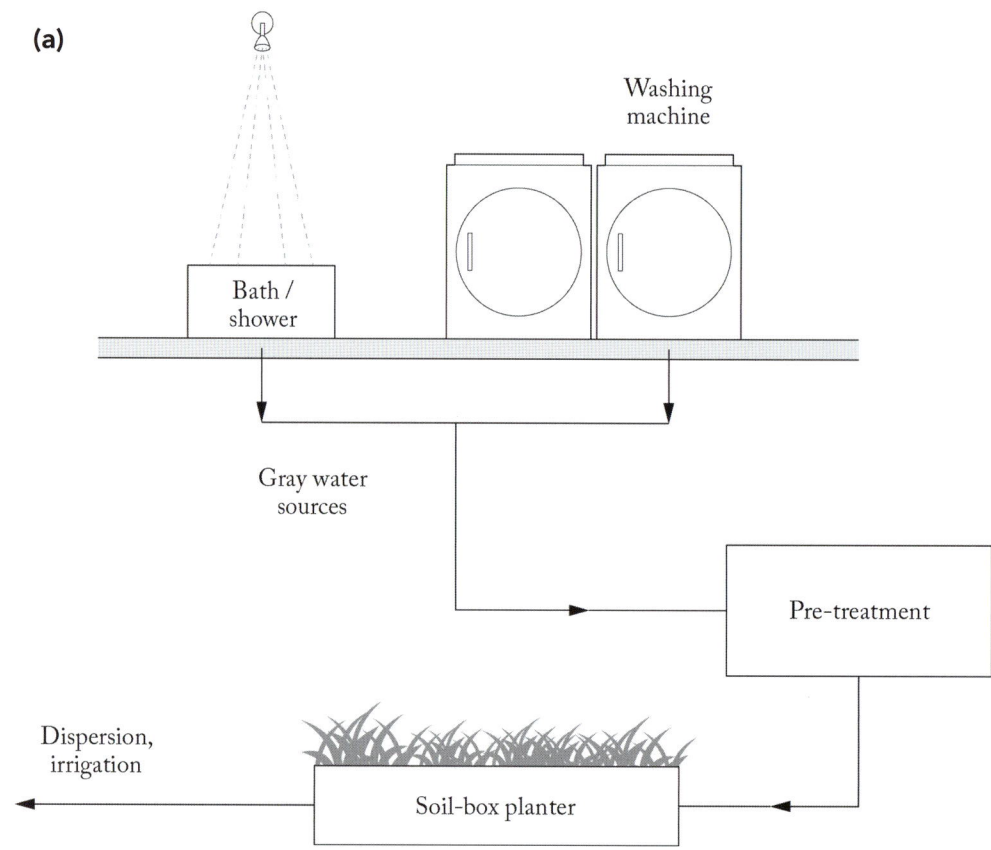

Figure 5.4.7 A simple gray water reuse system (a) and water reuse in Oberlin College (b) (Source: Courtesy of Oberlin College.)

Areas	Jan	Feb	Mar	April	May	June	July	Aug	Sept	Oct	Nov	Dec	Total
Northwestern Plateau (Gallup)	0	0.33	0.86	1.87	3.37	4.95	6.15	5.37	3.56	1.91	0.60	0	**28.9**
Northern Mtns. (Santa Fe)	0	0.30	0.68	1.56	2.82	4.26	5.05	4.51	3.02	1.63	0.52	0	**24.3**
Eastern Plains (Clovis)	0.35	0.55	1.27	2.53	4.31	6.23	7.00	6.30	4.26	2.42	0.91	0.45	**36.5**
Western Mtns. (Grants)	0.26	0.41	0.98	1.87	3.23	4.85	5.67	4.94	3.41	1.92	0.71	0.35	**28.6**
Central Valley (Albuquerque)	0.38	0.64	1.44	2.76	4.58	6.37	7.17	6.43	4.42	2.52	0.93	0.46	**38.1**
Central Highlands (Mountainair)	0.26	0.41	0.98	1.94	3.33	4.85	5.48	4.81	3.39	1.91	0.71	0.35	**28.4**
Southeastern Plains (Carlsbad)	0.52	0.78	1.68	3.10	4.95	6.79	7.33	6.66	4.69	2.84	1.17	0.66	**41.1**
Southern Desert (Las Cruces)	0.56	0.83	1.78	3.11	4.94	6.91	7.66	6.80	4.88	2.97	1.24	0.68	**42.3**

Figure 5.4.8 Average evapotranspiration for selected areas in New Mexico, in inches. (Source: www.ose.state.nm.us/water-info/.../Albq.../rainwater-harvesting.pdf.)

The above family produces enough gray water to water a lawn of 1,129 square feet.

Estimating How Many Trees and Shrubs this Family Can Have Instead of a Lawn

If this family's property had trees, another way to look at the gray water system is to determine approximately how much water an individual tree or shrub will need for one week during July (hot season):

1   Eight young fruit trees: 8 × 50 gal./tree = 400 gallons (medium water using, 50 foot canopy).
2   Eight medium-sized shade trees: 8 × 62 gal./tree = 496 (high water using, 100 foot canopy).
3   Seven large shrubs: 7 × 31 gal./tree = 217 (medium water using, 50 foot canopy).

Total: 1,113 gallons per week, which is less than the family's gray water production of 1,120 gallons per week.

The number of gallons of water per week a plant needs will vary from season to season, plant to plant, and site to site, but this will give a general idea about the number of plants one can successfully irrigate in July with gray water.

A sample table, Figure 5.4.8, illustrates evapotranspiration data for some areas in New Mexico. Similar data is available for other states from www.nws.noaa.gov/oh/hdsc/PMPrelated studies/TR33.pdf

Summary

Water is essential to life, and yet we continue to undervalue it. As water demands increase, designers must look to new ways of managing water use through installation of more efficient water fixtures, recycling, reusing gray water, water harvesting, and effective, innovative wastewater treatments. Management of water resources is just one of many approaches to reducing our use of fossil fuel energy and decreasing alarming levels of all waste worldwide.

Reference

[1] Allison Kwok and Walter Grodnizk, *The Green Design Studio Handbook* (New York: Architectural Press, 2011).

Further Reading

Paul Hawken, Amory Lovins, and Hunter Lovins, *Natural Capitalism* (New York: Little, Brown & Co., 1999).

Amy Vickers, *Handbook of Water Use and Conservation: Homes, Landscapes, Industries, Businesses, Farms* (Amherst, MA: WaterPlow Press, 2001).

Public Technology, Inc. and US Green Building Council, *Sustainable Building Technical Manual: Green Building Design, Construction and Operation* (Alexandria, VA: Public Technology, Inc., 1996)

Web Support

www.davidsuzuki.org/About_us/Dr_David_Suzuki/
Article_Archives/weekly05180101.asp
www.livingmachines.com
www.globalissues.org/TradeRelated/Development/
water

Exercises

1   Research *Blue Planet*, a BBC nature documentary, and *Water*, by National Geographic, to understand the current water situation in the world and write your critique on what our next steps should be to address the water problem.

2   How much water can be recovered from typical homes (average occupancy of four people) in a city of 200,000 for landscape irrigation?

3   Explain how minimizing water use reduces fossil fuel use. Remember that utilities use power to extract, purify, and pump water from some source.

CHAPTER SIX

Evaluation Tools and Case Studies

6.1 Evaluation of Sustainable Buildings

Establishing Performance Targets

Architecture 2030, a US organization, aims to transform the global building sector from being a major contributor of greenhouse gases to becoming a part of the solution. The goal is to achieve Zero Net Energy for buildings, which means that annually a building produces as much energy as it consumes. This initiative challenges the design community to

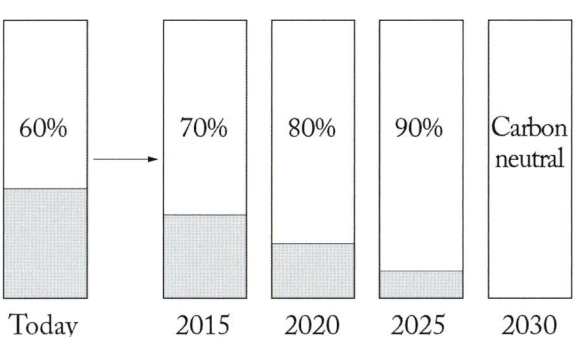

☐ Fossil fuel energy reduction

▨ Fossil fuel energy consumption

Figure 6.1.1 Architecture 2030: climate change action (see also Section 1.4).

adopt energy use reduction targets in increments until reaching carbon neutrality in 2030 (Figure 6.1.1)

To accomplish the goal of reducing global CO_2 emissions, the EPA has also established its own building performance program called *Energy Star*. Architecture 2030 and the EPA's Energy Star rating using the "Target Finder" tool are the two main pathways for setting up performance targets.

Energy Star, established in 1992, is an EPA voluntary program that helps businesses and individuals protect our climate through superior energy efficiency. Along with the US Energy Policy Act (2005), the program is used to identify and promote energy-efficient buildings and products, improve energy security, and reduce pollution through voluntary labeling. Many consumers are familiar with these labeling systems, which include stickers stating energy ratings and rankings of many household appliances such as refrigerators, water heaters, washers, and furnaces.

Calculations for Energy Star ratings are based in part on the Commercial Buildings Energy Consumption Survey (CBECS), which is a national sample survey that collects information on the stock of US commercial buildings (office, bank, courthouse, hotel, hospital, K–12 schools, medical office, supermarket, dormitory, big box retail, and warehouse), their energy-related building characteristics, and their energy consumption and expenditures. Commercial buildings include all buildings in which at least half of the floor space is used for non-residential purposes (www.eia.gov/consumption/commercial/Cached). For a selected building, the preliminary energy-use intensity (EUI) is calculated as below.

$$\text{EUI} \text{ (Energy Use Intensity)} = \frac{\text{Annual Building Energy Use (kBtus)}}{\text{Building Area (ft}^2)}$$

To earn the Energy Star rating, the commercial building designed for sustainability should have an EUI of 75 percent or more when compared to a typical CBECS building (see Figure 6.1.2). In order to help establish targets and to receive the Energy Star rating, the EPA offers online tools. How does one find what that energy use target should be in order to receive the Energy Star rating?

Target Finder is a no-cost online tool that enables architects and building owners to set energy targets to receive an EPA energy performance score for projects during the design process (www.energystar.gov/index.cfm?c=new_bldg_design. bus_target_finder).

Portfolio Manager is an assessment tool to verify energy performance of commercial buildings. Verification must be done by a licensed professional (professional engineer or registered architect) to be eligible for Energy Star recognition when the building achieves an energy performance score of 75 or higher. The licensed professional must verify that all energy use is accounted for accurately, that the building characteristics have been properly reported (including the square footage of the building), that the building is

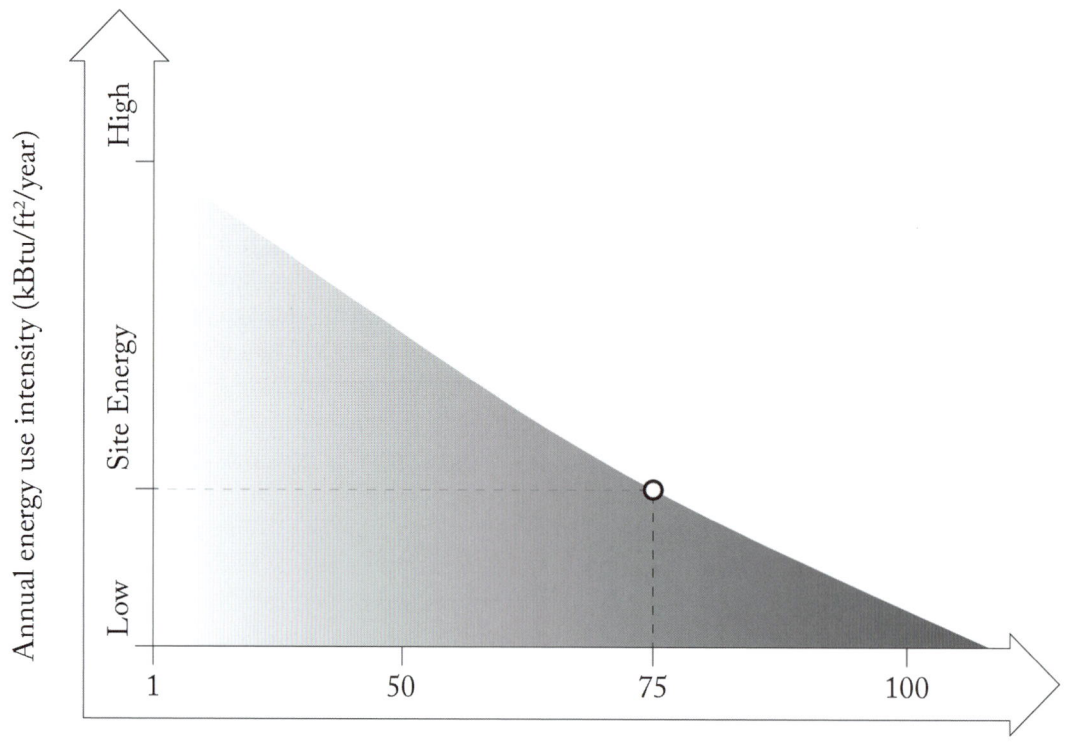

Figure 6.1.2 EPA energy performance score, percentage. (Source: US EPA.)

fully functional in accordance with industry standards; and that each of the indoor environment criteria has been met.

Architecture 2030 also uses CBECS for building data but requires more stringent energy reduction standards. Note that Architecture 2030 expects no fossil fuel energy need for buildings beyond 2030.

Evaluation Tools: Simulation Programs

One essential measure of building sustainability is the amount of energy it uses per square foot in heating and cooling seasons. That can be assessed using following analysis tools:

- Simple hand calculations (Sections 4.1, 5.1, and 5.2) and resultant EUI.
- Computer simulation programs such as Energy10, HEED, and RemRate for residential buildings and Energy Plus, Ecotect™, Project Vasari, IES VE, and Green Building Studio for simple commercial buildings.

Simulation programs like DOE2, eQuest, and EnergyPro for modeling medium to large buildings.

Energy 10 (www.sbicouncil.org/store)

This tool can be used to simulate smaller buildings, usually 10,000 sq.ft or below, to integrate and assess several options for energy-efficient design quickly and accurately. The program output clearly demonstrates the financial gain, quantifies the impact of design decisions, and also helps calculate energy credits of several programs such as LEED®. The program calculates hourly simulations and produces graphic reports indicating the building's thermal, HVAC, and daylighting performance over a full year of operation. Simulations from the Energy 10 program require actual energy and demand charges from utility bills.

HEED (www.aud.ucla.edu/energy-design-tools)

This free program for residential buildings considers several design variables. One of its major advantages

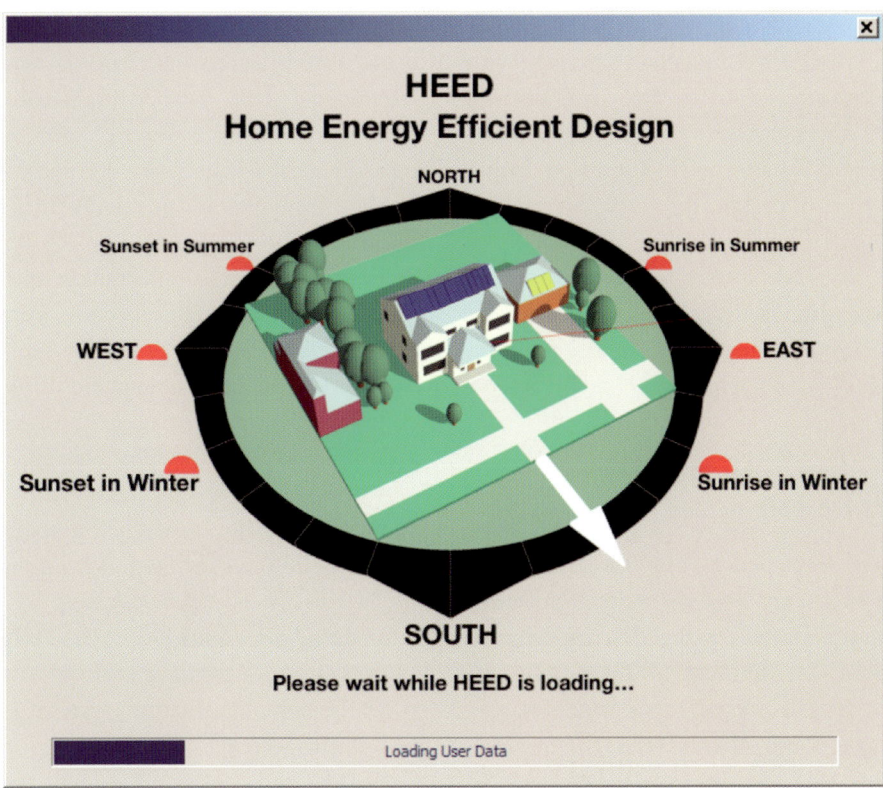

Figure 6.1.3 Simulation basics for HEED.
(Source: courtesy of Murray Milne, UCLA, www.energy-design-tools.aud.ucla.edu/heed.)

is that with only a few basic facts such as the location of the building in a city and the building type, size, height, and number of stories, the program can yield a base building. This easy-to-use program identifies how much *energy*, *money*, and *carbon* one can save by making various *design* or *remodeling* changes to a home. Initially a designer can draw the floor plan of a house, select from lists of typical wall and roof construction and then click and drag windows to their correct location. With this base information a designer can modify the building to make it sustainable.

ECOTECT™ (http://apps1.eere.energy.gov/buildings/tools_directory/software)

This a building design program that allows a designer to work easily in three dimensions and apply all the tools necessary for creating an energy-efficient and sustainable building. To encourage learning and investigation, ECOTECT™ simulations are visual and interactive and can analyze the building at any level of complexity. ECOTECT™ is one of the few tools in which performance analysis is simple, accurate, and, most importantly, visually responsive.

ECOTECT™ uses a 3D modeling interface with solar, thermal, lighting, acoustic, and cost analysis functions and is driven by the concept that environmental design principles are mostly addressed during the conceptual stages of design. The software responds by providing essential visual and analytical feedback from even the simplest sketch model. It has the capability of exporting facilities, which makes final design validation much simpler by interfacing with Radiance, EnergyPlus, and several other analysis tools.

EnergyPlus8.0.0 (http://apps1.eere.energy.gov/buildings/energyplus/energyplus_about.cfm)

This program was developed by the US Department of Energy. It is an energy analysis and thermal load simulation program. Based on the description of a building (location, size, number of floors, physical make-up, details of walls, floors, roofs, windows, and associated mechanical and other systems), EnergyPlus calculates heating and cooling loads necessary to maintain thermal comfort in the building. It also calculates the energy consumption of the building.

Integration of many building systems simultaneously reveals, by using the Energy Plus simulation, energy performance as it would operate in a real building.

DOE-2 (http://doe2.com/DOE2/)

This is a widely used and accepted free building energy analysis program that can predict the energy use and cost for all types of buildings. DOE-2 uses a description of the building layout, construction, usage, conditioning systems (lighting, HVAC, etc.) and utility rates provided by the user, along with weather data, to perform an hourly simulation of the building and to estimate utility bills. For over 30 years the US DOE has supported the development of DOE-2. Over its lifetime several versions of DOE-2 have been developed and released to the public. The latest is DOE-2.1E, which offers the most versatility to date.

eQuest (www.doe2.com/equest)

This is a quick energy simulation tool, built on the DOE-2 platform, that allows a designer to perform a detailed analysis of a building's design technologies using sophisticated building energy use simulation techniques. This is accomplished by combining building creation wizard, an energy-efficiency measurement wizard, and a graphical results display module from the advanced DOE-2 building energy use simulation program.

For designers it is important to know how well their sustainable design concepts are integrated into the design. ECOTECT™, HEED, and Green Building Advisor are helpful assessment tools in this regard. eQuest will guide a designer through the creation of a detailed DOE-2 building model, to automatically perform parametric simulations of design alternatives and to graphically highlight proposed design choices. The program requires the following input:

- building orientation
- area and total number of floors
- wall types and structural systems
- lighting systems
- heating and cooling equipment types
- window and door dimensions
- glass types

- occupancy load
- plug loads
- ventilation.

Example of Building Energy Use from a Typical eQuest Simulation

From Figure 6.1.4, electricity and natural gas consumption can be converted to total Btu/sq.ft/year, which helps in determining the EUI. This information, when compared with Energy Star or Architecture 2030 energy use targets, will illustrate how sustainable the building is. Note that when electricity use is peaking from April through September, natural gas use is at a minimum, confirming the seasonal energy use pattern.

Other formal rating systems exist for evaluating design and energy performance of buildings.

Complexity of Rating Sustainability of a Building and Site

Evaluating sustainability involves more than energy efficiency. It requires making judgments on how effectively a building has responded to the site environment; materials used in making the building and how sustainable they have been; efficiency and care in using water and wastewater; how well designers have minimized or eliminated toxic substances in building finishing products such as paints and in subsequent maintenance (cleaning products) used in the building; and the high quality of the building indoor air. Buildings that satisfy these requirements, when compared against an industry baseline, can be called sustainable.

Worldwide Sustainable Rating Systems

Today there are several sustainable building rating systems available in the market. In the public interest, the General Services Administration (GSA), a US Federal agency, requested a report on sustainable buildings rating systems to be completed by the Pacific Northwest National Laboratory. This laboratory is an independent, academically solid organization that is well acquainted with green buildings and known to maintain rigorous standards for peer review. These rating systems require varying levels of specialized sustainable design knowledge to be effectively used.

While building performance evaluation tools such as Energy Plus, DOE-2, eQuest, and other programs

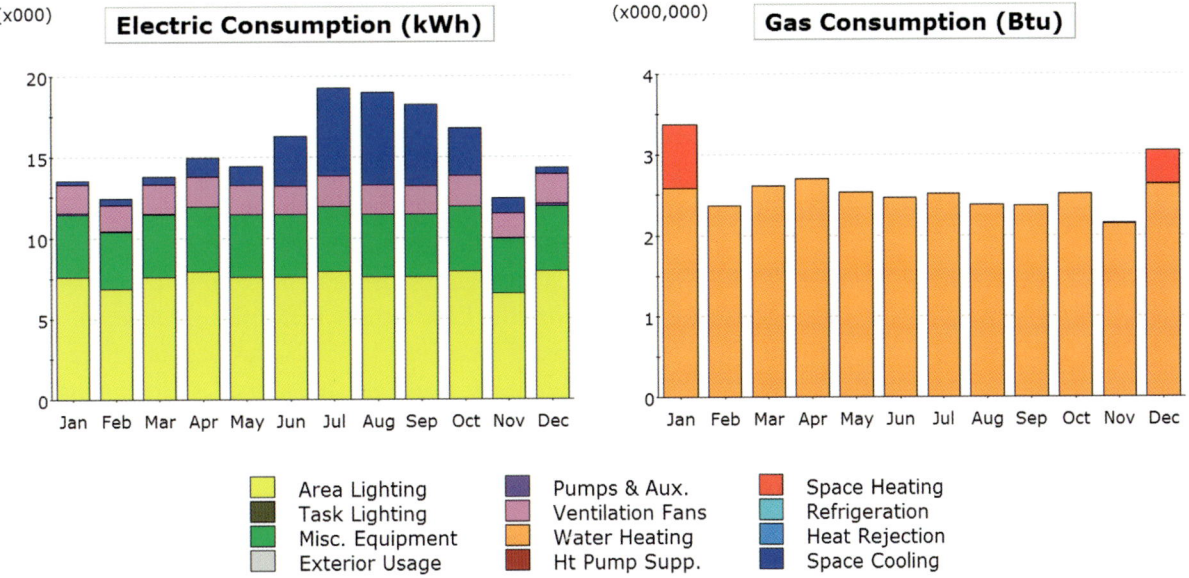

Figure 6.1.4 Example of energy use from an eQuest simulation.
(Source: Matt Higgins, Vibrantcy, Albuquerque.)

simulate the energy use in a building, the following worldwide leading rating systems evaluate overall performance of sustainable buildings.

- BREEAM (United Kingdom)
- Green Star (Australia)
- BCA Green Mark (Singapore)
- CASBEE (Japan)
- DGNB (Germany)
- Green Globes (Canada)
- Living Building Challenge (USA)
- LEED® (USA, Canada, India and over 130 countries).

Following is a brief summary of rating systems.

1. *BREEAM (Building Research Establishment's Environmental Assessment Method)* has a long track record in the UK since 1990, but it is not extensively used in the USA. The BREEAM assessment tool measures performance against a set of nine benchmarks. They are: building/construction, health and well-being, energy, transport, water, waste, materials, land use, and ecology and pollution. Each section gets a weighted score (credits) because each section deals with numerous environmental attributes. Credits range from 6 (water use) to 19 (energy). The BREEAM rating system can be used in the UK or internationally. However, it is neither used nor recognized by US design professionals.

2. *Green Star*, developed by the Green Building Council of Australia (GBCA) in 1994, is a comprehensive and voluntary rating system that assesses nine environmental impact categories. Buildings receive rating levels of 1 star (10 to 19 points) to 6 stars (75+ points – world leader standing). South Africa and New Zealand also use this system.

3. *BCA Green Mark* is a green building rating system in Singapore, used to evaluate a building for its environmental impact and performance. It provides a comprehensive framework for assessing the overall environmental performance of new and existing buildings to promote sustainable design, construction, and operations practices in buildings. The assessment criteria cover:

- energy efficiency
- water efficiency
- environmental protection
- indoor environmental quality
- other green features and innovation.

Depending on the overall assessment and point scoring, the building will be certified to have met the BCA Green Mark Platinum, Gold^{Plus}, Gold, or Certified rating.

4. *CASBEE (Comprehensive Assessment System for Building Environmental Efficiency)* is a relatively new system developed for the Japanese market that is available in English, but has not been tested in the USA. The system follows four basic sustainability criteria:

1 energy efficiency
2 resource efficiency
3 local environment
4 indoor environment.

The CASBEE rating system starts with a grade of C (poor) to S (superior) quality based on a building's "internal improvement for living amenities" to external space for reducing "negative environmental impacts." Buildings are assessed by trained, first-class architects who have passed the CASBEE assessor examination. A small number of buildings have used the system and all of those are in Japan; thus it is relatively unknown in the US market.

5. *The Deutsche Gesellschaft fur Nachhaltiges Bauen (DGNB)* system uses lifecycle assessments (LCAs) and benchmarks with two elements for its evaluation. The first element is fixed value of construction, derived from a German national research project that evaluates the relation between a building and its environmental impact. The second, a variable part, is derived from the German energy performance certificate, in accordance with the EU's Energy Performance Directive.

6. *Green Globes™ US* was adapted from Green Globes Canada in 2004 and is developing tools that address major renovation, tenant build-out, and operations and maintenance applications. The Green Building Initiative received accreditation as a standards developer by the American National Standards Institute (ANSI) and is working toward developing Green Globes™ US as an official ANSI standard. Currently, sustainable design and construction information is

submitted online for third-party verification, which is provided by a Green Building Initiative-approved and Green Globes-trained professional. Thus far it has not gained popularity in the USA.

According to General Services Administration (GSA) studies, the Green Globe program has projects in over 42 countries worldwide, with commitment to sustainable environmental outcomes. Like LEED®, this Canadian organization hopes to attract new customers to participate in their evaluation method. The Green Globe Standards are based on the Principles of Sustainable Development as detailed in the Mohonk Agreement. It is anticipated that this agreement enables compliance with present and future government legislation and industry acceptance. The emerging Green Globe evaluation programs in Canada include:

- Existing Office Buildings (available in the USA also);
- Green Globes for Existing Light Industrial Buildings;
- Green Globes Design (available in the USA also);
- Green Globes Fit-up;
- Green Globes Building Emergency Management.

The Green Globe program, in addition to sustainable benefits, hopes to address the following key environmental challenges of our times:

- reduction in greenhouse gas emissions;
- energy efficiency, conservation and management;
- reduction in the consumption of fresh water and resources;
- ecosystem conservation and management;
- support for local community development;
- improved management of social and cultural issues;
- improved land use planning and management;
- improved air quality and noise reduction;
- improved wastewater management;
- waste minimization, reuse, and recycling.

By monitoring and taking suitable actions in these key performance areas, an organization can reduce its carbon footprint and enjoy other environmental benefits.

7. *Living Building Challenge*, copyrighted by Cascadia Region Green Building Council and International Living Building Institute in 2009, is attempting to raise the bar. It defines the most advanced measure of sustainability in the built environment. This certification program covers all building at all scales and is a unified tool for transformative design, allowing us to envision a future that is socially just, culturally rich, and ecologically benign. The Living Building Challenge is composed of seven performance areas: site, water, energy, health, materials, equity, and beauty. These are subdivided into a total of 20 imperatives, each of which focuses on a specific sphere of influence. Two rules govern the standard: (1) All imperatives assigned to a typology are mandatory; and (2) certification is based on actual, rather than modeled or anticipated performance. See https://ilbi.org/lbc/LBC%20Documents/LBC2-0.pdf for details.

8. *LEED® (Leadership in Energy and Environmental Design)* is currently the dominant system in the US market and is being adapted to multiple markets worldwide. The currently available LEED® rating systems address all GSA building and project types. A *Product Development and Maintenance Manual* is publicly available, which governs how changes are made to the LEED® rating systems. The steps followed for the development of US Green Building Council rating system products include technical development by committee, pilot testing, a public comment period, approval by council membership, and then release for public use. A major revision, in 2009, attempts to streamline the rating process for existing and new buildings. Thousands of US buildings have received LEED® ratings and many more are seeking certifications. LEED® is often required of government buildings. The architectural profession has embraced the concept of designing sustainable buildings and is encouraging architects to become accredited LEED® professionals. LEED® is not only the US market leader, but is also the most widely used rating system by federal and state agencies, which makes it easy to communicate a building's sustainable design achievements with others.

LEED® Certifications

Since LEED® rating systems are dominant in the USA, understanding of the certification process is important to architects wishing to improve their sustainable practices and designs. According to the USGBC website, LEED® rating systems are developed through an open, consensus-based process led by LEED® committees. Each volunteer committee is composed of a diverse group of practitioners and experts representing a cross-section of the building and construction industry. The key elements of USGBC's consensus process include a balanced and transparent committee structure, technical advisory groups that ensure scientific consistency and rigor, opportunities for stakeholder comment and review, member ballot of new rating systems, and a fair and open appeals process.

The family of LEED® rating systems as of 2009 is listed below. Additional LEED® certifications are in development. Some projects may have only one applicable rating system, while others may have more. The USGBC encourages the project team to tally a potential point total using the rating system checklists for all possibilities. A project is a viable candidate for LEED® certification if it can meet all prerequisites and achieve the minimum points required in a given rating system. Currently nine rating systems are: LEED® for New Construction, Existing Buildings, Commercial Interiors, Core & Shell, Retail, Schools, Homes, Neighborhood Development, and Healthcare. Project Teams interact with the Green Building Certification Institute (GBCI), which has been a separate entity from USGBC since 2008, for project registration and certification. GBCI administers credentialing and certification programs related to green building practice. These programs support the application of proven strategies for increasing and measuring the performance of buildings and communities as defined by industry systems such as LEED®.

The LEED® 2009 Green Building Rating System for New Construction and Major Renovations is a set of performance standards for certifying the design and construction of commercial or institutional buildings and high-rise residential buildings of all sizes, both public and private. The intent is to promote architecturally sustainable designs through seven categories:

1 Sustainable Sites (SS) – *minimize the impact on ecosystems and water resources.*
2 Water Efficiency (WE) – *reduce potable water consumption.*
3 Energy and Atmosphere (EA) – *energy performance through innovative strategies.*
4 Materials and Resources (MR) – *sustainable building materials & reducing waste.*
5 Indoor Environmental Quality (IEQ) – *better indoor air quality, daylight and views.*
6 Innovation in Design (ID) – *sustainable building expertise.*
8 Regional Priority (RP) – *regional environmental priorities.*

LEED® 2009 for New Construction and Major Renovations certifications are awarded according to the following scale:

- Certified: 40–49 points
- Silver: 50–59 points
- Gold: 60–79 points
- Platinum: 80 points and above *(Possible points 100).*

Evaluation systems and categories show priorities for designers interested in sustainability. They can be used early in the design process for planning and programming, and later as evaluation or assessment during a walk-through.

Future Actions

Calls for sustainable practice are increasing. "By some conservative estimates, the building sector worldwide could deliver emissions reductions of 1.8 billion tons of CO_2," says UNEP Executive Director Achim Steiner. "A more aggressive energy efficiency policy might deliver over two billion tons or close to three times the amount scheduled to be reduced under the Kyoto Protocol."

The UNEP report, entitled *Buildings and Climate Change: Status, Challenges and Opportunities,* states that applying ambitious standards could yield quick results.

In response to the Architecture 2030 challenge, there are already a few high-profile projects focused on cutting emissions from buildings. In May 2007, the Clinton Climate Initiative launched the Energy Efficiency Building Retrofit Program, a $5 billion project that will reduce energy consumption in existing urban buildings with the involvement of city governments and corporate investment.

In addition, we are seeing more high-profile examples of sustainable building practices worldwide. Prominent buildings, such as the Swiss Re "Gherkin" building in London or the renovated Reichstag (Parliament) in Berlin, serve as famous examples of green buildings. Builders completed a stadium in Beijing for the 2008 Olympics that showcases the latest in ecological building technology. Designed by Swiss architects Herzog & de Meuron, the Beijing National Stadium incorporates solar power, rainwater collection, and innovative ventilation systems.

In early 2007 the building with the highest LEED® rating was the St. Louis headquarters of construction company Alberici. The office building supplies 18 percent of its energy from an on-site wind turbine and uses sustainable landscaping, rainwater harvesting, and solar energy. There are buildings in India such as Godrej in Hyderabad and Suzlon One Earth in Pune with the highest LEED® rating (Platinum), paving the way for similar attitudes in the developing world.

Many commercial buildings and homes are incorporating smaller-scale energy-saving strategies into their building or renovation plans to save money in the long run. Users are also proud to live and work in ecologically friendly buildings.

LEED®- or otherwise-certified buildings are not just more efficient, they also carry less risk. In October 2006 the Allianz subsidiary of Fireman's Fund became the first US insurer to integrate this statistical fact in its policy by offering a discount for LEED®-certified buildings. An upgrade package even allows owners to rebuild conventional buildings using green architecture and technology. In several architecture schools experiments are in progress to design buildings with a "zero net energy" concept where any fossil fuel energy used in a building is offset by some form of solar PV system or wind energy. In their book *The World's Greenest Buildings* [1], Jerry Yudelson and Ulf Meyer have identified several high-performance buildings all over the world. This is a testament to the design professionals' commitment to dealing with CO_2 emissions and sustainability.

Summary

Sustainable building rating systems help designers meet environmental challenges and reduce the carbon footprint of buildings through requirements for planning, design, and construction of high-performance facilities. Different rating systems are developed for different building types and for new or existing structures. Simple design assessment computer simulations such as ECOTECT™, Energy 10, HEED, and Energy Plus concentrate on the energy performance of the building more than whole-system design. The GSA reviewed information on several of these rating systems, eventually working with other groups to narrow the list to five main systems. Of these, Green Globe and especially LEED® systems offer evaluations and certification processes in Canada and the USA.

Reference

[1] Jerry Yudelson and Ulf Meyer, *The World's Greenest Buildings* (Abingdon: Routledge, 2013).

Further Reading

2009-LEED-NC-Checklist.xls; also found at www.usgbc.org/DisplayPage.aspx?CMSPageID=220

New Mexico Regional Priority Credits.xls; also found at www.usgbc.org/DisplayPage.aspx?CMSPageID=1984

2009 BD+C Reference Guide.pdf; also found at www.usgbc.org/ShowFile.aspx?DocumentID=55465.

Allianz: A Green Foundation for Architecture: https://acs.allianz.com/en/press/publications

Architecture 2030 Challenge: http://architecture2030.org/2030_challenge/the_2030_challenge

Web Support

www.wbdg.org/release_100606.php-2

Exercise

1 Explain the difference between evaluation tools and assessment tools. How can one use evaluation tools for modifying building designs for sustainability? Give examples.

6.2 Energy Sources and Sustainability Audit

A sustainability audit for new or existing buildings can reveal areas for improvement and guidelines for site, water, indoor air quality, structures, and materials. An energy audit provides insight into how and where major quantities of energy are being used and where waste occurs. Energy Star, LEED®, and other rating systems help the designer plan and assess a facility's energy systems.

Energy Use and the Benefits of an Energy Audit

If properly performed and understood, an energy audit can provide important guidelines to the designer or building owner regarding major areas of energy use. Most important is the insight into *how* and *where* major quantities of energy are being used. A person conducting an energy audit/survey must develop the ability to draw back and look at the overall situation before making important decisions. Energy audit of an existing building is useful for retrofitting a building for sustainability. The USGBC has developed LEED®-EB for encouraging the building owners to improve the sustainability of existing buildings, or retrofitting in the interest of mitigating CO_2 emissions. Costs can be acceptable to the owner/user when viewed over the entire lifecycle of the building. It is also important to review refrigerant management and make mandated changes.

General methodology should determine the amount of energy entering the site/building, energy produced on-site, how the energy is used in the site/building, energy leaving the site/building, how much is wasted and how much is recirculated. An audit poses typical questions:

1 What does the floor system contain structurally and mechanically (under-floor air ducts, double structural layers to allow for individual HVAC controls)?
2 Does the lighting system meet latest codes as well as Energy Star, ASHRAE 90.1 and/or Title 24 standards? If not, can it be brought to current standards cost-effectively?
3 Can the purchasing policies be modified to eliminate VOCs in the building?
4 How can the building be more efficient in the use of water and waste management, including recycle, retrofit and reuse?
5 Can energy simulations using eQuest or other simulations and comparing them with utility bills give insight into possible retrofit options?
6 Can any control strategies be improved for optimizing energy use, including building commissioning and/or retro-commissioning?
7 Most important of all, is there any potential for renewable energy source development?

Site and Building Energy Sources

An audit must look at the energy sources being used to operate the building. Site and building energy systems typically include electricity, fuel oil, natural gas, LPG, coal, steam, chilled water, hot water, compressed air, and potable water supply. These active energy systems are derived from coal, fuel oil, natural gas, LPG, hydro-electric plants, and nuclear power plants.

In a sustainable site, solar energy, including PV systems, and wind energy may contribute a considerable amount of energy needed to operate the site and the building. Is there any way these systems can be used either on-site or through purchasing to reduce active energy use?

In all building sites waste streams and waste energy include: wastewater, solid wastes and liquid wastes. In general, a facility receives energy in the form of purchased fuels or utilities, which are transformed, converted, and distributed among various building operations as energy end uses. Output from the building and/or the site includes some useful product(s) or service(s), some by-products, wastes, and wasted energy. How can the designer make the entire system work more efficiently from input through output?

Energy Star and LEED® ratings

The Energy Star energy rating is given by the EPA based on a statistical analysis of similar buildings in a region. If a building falls below the statistical baseline it gets a ranking indicating the relative energy efficiency. LEED® uses the Energy Star rating for energy efficiency as a part of overall LEED® credit and to determine the final LEED® rating.

As described in the opening to Chapter 6, the LEED® rating includes a whole range of issues such as the building construction, attention to resource efficiency, pollution mitigation, VOC abatement, recycling, solid waste, and wastewater management, and ongoing sustainable energy and indoor air quality management. Depending on the level of LEED® rating a building can apply for and receive a certificate (LEED® certified, Silver, Gold, and Platinum). This information can be a valuable guide to designing and implementing an audit of an existing structure. The ratings are also a tool for decision-making during renovations.

The Building Sustainability Audit

Audit procedures are used to assess how well buildings meet issues of sustainability. Audits can also help in correcting any deficiencies in buildings found over time or after new standards are adopted.

An assessment can be made of an existing building or can also be used as a quick reference guide in the case of a planned new construction. Sustainability opportunities resulting from an audit cover a wide range of issues, and the following guide serves as a preliminary checklist:

Site

Sustainability benefits can occur through careful site analysis.

General

1 Check the site for air, sunlight, and water quality, soil issues (not brownfield), and any potential for renewable energy development. Look for good grade levels or usable slopes for making attractive buildings.

Community Resources

2 Determine if the site is close to public transportation, the workplace, libraries, shops and schools.
3 Are affordable health facilities and community centers in the area to meet community needs?

Public Utilities

4 Assess the availability of clean water supply, electricity, natural gas, and other fuel supplies.
5 Note infrastructure and access to main highways to minimize automobile travel and thus reduce the use of fossil fuels.
6 Parks and recreation areas are added benefits.

Developmental Considerations

7 Any changes should not unduly disturb existing flora and fauna, or should aim to return native conditions to stripped land.
8 Seriously consider minimal damage to the land.
9 Restore environmental productivity.

Relationship of Landscaping to Building Design

10 Devote at least 50 percent of grounds to trees and plants and minimize hard surfaces.
11 Avoid cutting trees.
12 Blend with existing ecosystems.
13 Use gray water for landscaping.
14 Consider the use of rainwater harvesting.
15 Design landscaping as food gardens.

Location of building(s) on the site

16 The proposed buildings should respond to the local climate by taking holistic approaches to rectify site problems.
17 Location and siting should respond to seasonal changes.
18 The orientation of the building(s) should be east–west in the USA.
19 The building(s) should respond to land forms.

Water Management

To produce clean water takes energy from the moment it is harvested from lakes, aquifers, rivers, and other sources. To save water means preserving the supply for the future as well as using less fossil fuel in energy production.

Saving Water

1 Ensure all plumbing fixtures are efficient and use less water or no water.
2 See if automatic toilets and urinals are a possibility, including waterless fixtures.
3 Save water to protect fish, wildlife, and aquifers.
4 Install efficient and modern showerheads.

Efficient Landscaping

1 Select plants that are appropriate for the climate, soil, and location. Consult a landscape architect.
2 Choose drought-tolerant plants for arid zones.
3 Use "xeriscaping" (attractive landscaping requiring little or no irrigation).
4 Use drip irrigation to prevent water waste.
5 Avoid turf to save water.

Use of Wastewater

6 Collect and use gray water after treatment for landscape and toilets.
7 Collect rainwater wherever possible and store it for landscape use.
8 Although "biological wastewater" treatments are not easily used in many facilities, there are opportunities to use them in certain places. Investigate the use of living machines.

Solid waste management

1 Develop a solid waste management plan which includes recycling and reuse of several waste products generated in the building. Design a separation area and encourage occupants to use it by some incentives.

Buildings and materials

Shapes and Layout

1 Remember that optimum surface-to-volume has an impact on the energy use in a building.
2 Check if the building has proper solar orientation.
3 Determine if the building has been laid out to benefit from the wind.

4 Check for adequate and appropriate roof overhangs.

Daylighting Use

1 Check if best use of the sun has been made.
2 Look for passive cooling/heating opportunities.
3 Thoroughly explore light shelf and daylighting use.

Building Shell (Walls, Windows, Doors, Floor and Roof)

1 Ensure that proper insulation has been applied according to local codes or model codes such as California's Title 24.
2 Place radiant barriers correctly to reduce heat load on a building.
3 Check that a sufficient number of operable windows and double glazing with proper U-values exist. Explore use of spectrally selective glazing.
4 Determine if the building materials to be used in retrofitting as well as existing ones are environmentally responsible, such as FSC-approved wood.
5 Are all the paints, fabrics, adhesives, and other finishes free from VOCs? Are the roof and other structural systems made of recycled material?
6 In contemporary office buildings, install "intelligent façades" such as double glazing and proper sun controls.
7 Use recycled glass, paper, plastic, and other reusable materials in the building.
8 Check materials for durability. Buildings should be built for the long haul.
9 Remember that buildings should be of the correct size for strength and durability, and should not have oversized members, which are wasteful.
10 Avoid toxic materials such as asbestos and paints containing oils and VOCs.

Environmental impact and ecology

1 Check if the building materials used have low embodied energy. For example, structural lumber has a low embodied energy while aluminum has the highest.
2 Verify that over the lifecycle costs will be low. There is a user-friendly *lifecycle costing spreadsheet*

available in Excel and Office 97 for free from www. doe2.com.

3 Ensure that the air quality, air movement, and HVAC systems are working properly or design them for maximum performance for new constructions.

Indoor Air Quality

1 Make sure the quality of the air coming into the building is fresh and clean and the exhaust system is functioning properly.
2 Verify that filters are placed and maintained properly.
3 Place CO_2 monitors in the building.
4 Check for mold and other discoloration in the building.
5 Avoid outgassing (emission of toxic gases from building finishes and materials).
6 Do not use toxic cleaners for cleaning the building.
7 Development of a *green purchasing and durable goods policy* will enhance the sustainability of the building.

Summary

Tools to assess sustainability can also be used as guides for future projects. A sustainability energy audit reveals major areas of energy use, how and where energy is used, and reveals the energy efficiency of the building. It gives insight into how energy use might be improved. The rating systems of LEED® and Energy Star rank multiple aspects of sustainability, while a sustainability audit provides a checklist for assessment of the site, water use, waste, buildings and materials, interior air quality, and more. Audits assist designers to make the most of opportunities for efficient sustainable practice.

Exercise

1 How can a sustainability audit be used to prioritize system changes to improve energy performance of an existing building? Visit a building in your area and consider it in terms of sustainability, using some of the criteria presented for audits. Write a report.

6.3 Case Studies

Sustainable architectural design emphasizes an integrated design approach to arrive at its goal. The case studies selected are representative building types from the US Energy Information Administration (EIA). These buildings represent how a designer approached the architectural issues while adopting current technology and pushing the envelope in a creative way. They illustrate how a designer makes decisions that are responsive to climate, siting, materials selection, and other choices. Of particular interest is that these buildings respond primarily to architectural needs while respecting nature's gifts. All examine appropriate technologies for the building's needs in terms of users, context, site, landscape, building envelope, appropriate materials and evaluation of building performance through certification or award by third-party assessments such as LEED® or other methods. Summary descriptions of case studies follow.

1. Clear View Elementary School

Location: Hanover, PA
Use: elementary school
Size: 43,000 sq.ft
Architect: John Boecker, L. Robert Kimball & Associates

Sustainable Strategies

Site

• The elementary school was built on a previously developed site, avoiding use of agricultural land or removal of natural habitat.
• Site allows safe access for bicycle and pedestrian commuters. Bicycle racks and shower/changing facilities are provided.
• Site chosen for construction was low impact, located above the flood plain, and had minimal grade slope.
• New construction ties into existing underground storm sewer pipe.
• Trees were planted to shade parking areas and reduce heat island effect.

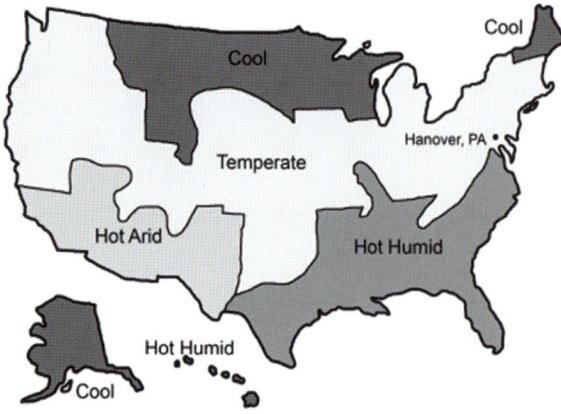

Figure 6.3.1 Clearview Elementary School.
(Source: photo by © Jim Schafer.)

- 50 percent of construction waste was recycled or reclaimed.

Building Envelope

- Insulated concrete forms (ICF) used for exterior walls provide high levels of building insulation.
- The building's orientation and form enhances winter heating and summer cooling.
- Wall and roof section R-value is greater than 25.
- Concrete slab perimeter is insulated, achieving an R-value greater than 11.
- High albedo roofing surface reduces solar heat gain.

Passive Strategies

- Curved building form serves as sunscreen for south-facing glazing, acoustical backdrop for outdoor assemblies, and functions as a sundial.

- The east–west building wings are long and narrow, allowing daylight to enter the center of the building, through the clerestories and windows provided.
- Skylights and clerestories supply high levels of daylighting, reducing the use of artificial lighting.
- Passive solar designed reverse-baffle solar shading devices, horizontal sunshades, and sunscreen walls, allow direct low winter sunlight to enter the building to provide passive heat, and only indirect summer sunlight to reduce heat gain.
- Thermal mass of masonry wall and terrazzo floor, in the main north corridors, help store solar heat for passive winter heating.
- Light-colored interior paint finishes were selected to maximize daylighting levels.

Water Efficiency

- Waterless urinals, low-flow toilets and shower-heads, and lavatories with automatic faucet controls reduce potable water use. Uses 30 percent less potable water than a traditionally designed school.
- Indigenous and drought-resistant landscaping further reduces water consumption.

Air Quality

- A floor-mounted air diffusing system that responds to changes in temperature, humidity, and carbon dioxide levels provides high-quality indoor air. Floor-mounted diffusers supply air that is closer to the breathing zone of the occupants, in this case, primarily children.
- Low- and zero-emitting volatile organic compound materials and interior finishes were used, providing improved indoor air quality.
- Demand-controlled ventilation using CO_2 sensors is provided throughout the building.
- Operable windows provide fresh air supply for the entire building.
- An indoor air quality management plan is implemented for the school.
- Entry sequence to school is designed to remove dirt tracked in from the occupants and other airborne particles before entering the building.
- Ventilation system is designed to exchange both heat and humidity between incoming and outgoing air.

Sustainable Materials

- 50 percent of the building materials have 20 percent post-consumer content, such as plastic toilet partitions made from recycled plastic, and heavy steel framing.
- 50 percent of the building materials have pre-consumer recycled materials, such as concrete masonry with industrial waste aggregates, recycled content rubber flooring, and agricultural waste product wheat board panels.
- Approximately 40 percent of all building materials were manufactured within 500 miles from the building site (hemlock siding), reducing transportation cost and energy usage.
- 30 percent of the cement in the concrete used was replaced with industrial waste flyash.
- Naturally rot-resistant wood species were specified for exposed applications.
- Low-maintenance and long-lasting building materials were used to decrease long-term replacement cost and embodied energy of the building.

Innovations

- Geothermal ground source heat pumps connected to a series of 150 foot deep geothermal wells are provided in each classroom for both heating and cooling purposes.
- An under-floor air system provides conditioned air at the breathing and body zone of the occupants, thus achieving a greater degree of efficiency. The air change effectiveness is greater than 90 percent.
- The school has a central space for materials separation and recycling.
- Building materials were selected based on lifecycle analysis (LCA). BEES software was used to produce basic comparisons, and further detailed material analysis was produced using Athena Environmental Impact Estimator software.

Energy

- Triple-glazed, high-performance windows were installed to increase building insulation and assist in reducing energy costs.

- Geothermal heat pumps connected to a series of 150 foot deep geothermal wells provide heat and cooling for the building, reducing energy consumption.
- Clear View Elementary School uses 40 percent less energy than a traditionally designed school of similar size, resulting in an annual cost saving of $18,000, with a nine-year payback time period for the increased material cost.
- Illumination sensors, high-efficiency fluorescent lights, dimmer switches, and compact fluorescent lamps reduce electrical use.
- HVAC system is commissioned.
- Light levels were designed for no more than 1 watt per square foot.
- Direct digital control systems are used for the HVAC system, optimizing performance.
- Heat recovery and demand controlled ventilation are provided to maximize mechanical efficiency and reduce electrical usage.
- PowerDOE software was used to calculate the electrical load of Clear View Elementary School, which was 23,628 Btu/sq.ft/yr.

2. Environmental Dynamics Incorporated

Location: Albuquerque, NM
Use: office space
Size: 7,300 sq.ft
Architect: EDI

Sustainable Strategies

Site

- Site selection was urban infill with an adaptive reuse of an existing building. Reducing embodied energy of the project and eliminating use of undeveloped site.
- 85 percent of construction waste was reused or recycled, reducing landfill volume and reducing embodied energy of building.
- Site permeability was increased, thus reducing the heat island effect of the site. Demolished pervious site material was reclaimed and utilized as low-height gambion site walls.

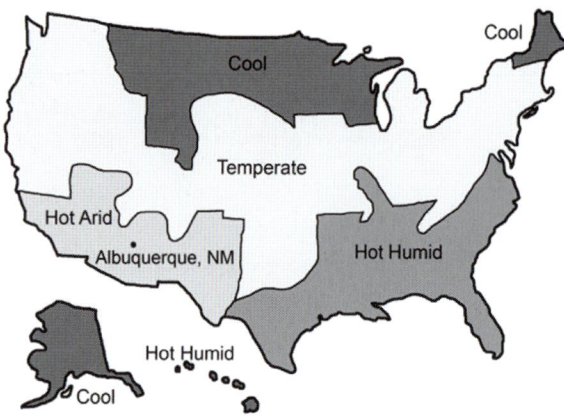

Figure 6.3.2 Environmental Dynamics Incorporated. (Source: photo by Patrick Coulie.)

- Sustainable transportation is fostered by the availability of bicycle storage and changing rooms for employees.
- Site is located adjacent to public transportation access.

Building Envelope

- Green roof installed to insulate the building and minimize the heat island effect.
- High-performance architectural windows installed to provide greater insulation and decreased solar heat gain, reducing building energy loads.
- A lime stucco applied as the exterior finish reduces the structure's heat island effect and protects the building's interior.

Passive Strategies

- Natural ventilation is used as the main source of cooling for the building. Large overhead doors oriented to an exterior courtyard provide copious amounts of natural fresh air and daylighting.
- Solar hot water panels use solar radiation to provide hot water to the building.
- Large amounts of daylighting delivered to the interior via skylights, clerestory windows, and overhead doors supply excellent levels of interior illumination. Daylight and views are provided for 100 percent of all regularly occupied spaces.

Water Efficiency

- Rainwater is captured, stored, and used for landscape watering.
- Water-efficient plumbing fixtures, with aerators, and gray water toilets reduce water usage by 30 percent.

Air Quality

- Low-emitting volatile organic compound interior finish materials such as paints, adhesives, carpets, and others, were used to reduce indoor air contamination.
- Operable windows and overhead doors provide large amounts of fresh outside air change.
- High-performance air filters were installed to increase the indoor air quality.
- Natural ventilation and thermal comfort provided by operable windows and overhead doors provide most of the building's fresh air supply, increasing workers' health and productivity.

Sustainable Materials

- Lime stucco made from regional and recycled materials was used as the building's exterior finish surface.
- Low-level volatile organic compounds interior finish materials with high recycled contents were used to increase indoor air quality and provide a healthier work environment.

- Salvaged, rapidly renewable, and regionally manufactured materials were used for construction when possible.

Innovations

- A natural lime stucco was used as an exterior finish material, taking advantage of lime's natural carbonization hardening ability, heat reflectivity, resistance to molds, and unique color rendition.

Energy

- Installed green roof provides additional insulation value and reduction in heat gain, lowering utility costs.
- Solar hot water panels used for hot water supply help reduce energy consumption.
- High-rated building insulation was used to further reduce heat gain and utility consumption.

3. Founding Farmers Restaurant

Location: Washington, DC
Use: restaurant
Size: 8,500 sq.ft
Architect: Core architecture + design

Sustainable Strategies

Site

- 90 percent of all construction waste was recycled or diverted from landfills.
- Site location is urban Washington, DC which is located along major bus routes. Bicycle racks located in front of the restaurant encourage employees to bike to work.

Passive Strategies

- Window shading reduces heat gain, reducing reliance on mechanical HVAC system.
- Daylighting is maximized to reduce the dependency upon electric lighting.

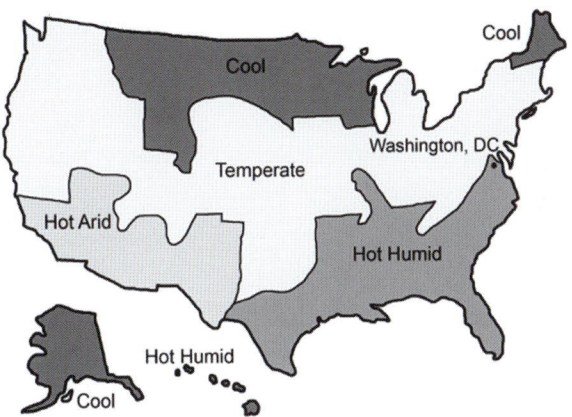

Figure 6.3.3 Founding Farmers Restaurant. (Source: photo by Michael Moran/OTTO.)

Water Efficiency

- In-house Natura water filtration system eliminates need for bottles, trucks required to deliver them, and tons of glass and plastic recycling waste.
- Waterless urinals and low-flow lavatories reduce water usage. The Founding Farmers Restaurant saves approximately 193,168 gallons of water annually.
- Water-efficient Energy Star-rated dishwasher and spray valve further reduces water consumption.

Air Quality

- CO_2 sensors are installed throughout the restaurant to monitor indoor air quality.
- Mechanical ventilation rates of the restaurant exceed the code requirements by 30 percent.

Sustainable Materials

- Flooring material is reclaimed from heart of pine support beams salvaged from an old textile mill located in Hickory, North Carolina.
- 15 percent of all construction materials are reclaimed, some of which are reclaimed brick, and salvaged beams, wood barn doors, stone flooring and a two-story wood portal made from reclaimed barn wood.
- 45 percent of all materials were manufactured within 500 miles of the construction project.
- Walnut tables, custom bar stools, and side chairs, were made from wood harvested from forests located in PA and Ohio, and manufactured in Greensboro and High Point, North Carolina.
- PaperStone countertops located in restrooms were made from 100 percent post-consumer recycled content paper, and a non-petroleum based phenolic resin. Bar counter tops are made from concrete.
- Recycled paper with soy-based inks are used for all menu printing.
- Low volatile organic construction materials such as paints and adhesives were used to reduce indoor air pollutants.
- Acrylic screens with 40 percent pre-consumer recycled resin were used as interior dividing screens. Interior graphics were printed on materials made from sustainable harvested wood pulp.
- Mezzanine guardrails are made from recycled steel.
- Restaurant booths are made from recycled steel and upholstered in a chemical-free cotton print.

Innovations

- Founding Farmers represents a unique farm-to-table dining concept. It is owned by a collective of over 40,000 family farmers, sourcing its food from locally producing farmers within the mid-Atlantic region. Growing, buying, and serving food that is healthy for people to eat, good for the farmers that grow and harvest it, and good for the animals that produce it.
- Founding Farmers practices environmental conservation and natural resource preservation, supporting sustainable farming and agriculture. Reducing pollution and transportation costs by sourcing locally.

- Biodiversity is supported by purchasing food products from organic farms that practice crop rotation and elimination of chemical pesticides.
- Animal welfare is practiced by Founding Farmers through the humane treatment of livestock animals, allowing open-range natural grazing and providing a natural diet appropriate to their species.
- Founding Farmers practices economic viability; paying farmers fair wages, supplanting dependencies on government subsidies, and strengthening rural communities.

Energy

- A high-efficiency HVAC system using heat pumps exceeds the Advanced Buildings Energy Benchmark, and the ASHRAE 90.1 standards by 10 percent.
- 100 percent of the electric consumption is purchased from green power credits.
- Motion sensor lighting reduces electrical use.
- Energy-efficient low-voltage mini-halogens, LED lighting, and compact fluorescent lamps were used to reduce energy consumption.
- The restaurant is 100 percent carbon neutral, purchasing offset credits through CarbonFund.org, leaving no measurable energy waste footprint behind. Seventy tons of CO_2 emissions were offset in 2009.
- Over 80 percent of the appliances are Energy Star-rated.

Recycling

- A kitchen waste recycling and compost area is provided for the restaurant, and used daily.
- Biodegradable bags are used for any non-organic products that cannot be recycled.
- Carry-out foods are packaged with biodegradable boxes, bags, and utensils.
- The use of bottled water is eliminated by in-house water filtration.
- Paper use in restrooms is reduced by the installation of high-powered hand dryers.
- Recycling is implemented with both front of house (seating area) and back of house (kitchen/service areas) measures.

4. Hawaii Preparatory Academy

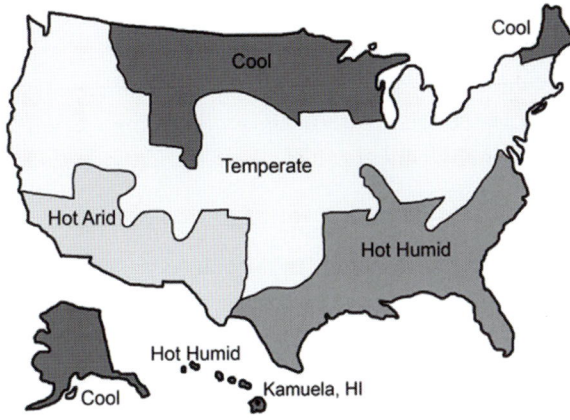

Figure 6.3.4 Hawaii Preparatory Academy.
(Source: photo by Matthew Millman Photography.)

Location: Kamuela, HI
Use: high-school science building
Size: 6,100 sq.ft
Architect: Flansburgh Architects

Sustainable Strategies

Site

- The science sustainable energy lab was built on a grayfield used previously as a bio-waste dumping area.
- Site was selected for the windward exposure to abundant trade winds that accelerate down from the hillside located above the site.
- Southern exposure of site optimizes solar thermal exposure for photovoltaic energy-generating panels.
- Orientation maximizes access to outdoor and ocean views. With outdoor courts that facilitate

natural ventilation, connect buildings with the site, and take advantage of Hawaii's favorable climate by providing exterior learning space.

- Buildings are terraced to coincide with the site's topography, maximize solar orientation, and provide shelter from strong winds.

Passive Strategies

- Daylighting is maximized and controlled by the use of skylights, wood sun screens, and interior roller shades to minimize the use of electrical lighting and provide pleasant interior lighting.
- The fenestration and building shapes were determined using energy modeling to maximize daylighting.
- The building's form, fenestration, and site location take full advantage of the hillside trade winds that accelerate down the hillside, directing, and modifying the wind velocity and volume to cool the interiors of the buildings.
- The building is entirely naturally ventilated. Low-level louvers on the windward side let in cool air and high-level louvers and clerestory windows allow spent air to escape. The pressure differential created by the roof form assists air circulation.
- The building's roof form provides protection from the dominant trade winds, creating usable exterior classroom space and courtyards.
- The building's water storage tanks, solar panels, and mechanical system location take full advantage of and follow the change in elevation of the site and buildings.

Water Efficiency

- All water used is harvested from rainwater on site (6,593 gallons annually) and/or a closed-loop system. Rain is gathered from the large, sloped roof surfaces. Water is stored in a 10,000 gallon storage tank, and filtered for potable drinking use and waste system use.
- An individual wastewater system provides treatment for domestic wastewater and on-site infiltration. Creating an additional degree of water treatment and cleaner end product by percolation via leaching fields.

- Waterless urinals and low-flow toilets and lavatories save 193,168 gallons per year.

Air Quality

- The building is completely naturally ventilated. Automated louvers maintain temperature and relative humidity levels to provide user comfort. Exhaust fans provide additional airflow if needed.
- 24/7 CO_2 sensors are installed throughout the building to monitor indoor air quality.
- Low- and zero-emitting volatile organic compound materials and interior finishes were used, providing improved indoor air quality.
- Operable windows covering approximately 19 percent of the total floor area are located in every space, providing 24 prescribed air changes per hour, as mandated by the Title 24 air change requirements.
- Green cleaning program is utilized to further indoor air quality.

Sustainable Materials

- All materials were supplied from sources within 500 mile radius of the building site.
- Use of red-list materials containing formaldehydes, PVC, and mercury were zero to minimum. Bio-luminescent exit lights that are mercury free were installed. Custom designed cotton core with FSC-certified wood frames and hemp fabric coverings were used as acoustic wall panels, without formaldehydes.
- Laminated wood beams were used that contained no urea formaldehyde in the adhesives.
- Concrete used for foundation walls and pre-cast countertops.
- Salvaged native Ohia wood column used for sustainable and aesthetic purposes.

Energy

- An experimental cooling system that absorbs cool nighttime temperatures via circulated water through panels is stored in a below-grade 10,000 gallon insulated storage tank, for daytime cooling

purposes, replacing the need for conventional air-conditioning, and thus reducing electricity use.

- The science buildings are powered by three roof-mounted solar photovoltaic arrays, totaling 26 kW of power, and two remote-located wind turbine generators. The science building used approximately 60 percent of the total power generated on site in its first year of operation.
- Solar PV panel systems are tied into the electrical grid, and augmented by a hybrid battery backup system that is charged by the mains and/or renewable sources on site. Energy that is not used by the science building is net metered back into the campus grid.
- A separate solar thermal array supplies the facility's hot water needs.
- The facility's energy efficiency is further augmented by the use of the BIS self-regulated monitoring system, which coordinates the building systems to maximize peak energy performance.

Innovations

- Carbon offsets purchased. Offsets produced from wind farms in North and South Dakota, Texas, and Washington, and solar farms in California.
- An experimental cooling system that collects cool nighttime energy via circulating water through roof panels to be stored as chilled water for use during the daytime was used to replace conventional air conditioning.
- A self-regulating building monitoring system uses over 600 building sensors to regulate the ventilation, cooling/heating, water use, and energy generation to optimize the building's sustainable performance.
- All water and power needs of the science building are met from on-site sources.

5. Proximity Hotel

Location: Greensboro, NC
Use: hotel, conference/event space, full-service restaurant
Size: 118,000 sq.ft
Architect: Centrepoint Architecture

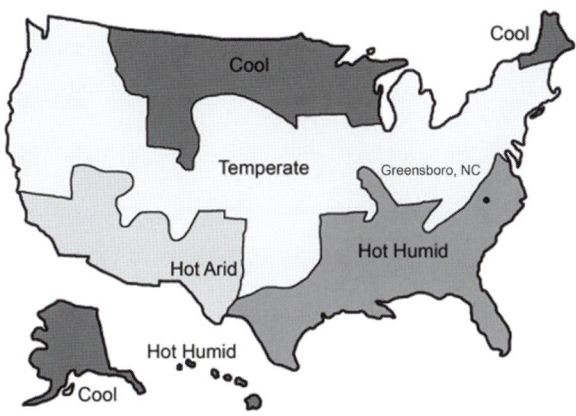

Figure 6.3.5 Proximity Hotel.
(Source: photo by Courtesy of Proximity Hotel, Greensboro, NC.)

Sustainable Strategies

Site

- 700 linear feet of stream was restored by reducing existing erosion through the planting of local adaptable species and by rebuilding existing buffers and banks.
- A floodplain bench was created by removing 700 cubic yards of soil.
- Grade control and the maintenance and creation of riffles and pools were provided by the addition of 376 tons of boulders and 18 logs.
- Minimum construction disturbance to site by use of pre-cast concrete panels for building shell.
- 87 percent of the generated construction waste was recycled, preventing 1,535 tons of waste from going to landfills.

Building Envelope

- High-performance insulated Carboncast wall panels consisting of EPS insulation sandwiched between two concrete wythes, and all connected with carbon-fiber trusses, creating a R-14 insulation rating, were used for the exterior envelope. The pre-cast insulated panels were formed from locally recycled materials.
- Carboncast panel faces came pre-finished, reducing toxic volatile organic compound emissions to the site.

Passive Strategies

- Large (7' 4" square) energy-efficient operable windows provided more than 97 percent of all regularly occupied spaces, providing a sightline to the outdoors as well as natural ventilation.
- A green roof is located above the restaurant to help reduce the urban heat island effect as well as energy needs for refrigeration and air conditioning.

Water Efficiency

- High-efficiency plumbing fixtures (low-flow toilets and faucets, waterless urinals) reduced water usage by approximately 34 percent, saving two million gallons of water annually, saving $13,000 in the first year of operations.

Air Quality

- Large amount of outside air (60 cubic foot per min) circulate into the guestrooms, utilizing an energy-efficient energy recovery system (utilizing heat from exhausted building air), improving interior air quality.
- Engineered variable-speed hoods whose power is determined by the kitchen needs (monitors heat, smoke, and pollutants) reduce energy needs by 25 percent, providing fresh air as well.
- Low-emitting volatile organic compound interior finish materials, paints, adhesives, carpets, and others reduce indoor air contamination.

Sustainable Materials

- Recycled building materials such as reinforced steel with 90 percent post-consumer recycled content, including gypsum wallboard 100 percent, asphalt 25 percent, and steel staircase with 50 percent post-consumer recycled content. Concrete used contained 4 percent (224,000 lbs) waste product flyash.
- Bistro bar is made of salvaged, solid walnut trees, harvested via sickness or storm. All room trays made of Plyboo (bamboo plywood).
- Guestroom shelving and bistro's tabletops are made of walnut veneer, with a SkyBlend substrate made from 100 percent post-industrialized recycled wood pulp without formaldehyde.

Innovations

- Local vendors and artists were used to reduce the transportation carbon footprint, and to reduce packaging material use and shipping needs. Forty-six percent of building materials were regionally sourced. Most furniture was fabricated within 18 miles of the site.
- An education center is provided to provide green tours for hotel guests, sustainable practices symposia, and student outreach programs.
- Bicycles are provided for guests to utilize the adjacent five-mile greenway.

Energy

- 100 rooftop solar photovoltaic panels utilized for hot water provide 60 percent of the hot water for the hotel and restaurant.
- The hotel and restaurant uses 39.2 percent less energy than a similar conventionally code built structure by using efficient materials and progressive construction technology.
- Geothermal energy is used for the restaurant's refrigeration equipment, in lieu of the standard water-cooled system, providing significant water-use savings.
- Regenerative-drive elevators that generate electricity as they descend provide much of the energy required for elevator ascent.

- An energy-efficient ground source heat pump refrigeration system exchanges waste heat with groundwater loops.
- Expected building and operational energy savings is $140,000.

6. Sokol Blosser Winery

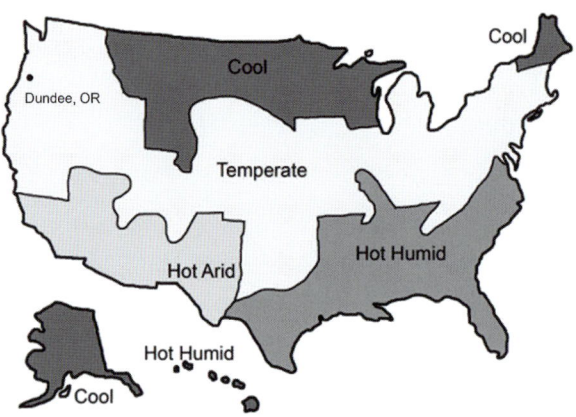

Figure 6.3.6   Sokol Blosser Winery.
(Source: image courtesy of Sokol Blosser Winery.)

Location: Dundee, OR
Use: Winery
Size: 5,805 sq.ft
Architect: SERA Architects

Sustainable Strategies

Site

- 94 percent of construction waste was recycled and diverted from landfill.

- Winery actively provides built habitat to assist with western bluebird recovery and salmon safe watershed restoration.
- Barrel cellar is built below grade, resulting in minimal site run-off, and minimal heat island effect.
- Winery estate has planted approximately 1,000 trees and plants to assist in the reduction of invasive plant species.
- Six acres of the estate have been voluntarily retired to protect environmentally sensitive land, decrease erosion, restore wildlife habitat, and protect the purity of surface and groundwater.
- Typical two feet of soil coverage provided over structure and continuous with adjacent grade level, provides habitat for a diversity of flora and fauna, including gophers, field mice, and song birds.
- Cut and fill of site was balanced so that no additional soil needed to be imported.
- Vegetation providing shade was planted along new paved access route to minimize heat island effect.
- North-facing site was chosen because it was not well suited for grape cultivation, and because of its greater temperature control due to less direct solar exposure.

Building Envelope

- The building was placed underground with a minimum soil coverage depth of two feet, to avoid the cost of an above-grade insulated structure, and also to benefit from the insulation value of the earth.
- In addition to the two feet of building soil coverage, a four-inch layer of rigid polystyrene was provided for additional thermal roof insulation.

Passive Strategies

- Heat generated from the wine fermentation process is dissipated through induced natural ventilation.
- Natural light from skylights reduces required electric lighting use.
- Underground wine cellar uses the constant cool earth temperature to minimize mechanical energy required.

- Rectangular building shape, oriented east–west lengthwise, reduces east–west solar heat gain and takes advantage of the desired cool temperature north orientation.
- Uninsulated concrete walls use the cooling thermal properties of soil to support desired cool interior temperatures. The concrete material provides thermal mass with a significant time lag in summer months, to assist in cooling the building.
- Natural ventilation and the rooftop heat stack system moderate temperature and provide night air flushing to dissipate heat during the summer months.

Water Efficiency

- No net increase in stormwater run-off due to earthen roof and minimized impervious coverage. Earthen roof allows percolation and drainage into surrounding landscape.
- On-site well provides potable water for barrel room washing and winery equipment cleaning.
- Trench drains within the barrel cellar direct run-off to a drainage area that filters the water for reuse for vineyard irrigation.
- Water-efficient regional wildflowers and grasses were selected for introduced landscaping.

Air Quality

- Three earth tubes each three feet in diameter, located along the northern elevation of the structure, provide large quantities of fresh air at a low velocity.
- Mechanically controlled vents in each of the earth tubes monitor carbon dioxide levels, providing fresh air during the carbon dioxide producing wine fermentation process.
- Low-emitting volatile organic compounds paints, sealants, and adhesives were utilized to increase air quality.
- Indoor humidity levels are controlled with evaporative cooling misting units, keeping humidity levels between 75 and 90 percent.

Sustainable Materials

- Half of all building materials contain 40 percent post-industrial or 20 percent post-consumer content.
- 75 percent of the materials were harvested within 500 miles of the building site.
- Materials selected for construction were chosen on the basis that they were durable, biodegradable, non-toxic, and produced from recycled, reused, abundant, or rapidly renewable sources.
- Building material palette was kept to a minimum to reduce cost, provide energy performance, and achieve desired aesthetics.

Innovations

- 50 percent of the vineyard tractors and trucks are powered by bio-diesel fuel.
- Winery is farmed organically and has received full USDA organic certification.
- 100 percent post-consumer waste recycled paper used for copy and brochures.
- Wine bottle foil capsules eliminated, wine labels are printed on recycled paper, kraft cases used for finished product.
- CO_2 emissions from employee transportation are reduced by the encouragement of employee carpooling, as well as the demand for on-site parking.
- The wine barrel storage facility was constructed as a 100-year building. The building plan was designed with simplicity and flexibility to accommodate future programmatic changes.

Energy

- One-third of power usage is purchased from renewable wind power sources, offsetting 62,656 lbs of CO_2 emissions.
- Underground placement of the building eliminated the need for refrigeration.
- 20 percent of power is supplied by 25 kW photo-voltaic panel system.
- The barrel cellar structure uses 57 percent less energy than a similar conventionally constructed building.
- The below-grade location eliminates the need for refrigeration equipment, reducing peak electric demand.
- An underground conduit links the new barrel storage facility with the vats located in the existing adjacent facility, allowing wine gravity flow transfer, thus minimizing use of electric forklifts.

Conclusion

I wrote this book as a tool to meet the challenges of the studio design process within the context of sustainable buildings. To attain the goal of approaching sustainable Net Zero or Net Plus buildings I recommended a three-step approach:

1 *Do it right the first time* through awareness of cultural and formal aesthetics, environmentally sound practices that take advantage of orientation, capturing the natural assets of the land and wind and sun.
2 *Use free energy* by understanding issues involved in sustainable design: the site, building envelope, materials used, indoor air quality, water management, and minimizing waste following some of the LEED® guidelines
3 *Minimize fossil fuel energy* by using the most efficient technical systems possible.

Thousands of sustainable buildings built all over the world meet the green building challenge, proving that it is possible to design and build great architecture integrating form, function, and delight without sacrificing affordability. These buildings all reflect the above three-step approach in one form or another.

Designing sustainable architectural buildings is a complex process requiring innate aesthetic sense and understanding to be able to access and keep in mind several disciplines at one time and how they work together to achieve sustainable goals.

Building designers can plan for the future and provide for coming generations if they make a pledge today to evaluate all of their projects for environmental, energy, and water efficiency. It is my hope that this book can help in that process.

Bibliography

AIA Research Corporation, *Regional Guidelines for Building Passive Energy Conserving Homes* (Washington, DC: US Department of Housing and Urban Development, 1980).

American Institute of Architects (AIA), *Glazing Design Handbook for Energy Efficiency* (Washington, DC: AIA, 1997).

American Institute of Steel Construction, *Manual of Steel Construction*, 9th edition, (Chicago, IL: American Institute of Steel Construction, 2006).

Anderson, Bruce and Michael Riordan, *The Solar Home Book* (Harrisville, NH: Cheshire Books, 1976).

ASHRAE, *ASHRAE Handbook of Fundamentals* (New York: ASHRAE, 2009).

Bahadori, M.N, "Passive Cooling in Iranian Architecture." *Scientific American* Vol. 238, No. 2, February 1978.

Baird, George, *The Architectural Expression of Environmental Control Systems* (London: Spon Press, 2001).

Bolin, Rob, *Sustainability of the Building Envelope* (New York: Whole Building Design Group, 2009).

Boyce, P., C. Hunter, and O. Howlett, *The Benefits of Daylight Through Windows* (Troy, NY: Rensselaer Polytechnic Institute, 2003).

Brown, G. and Mark DeKay, *Sun, Wind & Light* (New York: John Wiley & Sons, 2001).

Brown, Lester, *Future at Risk on a Hotter Planet* (New York: W.W. Norton & Company, 2009).

Brown, Lester R., *Plan B: Mobilizing to Save Civilization* (New York: W.W. Norton & Company, 2009).

BuildingGreen Inc., *Greening Federal Facilities* (Brattleboro, VT: NREL and DOE, 2001).

California Energy Commission, *Building Energy Efficiency Standards, Compliance Manual* (California: California Energy Commission, 2008).

California Energy Commission, *Residential and Non-residential Standards: Building Energy Efficiency Standards, Compliance Manual* (California: CEC, 2008).

California Institute for Energy Efficiency (CIEE), *Building Technologies Program, Tips for Daylighting with Windows – The Integrated Approach* (California: Lawrence Berkeley National Laboratory, 1997).

Daniels, Klaus and Ralph E. Hammann, *Energy Design for Tomorrow* (Germany: Edition Axel Menges, 2008).

Dent, Stephen (James C. Snyder and Anthony J. Catanese, eds.), *Introduction to Architecture* (New York: John Wiley & Sons, 1979).

Dent, Stephen D., Class notes, School of Architecture & Planning, University of New Mexico, 2010.

DiLaura, David *et al.*, *The Lighting Handbook* (New York: IES, 2011).

Douglas, J. Balcolm, *Passive Solar Heating Analysis: A Design Manual* (Atlanta, GA: ASHRAE, 1984).

Earth Journal, *Environmental Almanac and Resource Directory* (Boulder, CO: Buzzworm Books, 1993).

Electric Power Research Institute, *Technology Applications* (Palo Alto, CA: Electric Power Research Institute, 2000).

Evans, B.H., *Natural Air Flow Around Buildings* (College Station, TX: Texas A. & M. College, 1957).

Forest Stewardship Council Certification, *FSC US Forest Management Standard (v1.0)* (Bonn: FSC, 2004).

Givoni, Baruch, *Climate Consideration in Buildings and Urban Design* (New York: John Wiley & Sons, 1998).

Global Change Research Program, *National Climate Assessment Report* (Washington, DC: Global Change Research Program, 2014).

Hagan, Susannah, *Harvard Design Magazine* (Boston: Spring 2003).

Hawken, Paul, Amory Lovins, and Hunter Lovins, *Natural Capitalism* (Boston, MA: Little, Brown and Company, 1999).

Hawthorne, Christopher, Turning down the global thermostat, *Metropolis Magazine*, 2003.

Heat Pump Centre, *Annual Review of Energy* (Netherlands: International Energy Agency, 1978, pp. 176–177).

Heschong Mahone Group, Inc., Daylighting in Schools, 1999. www.daylighting.com/pdf/product_testing/Heschong_Mahone_Daylight_%26_Schools_1999.pdf

Inter-Ministry Coordination Committee to Mitigate Urban Heat Island, *The Policy Framework to Reduce Urban Heat Island Effects* (Japan: Inter-Ministry Coordination Committee to Mitigate Urban Heat Island, 2004).

International Energy Agency, *Day Light in Buildings* (July 2000).

Iyengar, Kuppaswamy, *Lighting the End of the Efficiency Tunnel* (Des Plaines, IL: Cahners Publishing Co., 1999).

Kammen, Daniel M., *The Rise of Renewable Energy* (New York: Scientific American, 2006).

King, Bruce, *Buildings of Earth and Straw* (Sausalito, CA: Ecological Design Press, 1996).

Knowles, Ralph, *Energy and Form* (Cambridge, MA and London: MIT Press, 1975).

Knowles, Ralph, *The Solar Envelope* (Golden, CO: Solar Energy Information Data Bank, 1999).

Knowles, Ralph, *Sun Rhythm and Form* (Oxford: Architectural Press, 2011).

Kwok, Allison and Walter Grodnizk, *The Green Design Studio Handbook* (New York: Architectural Press, 2011).

Lam, William M.C., *Perception and Lighting as Formgivers for Architecture* (New York: McGraw-Hill, 1977).

Lechner, Norbert, *Heating, Cooling and Lighting* (New York: John Wiley & Sons, Inc. 2009).

Lewis, Owen J., *A Green Vitruvius* (London: European Commission, 1999).

Lynch, Kevin, *Site Planning* (Cambridge, MA: The MIT Press, 1971).

MacGregor, James G., *Reinforced Concrete Mechanics and Design*, 4th edition (Englewood Cliffs, NJ: Prentice Hall, 2005).

Makela, E.J., J.L. Williamson, and E.B. Makela, "Comparison of Standard 90.1-2010 and the 2012 IECC with Respect to Commercial Buildings," US Department of Energy, 2011.

Mazria, Edward, *The Passive Solar Energy Book* (Emmaus, PA: Rodale Press, 1979).

McCarthy, Battle, *Wind Towers* (Chichester: Academy Editions, 1999).

McNeill, J.R., *Something New Under the Sun* (New York: Norton, 2000).

Meadows, Donella and Dennis Meadows, *The Limits to Growth* (New York: Universe Books, 1972).

Millennium Ecosystem Assessment, *Ecosystems and Human Well-being: Biodiversity Synthesis* (Washington, DC: World Resources Institute, 2005).

Morrow, Baker H., *Best Plants for New Mexico Gardens and Landscapes* (Albuquerque, NM: University of New Mexico Press, 1995).

National Renewable Energy Laboratory, *High Performance Building Research* (Golden, CO: NREL, 2005).

New York City Regional Heat Island Initiative, *Mitigating New York City's Heat Island with Urban Forestry, Living Roofs, and Light Surfaces* (New York: New York City Regional Heat Island Initiative, 2006).

Newell, Richard (administrator), Biomass in the United States Energy Economy: International Biomass Conference & Expo, May 3, 2011, St. Louis, MO. www.eia.gov/pressroom/presentations/newell_05032011.pdf

Oak Ridge National Laboratory, *Recommended Levels of Building Insulation by Energy Star* (Washington, DC: US Environmental Protection Agency, 2008).

Office of Energy Efficiency and Renewable Energy, *Building Energy Use* (US Department of Energy, 2007).

Olgyay, Victor and Aladar Olgyay, *Design with Climate* (Princeton, NJ: Princeton University Press, 1963).

Public Technology, Inc. and US Green Building Council, *Sustainable Building Technical Manual: Green Building Design, Construction and Operation* (Alexandria, VA: Public Technology, Inc., 1996).

Public Technology, Inc. and US Green Building Council, Tom McKeag, "How Termites Inspired Mick Pearce's Green Buildings," *Zygote Quarterly*, September 2009.

Reisner, Marc, *Cadillac Desert* (New York: Viking, 1986).

Richardson, K., Will Steffen, Hans Joachim Schellnhuber, Joseph Alcamo, Terry Barker, Daniel M. Kammen, Rik Leemans, Diana Liverman, Mohan Munasinghe, Balgis Osman-Elasha, Nicholas Stern, and Ole Waever, *Climate Change: Synthesis Report: Global Risks, Challenges and Decisions, Copenhagen 2009* (Copenhagen: University of Copenhagen, 2009)

Rocky Mountain Institute, *Green Development* (Golden, CO: RMI, 2001).

Rocky Mountain Institute, *Technical Briefs* (Winchester, CO: US Department of Energy, 2004).

Santamouris, M. (ed.) *Solar Thermal Technologies for Buildings: The State of the Art* (London: James & James Ltd., 2003).

Smith, Craig B. (ed.), *Efficient Electricity Use* (Elmsford, NY: Pergamon, 1978).

Smith, Craig B., *Energy Management Principles* (Elmsford, NY: Pergamon Press, 1981).

Smith, Peter F., *Sustainability at the Cutting Edge* (Oxford: Architectural Press, 2003).

Socolow, Robert and Stephen Pacala, Energy's future: beyond carbon – a plan to keep carbon in check, *Scientific American*, September 2006, p. 50.

Stein, Benjamin, John Reynolds, and William J. McGuinness, *Mechanical and Electrical Equipment for Buildings* (New York: John Wiley & Sons, 1992).

Stein, B., J. Reynolds, W. Grondzik, and A. Kwok, *Mechanical and Electrical Equipment for Buildings* (New York: John Wiley & Sons, Inc., 2006).

Stein, Benjamin, John Reynolds, Walter Grondzik, and Alison Kwok, *Mechanical and Electrical Equipment for Buildings*, 10th edition (New York: John Wiley and Sons, 2009).

Susca, T., S.R. Gaffin, and G.R. Dell'Osso, *Positive Effects of Vegetation: Urban Heat Island and Green Roofs* (Italy: Polytechnic University of Bari, 2011).

Sustainable Building Technical Manual: Green Building Design, Construction and Operation (Alexandria, VA: Public Technology, Inc., 1996).

Swift, John M., Jr. and Tom Lawrence, *ASHRAE Green Guide* (Atlanta, GA: ASHRAE Publications, 2010).

Thomas Derek, *Architecture and the Urban Environment* (Oxford: Architectural Press, 2002).

Torcellini, P., N. Long, S. Pless, and R. Judkoff, *Evaluation of the Low-Energy Design and Energy Performance of the Zion National Park Visitor Center* (Golden, CO: NREL, 2005).

UN Brundtland Report: http://conspect.nl/pdf/Our_Common_Future-Brundtland_Report_1987.pdf

University of Michigan, Urbanization and global change, 2002. www.globalchange.umich.edu/globalchange2/current/lectures/urban_gc.

US Department of Energy, *2007 Building Energy Use* (Office of Energy Efficiency and Renewable Energy, 2007).

US Department of Energy, *Energy Information Administration (EIA)* (May–July 2008).

US Department of Housing and Urban Development, *Regional Guidelines for Building Passive Energy Conserving Homes* (July 1980).

US Green Building Council, *LEED for New Construction* (Washington, DC: USGBC, 2009).

Vickers, Amy, *Handbook of Water Use and Conservation: Homes, Landscapes, Industries, Businesses, Farms* (Amherst, MA: WaterPlow Press, 2001).

von Frisch, Karl, *Animal Architecture* (New York and London: Harcourt Brace Jovanovich, Inc; 1974).

Watson, Donald, *Designing and Building a Solar House* (Charlotte, VT: Garden Way Publisher, 1977).

Werth, Andrew, "Cooling Towers," a paper presented in a Sustainable Design class at The University of New Mexico, 2006.

Wigginton, Michael and Jude Harris, *Intelligent Skins* (Burlington, MA: Architectural Press, 2003).

Womack, James and Daniel Jones, *Lean Thinking* (New York: Simon & Schuster, Inc, 1996).

WWF, *Living Planet Report* (2006): assets.panda.org/downloads/living_planet_report.pdf.

Yamamoto, Yoshika, Measures to mitigate urban heat islands, *Science and Technology Trends Quarterly Review*, 18, 2006, 65–83.

Yudelson, Jerry and Ulf Meyer, *The World's Greenest Buildings* (Abingdon: Routledge, 2013).

Index

Page numbers in *italics* indicate figures.